Controversies
in Minority
Voting

CONTROVERSIES
IN MINORITY
VOTING

The Voting Rights Act
in Perspective

BERNARD GROFMAN
CHANDLER DAVIDSON
Editors

The Brookings Institution
Washington, D.C.

Copyright © 1992 by
THE BROOKINGS INSTITUTION
1775 Massachusetts Avenue, N.W., Washington, D.C. 20036

Library of Congress Cataloging-in-Publication Data

Controversies in minority voting : the Voting Rights Act
  in perspective / Bernard Grofman and
Chandler Davidson, editors.
      p. cm.
  Includes bibliographical references and index.
  ISBN 0-8157-1750-4
  ISBN 0-8157-1751-2 (pbk.)
    1. Afro-Americans—Suffrage. I. Grofman, Bernard.
  II. Davidson, Chandler.
KF4893.C66 1992
342.73'072—dc20
[347.30272]   92-7370
                                               CIP

9 8 7 6 5 4 3 2 1

The paper in this publication meets the minimum requirements
of the American National Standard for Information Sciences—
Permanence of Paper for Printed Library Materials, ANSI
Z39.48-1984

฿ THE BROOKINGS INSTITUTION

The Brookings Institution is an independent organization devoted to nonpartisan research, education, and publication in economics, government, foreign policy, and the social sciences generally. Its principal purposes are to aid in the development of sound public policies and to promote public understanding of issues of national importance.

The Institution was founded on December 8, 1927, to merge the activities of the Institute for Government Research, founded in 1916, the Institute of Economics, founded in 1922, and the Robert Brookings Graduate School of Economics and Government, founded in 1924.

The Board of Trustees is responsible for the general administration of the Institution, while the immediate direction of the policies, program, and staff is vested in the President, assisted by an advisory committee of the officers and staff. The by-laws of the Institution state: "It is the function of the Trustees to make possible the conduct of scientific research, and publication, under the most favorable conditions, and to safeguard the independence of the research staff in the pursuit of their studies and in the publication of the results of such studies. It is not a part of their function to determine, control, or influence the conduct of particular investigations or the conclusions reached."

The President bears final responsibility for the decision to publish a manuscript as a Brookings book. In reaching his judgment on the competence, accuracy, and objectivity of each study, the President is advised by the director of the appropriate research program and weighs the views of a panel of expert outside readers who report to him in confidence on the quality of the work. Publication of a work signifies that it is deemed a competent treatment worthy of public consideration but does not imply endorsement of conclusions or recommendations.

The Institution maintains its position of neutrality on issues of public policy in order to safeguard the intellectual freedom of the staff. Hence interpretations or conclusions in Brookings publications should be understood to be solely those of the authors and should not be attributed to the Institution, to its trustees, officers, or other staff members, or to the organizations that support its research.

Foreword

THE VOTING RIGHTS ACT OF 1965 has arguably been the most successful legislation to have come out of the Great Society reforms of the 1960s. Millions of people who might otherwise be shut out of the political process have been assured the franchise, and thousands of minority members have thereby been able to hold office. Yet the law continues to generate controversy. The controversy is, however, no longer primarily between southern white conservatives and civil rights activists, although some members of both groups remain involved. Instead, erstwhile allies in the cause of civil rights have come to disagree about the fairness and continued usefulness of the act. Some question the interpretation of the law by the courts and the Justice Department. Others disagree as to whether congressional amendments in 1970, 1975, and 1982 have distorted the intent of the original framers. And some fear that the law is inadvertently encouraging racial and ethnic polarization. Such matters take on added importance as nationwide redistricting focuses public attention on the relevance of the act for jurisdictions with significant minority populations.

This volume, growing out of a conference sponsored by the Brookings Institution, explores these and other issues that have arisen in the past quarter century. The authors include scholars and lawyers representing diverse views and various disciplines. Some have had experience enforcing the act, others have litigated cases initiated under its authority, and still others have been expert witnesses during litigation or researchers exploring the law's impact. They share a belief in the importance of minority voting rights in America; they diverge in their conclusions as to how these rights can be secured. The resulting controversy sheds new light on the nature of voting rights, the problems of representing minorities, and the complex interplay between law and social science.

The editors would like to thank Thomas E. Mann for hosting the conference and for helpful suggestions about this volume. Secretarial assistance was provided by Dorothy Gormick, Ziggy Bates, and Cheryl Larsson at the University of California, Irvine, and Rita Loucks at Rice University. Research and editorial assistance was provided by Kerri Gantz and Cathy Monholland at Rice University. At Brookings, James Schneider edited the manuscript, Todd Quinn verified its factual content, Sue Thompson, Lisa Pace, and Antoinette Williams corrected it, and Susan Woollen prepared it for typesetting. Max Franke compiled the index.

Brookings would like to acknowledge support provided by the Rockefeller Foundation for the conference and the additional papers commissioned for the volume. Funding for this project was provided to the University of California, Irvine, by the National Science Foundation.

The views expressed in this book are those of the authors and should not be ascribed to the sponsors of the conference or the trustees, officers, or staff members of the Brookings Institution.

BRUCE K. MAC LAURY
President

Washington, D.C.
April 1992

Contents

TABLES

FIGURES

Preface

THOMAS E. MANN

THE TWENTY-FIFTH ANNIVERSARY of the Voting Rights Act of 1965 was an occasion for both celebration and controversy. Virtually everyone acknowledged that the act had been remarkably successful in securing and preserving the right to vote for blacks and other minorities and in giving them a direct voice in their government. In contrast to the bitter failure following the first Reconstruction, recent decades have witnessed a second Reconstruction in which implementation of voting rights statutes has been effective in the face of southern white resistance. Dramatic increases in black registration and black elected officeholders in southern states testify to the seriousness of the effort to ensure that blacks no less than other members of the electorate have the opportunity to participate in the political process and to elect representatives of their choice.

Yet this triumph of the Voting Rights Act paradoxically coincided with the decline of the political party embraced by the act's beneficiaries. Since the mid-1960s racial politics has severely weakened the Democratic coalition, contributing to its loss of five of the last six presidential elections. And now during the post-1990 legislative redistricting, many analysts have noted that an alliance of civil rights activists and Republican party strategists, each wishing for very different reasons to concentrate minorities into districts in which they are a majority, has threatened to erode the Democratic control of the House of Representatives.

The new rule of thumb in legislative redistricting—that a majority-black or Hispanic district should be created wherever it is reasonable to do so—has also raised the specter of racial quotas, deepening racial and ethnic cleavages, and minority political ghettoes. Although voting rights has generated much less controversy than other dimensions of civil rights policy—the public has a more benign, even disinterested, attitude toward voting rights enforcement than toward affirmative action in employment and education—critics have seen policy enforcement as raising larger questions about the desirability of race-conscious measures to overcome past discrimination.

Indeed, the twenty-fifth anniversary of the Voting Rights Act occurred at a time when some traditional supporters of civil rights were rethinking the validity of policies evolving in the past two decades to improve the status of minorities in American society. The liberal historian, Arthur Schlesinger, Jr., reacting to the growing demands for multiculturalism in American education, has bemoaned the shift from the ideal of assimilation to the celebration of ethnicity. "Instead of a nation composed of individuals making their own free choices, America increasingly sees itself as composed of groups more or less indelible in their ethnic character."[1] The black sociologist William Julius Wilson, grappling with the growing concentration of poverty and social isolation in the inner cities, has argued that race-neutral policies offer the best hope for addressing the plight of disadvantaged minorities.[2] Paul Starr, editor of the new liberal journal, *The American Prospect*, has acknowledged the legitimacy of compensatory arguments for affirmative action but has suggested its costs may well outweigh its benefits: "with the positive effects of racial preferences have come many unhappy ones—sustaining racism, stigmatizing much minority achievement as 'merely' the result of affirmative action, creating a sense of grievance among whites who then feel entitled to discriminate, and blocking the formation of biracial political alliances necessary to make progress against poverty."[3]

Just how relevant is voting rights to this gathering debate over how best to advance the interests of disadvantaged minorities? Some parallels are clear: the potential for political backlash, the need to count heads by race and ethnicity to overcome racial and ethnic discrimination. Yet critical differences are also apparent. The right to vote and to have one's vote counted fairly is fundamental in a democracy, and the history of mock compliance with voting rights law has been odious.

At a conference at the Brookings Institution in November 1990 and in subsequent writing and editing, the contributors to this volume have wrestled with the complex and controversial issues surrounding the past, present, and future of the Voting Rights Act. The differences among them that remain in this book serve to inform and enlighten a crucial national debate.

1. Schlesinger 1991, 2.
2. Wilson 1990.
3. Starr 1992, 14.

Editors' Introduction

BERNARD GROFMAN & CHANDLER DAVIDSON

THE VOTING RIGHTS ACT OF 1965 is widely recognized as one of the most successful pieces of American legislation in the twentieth century. The purpose of the present volume is to provide a twenty-five year perspective on the act: its aims, its accomplishments, and what have been claimed to be its unintended consequences. To that end we have asked a number of leading scholars with differing views to write essays on the act's history, its implementation by the courts and the Department of Justice, and the broader questions involved in defining the idea of voting rights.

The book is intended to provide the reader with the information needed to place the Voting Rights Act in historical perspective, but with a focus on the voting rights issues and controversies that are of greatest concern today. We see these controversies as involving a combination of historical, normative, and legal-technical issues. Perhaps the key dispute is over whether the act and related case law have evolved into a mechanism for enforcing "affirmative action" quotas. In particular, to what extent has the proviso included in the 1982 amendments denying a right to proportional representation been violated in cases such as *Thornburg* v. *Gingles* (1986)? Are the standards of vote dilution now so loose that they permit almost unlimited expansion to cover practices the framers of the act in 1965 would not have considered as violating its provisions?

A related dispute concerns whether the act has now outlived its usefulness. Some who argue that it has claim that voting along racial lines—at least for the majority of whites—is largely a thing of the past. Other critics believe that the current manner of the act's enforcement harms minority political interests, even as it increases the number of minority officeholders, by unduly concentrating minorities in districts where they become a majority and thus denying them a wider influence. Another concern is whether the act, by forcing race-conscious districting, keeps racial issues unnecessarily prominent in American politics, while driving a wedge between minorities and their traditional liberal white allies.

In addition to debate about normative and policy questions, there has

I

been considerable dispute over the legal standards that ought to govern voting rights cases, especially with respect to the operationalization of the three prongs of the *Gingles* test for vote dilution under section 2 of the act. Another controversy concerns Justice Department enforcement of the act. Has enforcement been limited and inadequate, as some critics have charged? Has it been guided by a vindictive and distrustful view of state and local officials, as others have claimed? Has enforcement been tilted so as to favor the political interests of the administration in power, as still others have charged? Or, as its supporters claim, has the department done a creditable job of enforcement?

The mere listing of a sample of these issues is sufficient to serve notice that, in spite of the plaudits the act has received in many quarters, it has generated a sharply contested body of law and normative theory around which swirl many controversies that are not easily resolved. Rather than attempt a comprehensive inventory or offer an editorial perspective on major issues, we have chosen to let our authors speak for themselves. In so doing, we believe they can convey to readers a good sense of the range of issues, positions, and intensity of feelings on the important controversies that will be shaping the policy debate on voting rights in the 1990s.

The chapters are organized into four sections. The first contains a historical overview of voting rights in the United States, from the first Reconstruction to the present. It contains a chapter by Chandler Davidson describing the history of the Voting Rights Act of 1965, a chapter by Drew Days focusing on section 5 of the act, a chapter by Laughlin McDonald focusing on section 2 of the act, and a chapter by Timothy O'Rourke with an alternative, more critical view of the act and its recent implementation.

The second section covers the broader ramifications of the Voting Rights Act in American politics and race relations. It contains a chapter by Edward Carmines and Robert Huckfeldt on race and the dilemma of liberal politics, a chapter by Morgan Kousser that seeks to explain the relative success of the second Reconstruction as compared to the first, and a chapter by Hugh Davis Graham that views the Voting Rights Act in the context of recent social regulation.

The third section includes two essays that focus on the role of lawyers, expert witnesses, and minority advocacy groups in implementing voting rights. Bernard Grofman looks at the role of expert witnesses in the evolution of voting rights case law and in deciding particular controversies over the meaning and operationalization of key terms such as "racial bloc voting." Gregory Caldeira looks at what he calls the voting rights bar, the civil rights advocacy groups, attorneys, and expert witnesses who have been involved in voting rights litigation.

The fourth section discusses the Voting Rights Act and the quest for a color-blind society. It opens with an essay by Bruce Cain that examines whether implementation of the act violates either color-blind or majoritarian norms of American democracy. The section also contains brief comments on some of the issues raised in Cain's essay from scholars representing different perspectives: Luis Fraga, Lani Guinier, Carol Swain, and James Turner.

The last essay in the volume is a postscript by the editors that discusses the special nature of voting rights controversies and presents our thoughts about some of the issues that must be resolved if the goal of a color-blind society is to be achieved.

We hope this volume will both frame and help clarify the debate over the issues of minority voting rights and the concept of effective representation.

Part One ─────────────────────
Key Provisions of the Voting Rights Act

The Voting Rights Act: A Brief History

CHANDLER DAVIDSON

AT HIS FAREWELL presidential press conference, a weary and beleaguered Lyndon B. Johnson was asked by a reporter what he regarded as his greatest accomplishment and his happiest moment during his tenure. Johnson responded with a single answer: signing the Voting Rights Act of 1965.[1] Undeniably, passage of the act was of great historical significance. The climax of the so-called second Reconstruction, it secured for black Americans what the Fourteenth and Fifteenth Amendments, passed during the first Reconstruction, had not—the right to vote, the very bedrock of democracy.

Taking the act's full measure requires a broad historical compass. The story of black disfranchisement in America began in 1619 when the first Africans debarked from a ship in Jamestown, Virginia. For the next two and one-half centuries most blacks in this country were enslaved, and so they were unable to vote. Neither, of course, could women of any color. But freedmen, too, were not usually given the opportunity. At the time the Constitution was framed, to be sure, free black men could vote in some of the original states, including the southern one of North Carolina.[2] Moreover, some thousands of free southern blacks had the franchise early in the nineteenth century.[3] But the situation deteriorated as the century progressed. On the eve of the Civil War, free blacks were denied suffrage everywhere but in New York and the New England states— except for Connecticut, where they were also disfranchised. In New York, only blacks possessing $250 worth of property could vote; no such barrier applied to whites.[4]

I wish to thank Edward Cox, Bernard Grofman, Lani Guinier, Thomas Haskell, Gerald Hebert, David Hunter, Samuel Issacharoff, Gerald Jones, Pamela Karlan, and Laughlin McDonald for their help.

1. Lawson 1985, 4.
2. Dinkin 1982, 41–42. Stephenson 1969, 284, states that until the Revolution free blacks could vote in all the original states except South Carolina and Georgia. Dinkin does not go so far.
3. Franklin 1961, 80.
4. McPherson 1964, 223.

Between 1865 and 1869, blacks in the North remained largely disfranchised, as whites in the region voted against equal suffrage in eight out of eleven referendums on the issue.[5] Disfranchisement in the North as well as the South was the target of those abolitionists, still active after the war, who supported the Fifteenth Amendment.[6]

Reconstruction and the Black Franchise

Given what is known about his views on reconstructing the South, Abraham Lincoln probably did not favor general enfranchisement of the largely illiterate black population, although he suggested at one point that "very intelligent" blacks and those who were Union veterans might be given the vote.[7] Lincoln's successor, Andrew Johnson, was opposed to giving blacks suffrage immediately and, in any case, believed that individual states should decide the question.[8] It was only as a result of the Republican-dominated Congress that southern blacks were finally enfranchised. In its Reconstruction Act of 1867, passed over Johnson's veto, Congress required as a condition for readmission to the Union that the rebel states call conventions, to which blacks could be elected as delegates, in order to devise new constitutions guaranteeing voting rights to black men. By the time registration was completed that year, more than 700,000 southern blacks were on the rolls, comprising a majority of registered voters in several former Confederate states.[9]

Additionally, three Civil War amendments gradually extended constitutional protection to the black franchise. The Thirteenth, ratified in 1865, forbade slavery and thus secured for all blacks a minimal degree of citizenship. The Fourteenth, ratified in 1868, carried the process a step further, granting citizenship to all persons "born or naturalized in the United States." The Constitutional Convention of 1789 had decided that in determining a state's number of representatives in Congress, each slave would be counted as three-fifths of a free person. The Fourteenth Amendment, by implication, required that all blacks be counted equally with whites. Further, if a state denied or abridged the voting rights of male citizens who were at least twenty-one years of age, its representa-

5. See the chapter by Kousser in this volume.
6. McPherson 1964, 424.
7. Stampp 1965, 47. Had Lincoln lived, his views on black enfranchisement might have become more expansive. See McCrary 1978, 3–18.
8. Stampp 1965, 77.
9. Franklin 1961, 80; McPherson 1990, 19.

tional base in Congress was to be diminished in proportion to the number of those whose rights were curtailed. (This part of the amendment, however, was not applied when blacks were disfranchised some years later.)[10] Finally, by guaranteeing the "privileges and immunities" of citizens, as well as due process and equal protection of the laws, the amendment provided blacks with a weapon against political discrimination—one, however, whose potential would only begin to be fully realized in the twentieth century.

What the Fourteenth Amendment failed to do was explicitly prohibit vote discrimination on racial grounds. This prohibition was accomplished by the Fifteenth, ratified in 1870, which stated simply, "The right of citizens of the United States to vote shall not be denied or abridged by the United States or by any State on account of race, color, or previous condition of servitude. The Congress shall have power to enforce this article by appropriate legislation." The voting rights of blacks in the North as well as in the South were thereby given explicit constitutional protection, although much stronger versions of the amendment favored by Radical Republicans and blacks—one that would have prohibited states from imposing nativity, property, or literacy tests; another that would have given the federal government complete control over voting rights—were rejected on the grounds that they could not be ratified.[11] The amendment also was silent about the right to hold office, which many Radical Republicans wanted guaranteed.[12] Even so, the Fifteenth Amendment was a major advance in providing constitutional protection for black voting rights.

10. Myrdal 1944, 515.

11. McPherson 1964, 424–25; Foner 1988, 447. It is ironic that Wendell Phillips, one of the most radical of the abolitionists, was largely responsible for passage of the version of the Fifteenth Amendment that many abolitionists at the time correctly perceived to contain gaping loopholes that could be used to disfranchise blacks. The problem was that this version, passed by the House of Representatives, was in competition with a much more thorough Senate version that seemed incapable of ratification. No compromise between proponents of the two versions seemed possible. Congress would soon adjourn, and there was fear that a delay would preclude any amendment in the foreseeable future. Phillips endorsed the weaker version in his abolitionist newspaper, which was credited with passage of the amendment. Another abolitionist, Lydia Maria Child, saw clearly that this version might yet "be so evaded, by some contrivance, that the colored population will in reality have no civil rights allowed them" (McPherson 1964, 428). Indeed, numerous contrivances were soon adopted in the southern states, in spite of a series of congressional statutes passed soon after the Fifteenth Amendment was ratified. For a concise description of these "enforcement acts," see Hyman 1973, 526–31, who describes them as "virtually dead letters" (534) after 1874.

12. Foner 1988, 446.

But intense and often violent white southern resistance to black voting—concurrent with the rise of the Ku Klux Klan—made it clear to congressional Republicans that enforcement legislation authorized by the amendment would be necessary. Between May 1870 and April 1871 three Enforcement Acts were passed to put teeth in the new constitutional guarantee of black voting rights. Yet they were no match for white southern intransigence and "proved wholly inadequate, especially when enforcement was left to the meager forces that remained in the South at the time of their enactment."[13] Two Supreme Court decisions in 1876 virtually gutted the Fourteenth and Fifteenth Amendments as protectors of the black franchise.[14] In the Compromise of 1877, northern Republicans, by withdrawing all federal troops from the three southern states in which they remained, tacitly gave southern white Democrats the message that the federal government was willing to let the white South deal with blacks as best it saw fit. The first Reconstruction was over.

Disfranchisement

Among the measures employed by southern white conservatives to undermine the Civil War amendments were violence, voting fraud, white officials' discriminatory use of election structures (such as gerrymandering and the use of at-large elections to prevent black officeholding), statutory suffrage restrictions, and, in the waning years of the century, revision of the "reconstructed" state constitutions to effect disfranchisement. As J. Morgan Kousser argues in this book, none of the approaches—even violence—was sufficient in itself; all worked together as interlocking barriers gradually and surely to stifle political participation.

The results were precisely what the white conservatives had intended. At the high point of southern black voting during Reconstruction, about two-thirds of eligible black males cast ballots in presidential and gubernatorial contests. In the early years of Reconstruction, moreover, these voters elected large numbers of black officials to legislatures and to Congress—324 in 1872 alone, and many more to lower offices (see Kousser, table 1). At this time "about 15 percent of the officeholders in the South were black," James McPherson has commented, "a larger proportion than in 1990."[15] But measures to prevent blacks from voting

13. Franklin 1961, 172.
14. See Derfner 1973, 523, 528. The cases were United States v. Cruikshank, 92 U.S. 542 (1876) and United States v. Reese, 92 U.S. 214 (1876).
15. McPherson 1990, 19. Of course, a larger percentage of the South was black in the nineteenth century.

were employed with increasing effect following Reconstruction. Beginning in 1890 the first of several southern disfranchising conventions was held. Ten years later, only five blacks were southern legislators or congressmen (Kousser, table 1). After Mississippi revised its constitution in 1890, black registrants dropped to 6 percent of the eligible black population; in 1906, Alabama's black registrants stood at 2 percent. By contrast, two-thirds of eligible Mississippi whites were registered, as were 83 percent of white Alabamians.[16] Throughout the South, the doors to black political participation were forcefully slammed shut.

Disfranchisement at the hands of Democrats, which was hastened in the 1890s by the alliance of many southern blacks with the Populists in a violent struggle against the white propertied classes, coincided with the rise of state-enforced Jim Crow institutions that prevented interaction between blacks and whites as equals in every aspect of southern society, perpetuating a harsh racial caste system. These disheartening events, coming after the brief springtime of freedom that followed 250 years of slavery, fully justify the characterization of the 1890s as "the nadir."[17]

The Struggle to Regain the Franchise

The twentieth century had hardly begun, however, before blacks and their white allies were at work to regain their voting rights. "Let not the spirit of Garrison, Phillips and Douglass wholly die out in America," wrote the young W. E. B. Du Bois in 1900, his ringing call to action invoking the famous abolitionists. "May the conscience of a great nation rise and rebuke all dishonesty and unrighteous oppression toward the American Negro, and grant him the right of franchise [and] security of person and property."[18]

In 1910 Du Bois was one of the founders of the National Association for the Advancement of Colored People (NAACP), the civil rights organization that would take the lead in challenging not only southern blacks' political exclusion but the entire legal underpinnings of the racial caste system. One of the organization's first legal victories came in challenging the Oklahoma grandfather clause, a subterfuge to excuse whites from taking the state's literacy test. The Supreme Court declared it unconsti-

16. Lawson 1976, 15.
17. Logan 1954.
18. Quoted in Aptheker 1976, 6.

tutional in 1915, although Oklahoma soon adopted a new version.[19] The
NAACP took aim at the white primary in 1924 in the first major test of
that institution's legality when it represented a black plaintiff in his challenge
of Texas's party primary law, a law that an NAACP lawyer described
as flying "right in the teeth of the Fifteenth Amendment."[20] The Supreme
Court soon held that the statute violated the Fourteenth Amendment and
later struck down as well a law Texas had subsequently passed giving
state party executive committees the right to bar blacks from membership.
But the court unanimously held in 1935 that the Texas Democratic party,
when acting through its state convention as distinct from its executive
committee, had the right as a "private" organization to exclude blacks.
Only in 1944 did the high court, in Smith v. Allwright, finally declare
the white primary an integral part of the state's election process and
hence impermissible under the Fifteenth Amendment.[21] A key attorney
in the case was Thurgood Marshall, the first director-counsel of the
NAACP Legal Defense and Education Fund, which had been established
in 1939. Marshall would also play a commanding role as strategist and
trial lawyer in the school desegregation cases leading up to and including
Brown v. Board of Education of Topeka in 1954.[22]

Although southern officials tried through various stratagems to overcome
the prohibition of white primaries in Smith v. Allwright, they ultimately
failed. Black registration increased significantly. In 1940 black voters in
the South were estimated at a maximum of 151,000, about 3 percent of
voting-age blacks in the region. This was a level not much higher than
that at the time of disfranchisement. By 1947, three years after Smith, it
had increased to 595,000 and in 1956 to 1,238,038—still a mere 25
percent of voting-age blacks compared with 60 percent of whites who
were registered.[23]

19. Guinn and Beal v. United States, 238 U.S. 347 (1915). Oklahoma promptly devised
another disfranchising mechanism following Guinn that still enabled whites to preclude
blacks from voting, and this was not held unconstitutional until 1939 (Lawson 1976,
18–19).

20. Lawson 1976, 26.

21. See Hine 1979 for an account of the Texas white primary cases, which included
Nixon v. Herndon, 273 U.S. 536 (1927); Nixon v. Condon, 286 U.S. 73 (1932); Grovey
v. Townsend, 295 U.S. 45 (1935); and Smith v. Allwright, 321 U.S. 649 (1944). As late
as 1953 the Court, in Terry v. Adams, 345 U.S. 461, struck down a white "pre-primary"
held by a local party in Fort Bend County, Texas, to select the white community's contestants
in the Democratic primary in order to prevent a split in the white vote in the primary.

22. Brown v. Board of Education of Topeka, 347 U.S. 483 (1954). See Lawson 1976,
52; Kluger 1976.

23. Garrow 1978, 6–7; Price 1959, 10.

The battle for black voting rights had far to go. The poll tax was a barrier in a number of southern states and a particularly formidable one in Alabama, Mississippi, and Virginia, where the tax was cumulative.[24] But the most effective barrier, aside from the ever-present threat of violence and economic reprisal in the Deep South, was the literacy test, which in 1944 was still operative in all states of the former Confederacy except Arkansas and Texas. Even its fair administration would have excluded many blacks because of their unequal education under the Jim Crow regime. But white registrars, a law unto themselves, were often arbitrary in giving the test; they could exclude literate blacks while allowing illiterate whites to vote.[25]

The struggle for the ballot waged by blacks and their allies over the two decades from *Smith* v. *Allwright* to the passage of the Voting Rights Act was difficult.[26] It took many forms, including voter canvassing in kudzu-bordered country lanes, violent confrontations between blacks and white registrars, legal actions in musty courtrooms, and impassioned floor debates in the national capitol. In the process, three civil rights acts, passed in 1957, 1960, and 1964, addressed the exclusion of blacks from the voting booth. With respect to their voting provisions, all three were tentative, piecemeal efforts that failed to breach the barriers maintained by southern white supremacists. The burden remained on black voters to seek relief in the courts case by case, a time-consuming and extremely inefficient process, especially inasmuch as the southern district courts were mostly presided over by conservative local judges.[27]

Even so, black voting in the eleven former Confederate states as a whole continued to increase. By November 1964 the number of blacks registered had doubled since 1952, constituting 43.3 percent of their voting-age population. In the Deep South, however, white resistance was fierce in many areas, particularly the rural ones: average black registration in Alabama, Georgia, Louisiana, Mississippi, and South Carolina was only 22.5 percent of those eligible. In Mississippi, a mere 6.7 percent were registered.[28]

24. Garrow 1978, 243, note 13. Georgia, which had also had a cumulative tax, abolished it in 1945.
25. Lawson 1976, 86–115; Commission on Civil Rights 1968, 13–19.
26. Lawson 1976.
27. Strong 1968. There were exceptions, such as J. Skelly Wright and Alabama's legendary Frank M. Johnson, Jr. For an account of progressive judges during this period, see Bass 1981.
28. Congressional Quarterly Service 1968, 115.

Selma

To overcome hard-core resistance in these states, civil rights organizations in the early 1960s began to mount intensive grass-roots campaigns. The Voter Education Project of the Southern Regional Council was formed in 1962 and played a major organizing role over the next year and a half. The Congress of Racial Equality was heavily involved in Louisiana. Then in 1964, largely through the efforts of the Student Nonviolent Coordinating Committee (SNCC), the "Mississippi Freedom Summer" was organized, in which black and white college students from across the country converged on the state, joining with local black workers primarily to conduct door-to-door voter canvassing.[29] Early in the project three civil rights workers—two white and one black—were murdered in Neshoba County, riveting the nation's attention on the area.[30] The Freedom Summer produced few black votes but a great deal of white violence: "35 shooting incidents with 3 persons injured; 30 homes and other buildings bombed; 35 churches burned; 80 persons beaten," and 6 murders.[31]

That November, one week after Lyndon Johnson's landslide victory over Barry Goldwater, leaders of the Southern Christian Leadership Conference (SCLC), including its president, the Reverend Martin Luther King, Jr., met in Birmingham to discuss strategy. When the question of voting rights came up, C. T. Vivian, one of the organization's leaders, told the group that the SCLC should have "a rallying point around which we can stir the whole nation." Amelia Boynton, a longtime Selma, Alabama, activist, suggested that her town, where the SNCC civil rights efforts were faltering under hard-line political oppression, would be an excellent place to begin a voting drive. Plans were made to look closely at this possibility.[32] President Johnson, for his part, decided in December to press forward with an administration bill providing for federal voter registration officials in the South.[33]

29. The volunteers were also joined by numerous lawyers from two national civil rights legal groups, the Lawyers' Constitutional Defense Committee and the Lawyers' Committee for Civil Rights Under Law. See Parker 1990, 79.

30. Belfrage 1965.

31. Watters and Cleghorn 1967, 139; Garrow 1978, 20–21.

32. Garrow 1988, 358–59.

33. Garrow 1978, 38. Johnson's motives were probably a mixture of genuine concern for voting rights and a fear that the Civil Rights Act of 1964 had so alienated white southerners from the Democratic party that only a vastly increased black vote could offset the party's losses. See Stern 1992, chap. 8.

The SCLC, satisfied before the year was out that Selma was the field on which a decisive battle for the vote should be fought, began its campaign on January 2, 1965, in a city whose resistance to black registration and voting was extraordinary, even by southern standards. In surrounding Dallas County, where slightly more than half the 30,000 persons of voting age were black, only 335 were registered in the fall of 1964, in spite of intense efforts over the previous three years by SNCC, SCLC, and the Justice Department. By comparison, 9,542 whites were registered by the all-white board of registrars. Although "the litigation method of correction has been tried harder here than anywhere else in the South," Justice Department attorney John Doar wrote at the time, Dallas County blacks still lacked "the most fundamental of their constitutional rights—the right to vote."[34]

The SCLC's choice of Selma to dramatize the plight of disfranchised blacks was a good one. Registration in Dallas County was possible only two days each month. An applicant was required to fill in more than fifty blanks on a form, write a part of the Constitution from dictation, read four parts of the Constitution and answer four questions on it, answer four questions on the workings of government, and swear loyalty to Alabama and the United States.[35] The choice of Selma was strategically sound for another reason as well. Its sheriff, James G. Clark, Jr., much like Police Commissioner Eugene "Bull" Connor in Birmingham two years earlier, could be counted on to overreact to peaceful civil rights demonstrations.

As blacks' efforts to register continued day by day, the resistance of Selma officials grew stiffer—and uglier. Demonstrations began. Right wing troublemakers drifted into town, including a leader of the American Nazi party and some of his hangers-on. Black and white supporters of the demonstrators, from Alabama and elsewhere, also came. Law enforcement officers roughed up civil rights workers. Sheriff Clark seemed spoiling for a chance to take out his racist feelings on the blacks rallying to the cause. In various confrontations he beat and jabbed black protesters and leaders. State troopers also used unjustified violence against demonstrators. Mass arrests occurred, including 500 demonstrating black schoolchildren. Martin Luther King and a companion were jailed.

The national press was now giving Selma detailed coverage. In January the White House had announced its intent to sponsor voting rights legisla-

34. Garrow 1978, 34; Congressional Quarterly Service 1967, 67.
35. Congressional Quarterly Service 1967, 67.

tion. In early March, with the Selma drama unfolding, Dr. King met with President Johnson to discuss both the crisis and a voting rights bill. The climax of the Selma campaign occurred on Sunday, March 7, the day on which civil rights forces had earlier announced their intention to complete a peaceful fifty-four-mile trek, led by King, along U.S. 80 to Montgomery, the state capital. Governor George Wallace had forbidden the march and declared that state troopers would "use whatever measures are necessary to prevent a march."[36]

King, who had left town earlier and was scheduled to speak in Atlanta that day, decided after conferring with colleagues in Selma not to return for the march because it was not likely to take place and his time could be better spent in Atlanta mobilizing support for a "larger thrust forward." About 600 marchers set out on Sunday afternoon, led now by SCLC's Hosea Williams and SNCC's John Lewis. On the Edmund Pettus Bridge leading out of Selma, they were met by state troopers and sheriff's possemen. When the marchers refused orders to turn back and instead knelt in prayer, they were set upon by club-wielding troopers, teargassed, and finally driven back into the black neighborhood. Ninety to 100 demonstrators were injured, some severely, with wounds including broken bones, deep head cuts, and smashed teeth. Lewis sustained a serious head trauma and was flown to a hospital in Boston. Amelia Boynton, who had suggested the Selma campaign to the SCLC leadership, was beaten and teargassed into unconsciousness.[37]

Bloody Sunday, as it was later called, and a subsequent march successfully led by King to Montgomery—once Federal District Judge Frank M. Johnson, Jr., had overruled Alabama officials' prohibition of the demonstration—stirred the national conscience, as did the murders of three civil rights volunteers connected with the Selma campaign. Sheriff Clark unwittingly played the role earlier assigned him in the SCLC script, and George Wallace unintentionally did his part for the protestors' cause as well. On March 15 President Johnson presented his voting rights bill in an electrifying address to Congress, watched by a nationwide television audience of 70 million people. "It was an emotional peak unmatched by anything that had come before [in the civil rights movement], nor by anything that would come after," wrote David Garrow. Watching Johnson on a television set in Selma, King cried, something his colleagues and friends had never seen him do before.[38]

36. Garrow 1988, 396.
37. Garrow 1978, 31–77; Garrow 1988, 396–97, 399.
38. Garrow 1988, 408–09.

Riding a crest of national outrage at the events in Selma, Congress began action on Johnson's program. On August 3 the House approved the new Voting Rights Act by a vote of 328 to 74. The next day the Senate followed suit 79 to 18. Passage of the bill was a bipartisan effort that split along regional lines: northerners of both parties overwhelmingly supported it, southerners of both parties opposed it.[39] On August 6 the president signed the bill, calling it "one of the most monumental laws in the entire history of American freedom." In a ceremony that self-consciously harked back to the Civil War, the signing took place in a room off the Senate chamber in which Abraham Lincoln, 104 years earlier to the day, had signed into law a bill freeing slaves whom the Confederacy had coerced into service.[40] Five days later, the Senate confirmed Johnson's nominee for solicitor general, Thurgood Marshall, an act not only of symbolic but also of substantive importance: in 1967, after ably performing in that role, Marshall was confirmed as the first black to serve on the Supreme Court, where he became one of the Voting Rights Act's most reliable supporters.

The Voting Rights Act of 1965

Lyndon Johnson had told his attorney general, Nicholas deB. Katzenbach, to compose the "goddamnedest toughest" voting bill he could write, and the product lived up to that command.[41] The act was a fundamental departure from the tepid voting measures of the civil rights acts of 1957, 1960, and 1964. Providing for direct federal action to enable blacks to register and vote, it placed the initiative for enforcement firmly in the executive branch and made unnecessary the case-by-case litigation that had been required. The act's purpose was to enforce the Fifteenth Amendment. Section 2, a permanent feature that forbade states or political subdivisions to apply a voting prerequisite "to deny or abridge the right of any citizen of the United States to vote on account of race or color," echoed the amendment's language.

Congress was well aware of the Fifteenth Amendment's failure to do its job after Reconstruction. The act's supporters were determined that such a fate should not befall the new measure, despite determined resistance in the South. New York Representative Emanuel Celler, chair of the House Judiciary Committee and floor manager of the bill, asserted in his speech opening

39. See Kousser's chapter in this volume, table 6.
40. Congressional Quarterly Service 1968, 70.
41. Raines 1977, 337.

House debate that the act would eliminate the "legal dodges and subterfuges" still in operation. He claimed that it would be "impervious to all legal trickery and evasion" of the sort that had enabled white racists from the 1870s forward to twist the intent of the Civil War amendments to their own purposes. The southern white politicians of the 1960s understood this purpose clearly. Echoing the Democrats' opposition to congressional enfranchising measures during the first Reconstruction, they argued vehemently against the bill. Howard W. Smith of Virginia, the House Rules Committee chair and a leading opponent of the bill, called it an "unconstitutional" vendetta against the former Confederate states. Senator Herman E. Talmadge, Democrat of Georgia, called the bill "grossly unjust and vindictive in nature." Senator Strom Thurmond, Republican of South Carolina, averred that if it passed, "we have a totalitarian state in which there will be despotism and tyranny."[42] Many southern congressmen of both parties, strident in their opposition, agreed.

At the heart of the original act were sections 4 through 9—the "special provisions," most of which were temporary and would be periodically renewed by Congress. In the spring of 1965 seven southern states still had literacy tests. By means of a triggering formula in section 4, the act abolished for five years literacy tests in all states of the Union or their subdivisions that had had a test or similar device as a voting prerequisite on November 1, 1964, and a voter registration rate on that date—or voter turnout in the 1964 presidential elections—of less than 50 percent of the voting-age residents.[43] On August 7, 1965, the day after the act was signed, Attorney General Katzenbach suspended tests in seven states entirely (including Alaska) as well as in twenty-six North Carolina counties and one Arizona county. Later in 1965 and 1966, other North Carolina and Arizona counties were added, as well as one each in Hawaii and Idaho. Some of these counties and one state, Alaska, were able during the 1960s to exempt themselves, or "bail out," from coverage by persuading the District Court for the District of Columbia that, as specified in

42. Congressional Quarterly Service 1968, 69; *Congressional Quarterly Almanac* 1966, 548. Senator James Eastland, Democrat of Mississippi, alleged that the administration's bill was written to exclude President Johnson's home state of Texas from the triggering mechanism of section 4, a claim denied by Attorney General Nicholas Katzenbach (*Congressional Quarterly Almanac* 1966, 556).

43. A "test or device," as defined by the act, was any voting or registration prerequisite requiring a person to "(1) demonstrate the ability to read, write, understand, or interpret any matter, (2) demonstrate any educational achievement or his knowledge of any particular subject, (3) possess good moral character, or (4) prove his qualifications by the voucher of registered voters or members of any other class."

the section 4 bailout requirements, they had not used a test or a device in a discriminatory way for five years.[44]

Thus while coverage in the beginning was not, strictly speaking, limited to the South, for practical purposes it was. Between 1965 and 1970 six southern states and much of a seventh were the primary areas of coverage: Alabama, Georgia, Louisiana, Mississippi, South Carolina, Virginia, and forty of the one hundred counties in North Carolina.[45] It is these states that are often referred to, with only slight inaccuracy, as the seven states originally covered by the act's special provisions.

Section 5, in which the triggering formula in section 4 again came into play, was another key part of the act—one that would grow in importance after a Supreme Court decision in 1969 provided an expansive interpretation of its scope. Those states and counties covered by the formula had their voting laws frozen pending federal approval of proposed changes. They were required to submit to the attorney general (who normally would have sixty days to object) or the District Court for the District of Columbia all planned changes in any "voting qualification or prerequisite to voting, or standard, practice or procedure with respect to voting" that had not been in force on November 1, 1964. The proposed changes would be precleared, jurisdiction by jurisdiction, after federal scrutiny of the particular facts only if the changes did "not have the purpose and . . . [would] not have the effect of denying or abridging the right to vote on account of race or color." This controversial preclearance requirement in the covered jurisdictions gave the Justice Department unprecedented authority to monitor the region's election machinery and to object to discriminatory changes. However, the initiative to submit changes for preclearance remained with the covered jurisdictions, and the Justice Department has never tried to determine in a systematic fashion whether all changes have been submitted—a policy for which it has sometimes been criticized.[46]

Sections 6 and 7 gave the attorney general discretionary power to appoint federal officials as voting "examiners" who could be sent into covered jurisdictions to ensure, in effect, that legally qualified persons could register in federal, state, and local elections. Section 8 provided for federal observers, or poll watchers, to oversee the actual voting process; they were to be assigned by the attorney general if needed. In the first

44. The original bailout provisions, as well as the changes in these provisions in 1970, 1975, and 1982, are described and analyzed by Hancock and Tredway 1985.

45. Commission on Civil Rights 1975, 13–14.

46. Commission on Civil Rights 1975, 28.

ten years of the act, examiners were used sparingly, being sent into only sixty southern counties, most of which were in Mississippi and Alabama. About 15 percent of the 1 million new minority registrants during this period were attributed to the examiner program. More than 6,500 federal poll watchers were assigned to the covered states during the period.[47]

If the attorney general or private parties brought voting suits outside covered jurisdictions, section 3 gave courts authority to send federal registrars and poll watchers to the locales as needed. If the suits demonstrated that tests or devices violated Fourteenth or Fifteenth Amendment rights, section 3 allowed courts to abolish the tests. And the same section empowered courts, in imposing a remedy in a voting case outside covered areas, to retain jurisdiction for a period of time during which any voting change in the locale had to be precleared by the court or the Justice Department.

The act did not prohibit the poll tax, which four states still used as a voting requirement. The Twenty-fourth Amendment, ratified in 1964, had already outlawed it in federal elections and primaries. But some in Congress worried that the courts might find such a prohibition unconstitutional, endangering the constitutionality of the act as a whole. Thus section 10, while declaring that Congress believed the tax violated the Constitution "in some areas," merely instructed the attorney general "forthwith" to challenge the constitutionality of poll taxes as voting prerequisites in state and local elections. Katzenbach did so quickly, and in 1966 federal courts struck them down in Texas, Alabama, Mississippi, and Virginia.[48]

Section 11 prohibited anyone "acting under color of law" from preventing qualified voters from voting or having their votes fairly counted; and it prohibited anyone "acting under color of law or otherwise" from intimidating, threatening, or coercing those attempting to vote or helping others to vote. It also prohibited voting fraud in federal elections, and provided jail terms and fines for it. Section 12 provided punishment, as well, for violations of others' voting rights.

Section 14, in a passage the courts would later fasten on, spelled out in comprehensive detail the meaning of "vote" or "voting" to "include all action necessary to make a vote effective in any primary, special, or general election, including, but not limited to, registration, listing [of

47. Commission on Civil Rights 1975, 33–35.
48. Commission on Civil Rights 1968, 166–67. In *Harper* v. *Virginia State Board of Elections*, 383 U.S. 663 (1966), the Supreme Court overruled its 1937 decision in *Breedlove* v. *Suttles*, 302 U.S. 277, that the payment of a poll tax did not violate the Constitution.

eligible voters] pursuant to this act, or other action required by law prerequisite to voting, casting a ballot, and having such ballot counted properly and included in the appropriate totals of votes cast with respect to candidates for public or party office and propositions for which votes are received in an election."

These were, in short, the most important features of the law of which Lyndon Johnson was so proud and in the passage of which he, as well as Martin Luther King and the civil rights movement and its martyrs, played a major role. In 1966 the Supreme Court in *South Carolina* v. *Katzenbach* declared constitutional those sections of the act, including most of section 4 and all of section 5, challenged by the state of South Carolina.[49]

The South's Response to the Act

Attorney General Katzenbach designated the first group of counties and parishes for federal action three days after the president signed the act, and examiners immediately began to register black voters. Before the month was out, the president announced that 27,385 blacks in Alabama, Louisiana, and Mississippi had been registered by the federal examiners in the first nineteen days. He also alluded to signs of voluntary compliance with the act in some other locales.[50]

Faced with a federal enforcement effort that included the possibility of jail terms for miscreants, the most obvious response of white southern officialdom, even in the strongholds of resistance, was grudging acceptance of the new black enfranchisement. In Mississippi, that stronghold within a stronghold, black voter registration increased from 6.7 percent before the act to 59.8 in 1967.[51] The act simply overwhelmed the major bulwarks of the disfranchising system. In the seven states originally covered, black registration increased from 29.3 percent in March 1965 to 56.6 percent in 1971–72; the gap between black and white registration rates narrowed from 44.1 percentage points to 11.2. The Justice Department estimated that in the five years after passage, almost as many blacks registered in Alabama, Mississippi, Georgia, Louisiana, North Carolina, and South Carolina as in the entire century before 1965.[52]

49. *South Carolina* v. *Katzenbach*, 383 U.S. 301 (1966).
50. Congressional Quarterly Service 1968, 70.
51. Commission on Civil Rights 1968, 246–47.
52. Commission on Civil Rights 1975, 43; *Congressional Quarterly Almanac* 1971, 198. Here and elsewhere, comparisons between black and white registration and turnout rates must be treated with great caution, given the difficulty in obtaining accurate estimates

Optimists at the time believed the act would soon accomplish its purpose; the political incorporation of blacks seemed to be at hand. Steven Lawson, the leading student of twentieth century black enfranchisement, admits to having held such a view, with qualifications. In the 1980s, however, he concluded that "suffrage problems have not been self-correcting, and the second phase of enfranchisement—the search for a greater share of political representation—has engendered a new round of racial conflict."[53] Other observers were less sanguine from the beginning.

With some oversimplification, voting rights controversies during the past quarter century have focused more on what Lawson calls minority "representation" than mere access to the ballot box. The oversimplification lies in the fact that almost immediately after passage, white officials in numerous southern venues continued to restrict access to the ballot locally—that is, to disfranchise blacks—not in a frontal and obviously impermissible manner but with some of those "legal dodges and subterfuges" that Congressman Celler had anticipated during the hearings on the act. Thus in 1973, eight years after passage, Armand Derfner catalogued the following still-existing practices:

> Withholding information about registration, voting procedures or party activities from black voters; giving inadequate or erroneous information to black voters, or failing to provide assistance to illiterate voters; omitting the names of registered voters from the lists; maintaining racially segregated voting lists or facilities; conducting reregistration or purging the rolls; allowing improper challenges of black voters; disqualifying black voters on technical grounds; requiring separate registration for different types of elections; failing to provide the same opportunities for absentee ballots to blacks as to whites; moving polling places or establishing them in inconvenient or intimidating locations; setting elections at inconvenient times; failing to provide adequate voting facilities in areas of greatly increased black registration; and causing or taking advantage of election day irregularities.[54]

of participation by race, no matter what the method of estimation used. Lichtman and Issacharoff 1991, using a method different from that employed by the Census Bureau, argue that the 1984 Current Population Survey showing that black voter registration in Mississippi actually exceeded white registration by a margin of 85.6 percent to 81.4 percent, was quite inaccurate. A more reasonable estimate, they believe, is 54 percent black and 79 percent white.

53. Lawson 1985, xiii.

54. Derfner 1973, 557–58. For further evidence of disfranchising attempts in the decade following passage of the act, see Washington Research Project 1972, chaps. 2, 4; Commission on Civil Rights 1975, chaps. 4, 5.

Derfner listed yet another set of practices, widespread in the South, that restricted the efforts of black candidates to win office—what have sometimes been called methods of minority "candidate diminution" as distinct from disfranchisement. He listed eight practices, including the abolition of offices, extending the terms of white incumbents, and "imposing stiff formal requirements for qualifying to run in primary or general elections," such as high filing fees or numerous nominating petitions.[55]

Finally, Derfner listed a third set of practices or laws under the heading of "vote dilution." Included were racial gerrymandering; decreasing the black proportion in a town or county by annexation, deannexation, or consolidation; imposing a majority runoff requirement, which can enable white voters to mobilize behind a single white candidate in the runoff after having split their votes among several whites in the first election; holding at-large rather than district elections, which allows white voters to overwhelm black ones when the latter are in the minority; enacting such devices as full-slate laws, numbered-place laws, and staggered terms, all of which can, under some circumstances, preclude the use of "single-shot" voting by blacks, a strategy that can help them in at-large systems to elect black candidates; and "splitting the vote for a strong black candidate by nominating additional blacks as 'straw' candidates for the same office." These devices, Derfner noted, operated in a dilutionary manner where, as in most of the South, racial bloc voting among whites as well as among blacks is a factor.[56]

Disfranchisement was largely curtailed during the first ten years of the act, although several remnants remained. For example, Mississippi's

55. Derfner 1973, 555–56.

56. Derfner 1973, 553–55. These operate in different ways to diminish minority officeholding. All depend for their effectiveness on racially polarized voting in the jurisdiction where they are used: the nonminority vote typically goes for one candidate or set of candidates and the minority vote for another. The racial gerrymander carves districts so as to diminish the minority percentage in districts or, alternatively, it packs almost all minority voters into one or a few districts to prevent their having influence outside that area. Annexation, deannexation, and consolidation rearrange a jurisdiction's boundaries to decrease the total minority percentage. The majority requirement forces the two top vote getters into a runoff election if neither has won a majority of votes in the first race. In instances in which a black is the front-runner, having won a plurality but not a majority in a contest against two or more white candidates, the runoff can force the black candidate to run against a single white, giving white voters an opportunity to coalesce behind the latter. Full-slate laws, numbered-place laws, and staggered terms all have the effect of preventing or minimizing the effects of single-shot voting, a practice minority voters have often resorted to in an at-large election to overcome the handicap of white bloc voting. For further evidence of widespread dilution in the late 1960s and early 1970s, see Washington Research Project 1972, chap. 5; Commission on Civil Rights 1975, chaps. 8–9.

notorious dual registration system, a relic of the disfranchising constitution of 1890, by which urban voters had to register twice—once for
federal, state, and county elections, and again for municipal elections—
was not abolished in its entirety until 1987, as a result of a lawsuit brought
under the Voting Rights Act.[57] But vote dilution continued to be widely
practiced.

The Problem of Vote Dilution

Ethnic or racial minority vote dilution may be defined as a process
whereby election laws or practices, either singly or in concert, combine
with systematic bloc voting among an identifiable majority group to
diminish or cancel the voting strength of at least one minority group.[58]
Thus conceived, it is a form of discrimination distinct from disfranchisement and candidate diminution. In its most easily recognizable forms—
gerrymandering and multimember election systems—it was an important
tool used by whites in the South both during and after Reconstruction
to diminish the political strength of newly enfranchised blacks.[59] A Texas
newspaper put the matter forthrightly in 1876 when it described districts
in heavily black areas as "elongated most absurdly." In a redistricting
process dominated by whites, the "districts were 'Gerrymandered,' the
purpose being, in these elections, and properly enough, to disfranchise
the blacks by indirection" so that black voters would not make up more
than "a third of the voters in each district."[60] In addition to racial
gerrymandering, white officials from Reconstruction through the Progressive Era abolished districts entirely in many cities and counties and substi-
tuted at-large election schemes that placed black voters in majority-white
multimember districts, with the same effect: so-called disfranchisement
by indirection.[61]

Precisely the same methods were employed by southern white officials
during the second Reconstruction, and for the same purpose, although

57. Parker 1990, 205. There is some evidence, according to Ellis Turnage 1991, a Greenville, Mississippi, attorney, that even today various Mississippi jurisdictions, such as the town
of Sunflower, refuse to abide by the court decision outlawing dual registration. For examples
of both disfranchising and candidate-diminishing devices existing into the 1980s or later, see
Cox and Turner 1981; Parker and Phillips 1981; Department of Justice 1990.

58. For a similar definition, see Engstrom and McDonald 1987, 245.

59. Foner 1988, 422, 590; Kousser 1984, 30–33.

60. Quoted in Rice 1971, 26. It was in the heavily black areas before they were
gerrymandered that blacks in Texas were able to win office. Barr 1982, 48.

61. Kousser 1984, 32–33; Rice 1977.

their motives were not so plainly advertised. Actually, as lawsuits and voting drives became more frequent in the 1950s and early 1960s, various states had already begun to change their election statutes. In Alabama, where numerous counties had switched from at-large to district elections following turn-of-the-century disfranchisement, the change back to at-large elections began not long after *Smith* v. *Allwright* outlawed the white primary. Between 1947 and 1971, twenty-five of the state's sixty-seven counties switched from single-member districts to at-large elections.[62] Further, in 1951 Alabama adopted a full-slate law, preventing single-shot or bullet voting, a strategy that sometimes enables blacks to elect representatives from multimember districts by withholding votes for all candidates on the slate but their preferred ones.[63] The 1951 law, which applied to every public election in Alabama, statewide or local, was sponsored by a legislator who had entered politics in 1949 out of concern about increased black registration. Another legislator said the law was necessary because "there are some who fear that the colored voters might be able to elect one of their own race to the [Tuskegee] city council by 'single shot' voting."[64]

Whites' fear of black enfranchisement had also been building in Georgia for some time before the Voting Rights Act was passed. In 1957, the same year Congress enacted its first civil rights bill since Reconstruction, the general assembly officially resolved that the Fourteenth and Fifteenth Amendments be repealed because they "were malignant acts of arbitrary power" and "are null and void and of no effect." When the county-unit system, a scheme that guaranteed malapportionment and worked to the

---

62. McCrary and others 1990, 21.

63. A minority group, in using the single-shot strategy, decides in advance on a single candidate whom it will support among the field of candidates running for office. The structural preconditions for this strategy to work are that all the candidates are in competition with each other, the top vote getters fill the available positions, and each voter has as many votes to cast as there are positions to be filled. If the group's voters cast only one of their votes for a predetermined candidate, its other votes are withheld from their candidate's competitors, and this can sometimes lead to the election of their candidate, although the price paid for this strategy is having a say in the election of one candidate only. A full-slate law invalidates all ballots on which the voter has withheld any available votes, thus making single-shotting impossible. The numbered-place law requires candidates to run for designated places (A, B, C, and so forth) on the ballot, thus breaking what would otherwise be a single contest into several minicontests. The voter can cast only one vote per contest; thus by withholding votes, he or she is not taking votes away from a candidate's competitors. This law, too, frustrates efforts to single-shot. Staggered terms can also sometimes frustrate a single-shot strategy.

64. Norrell 1985, 79; McCrary and others 1990, 20.

disadvantage of blacks, was struck down by the Supreme Court in 1963, the state legislature quickly responded with a new bill establishing a majority-vote requirement for election to all county, state, and federal offices. The bill contained an anti-single-shot provision as well. Its sponsor was reported in several newspapers as saying its purpose was "to thwart election control by Negroes and other minorities." He warned that the federal government had been trying to "increase the registration of Negro voters."[65]

In Texas the numbered-place system was increasingly adopted by cities and school districts following *Brown* v. *Board of Education,* a trend that continued into the 1960s. The place system is the equivalent of an anti-single-shot or full-slate law when whites vote as a bloc against minority candidates. Used increasingly in both school board and municipal elections during those years, it was a potential weapon against minority voters, a fact that caused several Texas communities to adopt the system.[66] When Texas was forced to redistrict its badly malapportioned legislative and congressional districts in 1966 following the Supreme Court's one-person, one-vote decisions, the legislature gerrymandered multimember districts to dilute black votes in the state's most populous county. Not long thereafter, the legislature adopted a majority runoff requirement in the Houston school district, the state's largest, after two blacks and a white liberal had won election to the seven-person board under a plurality rule. When the state's poll tax was declared unconstitutional by a federal court in 1966, conservative Democrats in the legislature, led by Governor John Connally, adopted highly restrictive registration laws to supplant the tax requirement, laws a scholar at the time described as "very similar to the poll tax system, minus the poll tax." (The new laws included a four-month registration period that ended nine months before the elections.) The Connally faction also worked to limit the holding of state elections to off years, a measure that, when finally adopted in the early 1970s, slashed voter turnout in gubernatorial elections, which had been gradually rising over the past twenty years, by a third.[67]

In North Carolina the election of a black to the Winston-Salem board of aldermen in 1947 provoked a racial gerrymander of the city's wards; then, as blacks continued to win election in 1953 and 1955, the legislature imposed an at-large system on the city, after which all aldermen were white once more. Also in the 1950s the legislature passed a full-slate law

65. McDonald, Binford, and Johnson 1990, 9, 13–14.
66. Young 1965, 21–22.
67. May 1970; Davidson 1972, 55–67; Davidson 1990, 54–55.

applying to fourteen counties located primarily in the state's black belt. In 1966, soon after the Voting Rights Act was passed, the general assembly in special session "authorized 49 boards of county commissioners, which had had some form of election or residency by districts, to adopt an at-large election system." Departing from past practice, the legislature also required the at-large election of all school boards.[68]

Various kinds of dilutionary responses to increased black voting developed in every southern state in the 1960s; but the boldest response, linked directly to passage of the Voting Rights Act, occurred in Mississippi. Convening in January 1966, the all-white legislature passed thirteen bills concerning the election process, with little floor debate and without public hearings. None of the bills directly denied blacks the vote; yet all seemed intended to diminish their voting strength, either through creating racial gerrymanders, switching from district to multimember election systems, changing public offices from elective to appointive, or increasing the qualifications for candidacy.[69] The changes wrought by these bills were massive, affecting numerous state and local governments. For example, all county boards of supervisors and all county boards of education in the state—bodies having considerable public power—would now be elected at large in each county rather than from districts, as they had been since the nineteenth century. While the legislature was unusually reticent in explaining the motives behind this spate of laws, a few members were as forthright as their nineteenth century counterparts had been. One state senator, for example, opined that the switch to countywide elections would safeguard "a white board [of education] and preserve our way of doing business."[70]

The Growing Importance of Section 5

Faced with the possibility that the effectiveness of the newly acquired black franchise would be blunted in southern states by systematic vote dilution, as had happened during Reconstruction, black Mississippi plaintiffs and their attorneys attacked the legislature's 1966 laws in six separate actions.[71] Three were consolidated on appeal and together with a Virginia

68. Keech and Sistrom, forthcoming.
69. Parker 1990, 37–41.
70. Parker 1990, 51–55.
71. Two lawyers' groups were deeply involved in Mississippi voting rights litigation at the time: the Lawyers' Constitutional Defense Committee and the Lawyers' Committee for Civil Rights Under Law. A third group—the NAACP Legal Defense Fund, separate

case were decided in 1969 by the Supreme Court in *Allen* v. *State Board of Elections.* Among the questions before the Court was whether the changes, including those that did not disfranchise blacks but diluted their votes, had to be precleared under section 5. The original plaintiffs believed they did; the state of Mississippi disagreed and had not submitted them to the Justice Department. The Court accepted the black plaintiffs' argument. In one of the last decisions written by Chief Justice Earl Warren, it held that the act "gives a broad interpretation to the right to vote, recognizing that voting includes 'all action necessary to make a vote effective.'" Addressing specifically Mississippi's change from district to at-large elections of county supervisors, the Court invoked *Reynolds* v. *Sims,* the one-person, one-vote decision it had rendered five years earlier, to conclude that "the right to vote can be affected by a dilution of voting power as well as by an absolute prohibition on casting a ballot. . . . Voters who are members of a racial minority might well be in the majority in one district, but in a decided minority in the county as a whole. This type of change could therefore nullify their ability to elect the candidate of their choice just as would prohibiting some of them from voting."[72]

The decision affected the evolution of the Voting Rights Act as a weapon to prevent minority vote dilution. Until *Allen,* section 5 had been little used. The Justice Department, in the three and one-half years between passage of the act and the *Allen* decision, had objected to only six proposed changes in election procedure in covered jurisdictions, and none of these concerned vote dilution. In the three and one-half years following *Allen,* there were 118 objections, of which 88 involved dilution schemes. These

since 1939 from the NAACP—also had offices in the state but was primarily concerned with school desegregation cases. See Parker 1990, 79–81.

72. *Allen* v. *State Board of Elections,* 393 U.S. 544 at 565–66, 569 (1969). The Court's broad interpretation of the act as prohibiting dilution was strongly criticized by Justice John Harlan on the grounds that a close reading of the act's legislative history did not bear out this interpretation. It seems clear in retrospect that Warren feared white resistance to voting rights legislation in the South could again lead to the restriction of black voting rights, as occurred following Reconstruction. Speaking in the early 1970s, after his retirement from the Court, he said: "What happened in the early part of this century could well happen again if there is any relaxation on the part of those who have fought through the years for the advancements we have made. I believe no one can read the news of these days without realizing that there is, in this nation, a movement to further denigrate the rights of the black people. Left to its own momentum, the nation could again retrace its steps backward and again deny our proud boast that all men are created equal" (Warren 1972). Warren, like President Johnson, considered his most important achievement to have been in the realm of voting rights. While Johnson took special pride in the Voting Rights Act, Warren considered *Reynolds* v. *Sims,* an antecedent of *Allen,* to be his most important decision as chief justice (Katcher 1967, 435).

included attempts to replace single-member district systems with multimember ones, to replace plurality rules by majority-vote requirements, to create numbered-place systems and staggered terms, and to annex disproportionately white suburbs.[73] A tally at the end of 1989 revealed that 2,335 proposed changes had been objected to under section 5.[74] The great majority of objections involved proposals that would have diluted the votes of racial groups or language minorities. Had it not been for section 5 and the *Allen* decision, almost all the proposals would have become law. Moreover, white officials in the South would surely have implemented a much larger number of dilutionary changes had there been no section 5 to deter them.[75]

In 1969 the battle commenced over renewal of the act's temporary features, including section 5, which were scheduled to expire the following year.[76] Many southern officials urged scuttling the act altogether, still asserting that it violated states' constitutional rights. Governor Lester G. Maddox of Georgia, who had earlier gained notoriety by barring blacks from his Atlanta restaurant with a pickax handle, told the Senate Judiciary Committee that the Voting Rights Act was "ungodly, unworkable, unpatriotic and unconstitutional." (He then went to the House restaurant and autographed souvenier pickax handles.) A. F. Summer, Mississippi attorney general, said the act was "rank discrimination." The Nixon administration, following through on the "southern strategy" that had guided the president's 1968 election campaign, originally opposed extension of the act, calling it "regional legislation." Senator Sam Ervin of North Carolina took the lead in opposing civil rights forces and introduced numerous amendments—all defeated—that would have weakened the act, particularly section 5.[77]

After a yearlong struggle the civil rights forces prevailed, and the special provisions of the act were extended for another five years. Had this not happened, covered states would have been able to reinstate literacy tests in 1970. Congress also amended the section 4 trigger formula to apply to 1968 registration and presidential election turnout data, thereby extending coverage to additional counties. And, as an

---

73. Department of Justice 1990.
74. Department of Justice 1991.
75. Commission on Civil Rights 1975, 30.
76. Technically, the special provisions were not "scheduled to expire," as Hancock and Tredway 1985, 392, point out. Rather, the provisions were to remain in effect until covered jurisdictions bailed out. But by 1970 the tests and devices would have been outlawed for five years, and this would presumably have enabled a general bailout.
77. *Congressional Quarterly Almanac* 1971, 193–98.

experiment, it suspended the use of literacy tests in all fifty states—not simply the covered ones—until 1975.[78] In addition, Congress amended the bailout provision by requiring covered jurisdictions to demonstrate that they had not used a discriminatory test or device for the previous ten years.

Constitutional Protection against Vote Dilution

Even before the 1970 extension, minority plaintiffs and their attorneys had begun challenging vote dilution practices under the Fourteenth and Fifteenth Amendments and under section 2 of the Voting Rights Act. These actions had roots in a case filed in the 1950s. In *Gomillion* v. *Lightfoot* the Supreme Court in 1960 held unconstitutional a law by which the all-white Alabama legislature redrew Tuskegee's municipal boundaries to exclude all but 4 or 5 of the city's 400 black voters (but none of its white ones). In disfranchising the city's blacks the legislature apparently hoped to prevent the rapidly growing black community from gaining representation on the Tuskegee council. In 1951 the legislature had already enacted a full-slate law to accomplish the same end in the same city, which had an unusually large black proportion. This dilutionary scheme had not been sufficient, and so the more straightforward step was taken to disfranchise blacks in municipal elections by redrawing city boundaries. The Supreme Court saw a clear violation of Fifteenth Amendment rights in this latter action.

As noted by the opinion's author, Justice Felix Frankfurter, the violation was one of vote denial rather than vote dilution. But the case drew attention to the importance of districting as an indirect means for curtailing black voting strength. The Court emphasized that subtle efforts to debase voting rights are constitutionally prohibited, citing one of its earlier decisions—also written by Frankfurter—in support of the proposition that the Fifteenth Amendment "nullifies sophisticated as well as simple-minded modes of discrimination." In the legislature's blatant effort to prevent Tuskegee's blacks from voting and electing candidates of their choice, it had not resorted to the straightforward means of literacy tests, fraud, poll taxes, violence, and the like; it had accomplished its goal

78. *Congressional Quarterly Almanac* 1971, 192–93. Congress had come to perceive literacy tests as a widespread barrier to voting that extended far beyond the South. See Commission on Civil Rights 1975, 19–20.

through boundary manipulation, an "essay in geometry and geography," as Frankfurter put it.[79]

Two years after *Gomillion,* the Supreme Court in *Baker* v. *Carr* held that the apportionment of votes among legislative districts was justiciable.[80] Like the *Gomillion* decision it invoked, *Baker* helped shift the focus in voting rights law from disfranchisement to dilution. Then, in quick succession, the Court handed down three apportionment decisions overturning practices that diluted the weight of votes through malapportioned districts. The most noteworthy was *Reynolds* v. *Sims,* announced the year before passage of the Voting Rights Act.[81] The complainants, white voters, argued that the apportionment of the Alabama legislature diluted their votes because the districts contained unequal numbers of voters. (The district populations varied as much as 41:1.) In so doing, plaintiffs argued, the scheme violated the equal protection clause of the Fourteenth Amendment. The Court agreed, and the legislature was required to reapportion itself, creating substantially equal districts in both houses.

Although race was not an issue in the Court's opinion, it had clear racial implications, as did *Gray* v. *Sanders,* which stated explicitly that the Fifteenth and Nineteenth Amendments prohibit a state from overweighting or diluting votes on the basis of race or sex, respectively.[82] As post-Reconstruction historiography makes clear, one form of minority vote dilution employed by southern whites was malapportionment, drawing overpopulated black districts and underpopulated white ones. *Reynolds* destroyed this as a legal option for whites in the Deep South immediately before the Voting Rights Act enfranchised blacks there the following year.

Within months of the act's passage, the Court in *Fortson* v. *Dorsey* went a step further toward finding unconstitutional forms of minority vote dilution besides malapportionment. In rejecting a claim by Georgia plaintiffs that multimember state senatorial districts diluted their votes, the Court held that while such districts were not inherently unconstitutional, they might be if they "designedly or otherwise" operated "to

79. *Gomillion* v. *Lightfoot,* 364 U.S. 339 at 342, 347 (1960), quoting *Lane* v. *Wilson,* 307 U.S. 268 at 275 (1939). On the implications of *Gomillion* for the Voting Rights Act, see Karlan and McCrary 1988, 755–59. It is ironic that the city of Tuskegee played a major role in black voting rights actions. It is the home of the Tuskegee Institute, whose first director, Booker T. Washington, had come close to renouncing the Negro's right to vote in his famous Atlanta speech in 1895. See Logan 1954, 280.

80. *Baker* v. *Carr,* 369 U.S. 186 (1962).

81. *Reynolds* v. *Sims,* 377 U.S. 533 (1964).

82. *Gray* v. *Sanders,* 372 U.S. 368 at 379 (1963).

minimize or cancel out the voting strength of racial or political elements of the voting population."[83]

This was an invitation to plaintiffs to specify the nature of evidence that would demonstrate such illegal cancellation of voting strength, and several cases were filed. Various district and appeals court decisions quickly invoked *Fortson* in upholding black plaintiffs' claims that certain at-large schemes were unconstitutional. However, none of these cases had reached the Supreme Court by the time *Allen* v. *State Board of Elections* was argued in 1969—a fact that apparently caused the black plaintiffs' lawyers in that case to cast the issue in terms of section 5 coverage rather than a constitutional violation.[84] In 1971 the Court gave a further hint as to how minimization or cancellation might be demonstrated. In *Whitcomb* v. *Chavis,* it reversed a district court's finding that an Indiana multimember legislative district diluted the vote of black ghetto dwellers. The issue, said the Court, was not whether black candidates were defeated. Rather, it was whether the defeat was simply the result of their running on a Democratic slate that usually lost or, on the contrary, the result of ghetto dwellers having "less opportunity than did other . . . residents . . . to participate in the political processes and to elect legislators of their choice."[85] In other words, was the absence of minorities from legislative bodies the result of racial discrimination as such, or did it stem from such extraneous factors as the unpopularity of Democratic candidates in a Republican stronghold? If it were the latter, then to require a remedy that guaranteed safe seats to blacks, as the trial court had ordered, might be taken to imply that any group whose interests were unrepresented in a legislative assembly had a constitutional claim to proportional representation.

In 1973 Texas plaintiffs took up the *Whitcomb* challenge and finally convinced the Supreme Court that the pathetically small number of minority legislators elected from their counties was the result of unconstitutional minority vote dilution. *White* v. *Regester,* which involved multimember House districts in Bexar (San Antonio) and Dallas counties, was a signal victory in the battle for minority voting rights, all the more so because it was rendered by a unanimous Court.[86] But it was a dubious decision, nonetheless; it left practically unanswered the question of what were the

83. *Fortson* v. *Dorsey,* 379 U.S. 433 at 439 (1965).
84. Parker 1990, 171.
85. *Whitcomb* v. *Chavis,* 403 U.S. 124 at 149 (1971).
86. *White* v. *Regester,* 412 U.S. 755 (1973).

criteria by which judges could determine if a voting system diluted minority votes.

Two Alabama voting rights attorneys, James Blacksher and Larry Menefee, described the decision this way:

> The trial court findings of fact selected for inclusion in the Supreme Court's opinion . . . are difficult to catalogue. There was a history of *de jure* discrimination against black voters in Texas, and Mexican Americans "had long suffered from . . . invidious discrimination and treatment in the fields of education, employment, economics, health, politics and others." In Dallas County, only two blacks had been elected to the house since Reconstruction, and in Bexar County only five Mexican Americans had been elected. The Court did not, however, say whether others had been defeated by racially polarized voting. There was a powerful, white-dominated Democratic Party organization in Dallas that ignored blacks' concerns and used racial campaign tactics to defeat candidates supported by the black community, but no mention was made of any similar slating group in San Antonio. Cultural and language barriers had resulted in depressed Mexican American voter registration in Bexar County, but no mention was made of the black registration rate in Dallas. The district court had found "that the Bexar County legislative delegation in the House was insufficiently responsive to Mexican-American interests." Requirements that candidates run for numbered places and win by a majority of the total vote, "neither in themselves improper nor invidious, enhanced the opportunity for racial discrimination . . ." The Court gave no hint of the priority it attached to any of these facts; instead, it approved the district court's conclusion of unconstitutionality based on the "totality of the circumstances."[87]

The "totality of the circumstances," including the "cultural and economic realities" as well as the existence of multimember systems, was said to reveal that blacks and Mexican Americans "had less opportunity than did other residents in the district to participate in the political processes and to elect legislators of their choice."[88] The most distressing fact, from the point of view of practicing voting rights lawyers such as Blacksher

87. Blacksher and Menefee 1984, 215–16.
88. *White* v. *Regester*, 412 U.S. 755 at 769, 766.

and Menefee, was that the Court did not even attempt "to explain exactly why the record in this case demonstrated an equal protection violation when that in *Whitcomb* v. *Chavis* did not."[89]

After *White*, minority plaintiffs who challenged multimember systems had to make what they could of the hodgepodge of criteria enumerated by the justices. Subsequent cases that did not reach the Supreme Court, most notably *Zimmer* v. *McKeithen*, refined and systematized the criteria mentioned in *White* without specifying which ones were decisive. *Zimmer*, decided the same year as *White* by the Court of Appeals for the Fifth Circuit sitting *en banc*, enunciated eight criteria, four "primary" and four "enhancing" ones, that became the guideposts for litigation during the remainder of the decade. Notably absent from the list was evidence of intentional discrimination in the creation of dilutionary election rules.[90]

Extending Section 5 Coverage to Language Minorities

In January 1975, the year the temporary features of the Voting Rights Act were again scheduled to expire, the Commission on Civil Rights issued a lengthy report evaluating the impact of the act, primarily in the South. It concluded that while impressive progress had been made, especially regarding black registration and voting, Justice Department enforcement had been uneven. Discrimination, both in terms of disfranchisement and dilution, still existed. The report noted that "some counties with substantial black populations have no black elected officials at any level of government." Moreover, black officeholders were underrepresented at every level in the seven covered states, but particularly at the highest levels. "There is only one black representative in Congress," the report said. "No black holds statewide office in the South and no black candidate for statewide office has even come close to election." The commission recommended extension of the act for ten years, and the Ford adminis-

89. Blacksher and Menefee 1984, 215.
90. *Zimmer* v. *McKeithen*, 485 F.2d 1297 (5th cir. 1973), appealed and reversed on other grounds. The *Zimmer* "factors" were as follows: "where a minority can demonstrate a lack of access to the process of slating candidates, the unresponsiveness of legislators to their particularized interests, a tenuous state policy underlying the preference for multi-member or at-large districting, or that the existence of past discrimination in general precludes the effective participation in the election system, a strong case is made. Such proof is enhanced by a showing of the existence of large districts, majority vote requirements, anti-single shot voting provisions and the lack of provision for at-large candidates running from particular geographical subdistricts. The fact of dilution is established upon proof of the existence of an aggregate of these factors" (485 F.2d 1297 at 1305).

tration pushed for five.[91] Congress extended it for seven and made several amendments. One made permanent the 1970 national ban on literacy tests; a second permitted the prevailing party in voting rights suits brought under the Fourteen or Fifteenth Amendments to be paid attorneys' fees; and a third allowed private parties to sue in order to impose on jurisdictions preclearance and federal examiner remedies.[92]

But undoubtedly the most important amendment was a broad expansion in section 5 coverage. In its first decade the act had focused primarily on protecting the rights of blacks. The decade after its passage, however, witnessed the "Chicano revolt," a movement stretching from California to Texas, characterized by an unprecedented militance among Mexican Americans, who had historically occupied the rung between blacks and Anglos on the caste ladder in the southwestern states. While voting discrimination typically had not been as severe against Mexican Americans as against southern blacks, the difference in degree of political subjugation was an academic one in the eyes of the militants. Both groups in Texas had historically been excluded from white primaries; both had suffered from the financial burden of the poll tax, from laws and practices that kept their candidates out of office, and from vote manipulation by Anglo-dominated machines. Texas had not been covered in 1965 by the act's special provisions, however, because it did not have a literacy test.[93]

Mexican Americans, blacks, and their allies persuaded Congress to add an additional trigger formula that would cause the special provisions of the act to apply to Texas and some other previously uncovered jurisdictions. The new formula had three criteria. Coverage would occur if more than 5 percent of the voting-age citizens in the jurisdiction belonged to one language-minority group (defined as Asian Americans, American Indians, Alaskan natives, and persons of Spanish heritage), fewer than 50 percent of the jurisdiction's voting-age citizens voted in the 1972

91. Commission on Civil Rights 1975, 61–62, 336–59; *Congressional Quarterly Almanac* 1976, 525.
92. An excellent summary of the 1975 amendments, including the language-minority provisions, is found in Hunter 1976.
93. For a general political and social history of Mexican Americans in Texas, see Montejano 1987. On their exclusion from white primaries, see Garcia 1989, 27; Kibbe 1946, 227; Montejano 1987, 144. See Simmons 1952, 277–78, on the heavy burden of the poll tax as late as the 1950s on Mexican workers in South Texas. For an account of Anglo efforts to dilute the votes of Mexican Americans in Texas, see Brischetto and others, forthcoming. Anders 1982 gives a detailed account of the machine manipulation of South Texas Mexican-American voters in the Progressive Era.

presidential election, and that election was conducted only in English.[94] Jurisdictions meeting these criteria were thenceforth required to provide election materials, including ballots, in the appropriate language in addition to English.[95] But the real impact of the new language trigger would not be the implementation of bilingual elections but section 5 coverage. This measure, sponsored by the black Texas representative Barbara Jordan—and opposed not only by the state's conservative governor and secretary of state but also by Jordan's fellow liberal Texas representative, Henry B. Gonzalez, who claimed it was not needed— would bring Texas with its large black and Mexican-American populations under the preclearance umbrella.[96] Both minority groups, moreover, would be able to take advantage of all the special provisions of the act. Two other states, Arizona and Alaska, as well as scattered counties throughout the nation, would also be brought under section 5 by the language trigger.

Opponents of the bill tried in numerous ways to restrict its impact. One proposal, which would be offered again in 1982, was to expand section 5 preclearance to the entire nation on the grounds that it was unfair to single out the South. This ploy was backed by various southern senators, including Herman E. Talmadge and Sam Nunn of Georgia and John C. Stennis of Mississippi, all three Democrats, and Republican Strom Thurmond of South Carolina. John V. Tunney of California, a Democrat, responded that such an amendment would be unconstitutional, inasmuch as the Supreme Court, in finding the original act's regional focus constitutional because of the unusual history of vote

94. Hunter 1976, 256. This trigger was in title II, section 4(f)(4), of the 1975 amendments. A separate trigger, meant to supplement that in title II, was included in title III, section 203(c): it required bilingual elections if more than 5 percent of the voting-age citizens of a jurisdiction were members of a single language-minority group and that group's illiteracy rate was higher than the national rate. However, the language-minority trigger in title III, while originally requiring bilingual elections for a ten-year period, did not entail section 5 coverage, as the trigger in title II did. See Hunter 1976, 256–58. The requirement of bilingual elections in section 203(c) was extended in 1982 to expire August 6, 1992.

95. The exception to requiring a bilingual ballot is when the minority language in question has no written form, as is true of some native American languages. In this case, spoken assistance must be provided. Hunter 1976, 264.

96. The extension of section 5 coverage to Texas was opposed during congressional debate by Gonzalez primarily on the grounds that no impediments to minority voting still existed. After attempting to amend the act to preclude coverage of Texas, Gonzalez voted present rather than no on the legislation (*Congressional Record* 1975; Gonzalez 1991). On the impact of the extension of section 5 to Texas and the Southwest, see Garcia 1986; Cotrell and Polinard 1986.

discrimination in the South, had indicated it would be impermissible for the federal government to interfere in the voting procedures of states where there was no serious denial of voting rights. Tunney called the proposal of Talmadge and others a smokescreen for a move that would spread Justice Department resources too thin.[97] In spite of pockets of spirited opposition to section 5 among southerners in Congress, including a disproportionate number of Republicans, who were leaders of the opposition this time around, a majority of the southerners ultimately supported final passage of a major civil rights bill, the first time this had happened since Reconstruction.[98]

Amending Section 2 to Include a Results Test

After *White* v. *Regester* was decided in 1973, a growing number of minority plaintiffs began to file class-action constitutional challenges to election structures they claimed diluted minority votes, especially at-large or multimember plans.[99] Each challenge, of course, could only apply to a single governmental body, such as a school board or commissioners' court in a specific locale. (This was true of challenges under the Voting Rights Act as well.) These constitutional cases were burdensome for plaintiffs to win. *White*'s "totality of the circumstances" approach encouraged plaintiffs to hire experts of various kinds to gather mountains of statistical and historical evidence on government unresponsiveness, long-term patterns of race relations within the jurisdiction, the effects of voting laws and practices on minority candidates' chances, voter registration and turnout over the years, and voting patterns within ethnic enclaves and in the community as a whole. Thus, while *White* and its progeny had opened a door through which minority plaintiffs could now enter and seek constitutional relief for dilution, it was no simple matter to get over the sill. Once over it, however, plaintiffs were able to obtain from the courts fairly drawn, single-member districts in place of multimember ones.

The nonpermanent features of the Voting Rights Act, including section 5, were to expire in 1982. In 1980 a sharply divided Supreme Court announced a constitutional criterion for demonstrating dilution that

97. *Congressional Quarterly Almanac 1976*, 525–33.
98. McDonald 1989, 1278.
99. The private litigation under the act undoubtedly increased after 1975 partly as a result of the amendment that authorized payment of the prevailing party's attorney's fees.

38   CHANDLER DAVIDSON

appeared to be sharply at variance with the standards of proof in *White* and *Zimmer*. A plurality of justices in *City of Mobile* v. *Bolden* held that the Fifteenth Amendment only applied to access to the ballot, not vote dilution, and that both the Fourteenth and Fifteenth Amendments required a showing of purpose to discriminate. This "intent standard" was not only absent in *White*, but it departed from the logic of the Court's reapportionment cases, where the motives behind dilution through malapportionment—a violation of the Fourteenth Amendment— were not considered relevant. This ruling imposed a tremendous additional burden on minority plaintiffs, for many dilutionary laws had been established in the distant past, and the difficulty of proving intent to discriminate could be prohibitive. *Bolden* was therefore a major setback. "A plurality of the Court concludes," wrote Justice Thurgood Marshall in an angry dissent, "that, in the absence of proof of intentional discrimination by the State, the right to vote provides the politically powerless with nothing more than the right to cast meaningless ballots."[100]

After the initial shock wore off, *Bolden* galvanized the civil rights lobby into action. In light of Ronald Reagan's election soon after the decision and his probable appointment of conservative federal judges and Justice Department officials, *Bolden* seemed to portend a rollback of voting rights advances made during the second Reconstruction. Orchestrated by the Leadership Conference on Civil Rights, a Washington-based umbrella group, a coalition was created in 1981 to accomplish three goals: extend section 5, extend the language-minority provisions, and overcome the effects of *Bolden*. Strategists decided that overcoming the effects of the decision could be accomplished by amending section 2 when the special provisions of the act came up for renewal the next year.[101] Section 2, a permanent feature applying nationwide, had served as little more than a symbolic preamble to the operative sections, in effect restating the Fifteenth Amendment. The proposed change, if enacted, bade fair to overshadow the Constitution as the major instrument for attacking vote dilution both in covered jurisdictions and outside them. It would do this, its proponents hoped, by restoring the *White-Zimmer* criteria

100. *City of Mobile* v. *Bolden*, 446 U.S. 55 at 104 (1980). For a penetrating account of the implications, see Blacksher and Menefee 1984.

101. A study by the Commission on Civil Rights 1981, 89–94, found evidence of continued resistance to black and Mexican-American political participation in many jurisdictions across the South and the Southwest. It urged renewing the special provisions of the act for another decade.

and explicitly stating that proof of discriminatory results, rather than intent, was sufficient to substantiate a claim of dilution.

Strongly opposing the measure were William French Smith, Reagan's new attorney general, William Bradford Reynolds, his assistant attorney general for civil rights, and Republican Orrin G. Hatch of Utah on the Senate Judiciary Committee, the leader of congressional opposition to the bill. All three argued that it would result in a minority quota system in elections.

The opposition, it soon became clear, was no longer concentrated among southern congressmen, although there were intense efforts to gut the act by southern Republican Senators Strom Thurmond—an enemy of the act since 1965—Jesse A. Helms, and John P. East. In 1979 political scientist Abigail Thernstrom had published an article in a policy-oriented magazine, *The Public Interest,* attacking what she called "the odd evolution" of the Voting Rights Act. Although she approved of the original act, she argued (albeit without presenting evidence) that after *Allen* v. *State Board of Elections* in 1969 it had become a tool in the hands of Justice Department attorneys with a "vested interest" in mandating districts as section 5 remedies for at-large dilution and annexation of white suburbs, remedies that in her view amounted to "proportional racial representation." The act, Thernstrom warned, was "creating a host of new problems," and in spite of the opportunity for it to expire in 1982, seemed "well on its way to becoming . . . a permanent part of our political landscape."[102] It was not the canards of aging reactionary southerners that the Republican opponents of the amendment embraced during the debates of 1981–82 but Thernstrom's argument and those of academicians such as law professors Donald Horowitz and William Van Alstyne, political scientists Timothy O'Rourke and John Bunzel, and philosophers Barry Gross and Michael Levin.

Whether section 5 and the proposed new section 2 were, in fact, devices to impose racial quotas in the ranks of officeholders was one of the most hotly debated questions during the hearings on extension.[103] While Thernstrom did not testify, her writings on the act were entered in the record, and a number of scholars testified along lines similar to hers. Other scholars, such as C. Vann Woodward, an eminent historian of the South who had marched with Martin Luther King from Selma to Montgomery in 1965, backed the extension of section 5. Still others

102. Thernstrom 1979, 59–60, 75–76. For a more detailed and current critique of the act, based on the major ideas in the 1979 article, see Thernstrom 1987.

103. See Senate 1983.

spoke on behalf of the amendment to section 2 and its results test, including representatives of the major civil rights groups, individual minority political activists, and a number of lawyers. Among the latter was Archibald Cox, solicitor general in the Kennedy and Johnson administrations, who had helped frame the original act and later argued its constitutionality before the Supreme Court.

Reflecting the centrality of the quota issue in the hearings, the final version of amended section 2 restoring the *White-Zimmer* results standard contained this proviso: "Nothing in this section establishes a right to have members of a protected class elected in numbers equal to their proportion in the population."[104] Whether the act mandates quotas is still the major point of controversy and is addressed at length in the present volume.

The amended act, including revised section 2, passed by huge veto-proof majorities in both houses of Congress and was signed by President Reagan on June 29, 1982. The special provisions, including section 5, were extended for twenty-five years, to 2007.[105] (Section 5 by this time covered nine entire states and portions of thirteen others; today, it is nine and seven, respectively.) Bilingual assistance in certain language-minority jurisdictions not covered by section 5, first begun in 1975, was extended to 1992.[106] A new provision enabled illiterate and handicapped voters to choose their own assistant at the polls rather than accept a person chosen by the officials. Significantly, the special provisions' bailout standard was changed to provide incentives for eradicating voting discrimination—incentives that had not existed before. However, the new standard would be difficult to satisfy: a jurisdiction must have complied fully with preclearance requirements over the previous ten years.[107] This difficulty became even greater in 1987 when the Justice Department officially incorporated section 2 standards into section 5 preclearance requirements.[108]

104. This proviso, commonly known as the Dole compromise, was formulated mainly by Senators Edward Kennedy, Democrat from Massachusetts, and Robert Dole, Republican from Kansas. Derfner 1984, 155.

105. The Commission on Civil Rights, as well as extensive hearings in Congress, including testimony from William Bradford Reynolds, established the continuing need for the special provisions seventeen years after the act was passed. See Hancock and Tredway 1985, 404–06.

106. See note 94 for the trigger formula for coverage of these jurisdictions.

107. Hancock and Tredway 1985, 415–19.

108. See Department of Justice 1989, 574. In effect, this incorporation means that preclearance requires a submitting jurisdiction not simply to show that the proposed change

The consequence of *Bolden,* therefore, whatever the motives behind the decision, was that the right of minority voters to elect candidates of their choice was more strongly protected than ever before. And in an anticlimax to the congressional battle, the Supreme Court, which had apparently been stung by the widespread criticism of *Bolden,* seemed in *Rogers* v. *Lodge* to soften its constitutional standard to allow circumstantial evidence as indicative of intent to discriminate.[109] As Bernard Grofman wrote, *Rogers* came "close to reestablishing the *Zimmer* standard in all but name, albeit cloaked in the language of intent."[110]

Just how strongly minority voting rights had been secured became clear when the Court in 1986 spelled out the standards of proof for dilution under section 2 in *Thornburg* v. *Gingles,* a case challenging the use of multimember districts in North Carolina's legislative reapportionment. The Court enunciated three primary criteria for determining if multimember districts resulted in dilution. First, the minority group must be "sufficiently large and geographically compact" to make up a majority in at least one single-member district. Second, the minority must be "politically cohesive" or, in other words, tend to vote as a bloc. Third, the majority must also vote "sufficiently as a bloc to enable it . . . usually to defeat the minority's preferred candidate."[111] This three-part test, while introducing at least one new hurdle for those who would challenge vote dilution—an explicit largeness and compactness test—nonetheless swept from plaintiffs' path some of the requirements of a results case that *White* v. *Regester* had imposed, including the burden of demonstrating defendants' lack of responsiveness to minorities' interests.[112]

Although civil rights forces in 1982 had argued that their proposed revision of section 2 was intended to restore the *White-Zimmer* guidelines, the court in *Gingles* established a rather different test that finally explicated

does not make a minority group worse off than before, but also that the change, even if it meets the first requirement, does not violate section 2.

109. *Rogers* v. *Lodge,* 458 U.S. 613 (1982).

110. Grofman 1985, 97.

111. *Thornburg* v. *Gingles,* 478 U.S. 30 at 50, 51 (1986).

112. The most difficult new barrier to plaintiffs stemming from *Gingles* is the Court's operational definition of ethnic or racial "insularity"—a key feature of a dilution claim— in narrowly geographical terms. This means, for example, that blacks who do not live closely enough together in a city to form a majority in a single-member district without increasing the number of districts already in existence have no remedy for the dilution of their votes, even if they have long been frozen out of the political process. The criterion of geographical compactness is not found in the statute. For a discussion of this problem, see Karlan 1989, 199–213.

a logic of minority vote dilution and laid down manageable standards for demonstrating it, something *White* had clearly failed to do.[113]

Not surprisingly, in recent years numerous section 2 cases have been filed by private parties, many of which have been settled before trial. In other instances, evidence suggests that jurisdictions have changed their election systems to preclude litigation.[114] One of the most noteworthy section 2 suits to reach the Supreme Court since *Gingles* involved the election of state judges from multimember districts in Texas and Louisiana. Federal trial courts had found section 2 violations in Texas but not in Louisiana.[115] The Fifth Circuit Court of Appeals, sitting *en banc* later concluded that the section 2 results test did not apply to the election of judges in any case. In 1991 the Supreme Court held otherwise and remanded both suits for further proceedings. Because forty-one states elect some or all of their judges, it seems likely that these decisions will result in nationwide changes in the election of trial and appeals judges and increased numbers of minority lawyers on the bench.[116]

Results of the Act: 1965–1990

A quarter century after passage of the act, there was good reason for voters under its protection to celebrate its birthday. Looking back to 1965, a prominent voting rights lawyer recently remarked that "nothing less than a quiet revolution in voting" had occurred.[117] It was a revolution achieved, in large measure, by the act as passed and amended. The magnitude of the change is suggested by increases in voter registration

113. I owe to Samuel Issacharoff my appreciation of the significant difference between the standards for dilution in *White* and *Zimmer*, embodied in amended section 2, and those later enunciated in *Gingles*.

114. See, for example, the state-by-state data on this phenomenon in southern states in Davidson and Grofman, forthcoming. However, numerous jurisdictions have still been willing to fight plaintiffs' section 2 lawsuits. The most noteworthy of these was Los Angeles County, which hired seven private law firms and spent at least $6 million—exclusive of plaintiffs' legal costs, which it is required to pay—to defend its drawing of county supervisors' districts. The court found that these boundaries discriminated against Latinos (Simon 1991).

115. For an account of minorities in the Texas judicial election system, see Issacharoff 1989.

116. *Houston Lawyers' Association* v. *Attorney General of Texas*, no. 90–813 (1991); *Chisom* v. *Roemer*, no. 90–757 (1991). See Greenhouse 1991.

117. McDonald 1989, 1252.

and minority officeholding as well as by the more open atmosphere for voting in southern jurisdictions.

While the best available estimates of registration by race may overstate black registration significantly, the following figures are at least suggestive of the changes that have occurred. Between 1964 and 1988 the percentage of voting-age blacks registered in the eleven southern states increased from 43.3 percent to approximately 63.7 percent. Black registrants in the five Deep South states increased in the same period from 22.5 percent to about 65.2 percent. The gap in black-white registration in the latter states narrowed dramatically by one reckoning—which almost certainly overstates the convergence—from 47.1 to −4.4 points (indicating a black rate higher than the white one).[118] Comparable figures for Hispanics from the 1960s are not available.

The number of black elected officials increased from fewer than 100 in 1965 in the seven originally targeted states to 3,265 in 1989. In 1989 blacks in these states comprised 9.8 percent of all elected officials as compared with about 23 percent of the voting-age population.[119] While no estimates for Hispanic officeholders in 1965 are available, their number in six states with especially large Hispanic concentrations—Arizona, California, Florida, New Mexico, New York, and Texas—increased from 1,280 in 1973 to 3,592 in 1990. Hispanic officials thus constitute about 4 percent of the elected officials in those states, as compared with the Hispanic voting-age population of approximately 17 percent.[120]

Scattered evidence suggests an increase in registration among American Indians in Arizona, Colorado, New Mexico, and Utah, although systematic surveys apparently do not exist.[121] There is also a growing number of Indian officeholders, primarily in those areas where they are in the majority or where single-member-district elections—some established through suits brought under the Voting Rights Act—have been adopted.[122]

118. Congressional Quarterly Service 1968, 115; Commission on Civil Rights 1975, 43; Garrow 1978, 19; Bureau of the Census 1989b, 36–39. The 1988 figures are derived from the Census Bureau's 1988 postelection survey and are not deflated to reflect a general tendency of respondents to overreport having voted. Nor do these figures reflect possible racial differentials in overreporting.

119. Bureau of the Census 1989a, 259; Joint Center for Political Studies 1989, 11–12.

120. Bureau of the Census 1989a, 259; Joint Center for Political Studies 1989, 11–12; National Association of Latino Elected and Appointed Officials 1990, vii.

121. McDonald 1989, 1253–54.

122. Wolfley and Henderson 1991, 22–30.

Although it is difficult to assign a precise weight to the impact of the act on increased turnout and officeholding among all these groups, there is strong evidence that it has had a significant effect on both.[123]

The Act in Perspective

From one standpoint the Voting Rights Act has been more successful than its supporters in 1965 had reason to expect, certainly with regard to the election of minority candidates. The special provisions of the act have gone far toward securing the fundamental rights guaranteed by the Fifteenth Amendment, not only for southern blacks but for large numbers of Mexican Americans in the Southwest and for various language minorities elsewhere in the nation. The amendment of section 2, moreover, has provided a potent weapon for minority groups outside the South to achieve fair representation, a fact symbolized by the lawsuit won in 1987 by black plaintiffs in Springfield, Illinois, the hometown of Abraham Lincoln and the site of a race riot in 1908 that, among other events, led to the founding of the NAACP two years later.[124]

Yet from a different perspective the results of the act have been disappointing. The standard for this judgment is the one the civil rights movement of the early 1960s embraced at its most optimistic moment.[125] Martin Luther King, Jr., spoke of the tremendous potential leverage he thought blacks could exert through their voting strength, given their strategic position in the large cities of the nation. "Today," he wrote in 1964, "a shift in the Negro vote could upset the outcome of several state

123. On the relation between the act and black voter turnout in the South, see Alt, forthcoming. On the relation between act-related litigation and minority officeholding in the seven states originally covered plus Texas, see Davidson and Grofman, forthcoming.

124. *McNeil v. City of Springfield*, 658 F. Supp. 1015 (C.D. Ill. 1987). See McDonald 1989 and Parker 1990 for recent accounts of the act's successes.

125. See Jones 1985. Guinier 1991b has written eloquently of the larger failure of the act, drawn from her experience as a member of the voting rights bar and her reading of the literature of the civil rights movement. Edds, a journalist, captures the differences in interpretation of the act's effects by erstwhile civil rights activists through comparing the views of John Lewis and Hosea Williams, "who walked side by side at the head of Selma's 'Bloody Sunday' march." Lewis, now a congressman from Mississippi, spoke of a profoundly different climate in the South. He said of the act: "it liberated black people, and it liberated white people, and it liberated white politicians especially." But Williams told Edds: "Political power has not delivered to its constituents as we predicted it would. . . . We said, 'Your vote is worth dying for,' and sure enough, they went out and died. We said, 'You've got to vote ol' whitey out and ol' blackie in.' So they did. But things haven't gotten better. In too many cases, they've gotten worse" (Edds 1987, 25).

contests, and affect the result of a Presidential election." But holding the balance of power was not enough. "Only with the growth of an enlightened electorate, white and Negro together, can we put a quick end to this century-old stranglehold of a minority [of white reactionaries] on the nation's legislative processes."[126] A year later Lyndon Johnson also expressed an exalted notion of the franchise as he signed the Voting Rights Act. "The vote is the most powerful instrument ever devised by man," he said, "for breaking down injustice and destroying the terrible walls which imprison men because they are different from other men."[127]

Today, a careful assessment of the facts compels one to reply to the ghosts of King and Johnson that the prison walls still stand. Many blacks—and to an important degree various other ethnic minorities—remain prisoners in a discriminatory society. This society is no longer characterized by the Jim Crow system that existed well into the 1960s, but it is far from providing equal opportunity for people of any race or color.[128]

The most interesting debates over the Voting Rights Act now concern questions about the role it should play in helping voters attack structural discrimination. There are essentially three positions. (These exclude, of course, the views of those racists and racial conservatives who argue that discrimination against blacks and other minorities of color is no longer a structural feature of American society, and locate the problem primarily in the ethnic minorities themselves.)[129]

One position, held by those who might be called narrow constructionists, is that the act should enforce the Fifteenth Amendment in two ways: first, through securing the right of racial minorities to cast a ballot and have it fairly counted; and, second, through prohibiting vote dilution in jurisdictions—allegedly few in number—where the minority groups in question have been entirely frozen out of the political system, as in a scattering of locales in the South and the Southwest. Once the ice is

126. King 1964, 149–50.

127. Lawson 1985, 3–4. Yet as Walton 1985, 73, reminds us, decades before this extremely optimistic assessment of the vote's potential was expressed, Ralph Bunche, the eminent black political scientist, observed that "the great masses of whites . . . who have long been enfranchised, have been able to make but little progress toward solutions of many of their own problems with the ballot."

128. On the current status of blacks, see Jaynes and Williams 1989; Reed 1990. On Hispanics, but particularly the more disadvantaged groups within this heterogeneous category—Mexicans and Puerto Ricans—see Bean and Tienda 1987, chap. 10.

129. See Levin 1990, for example, who argues that the relatively low-paying jobs of blacks (and women) in America are probably the result of lower intellect and motivation, deficiencies he believes are genetically determined.

broken by the election of a small number of minority officeholders, dilution should not be prohibited. This view holds that a minority group should have no right under the act to elect candidates of its choice except in very unusual circumstances.[130] It implies that Congress should have imposed a much narrower construction on section 5 in 1970 following *Allen*; the special provisions should have been allowed to lapse by now, or at least a more generous bailout policy adopted; and section 2 should not have been amended in 1982 to allow a results test. Some in this camp, including Thernstrom, also believe that section 5 coverage should not have been extended to language minorities, arguing that they are not victims of serious vote discrimination.

The outcome of such policies would probably have been a stasis or decline in minority officeholding. But—so the argument goes—by shifting minority voters' focus of concern from racial proportionality among officeholders to the best way to form winning multiracial coalitions of the kind King believed possible, the revisions of the act favored by narrow constructionists would have increased the likelihood of a united front of the disadvantaged and their allies, whose votes could have overcome structural discrimination not only along racial lines but along class lines as well.[131]

There are at least two major problems with this view, and critics have been quick to point them out. First, blacks and language minorities have had an extremely difficult time electing their candidates to office as a result of white bloc voting and dilutionary election laws. Even now only 1.4 percent of officeholders in the United States are black and 0.8 percent are Hispanic, compared with 12.4 percent and 8.0 percent of their respective proportions of the population. Throughout the nation's history, white Anglos have been overrepresented far out of proportion to their numbers, and white officials are almost everywhere a huge majority. As the political history of the southern states in the present era makes clear, whites have been quick to use the entire panoply of dilutionary measures to maintain their advantage in officeholding. And they probably would have contin-

---

130. Although Thernstrom's 1987 criticism of the act is clearer than her view of how it should ideally work, she seems to represent the narrow-constructionist position. However, some passages suggest that she has doubts as to whether structural discrimination is still a significant barrier to equal opportunity. For a brief, concise example of the narrow-constructionist position, see Taylor 1991. In the present volume, see, in particular, the views of O'Rourke and Swain. See also Butler 1985. The National Urban League may be the first major black civil rights organization to be won over to the narrow-constructionist view. See "Urban League Takes Neutral Position on Thomas" 1991.

131. Thernstrom 1979, 75.

ued to do so but for section 5 and the recent evolution of constitutional law. Fairness alone, critics argue, dictates that the act protect the ability of recently enfranchised minority voters to elect their candidates.

Second, the narrow constructionists are said to underestimate the difficulty of progressive biracial alliances, especially when disadvantaged white southerners are an essential part of the alliance.[132] Martin Luther King himself, in the same book in which he argued for biracial coalitions, admitted that "the underprivileged southern whites saw the color that separated them from Negroes more clearly than they saw the circumstances that bound them together in mutual interest."[133] He was killed in 1968 only months before southern blue-collar whites forsook the Democratic presidential ticket in droves for the racist demagogue George Wallace. Then, along with southern white-collar whites, many of them moved into the racially conservative Republican camp in the 1970s, where they have since remained, except in 1976, when they voted for Jimmy Carter. How does one reconcile these facts, the critics ask, with the strategy of a coalition of the disadvantaged?[134]

The second position is to stand pat. While its proponents believe that the election of minority officeholders brings benefits to minority voters beyond mere pride in seeing "one of one's own" in office, they are skeptical of the power of the minority vote in the present conservative period to provide the much greater benefits the civil rights movement hoped it would. Standpatters believe the act as it now exists has been necessary to provide fundamental voting rights protection, including protection against dilution, in the years following the second Reconstruction that the Fourteenth and Fifteenth Amendments did not provide following the first one. That failure in the nineteenth century caused a massive setback to racial equality on all fronts. The standpatters believe, in other words, that barriers to the election of minority candidates from predominantly white jurisdictions have not collapsed, in spite of such dramatic breakthroughs as those by Douglas Wilder, elected in 1989 as the first black governor of Virginia (or any other state), or Dan Morales, the first Latino attorney general of Texas, elected in 1990. At least until

132. I count myself among those who earlier underestimated the difficulty of biracial alliances based on class similarities. See Davidson 1972, chap. 8; but also Davidson 1990, 43–45.

133. King 1964, 36.

134. Carmines and Huckfeldt in this volume discuss the racial underpinnings of the realignment since 1964. See also Carmines and Stimson 1989; Huckfeldt and Kohfeld 1989; Davidson 1990, chap. 11.

the possibility for a genuine biracial progressive coalition develops at the national level, the standpatters contend, the Voting Rights Act must continue to safeguard the rights of minorities to vote and to elect candidates of their choice.[135]

Criticisms of standing pat emanate from different camps. Narrow constructionists argue that the vote dilution remedy of maximizing safe seats for minority officials (where the choice, for example, is between two seats for moderate-to-liberal whites or one seat each for a minority member and a conservative Republican) results in a net increase of racially conservative officeholders by depriving white liberals of crucial minority votes.[136] Thus, they say, the Voting Rights Act forces an unfortunate trade-off: an increase in the number of minority seats at the expense of a viable coalition. An assumption of this criticism, often unspoken, is that minority officeholders answerable to a primarily minority constituency are dispensable, or at least serve no special function that whites cannot perform as well or better.

Another criticism, from both the narrow constructionists and the camp whose views will next be discussed, is that single-member-district remedies as now imposed by the Justice Department and the courts may politically ghettoize minority voters and render them less effective than they otherwise would be by limiting them to one vote—the vote for their district representative—and thus prevent them from joining with potential white crossover voters throughout the jurisdiction to elect a larger number of candidates answerable to minority voters.[137]

The third view, endorsed by those whom I call expansive constructionists, holds, like the view of the standpatters, that section 5 and amended section 2 are still essential to prevent continuing efforts by white voters to dilute minority votes but contends that new remedies for dilution are also necessary. This position has recently been argued, among others, by Lani Guinier, a law professor with experience as a Justice Department official and a voting rights attorney for the NAACP Legal Defense Fund.[138] Guinier was instrumental in helping amend section 2.

135. Many members of the voting rights bar today belong to this camp. See also, in this volume, the chapters by Cain, Days, Fraga, Kousser, and McDonald.
136. For an example of this criticism, see Taylor 1991, 52. But see Brace, Grofman, and Handley 1987; Parker 1990, 143−44.
137. Critics of the standpatters cite notable cases in which minority candidates have won office in predominantly white jurisdictions. These include, in addition to Douglas Wilder and Dan Morales, the recent election of black mayors in New Haven, Connecticut; New York City; Gainesville, Florida; Rockford, Illinois; and Denver, Colorado.
138. Guinier 1991b. See also her comments in this volume. Other representatives of

As do proponents of the first two views, expansive constructionists start from the premise that even when minorities are elected in proportion to their numbers from single-member districts, they are often unable to realize the goals the civil rights movement hoped the black vote could achieve. Unlike the narrow constructionists, however, they believe that the ability to elect candidates of choice is an important one that minority voters should not be asked to give up as the price for joining a multiracial coalition.[139]

The benefit of single-member districts, they point out, is that they allow the creation of majority-minority districts from which minority candidates can be elected, even when the white majority in the jurisdiction as a whole votes as a bloc against minority candidates and systematically causes them to lose. But there are potential costs as well. In a typical American at-large system with, say, eight contested council seats, each voter has eight votes and can possibly (though not necessarily) affect who fills all those seats. In a single-member-district system, each voter has only one vote and can at most affect the outcome for one seat. The trade-off is between an arithmetical minority of relatively safe minority seats on the one hand and, on the other, the possibility of influencing an arithmetical majority of officeholders, all of whom may be white. If the minority candidates who win in a single-member-district system encounter racial polarization on the council as well as in the electorate, they

---

this school, although not necessarily in agreement with Guinier on all points, are Karlan 1989; Still 1984; Still 1992.

139. There are two issues here: first, whether minority voters have a right to elect candidates of their choice; and second, whether minority officials serve a unique function that could not be served by white officials in their stead. On the latter issue, treated as an empirical question about the policy benefits minority officials are able to obtain for their constituents, the evidence is mixed, the result, in part, of the difficulty of measuring benefits going to specific groups and attributing these benefits to specific causes. See Button 1989, 226–29; Browning, Marshall, and Tabb 1984, 141–43; Browning, Marshall, and Tabb 1990, 224–27; Eisinger 1982; Garrow 1978, 193–94; Karnig and Welch 1980; Keech 1968; Lawson 1985, 267–69; Mladenka 1989; Morris 1981; Parker 1990, chap. 5.

In spite of the variable findings, however, it is significant that Browning, Marshall, and Tabb 1984 and Button 1989, in two of the most methodologically sophisticated, fine-grained studies of multiple cities—one group in California, the other in Florida—found strong evidence for the unique policy impact on minority communities of elected minority officeholders. Moreover, contrary to the narrow-constructionist view, Button 1989, 227, 229, found that in cities without black voter majorities, "liberal coalitions were rarely dominant or black officials had difficulty gaining access to such groups," and that in minority-black cities in which black officials were elected at large, the pressure from the majority-white voting bloc "has usually forced black candidates to moderate their views . . . and as a result, black candidates make fewer demands on behalf of their constituents."

may find themselves and their community's interests still isolated. Indeed, as sometimes happens, they may also discover that the majority on the council changes the rules once minority officeholders are elected: for example, important positions may be abolished that council members had traditionally occupied in rotation.

A second problem with single-member-district elections is that, as with typical at-large elections, the winner in each district takes all, giving the voters who backed the winner disproportionate representation. The winner may have squeaked by with 51 percent of the vote, but because he or she is the sole winner in the contest, the votes for the losing candidates are wasted.

Expansive constructionists, following Edward Still's lead, thus advocate remedies for Voting Rights Act violations that are neither the typical at-large arrangement that prevents election of the minority group's candidates of choice nor a single-member-district system.[140] Citing European practices as relevant examples, expansive constructionists urge the adoption of such modified at-large remedies as limited voting, cumulative voting, and a lowering of the "threshold of exclusion"—the number of votes needed for a candidate to be declared a winner—from 50 percent plus one to as low as 20 percent. Such remedies, they claim, will allow minority voters to elect their candidates proportionally in the near term and also allow them "a fair chance to have their policy preferences satisfied" by joining effective multiracial coalitions if racial polarization declines.[141]

This position also has its critics. First, there is little knowledge of how the new remedies would work in an American multiethnic setting, even though two components, low thresholds of exclusion and cumulative voting, are widely used in other democratic nations. Would the necessary assumptions underlying this scheme usually be met? Would the scheme work when racial groups, not national parties, were the key electoral groups? Second, would lowering the threshold of exclusion encourage more involvement by small extremist groups with antidemocratic tenden-

140. Still 1984.
141. Guinier 1991b, 1136. See also Amy 1991; Engstrom and Barrilleaux 1991; Still 1984; Still 1992. Under limited-voting rules, the voter is able to cast fewer votes than the number of at-large seats contested. "In theory such a system prevents the majority from making a clean sweep of all seats by voting a straight ticket. Theory has usually been borne out in practice" (Still 1984, 253). Cumulative voting gives all voters as many votes as there are seats to be filled; voters may concentrate their votes on fewer candidates. If minority voters are agreed on the targets of their cumulative votes, they may overcome the effect of the majority bloc in an at-large system.

cies?[142] Third, American courts are chary of imposing remedies that are outside the American tradition: Would they be likely to order such remedies?[143]

Finally, if this approach is offered as a solution to the failure of minority voting to bring about the ambitious goals envisioned by the civil rights movement, it is important to note that the suggested remedies do not seem applicable at the level of presidential elections.[144] And, one might argue, it is here, not at the state and local levels, that the kind of winning progressive coalitions must be forged if fundamental improvements in opportunities for the disadvantaged are to occur.

In summary, these three positions represent the major points in the debate over the act as it has evolved so far. They are all premised, I reiterate, on the fact that the vote in the hands of blacks and other minority groups has not proved as effective a weapon as the civil rights movement had hoped. All three positions are ostensibly directed at the problem of how to devise such a weapon. But the differences between the narrow constructionists and the other two schools, although tactical rather than strategic, do not appear amenable to a resolution in the near future.

142. Bell 1987, 97.

143. Guinier 1991b, 1152, note 351, points out, however, that courts have found threshold-lowering measures constitutional.

144. In Europe the election of prime ministers and their "governments" is necessarily tied to the outcome of parliamentary elections. In the United States the presidential election is separate from legislative ones and thus not within the reach of a proportional representation scheme.

Section 5 and the Role of the Justice Department

DREW S. DAYS III

THE VOTING RIGHTS ACT OF 1965 is generally regarded as the most successful piece of federal civil rights legislation ever enacted. As a result of its passage and enforcement, blacks in the South, particularly, have registered, voted, and been elected to public office in record numbers, as have Hispanics in the Southwest and West. This success was not easily won, however. The Fifteenth Amendment, ratified in 1870, was designed to ensure that former black slaves, freed by the Thirteenth Amendment and granted citizenship by the Fourteenth, would not be denied the right to vote "by the United States or by any State on account of race, color, or previous condition of servitude." Nevertheless, for the remainder of the nineteenth century and well into the middle of the twentieth, black efforts to make good on these assurances were largely unavailing. Whites in southern and border states used grandfather clauses, white-only primaries, interpretation and literacy tests, poll taxes, and outright physical intimidation to keep all but a paltry number of the most courageous and persistent blacks from voting.

The Reconstruction Era Congress, pursuant to its authority under the Fifteenth Amendment, enacted legislation designed to remedy unconstitutional deprivations of the right to vote, but with increasingly restrictive Supreme Court interpretations of those laws and stiffer southern resistance to them in Congress, federal interest in their vigorous enforcement waned. Although federal enforcement employing criminal statutes revived somewhat during the first three decades of the twentieth century, private civil rights groups assumed most of the responsibility for challenging restrictive election practices. Congress did not readdress voting rights until it passed the Civil Rights Act of 1957, which authorized the attorney general to bring civil suits to remedy interference with the right to vote. Although the act represented a major advance in federal efforts to combat discrimination in voting rights, Congress soon recognized that further legislation was necessary. The Civil Rights Act of 1960 was enacted primarily to provide the attorney general with a mechanism for appointing federal registrars to place qualified blacks on the voting rolls in those jurisdictions with proven records of black disfranchisement. But the act required the attorney general to rely on litigation to address discriminatory practices, and state officials demonstrated time and again their ability to use lengthy and complex litigation to forestall any meaningful change in their procedures. Against this backdrop Congress confronted intense pressure from civil rights groups to guarantee voting rights of blacks in the South. Congress responded with the Voting Rights Act of 1965.[1]

The 1965 Voting Rights Act and Section 5

The 1965 statute has many parts, but people familiar with its provisions and enforcement generally consider section 5 to have contributed most over the intervening quarter century to the law's effectiveness. Section 5 is unique among federal civil rights laws. It prohibits the implementation of any changes affecting voting in certain jurisdictions covered by the act without the approval of the attorney general or a special three-judge federal district court in the District of Columbia.[2] To receive preclearance, a covered jurisdiction must establish that its proposed change does not have the purpose or effect of "denying or abridging the right to vote on account of race or color." Thus while other civil rights statutes place the burden of enforcement on the federal government or private parties to initiate litigation or administrative proceedings, section 5 shifts the burden of initiation and proof to the proponent of a potentially discriminatory voting change.[3] And as recent Supreme Court decisions have made clear, where the burden rests shapes profoundly the outcome of civil rights litigation.[4]

Section 5 has been the subject of criticism almost from the moment it was added to the legislation in Congress. The Supreme Court's 1966

1. For more detailed discussion of the background for the act, see Carr 1947; Commission on Civil Rights 1961; Lawson 1976; Garrow 1978; Lewis 1978; Bickel and Schmidt 1984, 908–90; Franklin and Moss 1988; Goldfield 1990.

2. Most jurisdictions have chosen to seek preclearance from the attorney general rather than file a lawsuit in the special district court for a declaratory judgment. Between 1965 and April 1, 1991, the Department of Justice reviewed 188,048 changes. The number of jurisdictions seeking judicial preclearance between 1965 and December 1989 was fewer than 20 (Department of Justice 1990; Department of Justice 1991).

3. Motomura 1983, 190–91.

4. *Wards Cove* v. *Atonio*, 109 S.Ct. 2115 (1989) (employment discrimination); Belton 1990, 1359.

54   DREW S. DAYS III

decision in *South Carolina* v. *Katzenbach* upholding the act's constitutionality prompted an impassioned dissent from Justice Hugo Black on
the threat to principles of federalism posed by section 5.[5] It is a theme
that has echoed down through the more recent dissents of Justices Lewis
Powell, John Paul Stevens, and William Rehnquist.[6] At root, these criticisms
appear to stem from a view that the Thirteenth, Fourteenth, and Fifteenth
Amendments were not intended to alter radically the relationship between
the federal government and the states on civil rights issues.[7] Even if they
were, these critics argue, enough time has passed to render unnecessary
an intrusive mechanism like section 5.[8]

Despite these reservations, however, section 5 has flourished, in a
manner of speaking. The Supreme Court, starting with *Allen* v. *State
Board of Elections* in 1969, has liberally construed the preclearance
mechanism to extend far beyond mere changes in provisions affecting
the physical act of voting or running for office.[9] Consequently, proposed
annexations, redistricting plans, shifts from district to at-large electoral
schemes, and changes in the location of polling places must be precleared.[10]
The Court has also upheld Department of Justice regulations imposing
the burden of persuasion on the submitting jurisdiction in section 5
preclearance; construed the act broadly to include all jurisdictions within
covered states; refused to require proof of discriminatory intent to deny

5. *South Carolina* v. *Katzenbach*, 383 U.S. 301 at 358 (1966), Justice Black concurring
and dissenting. See also, Rice 1966, 159. Justice Black subsequently referred to the section
5 mechanism as "reminiscent of old Reconstruction days when soldiers controlled the South
and when those States were compelled to make reports to military commanders of what
they did." He added that he doubted "that any of the 13 Colonies would have agreed to
our Constitution if they had dreamed that the time might come when they would have to
go to a United States Attorney General or a District of Columbia Court with hat in hand
begging for permission to change their laws." *Allen* v. *State Board of Elections*, 393 U.S.
544 at 595–96 (1969).
6. *City of Pleasant Grove* v. *United States*, 479 U.S. 462 at 801 (1987) (Justice Powell
dissenting); *United States* v. *Board of Commissioners of Sheffield, Alabama*, 435 U.S. 110
at 140 (1978) (Justice Stevens dissenting); *City of Rome* v. *United States*, 446 U.S. 156 at
206 (1980) (Justice Rehnquist dissenting).
7. See, for example, the debate between Justices Black and William O. Douglas in
Younger v. *Harris*, 401 U.S. 37 (1971).
8. See *City of Rome* v. *United States*, 446 U.S. at 193 (Justice Lewis Powell dissenting).
9. *Allen* v. *State Board of Elections*, 393 U.S. 544 (1969). *Allen* also held that private
citizens had an implied cause of action to seek equitable relief against covered jurisdictions
for failure to preclear changes (554–57).
10. For annexations, see *City of Richmond* v. *United States*, 422 U.S. 358 (1975). For
redistricting plans see *McDaniel* v. *Sanchez*, 452 U.S. 130 (1981). For changes in location
of polling places see *Perkins* v. *Matthews*, 400 U.S. 379 (1971).

preclearances and interpreted the bailout provision of the act strictly; and shielded the attorney general's preclearance determinations from direct legal challenge.[11] Recently the Court reaffirmed its view that section 5 also applies to judicial elections.[12]

The Supreme Court has rendered at least two decisions, however, that are generally viewed as making enforcement of section 5 more difficult. The first, *City of Richmond* v. *United States,* presented the question of how annexations that altered the racial composition of the annexing jurisdiction should be treated under section 5. In that case, Richmond, Virginia, sought approval to annex portions of a largely white area adjacent to its city limits. The consequence of this proposed enlargement of the city boundaries was that the population of Richmond would drop from 52 percent black before annexation to 42 percent afterward.[13] A reasonable reading of section 5 would have been that a 10 percent reduction in the black population within the expanded city would have the effect of "abridging the right to vote on account of race." However, the Supreme Court held that, assuming it could be established after further proceedings in the trial court that the annexation had no discriminatory purpose, section 5 could be satisfied if Richmond created an electoral system that afforded blacks "representation reasonably equivalent to their political strength in the enlarged community."[14] For example, a ward system that afforded blacks 42 percent rather than 52 percent representation would be acceptable.

The Supreme Court's reluctance to articulate a rule for annexations that would guarantee racial minorities no change in their preannexation political strength probably was based on a pragmatic concern that to do so would pose an obstacle to a number of municipalities economically pressed to enlarge their tax bases. Additionally, the Court viewed as an unacceptable form of black overrepresentation any approach that preserved preannexation black voting strength in the postannexation city.[15] However,

---

11. See, in order, *Georgia* v. *United States,* 411 U.S. 526 (1973); *United States* v. *Board of Commissioners of Sheffield, Alabama,* 435 U.S. 110 (1978); *City of Rome* v. *United States,* 446 U.S. 156 (1980); *Morris* v. *Gressette,* 432 U.S. 491 (1977). *Morris* was viewed by the advocates of a strong section 5 enforcement program as a setback since it insulated from judicial review the attorney general's refusal to interpose an objection to a discriminatory change. *Morris,* 507 (Justice Marshall dissenting).

12. *Brooks* v. *Georgia State Board of Elections,* 59 U.S.L.W. 3293 (October 15, 1990).

13. *City of Richmond* v. *United States,* 422 U.S. 358 (1975).

14. 422 U.S. at 370.

15. 422 U.S. at 371.

the proper institution for resolving the tension between minority voting rights and economic realities was Congress not the Court. The Court's *Richmond* rule has imposed upon the attorney general the difficult burden of proving discriminatory purpose in order to prevent the dilution of minority political strength by annexations of largely white areas. In other words, after *Richmond* the "effects" standard became irrelevant in annexation cases.[16]

The second case, *Beer* v. *United States,* has had an even greater impact on section 5 enforcement. At issue was whether a New Orleans plan, drawn up after the 1970 census, to reapportion seats on its city council satisfied section 5 requirements. The attorney general had denied preclearance and New Orleans had, as the act permits, brought suit before the special district court. The court rejected the plan on the grounds, among others, that it failed to afford black citizens a chance to elect representatives of their choice in numbers approximating their percentage of the total population. The court believed that reasonable alternative plans were available to New Orleans that would achieve that result.[17]

The Supreme Court reversed the decision. It found no violation of section 5 because the plan provided blacks with the prospect of electing at least one council member. Under the previous plan, based on the 1960 census, no blacks had been elected or could realistically have been elected by black voters alone. In so concluding, the Court announced the following guiding principles: section 5 precludes changes that have a retrogressive effect on the preexisting voting rights of minorities, and ameliorative changes, even if they fall short of what might be accomplished in terms of increasing minority representation, cannot be found to violate section 5 unless they so discriminate on the basis of race or color as to violate the Constitution. The New Orleans plan was ameliorative, not retrogressive, said the Court. As in the *Richmond* decision, the restrictive reading in *Beer* shifted the focus of section 5 from whether the proposed change had a discriminatory effect (as against other alternatives) to whether the plan was intentionally discriminatory.[18]

Congress has not, however, backed away from its original view that

16. For subsequent applications of the *Richmond* principle see *City of Port Arthur* v. *United States,* 459 U.S. 159, 103 S.Ct. 530 (1982); *City of Pleasant Grove* v. *United States,* 479 U.S. 462.

17. *Beer* v. *United States,* 425 U.S. 130 (1976).

18. 425 U.S. at 141. The *Beer* principles have been reaffirmed by the Court most recently in *City of Lockhart* v. *United States,* 460 U.S. 125 (1983). For a further discussion of the impact of *Richmond* and *Beer* on minority voting rights, see Binion 1979, 154; Ball 1986, 28.

section 5 preclearance was crucial to any effective attack on pervasive discrimination in voting. In 1970 the act was extended for five years and, because the trigger for section 5 preclearance was revised, several new jurisdictions, all outside of the South, were added to the list of those precluded from implementing voting changes without prior approval. Attempts by critics of section 5 to abolish Department of Justice preclearance were defeated.[19] In 1975 Congress extended the act once again, this time for seven years. This second extension incorporated new protections to ensure that there would be no voting rights discrimination against language minorities.[20] As a consequence of this change, the number of jurisdictions subject to section 5 preclearance increased significantly, largely because coverage was extended to all of Texas.[21]

In 1982 the act was extended still again. Section 5 was set to expire in twenty-five years.[22] And the "bailout" requirements for jurisdictions that wish to free themselves of having to obtain preclearance have become more detailed.[23] Perhaps the most far-reaching consequence of the 1982 amendments has been the incorporation of the new section 2 standards into the section 5 preclearance process. The Department of Justice has taken the position that such an incorporation was mandated by Congress.[24] Under the department's approach, of course, the retrogression standard of *Beer* no longer poses an obstacle to full evaluation of proposed changes. The question instead becomes whether the changes provide minority voters with the greatest feasible access to the political process in light of the "totality of the circumstances." This issue will have to be resolved ultimately by the Supreme Court.[25]

19. Graham 1990, 121–57.

20. Hunter 1976, 250; Commission on Civil Rights 1976.

21. *Briscoe* v. *Bell*, 432 U.S. 404 (1977).

22. See Commission on Civil Rights 1981 for an assessment of the act's effectiveness before the 1982 amendments.

23. Days and Guinier 1984, 167, 171–76; Phillips 1983.

24. Department of Justice 1989; letter from John R. Dunne, assistant attorney general for civil rights, to Roma Hague, attorney, Board of Supervisors, Jackson, Mississippi, July 19, 1991 (in my possession), denying preclearance of a redistricting plan in Hinds County.

25. There have been some references in Supreme Court and lower court opinions that support the department's view: see, for example, *City of Lockhart* v. *United States*, 460 U.S. 125 (1983) (Justice Marshall dissenting); *Chisholm* v. *Edwards*, 839 F.2d 1056 at 1064–65 (5th Cir. 1988). See also Haddad 1984, 139. The first direct challenge to the department's position has come in a declaratory judgment action filed in the three-judge federal court in Washington, D.C., *Georgia* v. *Thornburg*, No. 90-2065 (D.D.C. filed August 24, 1990).

Section 5 and Its Critics

Section 5 has not been popular, understandably, with those jurisdictions subject to preclearance. However, criticisms have also arisen among those originally supporting it. Abigail Thernstrom in *Whose Votes Count?* charged that section 5 has been transformed improperly from its original objective of "guarding against renewed disfranchisement, the use of the back door once the front one was blocked," to an instrument to "promote the election of blacks to public office."[26] She faults the Supreme Court, Congress (through its several extensions of the provisions), and the Department of Justice under both Democratic and Republican administrations for this alleged turn of events. For example, she sees the decision in *Allen* v. *State Board of Elections* as perhaps correct on its facts but argues that its expansion of the definition of what types of changes would be subject to preclearance was an unjustified interpretation of the Voting Rights Act that began its reshaping "into an instrument for affirmative action in the electoral sphere."[27]

The decision in *Richmond* v. *United States,* in Thernstrom's estimation, although not greeted warmly by civil rights advocates, imposed an improper burden on annexing jurisdictions to ensure fair representation for the postannexation minority population. This view is premised on the assertion that, as originally conceived by Congress, "'effect' and 'purpose' were close to interchangeable terms; the former was simply circumstantial evidence of the latter."[28] Armed with this reading of section 5, she searches for the many ways in which electoral changes have been denied preclearance on the grounds that they could not meet the effects test even when there was no evidence of discriminatory purpose. Hence, her assertion that annexations "are seldom discriminatory in purpose" forms the basis for a rejection of the Court's approach to annexations in *Richmond.*[29]

Thernstrom regards the decision in *Beer* v. *United States* requiring proof of retrogression to deny preclearance as an example of the Supreme Court's appropriate restraint of efforts by civil rights advocates and the Department of Justice to convert section 5 into an affirmative action device. However, she argues that *Beer* provided grounds for its own weakening by acknowledging that changes that violated the Constitution

26. Thernstrom 1987, 20, 38.
27. Thernstrom 1987, 22–30, quote on 27.
28. Thernstrom 1987, 26–27, 146–49.
29. Thernstrom 1987, 140.

could also justify denial. As a result the Department of Justice and the district court in Washington, D.C., have exploited those grounds consistently to sidestep the central requirements of *Beer*.[30]

This is not the occasion to offer a thoroughgoing response to Thernstrom's complex book, which attempts to demonstrate that the original purposes not only of section 5 but of the entire Voting Rights Act have been subverted since 1965. Moreover, others have already done so.[31] But a few observations would seem in order. First, Thernstrom is wrong that the concern of Congress in 1965 was simply to ensure that blacks had "the right to enter a polling booth and pull the lever."[32] The history of racial discrimination in voting had made clear to Congress that it could not anticipate the variety of stratagems officials in covered jurisdictions might use to maintain the status quo. Section 5 is a testament to Congress's view that flexibility should characterize the government's enforcement efforts and that discriminatory schemes, "sophisticated as well as simple-minded," should be denied preclearance.[33] The Supreme Court's decision in *Allen* correctly captures the spirit of that objective.

Second, Congress plainly required jurisdictions submitting plans to establish that proposed changes did "not have the purpose or the effect of denying or abridging the right to vote on account of race or color." Although Thernstrom prefers to give this language a crabbed reading, judicial and administrative interpretations cannot be said, at the very least, to do any violence to its plain meaning. Moreover, their interpretations are more in harmony than is Thernstrom's with the overall objectives of the act and section 5 to ensure that electoral legerdemain by racist officials would not continue to deprive blacks of an equal chance to participate in the political process.

One is certainly inclined to sympathize with Thernstrom's desire to see our nation transcend a focus on race in electoral matters and to embrace her optimism about American society and its political process. The problem, however, is that she overlooks or mischaracterizes the overwhelming evidence that minorities continue to be excluded from the political process. This same evidence has since 1965 persuaded Congress, the Supreme Court, and the Department of Justice that the protections of the Voting Rights Act and section 5 are still needed.

At the other end of the spectrum, Howard Ball and his colleagues have

30. Thernstrom 1987, 149–53, 157–91.
31. See, for example, Frickey 1988; Grunes 1988; Karlan and McCrary 1988.
32. Thernstrom 1987, 5.
33. *Lane* v. *Wilson*, 307 U.S. 268 at 275 (1939).

lamented in *Compromised Compliance* the absence of vigorous enforcement of section 5 by the Civil Rights Division of the Department of
Justice.[34] Their concern arises, first, because the attorney general's decision
to grant preclearance is, according to the Supreme Court's *Morris* v.
Gressette opinion, not subject to judicial review.[35] Consequently, for
minorities who believe that the attorney general has approved an electoral
change that denies or abridges their right to vote, their only recourse is
to file a constitutional lawsuit to establish that the change was intentionally discriminatory.[36] *Compromised Compliance* concludes, based on a
comprehensive review of the Voting Rights Act, relevant court decisions,
and the Department of Justice's administrative procedures for handling
preclearance submissions, that enforcement efforts have failed to achieve
the objectives Congress envisioned for section 5. Instead of ensuring
consistently that precleared changes promote full political participation
for racial minorities, the department has been willing, they contend, to
enter into negotiated settlements with submitting jurisdictions that produce
"suboptimal" results.[37]

Ball and his colleagues are certainly correct that the Department of
Justice largely ignored section 5 until after the *Allen* decision in 1969.
They are also correct that once geared up to enforce section 5 vigorously,
the department had to address two "technical-legal" problems that stood
in the way of achieving optimal compliance with the Voting Rights Act.[38]
The first problem was how to ensure that covered jurisdictions submitted
proposed changes for preclearance. Since the department's voting rights
implementation policy was indeed "fiscally dry," so that covered jurisdictions could not expect to get any financial reward for compliance, other
techniques had to be devised to induce submission. The second problem
was how to enforce section 5 within the context of a federal system in
which local jurisdictions continue to have broad discretion, even after
passage of the Voting Rights Act, to order their electoral systems.[39]

34. Ball, Krane, and Lauth 1982. See also Foster 1986, 17.
35. *Morris* v. *Gressette*, 432 U.S. 491 (1977).
36. This limitation has been significantly lessened by the amendment in 1982 of section
2 of the act, which prohibits any electoral requirement that "results in a denial or abridgement" of the right to vote on account of race or color. See Derfner 1984, 145. This amended
section was construed for the first time by the Supreme Court in *Thornburg* v. *Gingles*,
478 U.S. 30 (1986). Consequently, those dissatisfied with the granting of preclearance may
now sue the jurisdiction in question under section 2.
37. Ball, Krane, and Lauth 1982, 84–91, 135–37, 193–205.
38. Ball, Krane, and Lauth 1982, 77–78, 137.
39. Ball, Krane, and Lauth 1982, 28, 90–91.

Additionally, the department has had to operate in the midst of demands from civil rights organizations, on the one hand, that preclearance reviews be thorough and tough and from submitting jurisdictions, on the other, that the reviews be speedy and efficient. The department's response to the technical-legal problems has been to rely primarily on negotiation with submitting jurisdictions rather than on coercive measures. Undoubtedly, this process has produced second-best results in some instances or even, on rare occasions, results based purely on political considerations. But it has also achieved significantly high levels of compliance by covered jurisdictions in submitting their changes.

It is also generally incorrect to assume, as do the authors of *Compromised Compliance,* that the Justice Department negotiates with covered jurisdictions from a position of weakness. Quite the contrary, a denial of preclearance may result in overturning actions a jurisdiction has already taken or in suspending changes such as annexations and bond elections that have enormous economic consequences. At the very least, a denial may promise lengthy and expensive litigation.[40] These dire possibilities ensure that the department possesses the upper hand in most instances. This does not mean, however, that it may properly, in the face of contrary law or the absence of any principled basis, deny preclearance. Given these various considerations, what emerges from an assessment of the department's enforcement of section 5 since *Allen* is a picture of generally balanced and judicious use of this "extraordinary federal remedy," rather than "compromised compliance."[41]

Houston's experience offers an interesting example of how preclearance works. In April 1979 the city submitted to the Justice Department a proposed plan of annexations and deannexations. The department granted preclearance for two deannexations and one annexation because they were unpopulated areas and unlikely to affect minority voting strength in the city. Two other annexations were approved because they had substantial minority populations. However, fourteen other proposed

40. See Lamar 1988, 1765, recommending greater flexibility in devising remedies for unprecleared elections.

41. The General Accounting Office 1983, 8, reported, for example, "The Civil Rights Division has consistently applied the discriminatory purpose or effect analysis in making preclearance, objection, and withdrawal decisions under Section 5 of the Voting Rights Act. Its decisions have been made in accordance with existing legal standards and established procedures. We found no evidence that the division had applied arbitrary administrative standards in making decisions. Also, on the basis of our review of correspondence files, we found no evidence that parties outside of the division influenced its decisions."

annexations were not precleared on the grounds that they would have a discriminatory effect on minority voting strength.

The department's June 11, 1979, letter of objection pointed out that these annexations would reduce the black population from 26.0 percent to 24.8 percent and the Mexican-American population from 14.0 percent to 13.5 percent. Furthermore, there was evidence of racial bloc voting under Houston's at-large system for electing the eight-member city council and the mayor. As the letter noted further, although approximately two of every eight residents in Houston were black and one of every eight Mexican American, no Mexican American and only one black had ever served on the council. It closed by suggesting that an electoral system in which some council members were elected from single-member districts might satisfy section 5 requirements.[42]

On June 20, 1979, two delegations visited the Justice Department to discuss the letter. The first, comprising Houston's mayor and several members of the city council and its attorneys, urged the department to withdraw the objection and submitted a formal request for reconsideration, which Civil Rights Division staff promised to review promptly. The second delegation, led by Congressman Mickey Leland, was composed of black and Mexican-American citizens of Houston and representatives of minority organizations there who argued in favor of requiring the city to change its at-large system.[43]

After the Civil Rights Division reviewed thoroughly the city's request for reconsideration, Houston officials were notified by letter on July 18 that the objection would not be withdrawn. Moreover, the department objected to seven of eight referendum issues that were scheduled to be placed before the voters (including those in the proposed annexed areas) on August 11. The eighth issue, which, the letter said, "might provide a basis for curing the dilutive aspects of the annexations," involved a proposed change in Houston's electoral system under which the city council would be enlarged from nine members (including the mayor) elected at large to fifteen members, nine of whom would be elected from single-member districts and six (including the mayor) elected at large.[44]

When the department's refusal to withdraw the objection of June 11,

42. Letter from Drew S. Days III, assistant attorney general, to Robert M. Collie, Jr., city attorney for Houston, June 11, 1979. I have since been told that there were some black members during Reconstruction.

43. The chronology reported here is drawn from records that I kept during my tenure as assistant attorney general.

44. Letter from Drew S. Days III to Robert M. Collie, Jr., July 18, 1979.

1979, was received, Houston's city attorney informed the Civil Rights Division that the city would not comply with the restrictions imposed on the August 11 referendum election. On July 19, therefore, department lawyers joined an already-filed private federal court action under section 5 and sought an injunction against Houston's proceeding as planned with the election.[45] An injunction was granted, and only one issue, the proposed new electoral system, was presented to the voters in the referendum. The federal court also required Houston to report on July 23 on the steps it had taken to comply with the department's section 5 objections.

The referendum was held, the plan for the fifteen-member council was approved by the voters, and Houston's proposal to implement such a plan was submitted to the department for preclearance. Preclearance was given on August 31. Houston was informed that the department would make every effort to act expeditiously on any plan from the city that indicated exactly how the single-member districts would in fact be drawn. Of great concern to Houston was its desire to hold a referendum on a multimillion-dollar bond issue on September 25 that would also include voters from the objected-to annexed areas, as well as its hope of having elections for the city council under the new plan on November 6.

On September 12 Houston submitted the proposed configurations of the new single-member districts, and on September 17 representatives of Houston's black and Mexican-American communities again visited the department to provide their assessment. After reviewing the plan and community reactions, the department determined on September 21 that it should be given preclearance.

On November 6 Houston held its first election under the new plan. Two blacks and one Mexican American were elected from districts and one black was elected at large to the fourteen-seat council. The mayor continued to be elected at large. Houston's political process, like that of many other communities covered by the act, was forced to open up to previously excluded minority voters, thanks to the power given the attorney general under section 5.

To the criticisms of the Justice Department's section 5 enforcement by Thernstrom and by Ball and colleagues, one must add those of the General Accounting Office. In both 1978 and 1983 the comptroller general issued reports highly critical in two principal respects.

The GAO faulted the department, first, for not having in place effective

45. *United States* v. *City of Houston*, C.A. No. 78-4-2407 (S.D. Tex. July 19, 1979). See also, Department of Justice 1979, 117.

mechanisms to determine the extent to which covered jurisdictions were complying with section 5 by submitting proposed electoral changes. For example, in its 1978 report, the GAO noted that a private civil rights group had identified 44 allegedly unsubmitted election law changes made in Georgia between August 1965 and March 1976. Prior to hearings on the 1975 extension of the Voting Rights Act, the Department of Justice conducted reviews that determined that 316 state session laws passed between 1970 and 1974 in eight covered jurisdictions had not been precleared.[46] In its 1983 study the GAO reported that another private civil rights group found in a 1979–80 survey that 1,000 unsubmitted session laws had been enacted in six of eleven covered states between 1965 and 1980.[47]

The GAO's second concern was the Justice Department's lack of systematic follow-up procedures to ensure that jurisdictions did not attempt to implement changes that had been denied preclearance. As of 1978, according to the GAO, the attorney general had objected to 257 of the reported 13,433 submissions between 1965 and 1976 but had yet to initiate any formal monitoring program to determine compliance.[48] In its 1983 report the GAO indicated that the department had conducted a review in June 1981 of 262 objections interposed since January 1975 and found that 11 had been ignored. In these 11 cases, between three and seven years had elapsed since the objections were communicated to the respective jurisdictions.[49]

The GAO's concerns are well founded: the Justice Department had failed to monitor the level of compliance with the submission requirement and to ensure that changes denied preclearance were not implemented.[50] But the department has not had the resources to conduct compliance reviews, even if it wished to do so, and has not thought such reviews a wise allocation of resources. Its contention, for which there is some basis, is that most important electoral changes are submitted by covered jurisdictions voluntarily or are made public through the efforts of private civil rights groups. However, the department's attitude has been tempered by the GAO reports, and it has embarked on a new course of monitoring compliance.[51]

46. General Accounting Office 1978, 12, 13.
47. General Accounting Office 1983, 14–15.
48. General Accounting Office 1978, 15.
49. General Accounting Office 1983, 16–17.
50. Days and Guinier 1984, 168; McDonald 1983, 68.
51. General Accounting Office 1983, 22. Keady and Cochran 1980–81 have argued,

Conclusion

It would be difficult to imagine that any single legislative provision could successfully rectify the effects of centuries of discrimination against minorities in the electoral process. Section 5 of the Voting Rights Act certainly has not done so. However, at least since 1969 the preclearance process has proved a significant barrier against electoral practices that might retard even further the arrival of the day when racial and ethnic minorities become full-fledged members of the American political community. Congress was indeed wise to "shift the advantage of time and inertia from the perpetrators of the evil to its victims."[52]

---

however, that the section 5 administrative process has so many defects that it ought to be given over entirely to the federal courts. This proposal would, if adopted, make the preclearance process entirely unworkable. Whatever might be gained in the quality of the review would surely be lost in the delay that judicial preclearance would necessarily entail.

52. *South Carolina* v. *Katzenbach*, 383 U.S. 301 at 328 (1966).

The 1982 Amendments of Section 2 and Minority Representation

LAUGHLIN MCDONALD

SECTION 2 OF THE VOTING RIGHTS ACT OF 1965, a general prohibition on discrimination in voting, has become one of the most powerful weapons for protecting voting rights since it was amended in 1982 to incorporate a "results" test for violations.[1] Reinforced by other provisions, such as the requirement in section 5 that changes in electoral procedure be federally supervised and the ban on literacy tests contained in section 4, it has brought about the gradual demise of discriminatory at-large elections and has led to a substantial increase in officeholding by minorities.

The Crisis of 1980

In the spring of 1980 the campaign for equal voting rights faced a major crisis. In *City of Mobile* v. *Bolden* the Supreme Court had held that minority plaintiffs had to prove intent to discriminate on the basis of race if they were successfully to challenge discriminatory voting practices under the Constitution or section 2.[2] Meanwhile, section 5, which required jurisdictions with a history of discrimination in voting and low voter registration or turnout to get federal preclearance of any changes they wished to make in their election procedures, was on the verge of expiration. The combination of the *Bolden* decision and the expiration of section 5 was potentially disastrous. Unless Congress took corrective action, jurisdictions with long traditions of discrimination would be able to return to their old ways, and minorities would be powerless to stop them unless they could prove that state officials acted with specific racial animus.

Before *Mobile* v. *Bolden* the Court had held in *White* v. *Regester* (1973) that voting practices were unlawful if they denied minorities an equal opportunity "to participate in the political processes and to elect legislators of their choice."[3] Unequal opportunity could be shown by evidence of the effect of the practice and factors such as a history of

1. See the appendix to this volume for the text of the act as amended in 1982.
2. *City of Mobile* v. *Bolden*, 446 U.S. 55 (1980).
3. *White* v. *Regester*, 412 U.S. 755 at 766 (1973).

discrimination, the existence of cultural and language barriers, racially divisive campaign appeals, limited numbers of minority-elected officials, a depressed socioeconomic status for a minority, and the use of potentially discriminatory majority vote and numbered-post requirements.[4] The Fifth Circuit Court had later held in *Nevett* v. *Sides* (1978) that plaintiffs must also show that a challenged practice was racially motivated. The decision did not change the plaintiff's burden of proof, however, since the court held that evidence of the criteria identified in *White* v. *Regester* "raises an inference of intent and, therefore, that a finding under the criteria satisfies the intent requirement."[5]

The immediate impact of *Mobile* v. *Bolden* was dramatic. Because of the plaintiff's onerous new burden of proof, litigation challenging discriminatory voting practices under the Constitution and section 2 dried up. Some plaintiffs (both the Department of Justice and private parties) who had cases pending dropped them, and virtually no new cases were filed. Defendants became suddenly intransigent and refused to discuss settlement.[6]

The prospects for congressional relief seemed bleak. The resurgence of states' rights sentiment in the 1980 presidential election, the increased conservatism of Congress, and the defeat of the Fair Housing Act amendments in 1981 suggested that passage of any civil rights legislation would be doubtful, particularly legislation that challenged the increasingly popular idea that racially discriminatory intent was the proper standard for evaluating civil rights violations.

The Amendment of Section 2

Mobile v. *Bolden,* ironically, proved an opportunity rather than a reversal. It galvanized civil rights activists into a unified force and sharply focused a national debate on voting rights. Congress responded overwhelmingly in 1982 by extending the preclearance provisions of section 5 for another twenty-five years and amending section 2 to prohibit voting practices, regardless of their purpose, that result in discrimination.

4. A numbered-post requirement forces candidates for multimember offices, such as city councils or county commissions, to run for a particular post or seat, rather than for existing vacancies. The requirement produces individual, head-to-head contests, and limits the ability of a politically cohesive minority to concentrate its votes on one or a few candidates and withhold its votes from the opposition. See *Rogers* v. *Lodge,* 458 U.S. 613 at 627 (1982).

5. *Nevett* v. *Sides,* 571 F.2d 209 at 217 (5th Cir. 1978).

6. Parker 1981, 111–12.

According to the legislative history, Congress was unhappy with *Bolden's* requirement that plaintiffs prove intent to discriminate and amended the act to reinstate its earlier intention "that violations of the Voting Rights Act, including Section 2, could be established by showing the discriminatory effect of the challenged practice." Congress concluded that the intent standard was "unnecessarily divisive" because it required plaintiffs to prove that local officials were racists, the burden of proof was "inordinately difficult," and it asked "the wrong question." The right question was whether "as a result of the challenged practice or structure plaintiffs do not have an equal opportunity to participate in the political processes and to elect candidates of their choice."[7]

The House and Senate reports that accompanied the 1982 amendments set out certain readily verifiable factors derived from *White* v. *Regester* and other cases that courts ordinarily should consider in discovering whether minority populations of voters had been diluted. These factors included racially polarized voting, a history of discrimination, depressed levels of minority income and employment, and few minority officeholders. Congress also described subjective factors such as government responsiveness to minority communities and racial motives that courts should avoid considering. The factors were illustrative not exhaustive, and no particular number had to be proved. The ultimate question, as under *White*, was whether the challenged practice denied the minority an equal opportunity to participate in the political process and to elect candidates of its choice, a question that could be answered only by "a searching practical evaluation of the 'past and present reality.'"[8]

Two days after Congress amended section 2, the Supreme Court, in *Rogers* v. *Lodge*, essentially reversed *Mobile* v. *Bolden*. While the Court continued to require proof of discriminatory intent, it said that such intent could be inferred from circumstantial evidence: "discriminatory intent need not be proved by direct evidence. 'Necessarily, an invidious discriminatory purpose may often be inferred from the totality of the relevant facts. . . .'"[9]

Mobile v. *Bolden* and *Rogers* v. *Lodge* can scarcely be distinguished on their facts but can be understood as a reflection of changes in the membership of the Court and the vote of the chief justice. Justice Sandra Day O'Connor had replaced Justice Potter Stewart, who had written the

7. House of Representatives 1981, 29; Senate 1982b, 28, 36–37.
8. Senate 1982b, 30, quoting *White* v. *Regester*, 412 U.S. 755 at 769–70 (1973).
9. *Rogers* v. *Lodge*, 458 U.S. 613 at 618 (1982), quoting *Washington* v. *Davis*, 426 U.S. 229 at 242 (1976).

plurality opinion in *Bolden,* and she voted for the plaintiffs in *Rogers* v. *Lodge.* Chief Justice Warren Burger, confronted with the egregious facts in *Rogers* and, according to one observer, "stung by nationwide criticism of the *Bolden* decision," changed sides and voted with the majority in *Rogers.*[10]

Still, despite the greater receptivity shown by the Court to constitutionally based claims in *Rogers* v. *Lodge,* section 2 remains the principal basis for challenging possible voting rights abuses. That is true not only because it dispenses with any requirement that plaintiffs prove a discriminatory purpose, but because the courts are obligated to resolve cases where possible on statutory grounds and avoid a constitutional decision.[11]

Judicial Construction of Section 2

The Supreme Court construed amended section 2 for the first time in 1986 in *Thornburg* v. *Gingles.* A majority of the Court (Justices William Brennan, Thurgood Marshall, Harry Blackmun, John Stevens, and Byron White) established a three-part test for determining when at-large voting in multimember legislative districts violated the results standard of the statute. First, the minority must be able to show that it is sufficiently large and geographically compact to constitute a majority in one or more single-member districts. Second, it must be able to show that it is politically cohesive or tends to vote as a bloc. Third, it must show that the majority votes sufficiently as a bloc "usually to defeat the minority's preferred candidate." The other factors discussed in the 1981 and 1982 House and Senate reports, such as the lingering effects of discrimination, racially directed campaign appeals, and the use of election devices that abet discrimination, were deemed supportive of, but not essential to, a finding of voting rights violation.[12]

The Court also simplified proof of racial bloc voting and made clear that plaintiffs were not required to prove that voters were voting for reasons of race rather than for some other reason, such as religion, party affiliation, age, or name identification. According to the Court, "all that matters under § 2 . . . is voter behavior, not its explanations." Bloc voting exists "where there is 'a consistent relationship between [the] race of the voter and the way in which the voter votes' . . . or to put it differently, where 'black voters and white voters vote differently.'" While no simple

10. Derfner 1984, 161.
11. *Escambia County, Florida* v. *McMillan,* 466 U.S. 49 at 51 (1984).
12. *Thornburg* v. *Gingles,* 478 U.S. 30 at 48, 51, 82–83 (1986).

doctrinal test is applicable in all cases, legally significant racial bloc voting exists in general where "a white bloc vote . . . normally will defeat the combined strength of minority support plus white 'crossover' votes."[13]

Thornburg v. *Gingles* was enormously significant because it simplified decisions in voting cases and added greater predictability. By focusing almost exclusively on racial patterns in elections and demographics, the three-part analysis placed claims of racial discrimination in voting on the same evidentiary footing as claims based on population disparities. The *Gingles* inquiry avoids, or seeks to minimize, unnecessary investigation into historical, social, and economic dynamics and intent, and attempts to measure dilution in the same objective way as does the "one person, one vote" rule. The analysis in *White* v. *Regester* and the legislative history is still relevant, but proof of the *Gingles* factors is ordinarily enough to establish a violation of section 2.[14]

The Impact of Amended Section 2 on Litigation

The amendment of section 2 and the decision in *Rogers* v. *Lodge* in 1982, together with the *Thornburg* v. *Gingles* decision in 1986, represented a strong congressional and judicial commitment to equality in voting and support of claims of voting rights violations. They also accelerated the pace of litigation.

Before the 1980s, voting cases often involved seemingly endless appeals and remands for further consideration of the factors mentioned in *White* v. *Regester*. Judges frequently viewed the same or nearly the same evidence and reached opposite conclusions.[15] Because proving a violation was expensive and time consuming, the number of discriminatory practices the minority and civil rights communities had the resources to challenge was limited. *Mobile* v. *Bolden*, for example, took eight years to litigate; the plaintiffs' lawyers spent 5,525 hours and $96,000 in out-of-pocket costs to prosecute the case.[16] A 1979 survey of federal district court judges recognized the complexity of

13. *Thornburg* v. *Gingles,* 478 U.S. at 53, 56, 73.
14. Compare *Solomon* v. *Liberty County, Florida,* 899 F.2d 1012 (11th Cir. 1990) (concurring opinions of Judge Kravitch and Chief Judge Tjoflat).
15. See, for example, *Cross* v. *Baxter,* 604 F.2d 875 (5th Cir. 1979), *aff'd,* 639 F.2d 1383 (5th Cir. Unit B Mar. 1981), *modified,* 688 F.2d 279 (5th Cir. 1982), *vacated and remanded,* 460 U.S. 1065 (1983).
16. *Bolden* v. *City of Mobile,* Civ. No. 75-297-P (S.D. Ala. Dec. 12, 1983).

such litigation by giving voting cases a weight of 2.842, as opposed to an average case weight of 1.000 on a scale that measured the complexity of cases and the judicial resources various categories needed. Voting cases were exceeded in complexity by only ten of the fifty-five categories listed in the survey.[17]

Before the adoption of the results standard in 1982, about 150 voting cases of all kinds were brought in federal court each year.[18] Since then, with the streamlining and greater predictability of section 2 challenges, the number has jumped to 225 a year. As a result of the increase in litigation or the threat of litigation, more and more jurisdictions have abandoned the discriminatory features of their election systems, particularly at-large voting. According to the Department of Justice, in the three years before 1982, fewer than 600 jurisdictions in the states covered by section 5 changed their method of election; 1,354 did so in the three years following the amendment of section 2.[19]

As these figures suggest, voting cases are being settled at a much greater rate than in the past. In Edgefield County, South Carolina, for example, the first challenge to at-large elections was filed against the county council in 1974 and was litigated for more than ten years, including an appeal before the Supreme Court.[20] A similar suit was filed against the county school board in 1985. Following the decision in *Thornburg* v. *Gingles,* and a trial court decision for the plaintiffs, the defendants decided not to appeal.[21] Voting rights suits were then filed against the two largest towns in the county, Johnston and Edgefield, and both municipalities settled without going to trial.[22]

Dillard v. *Crenshaw County* further illustrates the quickened pace of voting rights litigation and the increased willingness of defendants to settle. The case was filed by blacks challenging at-large elections in the nine counties in Alabama that used such procedures and were not already subject to federal lawsuits. Three of the nine counties reached full agreement with the plaintiffs shortly after the litigation was begun. Following issuance

17. Administrative Office of the United States Courts 1980, A-161.
18. Administrative Office of the United States Courts 1980, A-16.
19. Department of Justice, Civil Rights Division 1987, 2.
20. *McCain* v. *Lybrand,* 465 U.S. 236 (1984).
21. *Jackson* v. *Edgefield County, South Carolina School District,* 650 F. Supp. 1176 (D.S.C. 1986).
22. *Jackson* v. *Johnston, South Carolina,* Civ. No. 9:87-955-3 (D.S.C. Sept. 30, 1987); *Thomas* v. *Mayor and Town Council of Edgefield, South Carolina,* Civ. No. 9:86-2901-16 (D.S.C. May 27, 1987)).

of a preliminary injunction by the district court, three more counties reached a full settlement and the remaining three partial settlements.[23] The plaintiffs eventually amended their complaint to add 183 cities and county school boards that used at-large elections, alleging that they too were tainted by racially inspired enactments of the Alabama legislature. All but 7 of the jurisdictions entered into an interim consent decree, agreeing to a resolution of the plaintiffs' claims in the district court.[24]

Another factor contributing to change is that jurisdictions losing in court are required to pay the plaintiffs' costs and attorneys' fees. In *Lodge* v. *Rogers*, the Burke County, Georgia, defendants not only had to pay their own lawyers, but they had to pay the plaintiffs' lawyers $294,584.41.[25] The odds of losing and the consequent costs have thus been strong incentives for jurisdictions not to fight to keep at-large voting systems. According to a survey of probate judges in Georgia conducted by the *Atlanta Constitution* two years after the *Lodge* decision, the threat of lawsuits was prompting more and more local officials to adopt district elections.[26]

The Expanded Scope of Section 2

In addition to the increase in the number of voting rights cases being brought and the jurisdictions affected, the scope of section 2 litigation has broadened. While most challenges have been to at-large elections, districting plans, and other electoral structures, section 2 also applies to all practices or procedures related to voting rights, including those that are episodic and do not involve permanent structural barriers.[27] The courts have, accordingly, usually given it a generous construction and have held that such practices as the failure to appoint blacks as poll officials, requiring separate or dual registration for city and county elections, referendums that cover several issues in a single question, and a sole commissioner (one person) form of government were subject to challenge under the statute.[28]

23. *Dillard v. Crenshaw County*, 649 F.Supp. 289 (M.D. Ala. 1986), *aff'd in part, remanded in part*, 831 F.2d 246 (11th Cir. 1987).
24. *Dillard v. Baldwin County Board of Education*, 686 F.Supp. 1459 at 1461 (M.D. Ala. 1988).
25. *Lodge v. Rogers*, CIV 176-55 (S.D.Ga. Mar. 23, 1983).
26. Hansen 1984, 16A.
27. Senate 1982b, 30.
28. See *Harris v. Graddick*, 615 F.Supp. 239 (M.D. Ala. 1985); *Mississippi State Chapter, Operation PUSH v. Allain*, 674 F.Supp. 1245 (N.D. Miss. 1987); *Lucas v. Townsend*, 908 F.2d 851 (11th Cir. 1990), *vacated and remanded on other grounds sub nom.*,

Section 2's prohibition of vote dilution has also been held to cover the election of judges. In *Chisom* v. *Roemer,* the Supreme Court rejected Louisiana's contention that judges were not "representatives" and held that "state judicial elections are included within the ambit of §2 as amended."[29] In a companion case, *Houston Lawyers' Association* v. *Attorney General of Texas,* the Court ruled that trial judges were not special "single-member offices" exempt from section 2 coverage.[30]

It seems equally clear that section 2 applies to the election of any public official where vote dilution is subject to remedy. In *Dillard* v. *Crenshaw County, Alabama* the court of appeals rejected the suggestion that elected administrative positions are excluded from section 2 coverage: "nowhere in the language of section 2 nor in the legislative history does Congress condition the applicability of section 2 on the function performed by an elected official."[31]

When it was enacted in 1965, the Voting Rights Act essentially targeted seven states of the old Confederacy that had systematically discriminated against blacks. Reflecting the expansion of the act in 1975 to cover language minorities, section 2 is now being increasingly used on behalf of Hispanics and native Americans, and in the North, the West, and the Southwest. Suits by Hispanics challenging at-large elections are now commonplace, as to a lesser extent are those by native Americans.[32]

Single-Member Districts and Increased Minority Officeholding

When the Voting Rights Act was enacted there were fewer than 100 black elected officials in the seven targeted southern states and fewer than 200 nationwide. By January 1990 there were 3,394 in the targeted states and 7,370 nationwide.[33] Statistics for nonblack minorities from years before 1965 are not generally available, but as of the mid-1980s there were an estimated 3,360 elected officials of Latin American descent

---

Board of Public Education and Orphanage for Bibb County v. *Lucas,* 111 S.Ct 2845 (1991); *Carrollton Branch of NAACP* v. *Stallings,* 829 F.2d 1547 (11th Cir. 1987).

29. 111 S.Ct. 2354 at 2368 (1991).

30. 111 S.Ct. 2376 at 2380 (1991).

31. 931 F.2d 246 at 251 (11th Cir. 1987).

32. For Hispanics see, for example, *Gomez* v. *City of Watsonville,* 863 F.2d 1407 (9th Cir. 1988). For native Americans see *Windy Boy* v. *County of Big Horn,* 647 F.Supp. 1002 (D. Mont. 1986).

33. Commission on Civil Rights 1968, 15; Joint Center for Political and Economic Studies 1990, 10-1.

and 852 native Americans (in nontribal offices).[34] The increase in minority
officeholding can be traced to the operation of the Voting Rights Act as
a whole—to the abolition of discriminatory tests for voting, the expansion
of minority registration, and the requirement of preclearance of new
voting practices under section 5. Equally critical, however, has been the
adoption of effective minority voting districts, many as a result of litigation or the threat of litigation under section 2.[35]

In Mississippi and Alabama every black in the state legislature in 1988
was elected from a majority black district.[36] In Big Horn County, Montana,
the only native American who served on the county commission was
elected from a majority Indian district. In Georgia, of the six black state
senators and twenty-two representatives, only one, Michael Thurmond,
whose district includes the University of Georgia at Athens, was elected
from a majority white (57 percent) district. Districts of the remaining
black members ranged from 56 percent black to 99 percent.[37] In cities
and counties in Texas that have adopted single-member districts or redrawn
district lines, "the results have in all cases been favorable to ethnic minorities: registration, voter turnout, and minority representation have
increased.[38]

The Omnipresence of Racially Polarized Voting

The assumption was implicit in the Voting Rights Act that increased
participation by minorities would gradually diminish the significance of
race in politics. Chief Justice Earl Warren expressed this view in his
opinion for the Court in *South Carolina* v. *Katzenbach* holding the act
to be constitutional.

Hopefully, millions of non-white Americans will now be able to participate for the first time on an equal basis in the government under
which they live. We may finally look forward to the day when truly
'[t]he right of citizens of the United States to vote shall not be denied
or abridged by the United States or by any State on account of race,
color or previous condition of servitude.'[39]

34. NALEO Educational Fund 1988; National Indian Youth Council 1986.
35. Joint Center for Political Studies 1986, 1, 5.
36. McDonald 1988, 31.
37. May and Palmer 1988, 4B.
38. Montejano 1987, 298.
39. *South Carolina* v. *Katzenbach*, 383 U.S. 301 at 337 (1966).

Although the act undoubtedly has had an ameliorating effect on attitudes, race is still a dynamic consideration in American politics, particularly as reflected in the strong continuing patterns of voting along racial lines. In contests where voters are given a racial choice, whites tend to vote white and blacks to vote black.

In Burke County, Georgia, in 1978 a trial court found "overwhelming evidence of bloc voting along racial lines."[40] Ten years later voting was still overwhelmingly polarized. In the 1988 primary election for coroner, 95 percent of whites voted for the white candidate and 80 percent of blacks for the black candidate. In the election for county school superintendent the same year, all the whites voted for the white candidate and 77 percent of blacks for the black candidate. In the 1982 and 1984 legislative elections, white voters cast an estimated 100 percent of their votes for the white candidates and none for the black.

The analysis of Burke County elections was part of a larger study conducted by the American Civil Liberties Union in connection with a challenge to the at-large, circuitwide election of superior court judges.[41] The ACLU analyzed all judicial, legislative, and at-large county office elections in Georgia since 1980 in the counties involved in litigation in which there had been a serious black candidate, defined as one who received as least one-half of the black vote. In all fifty-one such elections from twenty counties, a majority of whites (on the average, 86 percent) voted for white candidates and blacks (84 percent) for the black candidates.[42] Given this pattern, it is apparent why black candidates have found it difficult to win in majority white districts and why they have enjoyed success primarily in districts where blacks were in the majority.

Polarized voting is not simply a feature of states in the Deep South: border states and nonsouthern states also show the pattern. In Chattanooga a court found that "black and white voters . . . do vote differently most of the time." In Arkansas, in areas of the state where blacks make up a significant part of the population, voting patterns were called "highly racially polarized." In Watsonville, California, the non-Hispanic majority usually voted sufficiently as a bloc to defeat the minority votes. And in Springfield, Illinois, the evidence "overwhelmingly" supported the finding that "extreme racially polarized voting exists."[43]

40. *Rogers* v. *Lodge*, 458 U.S. 613 at 623 (1982).
41. *Brooks* v. *State Board of Elections*, Civ. No. 288-146 (S.D.Ga. 1989).
42. American Civil Liberties Union 1988.
43. *Brown* v. *Board of Commissioners of Chattanooga, Tenn.*, 722 F.Supp. 380 at 393 (E.D.Tenn. 1989); *Jeffers* v. *Clinton*, 730 F.Supp. 196 at 208 (E.D.Ark. 1989); *Gomez* v.

Some minority candidates, particularly those who have previously held elective office or run with the advantages of incumbency, have succeeded in winning a significant number of white crossover votes. In 1986 Mike Espy became the first black elected to Congress from Mississippi since Reconstruction as the result of reapportionment and the creation of a majority black district in the Delta area of the state. He won 52 percent of the vote overall, but just 10 percent of the white vote. In 1988, running as an incumbent, he won reelection with 40 percent of the white vote and 66 percent of the vote overall.[44] But encouraging as this crossover vote was, particularly in a state that traditionally has taken the lead in discriminating against blacks, Espy's election still reflects racially polarized voting by almost any accepted definition of the term—for example, whites and blacks voting differently or a majority of each race voting differently.[45]

The same is true of Douglas Wilder's successful campaign for governor of Virginia in 1989. Although not an incumbent, he had first been elected to the state senate from a majority black district and had served as lieutenant governor. He received about 39 percent of the state's white votes.[46] Thus his election, though exceptional, was nonetheless characterized by polarized voting.

Despite the Espys and Wilders, for most minority candidates strong voting along racial lines is still the reality. Sometimes even the exceptions later serve to prove the rule. Andrew Young was elected to the majority-white Fifth Congressional District of Georgia in 1972 with a solid black vote and, in the afterglow of the civil rights movement, 25 percent of the white vote. In 1981, however, after serving in Congress for three terms, serving as ambassador to the United Nations under President Carter, and raising more money than in his previous campaigns (and after, it should be noted, the often confrontational administration of Maynard Jackson, the city's first black chief executive), he won only 9 percent of the white vote in his election as mayor of Atlanta.[47] Given Young's showing, polarized

---

City of Watsonville, 863 F.2d 1407 at 1417 (9th Cir. 1988); McNeil v. City of Springfield, 658 F.Supp. 1015 at 1027 (C.D.Ill. 1987).

44. Hall 1988, 7.

45. In Thornburg v. Gingles, 478 U.S. 30 at 53, note 21 (1986), the Court defined racial bloc voting as "'black voters and white voters vot[ing] differently.'" Other cases have used different definitions, such as a majority of each race voting differently. See Brown v. Board of Commissioners of Chattanooga, Tenn., 722 F.Supp. 380 at 392 (E.D. Tenn 1989).

46. Shapiro 1989, 54.

47. Busbee v. Smith, Civ. No. 82-0665 (D.D.C.), deposition of Andrew Young, p. 9.

voting in the metropolitan Atlanta area, even for a candidate with extraordinary credentials, still seems a political fact of life.

Resegregation and Racial Quotas

Critics of section 2 have argued that the greater number of minority voting districts and the resulting increase in minority elected officials is what is *wrong* with the outcome of the Voting Rights Act. The statute has become, they argue, an unwanted quota system for minority office-holding and leads to resegregation and racial polarization.[48] These same arguments were made in 1982, when witnesses testified that section 2 would "stigmatize minorities" and "compartmentalize the electorate," that it would "pit race against race" and would restrict minority political influence to "the bounds of their quota."[49] Members of the Senate Subcommittee on the Constitution also argued that adopting a results standard for section 2 would lead to the creation of black single-member districts that would be nothing more than "political ghettoes for minorities" and that "minority *influence* would suffer enormously."[50] Congress weighed these arguments but determined that the amendments were justified to combat racial discrimination and polarization in the electorate.

According to a 1982 Senate report, the testimony and other evidence presented to the committee belied speculations that the amendment of section 2 would be divisive and would polarize communities on the basis of race. Numerous courts had applied the results test before 1980 and the decision in *City of Mobile* v. *Bolden,* and none of the dire consequences predicted by the opponents of the 1982 amendment had occurred. "There is, in short, an extensive, reliable and reassuring track record of court decisions using the very standard which the Committee bill would codify. The witnesses who attacked the 'result standard' virtually ignored those decisions in their analysis and, in most cases, admitted unfamiliarity with them, as well." Criticism of the application of the results standard and the use of single-member districts in racially polarized jurisdictions is, the report continued, "like saying that it is the doctor's thermometer which causes high fever."[51] Indeed, one of the most vocal critics of amended section 2 has conceded that "when black voters are 'isolated'

48. Fund 1987, 18; Schuck 1987, 51.
49. Senate 1982a, 1115 (statement of Robert M. Brinson); Senate 1982a, 745 (statement of Michael Levin).
50. Senate 1982b, 103 (additional views of Senator Orrin G. Hatch).
51. Senate 1982b, 32, 34.

within the political system," or "when the electoral process is distorted by racism," blacks "become entitled to single-member districts."[52]

Section 2 does not impose a quota for officeholding, although the outcome of elections is certainly a factor in determining whether a challenged practice violates the results standard of the statute. Congress made that clear by incorporating a disclaimer in the act, that nothing in section 2 established "a right to have members of a protected class elected in numbers equal to their proportion in the population." According to the Senate report, the disclaimer means that minorities cannot establish a violation of the statute merely by showing that they were not proportionately represented in public office.[53]

Thornburg v. *Gingles* similarly disavowed that section 2 was a quota system for minority officeholding: "the conjunction of an allegedly dilutive electoral mechanism and the lack of proportional representation alone does not establish a violation."[54] Instead, a plaintiff has the burden of establishing the *Gingles* factors or, in appropriate cases, the other factors identified in the legislative history. *Gingles* has been interpreted as requiring jurisdictions in which voting is racially polarized to create, where possible, reasonably contiguous and compact minority-controlled districts so as to provide minorities an equal opportunity to participate in the political process.[55] But section 2 does not set quotas for officeholding or require proportional representation.

Some of the criticism of the results standard and the increased use of district voting that has flowed from it is undoubtedly a rationalization for protecting incumbents and maintaining the status quo or simply a mask for opposition to minority political participation. During the 1981 congressional reapportionment in Georgia, for example, a member of the general assembly criticized a plan introduced by Senator Julian Bond creating a 69 percent black Fifth Congressional District in the Atlanta metropolitan area because it would bring "resegregation in a fine county like Fulton and resegregation in a fine city like Atlanta." The plan would disrupt the "harmonious working relationship between the races" and would cause polarization and white flight. Other members said that a majority black congressional district would be merely a black ghetto. One of the black members of the general assembly, indicating that the opposition was racially based, defended the Bond plan and charged that

52. Thernstrom 1987, 240.
53. Senate 1982b, 23–24.
54. *Thornburg* v. *Gingles*, 478 U.S. at 46.
55. *Jeffers* v. *Clinton*, 730 F.Supp. 196 at 198 (E.D.Ark. 1989).

no one seemed concerned about "working relations" in the other nine (majority-white) congressional districts but expressed racial concerns only about the single district in which whites might constitute the minority.[56]

The general assembly rejected the Bond proposal and adopted instead a plan that divided the black population in metropolitan Atlanta among several congressional districts and thus minimized the percentage of minorities in the Fifth District. Joe Mack Wilson, chair of the House Reapportionment Committee and the person who dominated the process in the lower chamber, frankly explained to his colleagues, "I don't want to draw nigger districts."[57] The state sought section 5 preclearance of its plan but preclearance was denied. The District Court for the District of Columbia, which has jurisdiction in section 5 preclearance litigation, in an extraordinary finding, concluded that "Representative Joe Mack Wilson is a racist," and that the state's plan "has a discriminatory purpose in violation of section 5."[58]

The Politics of Inclusion

Social science data tend to confirm the findings of Congress that increased minority officeholding associated with single-member districts has not itself created division but has resulted in greater political and social responsiveness to minority interests and the inclusion of minorities in decisionmaking.[59] A study of ten cities in California found that minority political participation, facilitated by single-member districts, was "associated with important changes in urban policy—the creation of police review boards, the appointments of more minorities to commissions, the increasing use of minority contractors, and a general increase in the number of programs oriented to minorities." The report also found that the mere presence of black and Hispanic council members tended to break down polarization and racial stereotyping and "has increased minority access to councils and changed decision-making processes."[60]

A 1979 study in Alabama found "a causal relationship between growth and black political participation and policy change: the greater the change in political mobility, the greater the change in social welfare policy."[61]

56. *Busbee* v. *Smith,* 549 F.Supp. 494 at 507 (D.D.C. 1982).
57. 549 F.Supp. 494 at 501.
58. 549 F.Supp. 494 at 500, 517.
59. Morris 1981, 164, 180.
60. Browning, Marshall, and Tabb 1984, 141, 168.
61. Quoted in Hamilton 1984, 15.

A study of Newark concluded that under a black mayor more blacks "were appointed to higher offices as well as employed throughout the city government," and that there was a strengthening of the city human rights commission and the implementation of affirmative action policies.[62] Black electoral participation also brought changes in the outcome of elections and the distribution of services in Tuskegee, Alabama, and Durham, North Carolina.[63]

Increased minority political participation has also had a significant effect on national policy. Just a decade after the 1965 Voting Rights Act, for the first time since Reconstruction, a majority of the white members of Congress from the South supported, on final passage, a major civil rights bill, the 1975 amendments to the act. This watershed political event can be traced directly to the increased participation of blacks in the region's electoral process.[64]

Southern congressional support for the 1982 amendments of the Voting Rights Act, as well as support for the Civil Rights Restoration Act and the Fair Housing Act of 1988, are similar manifestations of the expansion of black suffrage. The Civil Rights Restoration Act passed the House 315 to 98 and in the Senate 75 to 14. The Fair Housing Act passed in the House 376 to 23 and the Senate 94 to 3.[65] The members of Congress from Alabama, Georgia, Louisiana, Mississippi, North Carolina, South Carolina, Tennessee, and Texas cast 138 votes for and only 41 votes against the two bills, a pattern unthinkable twenty years before.

Increased minority political participation and officeholding, while it has certainly not redressed all the legitimate grievances of minority communities nor realized all the goals of the civil rights movement, has conferred other undeniable benefits.[66] It has reduced election-related violence and made racist politics generally unfashionable. It has made it possible for minorities to pursue careers in politics and thus made the political resources of minority communities more available to society as a whole. It has provided minority role models, conferred racial dignity, and helped dispel the myth that minorities were incapable of political leadership. It has also required whites to deal with minorities more nearly as equals, a change in political relationships whose implications have been profound.

62. Yatrakis 1981.
63. Keech 1968, 2, 93.
64. Black 1978, 448–49; Stern 1985, 114, 117–18.
65. American Civil Liberties Union 1988, 4, 6–9, 12–17.
66. On realization of the goals, see Guinier 1991b, 1101–34.

White Backlash

Although section 2 enforcement has not caused resegregation in the sense of creating racial division and isolation where none existed before, it has to some extent precipitated a white backlash in the form of political realignment. One observer has noted the changing composition of the Democratic party in the United States caused by more blacks participating in Democratic primaries and voting for and electing black candidates.[67] Increased minority participation has in turn caused an exodus of conservative white Democrats to the Republican party. If the exodus continues, some have argued, the result could be an increasingly black but politically impotent Democratic party opposed by an increasingly white and dominant Republican party pursuing ever more racially regressive policies as the realignment unfolds.

It would be unprecedented if the mobilization of minorities were not met with a response of some kind from the majority. Earlier examples of black mobilization and white reaction abound in the South, where political change has been most dramatic and, from the white perspective, most traumatic. In South Carolina the abolition of the white primary in 1947 in *Elmore* v. *Rice* caused a surge of black registration.[68] In 1940 there had been perhaps 3,000 blacks registered to vote in the state; soon after the decision in *Elmore* black registration jumped to 50,000.[69] The Democratic party attempted to blunt the impact of the decision by organizing itself into clubs open only to whites. Blacks could vote in the primaries, but only if they took an oath to support the social and educational separation of the races and swore to their belief in state's rights and their opposition to federal laws prohibiting employment discrimination. The oath was challenged by a Beaufort County man, David Brown, and was held unconstitutional.[70] Two years later the state passed two statutes to limit the effect of increased black registration and participation in the Democratic primary—one imposing a majority vote requirement in the primaries and the other a full-slate law.[71]

---

67. Baxter 1990. See also the chapter by Carmines and Huckfeldt in this book.

68. *Elmore* v. *Rice,* 72 F.Supp. 516 (E.D.S.C. 1947).

69. Lawson 1976, 134.

70. *Brown* v. *Baskin,* 78 F.Supp. 933 (E.D.S.C. 1948); 80 F.Supp. 1017 (E.D.S.C. 1948).

71. 1950 S.C. Acts 2059, 2098, no. 858. A requirement that a candidate for nomination or election to office receive a majority of the votes cast, as opposed to a simple plurality, allows a politically cohesive majority, even though its votes may have been divided in the

In Mississippi a dramatic increase in black voter registration following passage of the 1965 Voting Rights Act triggered a massive resistance campaign by the state's white leadership.[72] The state legislature enacted a number of retaliatory measures, including gerrymandering congressional district lines to fragment the black community and authorizing counties to switch from district to at-large elections for boards of supervisors and county school boards. These acts were primary factors in the defeat of black candidates in elections in the 1960s but were ultimately set aside by the courts and during preclearance under section 5.

Political backlash among whites is probably as unavoidable as white flight to escape school desegregation. Both are evidence of the continuing, debilitating influence of race in American life, but neither is a principled basis for weakening the enforcement of civil rights laws.[73] If they were, it would give intransigent whites a virtual veto over racial equality.

Incomplete Progress

Progress under section 2 and the act as a whole, substantial as it has been, is incomplete. In Georgia blacks are nearly one-third of the population but account for only 8 percent of elected officials. In Mississippi, which has the largest black voting-age population (33 percent of the total) and the largest number of black elected officials (669) of any state, blacks make up only 13.5 percent of elected officeholders. Nationally blacks comprise 12 percent of the population but hold just 1.5 percent of elected offices. Hispanics are 7 percent of the population but less than 1 percent of officeholders, and the percentage of native American officeholders is similarly low.[74]

Minority voter registration and turnout also remain depressed. According to a survey taken by the Bureau of the Census after the 1988 presidential election, 68 percent of eligible whites reported that they were registered and 59 percent reported they had voted. But less than 65 percent of

initial election, to select a candidate of its choice in the ensuing runoff. See *White* v. *Regester*, 412 U.S. 755 at 766 (1973). Requiring voters to vote a full slate, that is, vote for every position up for election, deprives a cohesive minority of the opportunity to single-shot vote. See *Dunston* v. *Scott*, 336 F.Supp. 206 at 212–13 (E.D. N.C. 1972).

72. Parker 1987.

73. *Cooper* v. *Aaron*, 358 U.S. 1 at 16 (1958).

74. Joint Center for Political Studies 1990, 17; NALEO Educational Fund 1988.

blacks reported having registered and less than 52 percent voted; less than 36 percent of Hispanics had registered and 29 percent voted.[75]

This incomplete progress is the result of continuing racial polarization, as well as poverty, lack of education, and other discrimination-related barriers to mobilizing minority voters. It is also the result, ironically, of the general reliance on single-member districts as the preferred (or required, as some courts have indicated) remedy for section 2 violations.[76] The creation of single-member districts does not always provide minorities the equal opportunity to elect candidates of their choice: the minority population, for instance, may be too dispersed to construct any, or only a few, districts in which they are a majority.[77] In some cases, therefore, to provide the "complete and full" remedy for section 2 violations mandated by Congress, it may be desirable or necessary to adopt other remedial measures.

Among these measures are a limited voting system, in which each voter has fewer votes than the number of seats to be filled, or a cumulative system, in which each voter has as many votes as seats to be filled but may express a preference by giving all his or her votes to one candidate or dividing the votes among several candidates. Either system can ensure that a politically cohesive minority will be able to elect candidates of its choice, even where it is too dispersed to allow for the creation of minority-controlled single-member districts.[78] And despite claims that they are exotic procedures and antithetical to democratic traditions, the systems have often been used by American jurisdictions and have consistently withstood constitutional challenges.[79] They have also been approved by the courts in a number of recent consent decrees in section 2 cases challenging at-large elections and have been precleared by the attorney general.[80]

Where limited and cumulative voting have been implemented, they have been an effective remedy for section 2 violations; there is no evidence that they have had an adverse impact on local politics or undermined American democratic traditions. In Alabama, either limited or cumulative voting was adopted by consent in twenty-seven jurisdictions in the *Dillard*

75. Bureau of the Census 1989, 3, 5.
76. *McGhee v. Granville County*, 860 F.2d 110 (4th Cir. 1988).
77. Grofman 1985, 160.
78. Karlan 1989, 223–36.
79. *Cintron-Garcia v. Romero-Barcelo*, 671 F.2d 1 at 6–7 (1st Cir. 1982); *Orloski v. Davis*, 564 F.Supp. 526 at 529–30 (M.D.Pa. 1983).
80. See, for example, *United States v. City of Augusta*, CIV 187-004 (S.D.Ga. July 22, 1988); *Harry v. Bladen County*, CIV 87-72-7 (E.D.N.C. April 21, 1988).

v. *Crenshaw* litigation, and seventeen black candidates were elected in the sixteen jurisdictions where blacks qualified to run for city council seats. Jerome A. Gray, field director of the Alabama Democratic Conference, has stated that

> the tremendous success rate in which black candidates were elected under these new systems attests that they are yet another effective way to remedy section 2 violations of at-large elections, especially in localities where it is impractical to draw districts or where the black population may be too dispersed, but where there is still a definite minority community of interest.[81]

Conclusion

Unlike the preclearance provisions of section 5 of the Voting Rights Act or section 4's ban on literacy tests, section 2 does not depend upon voluntary compliance nor is it self-executing. It is enforced by lawsuits, of which there have been hundreds, particularly since the amendment of the statute in 1982 to incorporate a results standard for proving violations. The litigation has been arduous, and its burdens have been borne principally by minority communities and civil rights organizations. The success of section 2, in the extent to which it has opened the political process to minority voters and candidates, has been significant and gratifying, but it is not complete. Minority officeholding is disproportionately low and polarized voting a fact of political life. Much remains to be done to fulfill the hopes of Chief Justice Earl Warren that one day the equal right to vote would truly be a reality. There is no better time than now to renew the commitment to realize those hopes.

81. Jerome Gray, 1988 affidavit on file with author.

The 1982 Amendments and the Voting Rights Paradox

TIMOTHY G. O'ROURKE

Concerning the Voting Rights Act, I hope I never live to see it changed. . . . After forty years of living in my community, trying to get people to participate, after thirty years in one precinct, fifteen years as a clerk of election, I've seen it all. . . . And none of it, sadly to say, came about voluntarily with our General Assembly and all of our elected officials. . . . [To take] just one issue. As a clerk of election . . . I go to the precinct, set up with the judge the machines for voting, and can't find the machine. People lined up at six o'clock, five-thirty in the morning, because the polls was supposed to open at six. At six o'clock, neither the judge nor any of the clerks can find the machine. It had been moved, without notifying officers of election. Had it not been for the Voting Rights Act, I would have had no power behind me to demand that the machine be put back. . . . These are shenanigans that go on continually, and each time you must go through, fighting individually. Without the Voting Rights Act, Virginia would revert to the very same things she did a hundred years ago. Don't believe that it would change voluntarily. Thank God for the Voting Rights Act.[1]

V IRTUALLY EVERY COMMENTARY on the Voting Rights Act of 1965 begins by acknowledging the extraordinary impact of the law on the contours of American, and particularly southern, politics. On the first page of *Whose Votes Count?* Abigail M. Thernstrom points to the

I am grateful to Katharine I. Butler, Bernard Grofman, Paul W. Jacobs II, Abigail M. Thernstrom, Tracy Warren, and Sandra Wiley for helpful comments on earlier drafts. In attempting to develop a perspective on the entire twenty-five-year history of the Voting Rights Act, I have of necessity revisited some issues and cases that I have dealt with in previous writings; these are cited in the text and bibliography.

1. Observations offered by a woman who attended a public forum, "Suffrage and the Constitution: The Future of Voting Rights in Virginia," in Roanoke, Virginia, September 5, 1985. The meeting was one of twenty Virginia Court Days forums on constitutional issues conducted by the University of Virginia's Center for Public Service (from which an edited transcript is available).

86   TIMOTHY G. O'ROURKE

"breathtaking changes in southern politics" that can be traced to the influence of the act. And in *Black Votes Count*, Frank R. Parker begins, "Since 1965 America has witnessed a renaissance of black political participation." The "dramatic progress," he adds, "is due in large measure" to the passage of the 1965 law.[2] These observations suggest that the act has taken on a symbolic importance that extends well beyond the increased numbers of black and Hispanic voters and minority elected officials. Plainly, passage of the act was an event that transformed American political life, moving the nation closer to the ideal of genuine political equality. Appropriately, then, the twenty-fifth anniversary of its passage was celebrated because the act had so clearly marked a turning point in American constitutional and political history.

It is a measure of the impact of the original law that it now enjoys broad political support. Its very success has generated support for its continuation, as southern congressmen and senators with substantial numbers of black constituents have become advocates of its extension. Indeed, Morgan Kousser documents in this volume that most southern congressmen and senators backed extension of the act in 1975 and even more did so in 1982.[3] Moreover, in supporting the 1982 extension of the act, southern congressmen were not merely reconciling themselves to the terms of the original law but were voting for a substantial enlargement in its scope.

Although Justice Hugo Black once described the preclearance of changes in voting laws that the act requires of covered states as Reconstruction revisited, preclearance, like the act itself, has become less controversial.[4] At the grass-roots level, resistance to the principle of preclearance has diminished because minority officials and white officials more attuned to minority interests now sit in the state legislatures and on the local governing bodies that make submissions under section 5. Moreover, state and local officials have simply become accustomed to the process. To be sure, compliance with section 5 can prove burdensome for particular jurisdictions confronted with objections that are not always predictable. In the ordinary course of events, however, preclearance has amounted to more of a paperwork burden than a practical political one. From 1965 through 1988, more than 155,000 changes were submitted; the Justice

2. Thernstrom 1987, 1; Parker 1990, 1.
3. The 1982 extension was even supported by a majority of representatives and senators in the nine states wholly covered by the preclearance provisions of the act. Parker 1990, 190–91.
4. For Black's comments, see *Allen v. State Board of Elections*, 393 U.S. 544 at 595 (1969).

Department objected to fewer than 2,200 or less than 1.4 percent.[5]

Indeed, the impact of section 5 should not be assessed primarily in terms of objections but in the efforts of covered jurisdictions to avoid objections. Section 5 encourages jurisdictions to include minority interests in political decisions affecting voting and elections: unless blacks are involved in decisionmaking, the decisions themselves become vulnerable to objection. To the extent that minority interests are included, the decisions are more likely to be in accord with the minority political agenda.[6]

Thus the Voting Rights Act—the focus of divisive congressional debate in 1965, when it was viewed as an emergency and temporary measure— has become less contentious, even as it has become more far-reaching and permanent. It is almost axiomatic to refer to the act as the most successful modern civil rights measure.

And yet the several extensions and expansions of the act create a contradictory impression—one that suggests its successes have really been modest, that the nation is now only marginally closer to achieving full minority political participation than it was in 1965. Despite the dramatic growth in the number of minority voters and minority candidates elected to office since the passage of the original act, Congress has, with each extension, identified new obstacles to political equality and required ever greater federal oversight of state and local electoral processes. Thus the longer the history of the act, the longer its projected future has become. The 1965 act was renewed in 1970 for five years, renewed in 1975 for seven years, and renewed in 1982 for twenty-five years.[7] Although the number of Justice Department objections has been small in relation to the number of changes submitted, the absolute number of section 5 objections has grown with each round of postcensus redistricting.[8]

One reason for the growing number of objections is that the scope of the law has expanded geographically and substantively. After the 1970 amendments, for instance, three counties in New York City became subject to the act's preclearance provisions. The 1975 amendments brought language minorities—principally Hispanics—under the protection of the

5. Calculated from data in Parker 1990, 183.

6. The regulations of the Department of Justice on administration of section 5 state that one factor to be considered in the review process is the "extent to which the jurisdiction afforded members of racial and language minority groups an opportunity to participate in the decision to make the change." 28 C.F.R. 51.57(c) (1990).

7. P.L. 91-285, 84 Stat. 314 (1970); P.L. 94-73, 89 Stat. 400 (1975); P.L. 97-205, 96 Stat. 131 (1982).

8. From 1971 through 1980 the Justice Department objected to 789 changes; from 1981 through 1988, to 1,353 changes. Derived from data in Parker 1990, 183.

act and extended section 5 coverage to Texas and Arizona. Still another reason for the growth in objections is that practices that might have been regarded as nondiscriminatory in, say, 1970, are now viewed as barriers to minority political influence. Even as covered jurisdictions have become accustomed to, and complied more fully with, the preclearance provisions, they find themselves chasing an elusive standard.

Section 5 aside, another aspect of greater activity involving the act is the dramatic increase in the volume of voting rights litigation that has followed in the wake of the 1982 revision of section 2.[9] Unlike section 5, which is essentially regional in application, section 2 is a national prohibition against discrimination in voting. Under the new results test of section 2, a plethora of lawsuits have been filed from Los Angeles County to Springfield, Illinois, to Pittsburgh.

The paradox of the Voting Rights Act, then, is that success has bred a seemingly greater need, not a lesser one, for action against discrimination in voting. The scope of the law, the volume of voting rights litigation, and the level of Justice Department activity have expanded dramatically, even though virtually all commentators agree that the status of voting rights in America has manifestly improved since 1965.

Part of the explanation of the paradox is that the goals of the act have changed and have brought another, although not necessarily new, set of problems. The principal purpose of the original law was to enfranchise southern blacks. After 1969 the central concern shifted from suffrage to representation.[10] If the original act targeted literacy tests, the evolving act took aim against discriminatory redistrictings, annexations, and at-large elections. Progress came to be measured more in terms of increasing the number of minority officeholders than of increasing the number of minority voters.

But if changing goals provide a clue to the paradox, a larger part of the explanation lies in the way enforcement of the act changed after 1969. The 1965 act translated the goal of equal suffrage into concrete, precise operational terms. The law suspended literacy tests in much of the South and cleared the way for black citizens to register and cast ballots. For southern jurisdictions covered by the act, the law was largely self-enforcing (indeed, it was intended to provide a legislative solution to problems that had been ineffectually addressed through litigation in

9. The 1982 revision of section 2 (see the appendix to this volume) is the focus of more extended discussion later in this chapter.

10. On the changing goals of the act, see Morgan Kousser's chapter in this volume; also see Thernstrom 1987, 20–27.

the late 1950s and early 1960s). As the focus on suffrage gave way to the concern with representation, Congress did not change the form of the law so as to give precise operational meaning to fair representation. Instead, it merely extended the act and left the task of defining fair representation to be worked out by the Justice Department and federal courts. As this locus of decisionmaking changed, the terms of enforcement changed. While the original act banned certain practices in specific areas, the evolving act permitted the Justice Department and the courts to define discrimination case by case. The act, which had begun as a precise ban on particular legal devices, developed into a more conditional limitation on almost any kind of electoral procedure, depending on the circumstances in individual situations.

As the Justice Department and the courts took over defining and redefining the parameters of the Voting Rights Act, congressional opposition to it became more difficult. The congressional vote on the 1982 amendments was tantamount to a vote on whether one opposed or favored discrimination in voting, since the actual impact of the amendments could hardly be predicted. The contrast between the 1982 amendments and the original law could not be more stark. A member of Congress who supported the 1965 act voted to suspend the literacy test in certain states. A member who supported the 1982 amendments voted to encourage litigation anywhere in the nation where an electoral practice resulted in "less opportunity [for minority citizens] . . . to participate in the political process and to elect representatives of their choice."[11]

To trace the development of the paradox, the remainder of this chapter examines the evolution of the act and the emergence of fair representation as its principal focus. Because the goal of fair representation was grafted onto what was essentially a suffrage law, by the early 1980s the act had come to have serious internal inconsistencies. Congress sought to deal with these inconsistencies in the amendments of 1982, but these amendments and their subsequent interpretation and application by the courts have effectively elevated proportional representation as the operative standard of political equality.

In passing the 1982 amendments, Congress rightly recognized the need to extend the preclearance provisions of the law to continue protecting the citizenry. But in going beyond a simple extension, it modified the law in ways that threaten to undermine the progress toward political integration generated by the original 1965 act.

11. Section 2 as revised in 1982; see the appendix to this volume.

The Evolution of the Voting Rights Act, 1965–1982

The purpose of section 5 of the Voting Rights Act was to prevent jurisdictions from erecting new barriers to registration and voting in place of the discarded literacy tests. If a covered state changed its requirements for voter registration, the new requirements would be subject to preclearance. But what if a state, faced with the prospect of rising numbers of black voters, sought to undermine black voting strength not by modifying the rules for voter registration but by altering the format of elections? In *Allen* v. *State Board of Elections,* the Supreme Court considered whether section 5 covered a Mississippi law that allowed the basis of elections for county supervisors to be converted from ward to at large.[12] A thinly veiled purpose of the change was to submerge new black votes in predominantly white, at-large constituencies.[13] The Court held that section 5 encompassed not only the right to vote, but also the right to an effective vote (citing its "one person, one vote" principle for authority).[14]

The Transformation of Section 5

Allen substantially enlarged the scope of section 5, shifting the focus of the act beyond suffrage to include representation. In the years after the decision, the impact of section 5 would be felt in Justice Department objections to at-large elections, legislative redistricting plans, and annexations.

In changing the focus of the Voting Rights Act, however, *Allen* also changed the act's workings. In this regard it is useful to recall that section 4 of the law was self-enforcing, automatically suspending the literacy test in jurisdictions with low voter turnout. In short, the trigger formula— in its coverage and effect—was precise and unequivocal (although a covered area might, in rare circumstances, "bail out" from coverage). The original act effectively, although only temporarily, banned the literacy test in certain parts of the country; later amendments would make the ban national and permanent. As the focus of the act shifted to section 5

12. *Allen* v. *State Board of Elections,* 393 U.S. 544. In *Allen* the Court decided the named case and three others, one of which, *Fairley* v. *Patterson,* centered on the Mississippi law described in the text. For differing perspectives on *Allen,* see Thernstrom 1987, 20–30; Parker 1990, 91–101, 189–97.

13. See Parker 1990, 51-54.

14. 393 U.S. at 569, citing *Reynolds* v. *Sims,* 377 U.S. 533 at 555 (1964).

after *Allen,* its application to discriminatory election practices became more uncertain. This is because section 5 established a process for evaluating voting rules in the Justice Department and the courts; it did not prohibit any particular practice, as did section 4.

Thus *Allen* touched off an ongoing debate on the questions of when and under what circumstances an otherwise legitimate election procedure might be discriminatory. The case not only changed the focus of the law from vote denial to vote dilution but it also changed the terms of the law from precise to indefinite, opening up possibilities for expansion of the law but at the same time making interpretation more difficult.[15]

Three months after the Supreme Court decided *Allen,* it dealt with another, less noticed case that would also have a major impact on the evolution of the act. In response to the charge that the coverage formula of section 4 was arbitrary, Congress had included in the 1965 act a proviso that permitted a covered jurisdiction to win exemption from coverage (and thus the preclearance requirement). To "bail out," a covered jurisdiction had to file suit against the United States in the District Court for the District of Columbia, asking for a declaratory judgment that the jurisdiction had not used a literacy test in the preceding five years "for the purpose or with the effect of denying or abridging the right to vote."[16] Gaston County, North Carolina, filed an action to bail out and to reinstitute its literacy test. The county was able to demonstrate that, in the five years leading up to its suit, it had not applied its literacy test in a discriminatory manner. The district court, however, rejected the county's claim. In *Gaston County* v. *United States,* the Supreme Court affirmed both the holding and the reasoning of the district court. Although the test itself had been administered fairly, the fact that the county had operated segregated schools "for its Negro residents who are now of voting age" made the test discriminatory.[17]

---

15. Chandler Davidson 1984, 4, defines vote dilution as "a process whereby election laws or practices, either singly or in concert, combine with systematic bloc voting among an identifiable group to diminish the voting strength of at least one other group. Ethnic or racial minority vote dilution is a special case, in which the voting strength of an ethnic or racial minority group is diminished or cancelled out by the bloc vote of the majority. In extreme cases, minority vote dilution results in the virtual exclusion of one or more groups from meaningful participation in a political system."

16. The bailout language in this section has since been supplanted by a new bailout procedure, discussed later in this chapter.

17. *Gaston County* v. *United States,* 395 U.S. 285 at 293 (1969).

Under the logic of *Gaston,* virtually no covered southern jurisdiction could bail out, no matter what its record on voting rights before 1965.[18] Of course, since the 1965 act had suspended the literacy test in covered areas, almost every covered jurisdiction could have bailed out in 1970. The 1970 amendments to the act, however, changed the terms of bailout so that a jurisdiction would have to show that it had not applied a discriminatory test for the preceding ten years, and the 1975 amendments extended the period to seventeen years.[19] Thus the extension of the act in 1970 and 1975 was effectively an extension of the bailout requirement (since the provisions of the act are permanent). By blocking bailout, the extensions mandated continued preclearance for covered jurisdictions.[20] The *Gaston* decision, when coupled with the extensions of the act, made preclearance virtually inescapable for southern jurisdictions. While *Gaston* locked in the geographic coverage of the act, *Allen* opened the doors to a far more expansive interpretation of preclearance. The two decisions, then, combined to make covered jurisdictions—at least those making changes that had to be submitted for preclearance—subject to a much more stringent standard of political equality (one that embraced fair representation as well as equal suffrage). Plainly the combined force of *Allen* and *Gaston* increased the prospects for more far-reaching political reform in those areas that Congress had identified as having a long history of discrimination in voting. At the same time, however, regional preclearance as a mechanism of political reform had inherent limitations in both practical and constitutional terms.

18. In 1967 the Justice Department consented to the bailout of Wake County, North Carolina, the only jurisdiction in the seven southern states covered in whole or in part by the 1965 act to win exemption. No covered state or subdivision has bailed out without the consent of the Justice Department. See O'Rourke 1983, 774–75.

19. The seventeen-year period applied to jurisdictions covered by the original 1965 law. Jurisdictions brought under the coverage of the act by the language provisions of the 1975 amendments were subject to a ten-year period. O'Rourke 1983, 775, note 52.

20. In *City of Rome* v. *United States,* 446 U.S. 156 (1980), the Supreme Court held that Rome, Georgia, could not bail out because Georgia as a state was covered by the act. The Court also rejected Rome's claim that the extension of the act in 1975 was unconstitutional, since the continuation of preclearance, as an extraordinary use of federal power, could no longer be justified (446 U.S. at 180–82). In a dissenting opinion, Justice Lewis Powell argued that the constitutionality of preclearance depended on the availability of bailout for individual jurisdictions such as Rome that, in his view, had not engaged in voting discrimination in at least seventeen years (446 U.S. at 200–06).

The Limits of Preclearance

A 1976 Supreme Court case, *Beer* v. *United States,* illustrates the complexities of applying section 5 to representational issues. After the 1970 census the seven-member New Orleans City Council, then consisting of five ward seats and two at-large seats, sought a declaratory judgment in favor of a new redistricting plan for the five ward seats. Under the existing plan, only one of the five wards contained a black majority among registered voters. The new plan slightly enlarged the percentage of black registrants in this district, pushing the black percentage from 50.2 percent to 52.6 percent; it also increased the black percentage of the population in a second district from 49.4 percent to 50.6 percent (although blacks remained a minority of registered voters). The population of the city at the time was 45 percent black, and no black had been elected to the council from 1960 to 1970. The Court, speaking through Justice Potter Stewart, held that the new plan did not violate the discriminatory effect standard of section 5 because the new alignment was not retrogressive. According to the Court's rationale, if a redistricting plan did not reduce minority voting strength, it was entitled to approval (so long as the plan was free of discriminatory intent).[21]

In a dissenting opinion, Justice Byron White, citing racially polarized voting and the lack of black success in council races, called for a different test. The plan should not be precleared, said White, unless it gives blacks "the opportunity to achieve legislative representation roughly proportional to [their] population." In a separate dissent, Justice Thurgood Marshall took issue with the Court's view that the city's at-large seats, which had not been changed by the new plan, were wholly beyond the reach of section 5. While agreeing that the at-large seats were "not themselves before the Court," Marshall contended that the fairness of the plan "should be assessed" in relation "to the seven-member council it is designed to fill." Marshall went on to observe that "focusing only on five districts would allow covered municipalities to conceal discriminatory changes by making them a step at a time."[22]

In essence, Justices White and Marshall were asserting that the Court's narrow application of the retrogression rule would permit preclearance of discriminatory changes and leave underlying discriminatory systems in place. But if a weakness of the retrogression test was that it offered

21. *Beer* v. *United States,* 425 U.S. 130 (1976).
22. 425 U.S. at 143 (White dissenting); at 158–59 (Marshall dissenting).

only a partial cure for discriminatory electoral practices, the approach of White and Marshall suffered from a different and more profound sort of weakness. If a proposed change in one aspect of an election system were to open the entire system to a preclearance inquiry, jurisdictions might well avoid making any changes at all (since even changes that improved the position of minority voters might lead to the Justice Department's imposition of more radical changes).[23] Moreover, the White and Marshall dissents seemed to suggest that, within the context of section 5, the fairness of a procedure ought to be measured against the standard of proportional representation. But according to the Supreme Court's previous holdings, a racial minority had no presumptive constitutional right to proportional representation.[24]

In short, whatever the drawbacks of the retrogression test, it seemed to offer a manageable standard that avoided larger problems associated with White's and Marshall's approach.[25] Even under the retrogression rule, section 5 proved to be a powerful tool for political change, particularly in state legislative redistricting. Covered states had to redraw legislative district boundaries after the 1970 and 1980 censuses, thus giving the Justice Department the opportunity to review new plans.[26]

But a major limitation of section 5 is that it comes into play only when covered jurisdictions make changes in voting procedures. Until the 1982

23. As Thernstrom 1987, 150, points out, the retrogression rule was more consistent with the original intention behind section 5, that is, to prevent jurisdictions from backsliding.

24. See *Whitcomb v. Chavis*, 403 U.S. 124 at 149, 156–60 (1971); *White v. Regester*, 412 U.S. 755 at 765–66 (1973). The Court's opinion in each case was written by Justice White.

25. In *City of Richmond v. United States*, 422 U.S. 358 (1975), the Court set out a somewhat different test for annexations, holding that an annexation that reduced the black percentage of the city's population would be permissible so long as the city took steps to ensure that minority voters had representation in proportion to their numbers in the enlarged city. Richmond had replaced an at-large electoral plan with a ward system designed to give blacks a proportional share of power in the expanded city. Pointing to the fact that Justice White wrote the opinion, Thernstrom 1987, 151, considered the *Richmond* test to be at odds with *Beer*. I disagree. Arguably, any annexation that increased the white population percentage of a city could be viewed as retrogressive. By permitting municipalities to engage in annexations, even when such annexations led to a reduction in the relative voting strength of minorities, the *Richmond* approach, like the *Beer* standard, can be seen as a pragmatic, limited interpretation of section 5.

26. On the impact of section 5 on state legislative redistricting in the 1970s, see Civil Rights Commission 1975, 211–49. For a case study of the effects of section 5 on redistricting in the 1980s, see Parker 1982.

amendments, aggrieved minority groups could work around this obstacle only by filing lawsuits challenging existing voting procedures on constitutional grounds.[27] Such suits were expensive and the results unpredictable. Whatever one's view of the merits of the Supreme Court's 1980 decision in *City of Mobile* v. *Bolden,* requiring plaintiffs to show that voting practices were intentionally discriminatory clearly made lawsuits more difficult to win.[28] Because of the difficulty of pressing constitutional challenges, the impact of section 5 on covered areas was uneven, even anomalous. A city undertaking an annexation might be forced to convert from at-large to ward elections to win preclearance under section 5; a similar at-large city, making no change in election procedures, would be untouched by section 5 and perhaps largely immune (in fact if not in theory) to a constitutional challenge.[29]

A different kind of anomaly arose, of course, between covered jurisdictions and those not covered. As the Voting Rights Act transformed southern politics, minority voter registration and turnout and minority electoral success in covered states often compared favorably with that in noncovered states and made it more difficult to justify the peculiarly southern focus of the act.[30] Moreover, objections under section 5 increasingly targeted practices, such as annexations and at-large elections, that were commonplace inside and outside the South.[31] Comparison between covered

27. During the 1970s the leading precedents for constitutional challenges of vote dilution were *Whitcomb* v. *Chavis,* 403 U.S. 124 (1971); *White* v. *Regester,* 412 U.S. 755 (1973); *Zimmer* v. *McKeithen,* 485 F.2d 1297 (5th Cir. 1973) (*en banc*). These cases are discussed in Senate 1982b, 19–24. See also O'Rourke 1982.

28. *City of Mobile* v. *Bolden,* 446 U.S. 55 (1980). The Court upheld the constitutionality of at-large elections for Mobile's three-member commission; in nearly seventy years, no black had been elected to the commission, although the city was about one-third black. In a plurality opinion, Justice Stewart stated that neither the Fifteenth Amendment nor section 2 of the Voting Rights Act, which he regarded as a restatement of the amendment, applied to vote dilution. Furthermore, a showing of vote dilution under the Fourteenth Amendment would require a demonstration that the challenged practice was adopted or maintained with discriminatory intent. On the impact of *Mobile* on vote dilution litigation, see McDonald's chapter in this volume. See also Senate 1982b, 26–27; Thernstrom 1987, 81; Parker 1990, 174–75.

29. See note 25.

30. On this point, see Senate Committee on the Judiciary, *Voting Rights Act: Report of the Subcommittee on the Constitution,* reprinted in Senate 1982b, 159–69.

31. In *City of Rome* v. *United States,* 446 U.S. at 217, Justice William Rehnquist raised this argument in a dissenting opinion: "while most States still utilizing literacy tests [in 1965] may have been doing so to discriminate, a similar generalization could not be made about all government structures which have some disparate impact on black voting strength.

and noncovered areas thus posed two issues: whether the act ought to make it easier (possible really) for covered jurisdictions with good records to bail out, and whether it ought to be extended beyond the traditional boundaries of coverage (principally the South).[32]

The 1982 Voting Rights Amendments

The 1982 amendments addressed these inconsistencies in three ways. They provided for a new bailout process under which covered jurisdictions with exemplary records on voting rights could win exemption from preclearance. The new results test of section 2 applied nationwide and so facilitated litigation against discriminatory election systems both within and outside covered areas. And finally, the amendments had an indirect impact on the standards for preclearance under section 5.[33]

The New Bailout Provisions

The 1982 amendments provided for a two-year extension of the old bailout formula, with the new provision, section 4(a), to take effect on August 5, 1984. Although it has been portrayed as a genuine compromise resisted by civil rights leaders, they effectively dictated the stringent terms of the new provision.[34] Indeed, they embraced the idea—if not the reality—of bailout because it provided a pretext for a lengthy extension of preclearance. Thus the terms of the new bailout were worked out in the House of Representatives (primarily in the Judiciary Committee), which proposed to extend preclearance in perpetuity. The Senate, recognizing the questionable constitutionality of making emergency legislation permanent, countered with a

---

At the time Congress passed the Act, one study demonstrated that 60% of all cities nationwide had at-large elections for city officials, for example. . . . Obviously, annexations similarly cannot be presumed to be devoid of legitimate uses. Yet both of these practices are regularly prohibited by the Act in most covered cities."

32. In fact, these questions have been raised each time the Voting Rights Act has come up for renewal, although the political circumstances have varied. For instance, the Nixon administration proposed in 1969 both to eliminate the general requirement for preclearance and to ban the literacy test nationwide, in part "so that the 'regional' character of the act . . . would be removed." Garrow 1978, 194.

33. For background, see Boyd and Markman 1983.

34. See Hancock and Tredway 1985, 423; Thernstrom 1987, 90–103.

twenty-five year extension, to which the House acceded.[35]

Under the new provision, a jurisdiction (generally a county) in a covered state can bail out separately from the state, something it could not do before, but only if all the governmental units "within its territory" have met the criteria for bailout. The criteria can be divided into two categories: compliance and affirmative efforts. Under the first, a jurisdiction must demonstrate that it (and all subunits of government) has complied fully with the terms of the act during the preceding ten years, that it has not employed a literacy test as a prerequisite to voting, that no federal examiners have been sent to the area, and that it has made all relevant submissions under section 5 and none has encountered objection. In addition, the jurisdiction must show that there have been no successful voting rights suits against it and that none is pending.

Under the affirmative efforts criteria, the jurisdiction must

(i) have eliminated voting procedures and methods of election which inhibit or dilute access to the electoral process;

(ii) have engaged in constructive efforts to eliminate intimidation and harassment of persons exercising rights protected under this Act; and

(iii) have engaged in other constructive efforts, such as expanded opportunity for convenient registration and voting for every person of voting age and the appointment of minority persons as election officials throughout the jurisdiction and at all stages of the election and registration process.

At the time the 1982 amendments were adopted, proponents argued that one-fourth of the counties in the seven southern states covered wholly or in part by the 1965 act would be eligible to bail out as soon the new provision took effect. Such estimates, based entirely on the compliance criteria, undoubtedly overstated the extent of real eligibility.[36] In the new bailout's first year only Alaska filed for relief, an effort aborted before

35. See House of Representatives 1981, 1–2; Senate 1982b, "Additional Views of Senator Orrin G. Hatch of Utah," 101–02. On the dubious constitutionality of a permanent extension, see House of Representatives 1981, "Additional Views of Hon. Henry J. Hyde and Hon. Dan Lungren," 57–58.

36. O'Rourke 1983, 791, note 130. In theory if all jurisdictions began meeting the ten-year compliance criteria in 1982, all would be eligible for bailout in 1992; O'Rourke 1983, 789. The absence of bailout activity, however, suggests that the 1990s are unlikely to bring a surge in bailout actions.

trial. In an article written in early 1985, two Justice Department attorneys expressed puzzlement that the provision had not brought an onslaught of lawsuits from jurisdictions seeking exemption. They suggested that jurisdictions might be "laying the required groundwork."[37] By early 1992, no jurisdiction except Alaska had tried the new bailout.[38]

The absence of such actions is easy to explain. For a covered jurisdiction, the costs of attempting bailout—both in terms of political fallout and legal fees—would be large, the chances of success small, and the benefits even smaller. A jurisdiction attempting to bail out might open itself to the charge that it was attempting to evade the force of the law. Although a successful bailout might remove the stigma that attaches to preclearance, a failed action could enhance the stigma. If a jurisdiction did bail out, however, it would remain on probation for ten years and be subject to being covered again.[39]

Even by 1984, whatever appeal bailout might have had for covered jurisdictions had been undermined, in part because a jurisdiction, having bailed out, could still be the object of a lawsuit under the provisions of section 2. But in addition, the early success of section 2 lawsuits had an indirect effect on the terms of bailout itself, plainly strengthening the criteria for exemption. The affirmative efforts criteria of the new bailout provision effectively require a jurisdiction to prove that each element of its electoral system is free of discriminatory results. In short, as the results test of section 2 came to embody a standard of proportional representation, it also demanded more in the way of constructive efforts for bailout, thus effectively making bailout nearly impossible.[40]

The Section 2 Results Test

Before passage of the 1982 amendments, section 2 was a close paraphrase of the Fifteenth Amendment and had little impact on voting rights litigation. In response to the decision in *City of Mobile* v. *Bolden*, Congress modified section 2 to create a statutory results test for vote dilution. To show a violation under section 2, an aggrieved minority group must demonstrate that, "based on the totality of circumstances . . . its members

37. Hancock and Tredway 1985, 382, 422.
38. Letter from John R. Dunne, assistant attorney general, October 15, 1990; telephone conversation with David H. Hunter, Justice Department Voting Section, January 7, 1992.
39. Section 4(a)(5). See also Senate 1982b, 56.
40. This outcome was predicted by the *Subcommittee Report*, reprinted in Senate 1982b, 165.

have less opportunity than other members of the electorate to participate in the political process and to elect representatives of their choice" (see the appendix to this volume). The language closely tracks the Supreme Court's holding in *White* v. *Regester* (1973), which, according to the architects of the revised section 2, had established the proper, results-oriented basis for vote dilution claims.[41] The report of the Senate Judiciary Committee on the 1982 amendments drew on the language of *White* and *Zimmer* v. *McKeithen*, a 1973 Fifth Circuit case applying *White*, to explain the meaning of the new section 2. In particular, the report listed the "typical" factors that a plaintiff might show in a vote dilution claim: a "history of official racial discrimination" in voting; "racially polarized" voting; practices such as majority-vote rules that "may enhance the opportunity for discrimination"; a discriminatory slating process; socioeconomic disparities that impede minority political participation; "racial appeals" in campaigns; and the lack of minority electoral success. Two additional factors included the absence of official responsiveness to minority group interests and a "tenuous" policy in support of the challenged voting practice. The report made clear "that there is no requirement that any particular number of factors be proved."[42]

During debates on the 1982 amendments, proponents of the results test portrayed it not as a fundamental change in voting rights law but as a modest one designed to undo the harm created by the Supreme Court. The Senate report, for instance, asserted that amended section 2 "restores the legal standards . . . which applied in voting discrimination claims prior to the litigation involved in *Mobile* v. *Bolden*." Under that standard, the report argued, there was no right to proportional representation and plaintiffs did not always prevail. The report further noted that the amendment to section 2 is "careful, sound, and necessary, and will not result in the wholesale invalidation of electoral structures."[43]

Such predictions, if ever intended to be taken seriously, have been far off the mark. The introduction of the results test brought a surge in

41. See Senate 1982b, 27–28. Curiously enough, Justice White, the author of the Court's opinion in *White* v. *Regester,* said in *Rogers* v. *Lodge,* 458 U.S. 613 at 619 (1982), that the 1973 case rested on an intent standard. Following this reading, the difference between *Mobile* and *White* is that the former required an explicit showing of discriminatory intent while the latter allowed for a demonstration of intent based on circumstantial evidence. Disagreement over the meaning of *White* was a central element in congressional debate over the section 2 results test. Compare Senate 1982b, 27–28, with *Subcommittee Report,* reprinted in Senate 1982b, 130–31.

42. Senate 1982b, 28–29.

43. Senate 1982b, 2, 32–33, 35.

voting rights litigation, with most of the cases being won by plaintiffs.[44] The groundswell in litigation has occurred in part because courts have read the results test liberally. In *Thornburg* v. *Gingles,* the Supreme Court's principal exposition of section 2, Justice William Brennan effectively discarded the complex fact-finding inquiry suggested by the legislative history of the 1982 amendments. Instead, he set out a "functional analysis" centered on three preconditions:

> unless there is conjunction of the following circumstances, the use of multimember districts generally will not impede the ability of minority voters to elect representatives of their choice. Stated succinctly, a bloc voting majority must *usually* be able to defeat candidates supported by a politically cohesive, geographically insular minority group. . . . These circumstances are necessary preconditions for multimember districts to operate to impair minority voters' ability to elect representatives of their choice for the following reasons. First, the minority group must be . . . sufficiently large and geographically compact to constitute a majority in a single-member district. . . . Second, the minority group must be able to show that it is politically cohesive. . . . Third, the minority must be able to demonstrate that the white majority votes sufficiently as a bloc to enable it . . . usually to defeat the minority's preferred candidate.[45]

As Justice Sandra Day O'Connor noted in her concurring opinion, the Court had effectively "made usual, roughly proportional success the sole focus of its vote dilution analysis."[46]

44. In Virginia there were no successful vote-dilution lawsuits based on constitutional grounds before the 1982 amendments. By mid-1990 there had been at least twenty-two section 2 suits against county, city, and town electoral systems, and plaintiffs had won at least nineteen; Morris 1990, table 1. Laughlin McDonald, in his chapter in this volume, notes that voting rights cases increased by 50 percent after 1982. Moreover, the number of electoral changes made by jurisdictions covered by section 5 was twice as high in the three years after the change in section 2 as in the three years before. Compare McDonald's analysis with his testimony in 1982 in which he predicted that the results test would not lead to a "flood" of litigation. Senate 1982a, vol. 1, 369.

45. *Thornburg* v. *Gingles,* 478 U.S. 30 at 48–51 (1986). The case involved a section 2 challenge to five multimember state legislative districts in North Carolina.

46. 478 U.S. 30 at 102. In my view, Justice O'Connor's interpretation of the results test is more consistent with the legislative history of amended section 2 than is Justice Brennan's. Justice O'Connor argues that courts should take into account "all relevant factors" bearing on minority participation, rather than focusing almost exclusively (as Justice Brennan does) on minority candidates elected to office (478 U.S. at 97–100, quoted at 99).

The 1989 decision of the Fourth Circuit Court of Appeals in *Collins* v. *City of Norfolk* demonstrates the application of the results test.[47] The case concerned a section 2 challenge by black voters to the at-large election of a seven-member city council in Norfolk, Virginia, a city 35 percent black in 1980. When the suit was filed in 1983, a black had held one seat continuously since 1968; before the case went to trial in 1984, a second black was elected to council. In the course of complex and protracted litigation, a federal district court twice ruled in favor of the defendant city, but the plaintiffs ultimately prevailed, the Fourth Circuit Court holding that at-large elections in Norfolk violated section 2, even though, arguably, only two of the nine factors listed in the Senate report were satisfied. The appellate court overturned the district court's holding that plaintiffs had not demonstrated racially polarized voting and a lack of minority success.[48] Even on these two factors, the Fourth Circuit Court's holding was curious. In fact, as the appellate court recognized, "black candidates [had] won in seven of ten elections from 1968 to 1986." Moreover, seven of thirteen black candidates who had received 70 percent or more of the black vote had been elected. Eleven of nineteen candidates, black and white, who had received a majority of the black vote had been elected.[49]

In the face of strong evidence of usual black success, the Fourth Circuit Court distinguished between what it regarded as legitimate black successes and tainted ones. In its view the figures demonstrated only "the black community's ability to elect a single black member of the council. The statistics ignore the fact that from 1968 until this action was brought, the black community was unable to elect a second representative to council." To reach this conclusion, however, the court had to disregard the success of two white candidates elected with

47. *Collins* v. *City of Norfolk*, 883 F.2d 1232 (4th Cir. 1989), *cert. denied*, 112 L. Ed. 2d 305 (1990). The history of the case is summarized in the Fourth Circuit's decision, 883 F.2d at 1234–35, note 2. For the record, I was an expert witness for the city in this case.

48. 883 F.2d at 1236, note 3, and 1243. See also *Collins* v. *City of Norfolk*, 679 F.Supp. 557 at 561 (E.D. Va. 1988), in which the district court noted as settled facts that blacks in Norfolk registered and voted in higher percentages than did whites, that socio-economic differences between blacks and whites did not impede black political partici-pation, that there were no racial appeals in campaigns, that the city did not use a majority vote rule or other device to hinder single-shot voting by black voters, and that the policy behind at-large elections was not tenuous. The district court also found that the city's policies were responsive to black interests and that there was no discriminatory slating (679 F.Supp. at 581–86); neither of these findings was upset on appeal.

49. 883 F.2d. at 1240, and Judge Chapman's dissent at 1247.

majority black support. One of the two was elected three separate times with majority black support; both had been endorsed by the leading black political organization in Norfolk. In the court's analysis, these candidates could not count as representatives since each was elected with less black support than a black candidate who was defeated. For example, a white candidate won 72.9 percent of the black vote in 1980 but did not count as a minority representative because a black candidate polled 92.9 percent of the black vote in the same election and lost.[50]

Oddly enough, however, the court cited the 1976 election as an example of a failed effort by the black community to elect a white candidate to the second council seat. In that election a black incumbent won a new term with 97.3 percent of the black vote, while a white, who received 76.3 percent of the black vote, lost. Thus the court declared black voters could not pick a second councilor, "regardless of the race of the candidate."[51] It is not clear, however, why the white candidate who finished second among blacks in 1976 counted as a preferred candidate of black voters, when the white candidate who finished second among blacks in 1980 did not.[52] Even more curious is that the court ignored

50. 883 F.2d at 1237–40; see also the dissenting opinion at 1244 (Chapman dissenting).
51. 883 F.2d at 1241.
52. The Fourth Circuit Court cited as support for its opinion *Citizens for a Better Gretna* v. *City of Gretna*, 834 F.2d 496 at 502 (5th Cir. 1987), when a Fifth Circuit panel held that a black candidate could count as a candidate of choice of the black community in an election in which two white candidates garnered a larger share of the black vote. As the dissenting judge noted in *Collins*, it is hard to avoid the conclusion that the race of a candidate is now the key factor in assessing whether he or she is a representative of the minority community. Had the white candidates elected with majority black support in Norfolk been treated as preferred candidates of the black community, he continued, the black community would have had proportional representation from 1974 forward. See 883 F.2d at 1245, 1247 (Chapman dissenting).

While *Collins* v. *City of Norfolk* adopted a test of the "preferred candidate" that excluded certain white candidates elected at large, an Eleventh Circuit panel suggested that even a black candidate elected at large with black support might not qualify as a preferred candidate. In *Meek* v. *Metropolitan Dade County*, 908 F.2d 1540 at 1548 (11th Cir. 1990), the court hypothesized that, under an at-large format, the black candidate "may be a person for whom Blacks are willing to vote when the alternative would be the election of a White candidate, but that does not mean that the same candidate would be elected in a single-member district plan. . . . In short, the at-large scheme may cause the Black candidate to be someone other than the preferred candidate of Black voters." The appellate court offered no guidance to trial courts on a method to determine whether a candidate elected at large could also win in a projected single-member district. See also Guinier 1991a, 1141–42, who contends that even where blacks enjoy proportional success under at-large voting

the outcome of the 1978 election, when the top two choices of the black community were elected: a black candidate with 96.1 percent of the black vote and a white candidate with 68.5 percent of the black vote.[53]

The *Norfolk* case appears to represent exactly the kind of outcome that the architects of the new results test claimed could not occur: "some have suggested that plaintiffs could win under the results test by merely showing (a) at-large elections; (b) underrepresentation of minorities; and (c) 'a scintilla' of evidence, i.e., proof of one additional factor from among which *Zimmer* lists as relevant."[54] Plainly, however, the teaching of *Thornburg* v. *Gingles* as applied in *Collins* is precisely the abbreviated test eschewed by the Senate report. The new shortened test condemns both at-large elections and single-member districting plans that yield less proportional results than would be produced by single-member districts drawn to create a maximum number of black (or Hispanic) majority districts.

The Results Test and Section 5

The incorporation of a results test into section 2 has had a profound impact on the interpretation of section 5, even though the 1982 amendments made no change in the language of section 5. First, the surge in lawsuits that followed the creation of the results test raised important questions about the sufficiency of section 5 review under the retrogression standard. In Virginia, for instance, section 2 lawsuits were filed in the mid- and late 1980s against fourteen county districting plans that had previously gained section 5 preclearance (generally before passage of the 1982 amendments). Nearly all were successful, typically requiring a recon- figuration of districts to create a proportional number of majority-black districts.[55]

As a purely legal matter, preclearance plainly does not insulate a plan against a subsequent section 2 challenge, but it ceases to have much significance—legal or otherwise—when courts routinely rule that precleared

---

schemes, a winning black candidate may not fully voice black interests since he or she must take care to "appease the white voters."

53. The 1978 election results appear in *Brief for Appellants, Collins v. City of Norfolk, United States Court of Appeals for the Fourth Circuit*, Docket No. 88-3950 (1988), p. 11; and *Brief of Appellees*, in the same case, pp. 22, 34. See also the district court's original decision in this case, *Collins* v. *City of Norfolk*, 605 F.Supp. 377 at 388 (E.D. Va. 1984).

54. Senate 1982b, 33.

55. This summary relies on Morris 1990, table 1, and my own collection of newspaper articles and court cases in Virginia.

plans are discriminatory. It would appear, from a practical standpoint, that section 5 must encompass a results test; otherwise, a section 5 review would amount to a mere way station en route to a section 2 lawsuit.[56]

In a backhanded way, Congress signaled its intention that section 5 should encompass a results standard. Noting that *Beer* v. *United States* had held that a plan that passed the retrogression test might yet be so discriminatory "as to violate the Constitution," the Senate report on the 1982 amendments held that a change which violated the results test of section 2 could be denied preclearance under section 5.[57] Although the 1982 amendments did not modify the language of section 5 itself, the Justice Department in 1987 adopted the logic of the Senate report in fashioning regulations on substantive standards applicable to section 5 submissions.[58] The essence of these new regulations is that resultsrather than retrogression is the standard governing section 5 submissions.[59] The retrogression test called for a comparison of a new planwith what was; the results test permits a comparison between the new plan and what could be. What could be, of course, is proportional representation.

It would be more accurate to say that the operative standard is a qualified proportional representation. So far the favored remedy in vote dilution litigation has been the creation, to the extent feasible, of single-member districts in which minority voters constitute a majority of the electorate. In a vote dilution challenge to a city council elected at large, for instance, the basis for both the claim and the remedy is how many districts minority voters might control under a single-member-district plan. In a claim against a plan involving only single-member districts, the beginning point would

56. The tension between section 5 and section 2 is illustrated by a 1983 case in which the Justice Department gave its approval to an Anniston, Alabama, proposal for new residency district boundaries for council seats elected at large. The department warned the city, however, that the at-large system itself probably violated section 2. "In order to avoid an expected section 2 lawsuit by the Department of Justice, the city voluntarily abandoned the at-large system and adopted a single-member district election plan that allows black citizens a fair opportunity for effective political participation." Hancock and Tredway 1985, 420, note 195.

57. Senate 1982b, 12, note 31, citing *Beer,* 425 U.S. at 141–42. For a critique of the Senate report on this point, see Butler 1984, 32–34. It should be noted that the Court specifically stated that the plan at issue did not violate the constitutional standards of *White* v. *Regester,* which is the basis of the results test. Now, however, a plan like the one upheld in *Beer* would almost certainly violate a results test analysis under section 5.

58. 28 C.F.R. 51.55(b)(2) (1990).

59. Butler, 1984, 28–32, 59–67, argues that the Justice Department and the courts were moving toward a results test and away from the retrogression test even before the 1982 amendments.

be how many black or Hispanic majority districts could be drawn using the existing council size as a benchmark.[60] To the extent, then, that single-member districts provide the measure of and remedy for vote dilution, the results test may not require full-fledged proportional representation (such that a minority group's percentage of seats matches its percentage of the population).[61] It may be impossible, given a fixed number of districts, to draw a proportional number of single-member districts with a majority black or Hispanic electorate. Moreover, minority districts, once drawn, do not guarantee that a minority candidate will win.

Proportional What?

Many supporters of the results test as it has evolved deny that it is tantamount even to qualified proportional representation. As evidence, Frank R. Parker, for example, comments that blacks held only 13 percent of the seats in the Mississippi legislature and about 18 percent of the seats on local governing bodies in 1989, even though the state's population is more than one-third black. Thus, he argues, for Mississippi, the minority vote dilution principle "has not come close" to producing proportional representation. But if the principle has not yielded proportional results, perhaps it ought to. "If anything, black citizens have a valid complaint that the legal and political system still has failed to provide them with political equality, and that they continue to be victimized by the racism of a political system that confines them to black representation only in black majority districts."[62]

60. See, for example, *Jeffers* v. *Clinton,* 730 F.Supp 196 (E.D. Ark. 1989) (*three-judge court*), aff'd 112 L. Ed. 2d 656 (1991). In this case, a three-judge court struck down an apportionment plan for the Arkansas state legislature as a violation of section 2. "The 1981 apportionment plan created only five legislative positions . . . representing districts in which a majority of the voting-age population was black. We find that a total of 16 such districts . . . could have been created, and that these districts would have been reasonably contiguous and compact" (730 F.Supp. at 198). In late 1991 the Justice Department objected to a North Carolina congressional resdistricting plan that created only one majority-black congressional district when, in the department's view, two could have been created. Citing *Jeffers* v. *Clinton,* the department noted, "it appears that the state chose not to give effect to black and Native American voting strength in [the southeastern] area, even though it seems that boundary lines that were no more irregular than found elsewhere in the proposed plan could have been drawn to recognize such minority concentration." Letter from John R. Dunne, assistant attorney general, Civil Rights Division, to Tiare B. Smiley, special deputy attorney general, state of North Carolina, December 18, 1991.
61. See McDonald's chapter in this volume.
62. Parker 1990, 195–96. I am indebted to Daniel O'Connor for pointing out the significance of this passage.

Parker also points to section 2 itself as evidence that the results test does not mandate proportional representation. Section 2, of course, contains a disclaimer that there is no "right to have members of a protected class elected in numbers equal to their proportion in the population." The disclaimer is undermined, however, because the section also recognizes that the extent to which minority group members have been elected to office is the starting point for a dilution claim.

In truth, Congress inserted the disclaimer in 1982 not so much to guide judicial interpretation of the results test but to provide political cover against the charge that the new language was designed to bring about proportional representation.[63] But even if the disclaimer is taken at face value, its impact is mitigated because the overriding message of section 2 is that the test of vote dilution is results, not intent. While the disclaimer means that results cannot be equated with mere disproportionate impact, the rejection of intent means that courts cannot explain away disproportionate impact by suggesting that harmful results were not intended. Thus Justice Brennan argued in *Thornburg v. Gingles* that a defendant jurisdiction could not minimize the significance of the defeat of minority candidates by suggesting that white voters may have voted against minority candidates for nonracial reasons. "It is the *difference* between the choices made by blacks and whites—not the reasons for that difference—that results in blacks having less opportunity than whites to elect their preferred representatives."[64]

Thus the line between the results test of section 2 as interpreted by *Gingles* and mere disparate results is indeed very thin. If in fact a minority group does not enjoy proportional representation, the group apparently can prevail under *Gingles* merely by showing that it is large enough to control a single-member district and that it votes cohesively—since the group would, by implication, enjoy proportional representation but for white bloc voting.[65]

---

63. See Thernstrom 1987, 120–30.

64. 478 U.S. at 63. Justice Brennan spoke for himself and only three other members of the Court on this point. See also *Collins v. City of Norfolk*, 883 F.2d at 1238, 1242. The Fourth Circuit Court discounted the election of a second black candidate to the city council in 1984 on the grounds that the election was intended to derail the lawsuit. As noted in the text, the Fourth Circuit also discounted the election of two white candidates who received a majority of the black vote. Thus while courts may not explain away the defeat of black or black-supported candidates, they may explain away black victories.

65. This follows the analysis of the special concurrence of Chief Judge Tjoflat in *Solomon v. Liberty County, Florida*, 889 F.2d 1012 at 1021 (11th Cir. 1990) (*en banc*). While he argues that this reading of section 2 is inconsistent with the legislative history,

The Costs of a Results-Oriented Voting Rights Act

The enshrinement of proportional representation as the centerpiece of voting rights law is insupportable as a matter of legal interpretation. The courts and the Justice Department have brought us to a point that *seemingly* should alarm the congressional drafters of the results test. I say seemingly, because the real congressional purpose behind the new results test was less to provide a clear standard to govern claims of vote dilution than to delegate the task for developing the standard back to the courts—but with the proviso that intent be no part of the test. Thus Congress reaped the political benefits of endorsing voting rights and reigning in a rightward-tilting Supreme Court. At the same time it avoided any responsibility for the undesirable consequences that might follow. It held that the new results test would not require proportional representation and refused to say exactly which particular cities or counties or states might be vulnerable under the new test.[66] At least one casualty of the results test, then, has been candor in political debate.

The institutionalization of proportional representation on publicly elected bodies is unlikely to stir much popular resistance. There is little resistance among white elected officials themselves because few of them, even those whose positions will or might be jeopardized by compliance with the act, wish to be seen as opponents of equity in voting rights. For reasons that stand apart from race, the public is not much interested in the design of electoral districts. (Indeed, the reapportionment revolution of the 1960s barely intruded into the public consciousness.)[67] Even taking race into account, however, white voters are largely indifferent to voting rights issues. As Frank Parker comments, "white opposition to remedies protecting minority voting rights is not as pronounced as it is to the remedies developed in other civil rights areas. Contrary to the argument of Thernstrom and others, the question of strong protections for minority voting cannot properly be characterized . . . as an affirmative action issue because the impact on the personal lives of most whites is substantially less than, say, busing or hiring quotas."[68] He further observes that white officials do not enjoy any legal claim to hold office.

Despite Parker's portrayal of her views, Abigail Thernstrom agrees

---

he acknowledges that some of the language in *Gingles* seems to support this simple test of dilution.

66. Senate 1982b, 35.
67. Elliott 1974, 11.
68. Parker 1990, 208.

that voting rights does not provoke the same sort of controversy as quotas: "Whites denied medical school admission as a consequence of minority preference have been arguably denied a right; those disadvantaged by a change in the electoral rules cannot make that claim." In contrast to Parker, however, she goes on to say that the introduction of a proportional results mandate into electoral matters does carry a real cost, which falls equally on white and minority citizen: "categorizing individuals for political purposes along lines of race and sanctioning group membership as a qualification for office may inhibit political integration."[69] Indeed, voting rights law has now been set on a course toward racially separate electorates, even though progress toward political integration is substantial. As Thernstrom rightly observes, "Racially mixed dinner parties may still be rare, but a mix of blacks, browns, and whites in politics is not."[70]

69. Thernstrom 1987, 242. See also Butler 1984. There are other costs as well. Within the context of single-member districting plans, the effort to create a maximum number of safe minority districts requires redistricting agencies to ignore other important values, such as respect for political subdivision boundaries and communities of interest and a preference for compact, contiguous districts. In 1991 the Virginia General Assembly fashioned new boundaries for the state Senate and House. The new plans, as finally approved by the Justice Department (which objected to the initial House plan) increased the number of majority-black districts from two to five in the Senate and nine to twelve in the House. When compared to the old district maps, however, the new plans sharply increased the number of cities and counties that are split between two or more districts. Under the new Senate plan, the number of split cities and counties rose from eighteen to thirty-six; the number in the House from forty-two to sixty-two (these data were derived from Virginia General Assembly 1990–91). In fact, the figures understate the extent to which local boundaries were disregarded in 1991, since they do not count the number of towns split and they do not reflect the number of cities and counties split more than once. Two of the most egregious examples of irrational district lines are the Fifteenth and Eighteenth Senate Districts; both were drawn to have black majorities. The Fifteenth encompasses six counties, portions of six more, and three independent cities. The Eighteenth District stretches for about 180 miles across Southside Virginia, from the city of Portsmouth to rural Halifax County; it includes all or parts of six counties and six cities (see Virginia General Assembly 1990–91; McKelway 1991). To be sure, the Voting Rights Act is only one of several factors contributing to the creation of oddly shaped, locality-splitting districts in Virginia (and elsewhere); the mandate of one person, one vote, changing demographics, partisan politics, incumbency interests, and the new technology of redistricting have also contributed. The result, however one sorts out the causes, is a configuration of legislative districts that already has proved confounding to voters and candidates alike. See "Redistricting's Harvest" 1991; "Virginia Choices '91" 1991. For additional evidence on this point, see the review and illustrations of the new congressional district boundaries in Illinois, North Carolina, and Texas in "Special Report" 1992, 45–46, 86–88, 100–05.

70. Thernstrom 1987, 241. My own views are close to those of Thernstrom 1987,

In Virginia, one of the half dozen southern states targeted by the 1965 act, minority candidates running at large have since the late 1960s regularly won seats on local councils. Fredericksburg and Roanoke—overwhelmingly white cities—have elected and reelected black mayors. Both parties have run black candidates for statewide office, and in recent years a black candidate has been elected lieutenant governor and then governor. These developments are most assuredly attributable to the Voting Rights Act. But they are not successes attributable to section 5 or section 2. Instead they are attributable to the gradual workings of the original law—the enrollment of minority voters, the large-scale entry of minority voters into the rank and file of the political parties, the entry of minority candidates into politics, and a growing receptiveness of a predominantly white electorate to minority candidates.

Yet it is a measure of the fantastical quality of the contemporary discussions of voting rights law that such successes are so easily explained away. Elsewhere in this volume, for instance, Laughlin McDonald dismisses L. Douglas Wilder's election as governor of Virginia as exceptional and as an example of "racially polarized voting" (since Wilder received only two-fifths of the white vote).[71] Such successes, of course, must be explained away to preserve the legal momentum for creating safe minority districts.[72]

Nevertheless, to the extent the courts and the Justice Department make clear that proportional representation is the standard and provide clear

---

which I reviewed in O'Rourke 1988. Parker apparently intended his *Black Votes Count* to serve, in part, as a rebuttal to Thernstrom. While he takes issue with her analysis of various legal questions, he focuses almost exclusively on the impact of the act on Mississippi. He argues, however, that voting rights problems in Mississippi, such as "at-large elections that perpetuate all-white government," have their counterparts throughout the nation (Parker 1990, 197). Thernstrom seeks to draw distinctions between the status of voting rights inside and outside the South. She contends that the original act appropriately focused on the distinctive voting rights problems of the South (and especially the Deep South); expansions of the act beyond the South (for example, the extension of preclearance to three New York counties in 1970) undermined "the difference between protection for minorities in localities with well-documented histories of blatant Fifteenth Amendment violations, on the one hand, and protection where the barriers to political equality were either linguistic or socioeconomic, on the other" (Thernstrom 1987, 41).

71. Interestingly, McDonald (in this volume) refers to "the omnipresence of racially polarized voting." In contrast, the Senate report suggests that racial bloc voting of the sort that would give rise to a section 2 violation is fairly rare: "Unfortunately . . . there still are some communities in our Nation where racial politics do dominate the electoral process" (Senate 1982b, 33). For a discussion of the role of racially polarized voting in voting rights litigation, see Jacobs and O'Rourke 1986.

72. When the results of the 1990 census gave Virginia an additional congressional seat,

guidance to states and localities about the application of that standard to particular circumstances, state legislatures and local governing bodies might well find the task of complying with the Voting Rights Act (both sections 2 and 5) simpler than fighting it and less costly in legal fees. Within the context of section 5, in particular, if the Justice Department would just tell states and localities what to do, they could avoid protracted legal proceedings that might arise from bad guesses about what might be permissible.[73]

Still, what might be permissible in voting rights law is not likely to remain fixed for very long. The evolution of the act from suffrage to representation to proportional results no doubt will continue. Indeed, the real problem with the current version is that it is anchored by no concrete standards at all. The original act could be judged a success precisely because its objectives could be described in terms of banning literacy tests and registering voters. The current act must always fall short of success because its goal of fair results will be continually redefined so as to lie just beyond the current reality.

So the act now requires, at least in the view of the Justice Department and lower federal courts, the creation of majority-black districts wherever possible. The next questions are whether and how the act covers situations in which such districts cannot be created. Does it offer remedies to minority groups who are not sufficiently compact to benefit from single-member districts? Suppose a city is fashioning boundaries for single-member districts. If black voters cannot constitute a majority in a single-member district, are they entitled to be drawn together in a maximum-influence district?

Or suppose blacks constitute 15 percent of the electorate in a county that elects a seven-member council at large. Suppose further that there are no blacks on the board and that blacks are evenly distributed through-

---

a debate began about whether the new seat should be—indeed, whether it had to be, under the terms of section 5—a majority-black district so as to ensure the election of a black to Congress. When faced with the question in 1990, Governor Wilder correctly noted, "In Virginia, if it hasn't been shown that you don't have to do that to be elected to Congress, then my election meant absolutely nothing." "Wilder Faces Fight over Redistricting" 1990. In late 1991, however, the governor signed a congressional redistricting measure that created a 64 percent black district. "Special Report" 1992, 109.

73. The Justice Department's regulations on section 5 are a monument to circumlocution. For instance, 28 C.F.R. 51.58 (1990), on "representation," begins, "This section and the sections that follow set forth factors—in addition to those set forth above—that the Attorney General considers in reviewing redistrictings (see §51.59), changes in electoral systems (see §51.60), and annexations (see §51.61)."

out the county (a situation not all that unusual in rural areas) so no majority-black district can be drawn. Are blacks entitled to demand that a court impose some kind of formal, semiproportional voting scheme, involving elections at large with cumulative or limited voting?[74] Or suppose, instead, that in the same county the governing board has only three seats. Can minority voters demand that the board be expanded to seven?

That such questions can be asked tells us why the Voting Rights Act, once regarded as a temporary measure, has now become a permanent part of the American political landscape two decades after the Supreme Court in *Allen* v. *State Board of Elections* made fair representation the focal point of the act. What has evolved is an ever changing notion of political equality that requires a growing intrusiveness into the design of electoral mechanisms by judges, Justice Department bureaucrats, and academicians who, as expert witnesses or contributors to law reviews, help shape the movement of the law. Southern jurisdictions subject to section 5 preclearance have in effect been told that there is virtually no route of escape—no matter how good their record of compliance—from the monitors at the Justice Department.[75] The revision of section 2, however, has made bailout almost pointless in any case, since the test has swept away voting practices outside as well as inside areas subject to preclearance.

The results test, of course, continues to evolve, driven almost solely by the pursuit of proportional representation: at-large elections, which a decade ago were seen as the principal impediment to minority representation, have now been revived as the remedy of the future for voting rights claims. To be sure, these elections are now coupled with more curious procedures—cumulative and limited voting—that are frankly called semiproportional systems.[76] These new systems offer what single-member districts often cannot—real proportional representation—and so promise to enjoy increasing popularity among the lawyers and judges whose task it is to instruct local governments in the practice of democracy.

74. See McDonald's chapter in this volume.
75. Lest my argument be misinterpreted, I support section 5 preclearance because it ensures that minority interests will be able to participate in decisions about electoral practices. But I favor a preclearance standard rooted in the retrogression rule of *Beer,* not the results test of section 2. Moreover, achievable bailout should be available for jurisdictions with good records.
76. See McDonald's chapter in this volume. Also see Guinier 1991b, 1135–54, who argues that the ultimate goal of voting rights reform should be "proportionate interest representation." Under this theory, blacks would be better served by at-large, multimember

Recent developments in voting rights law represent the legal enthrone-
ment of what Ward E. Y. Elliott has called the Guardian Ethic. The
special province of lawyers, judges, academic experts, and journalists,
the ethic requires constant tinkering with the messy results of the multifa-
ceted electoral systems of a federal republic. Precisely because they are
not politicians, the Guardians are, indeed, more concerned with fixing
the results than with improving the politics that gives rise to the results.[77]
Thus at the Brookings conference that led to this volume, there were no
elected officials, no registrars, no party leaders; there were many lawyers

---

districts with cumulative voting than by single-member districts. The former would not
only guarantee black electoral success but would also expand the electoral influence of
black voters beyond the narrow confines of geographic districts that are majority black.
In addition, a proportional election system might fragment the interests of a white majority,
opening up more opportunities for blacks to bargain effectively in both electoral and
legislative matters. The theory also calls for modification of decisionmaking rules on legislative bodies to protect minority groups against a hostile majority. A minority group
might, for example, be accorded a veto over certain kinds of legislation.

77. Elliott 1974, 9-13. Several very recent Supreme Court decisions will have a profound
impact on the future of the Voting Rights Act. In *Chisom* v. *Roemer,* 59 LW 4696 (1991),
and *Houston Lawyers' Association* v. *Attorney General of Texas,* 59 LW 4706 (1991),
the Court held that protection against vote dilution under section 2 applies to state judicial
elections, thereby raising the prospect of widespread federal judicial intervention into the
design of election methods for state judges.

More recently, however, the Court rejected what would have been a radical—and
unwarranted—enlargement of section 5. In *Presley* v. *Etowah County Commission,* 60
LW 4135 (1992), the Court said that section 5 did not apply to alterations in the internal
distribution of power on two Alabama county commissions. The primary responsibility of
each commission was to oversee the maintenance of roads. One commission shifted budget
authority over road maintenenace from individual commissioners, who had supervised
spending in their respective districts, to the entire board; the shift occurred within months
of the election of the first black to the commission. A second commission transferred
control from individual commissioners to a county engineer appointed by the commission;
this change occurred seven years before the election of the first blacks to the commission.
Writing for the Court, Justice Anthony M. Kennedy held that modifications in the decisionmaking authority of elected officials are not covered by section 5, which reaches only
changes affecting voting (such as the qualifications of candidates, procedures for holding
elections, offices subject to election, and the relative influence of voters over electoral
outcomes). Reading the statute to cover modifications in the power of elected officials, in
Justice Kennedy's view, would require preclearance of changes in legislative committee
assignments, budgets, and state statutes affecting powers of local governments. The Voting
Rights Act would be converted into "an all-purpose anti-discrimination statute" and federalism would be reduced to "a mere poetic ideal." In dissent, Judge John Paul Stevens
endorsed the expansive view, arguing that it would not overwhelm covered jurisdictions,
especially in light of the fact that the Justice Department (which endorsed the expansive
view) had already processed 17,000 preclearance requests in the current fiscal year, ap-

and social science experts. There was much talk about lawsuits, but virtually no discussion of ways to increase voter turnout, to build biracial coalitions during political campaigns, or to energize the political parties at the grass roots.[78] Thus the meaning of voting rights has come to have more to do with rights than with voting. And political equality has come to focus on equality more than on politics. And the democratic process has given way to judicially decreed results.

---

proving more than 99 out of every 100. Yet the sheer volume of requests, in my view, should give one pause about a manifest enlargement in their number and content.

78. While I disagree with the conclusions reached by Guinier 1991b, 1091–1101, she offers an insightful critique of the limitations of "the black electoral success theory," which approaches equal political opportunity primarily, if not exclusively, in terms of the election of black candidates to office. As she observes, this approach has proved useful as a matter of legal strategy (since courts can readily ascertain whether black candidates are winning), but it does not suffice as a political strategy for genuine black empowerment. "Litigation to enforce the Voting Rights Act transformed the original goals of broad-based voter participation, reform, and authentic representation into the shorthand of counting elected black officials" (Guinier 1991b, 1091).

Part Two

Social Science Perspectives on the Voting Rights Act

Party Politics in the Wake of the Voting Rights Act

EDWARD G. CARMINES & ROBERT HUCKFELDT

THE VOTING RIGHTS ACT OF 1965 was both the culmination of a struggle for civil rights and a key event in the transformation of American politics. It solidified, extended, and institutionalized gains that had already been achieved, but in so doing the act created a new political reality that has reached into every community and affected almost every political process in the nation. It has altered the racial composition of the electorate, the party coalitions, and the officeholders. It has transformed the appeals of politicians, the lines of political debate, and the bases of political cleavage. Most important, it has transformed the strategies and agenda of American politics. This chapter considers the changes more fully by examining the strategic dilemma of the Democratic party that made the act possible, the consequences of the act for electoral politics, and the new strategic political environment that has resulted.

Strategic Imperatives since the New Deal

After World War II the Democratic party faced a severe challenge. The party of Roosevelt and Truman, a coalition of southern whites and northern urban ethnics with an appeal to the disadvantaged in American society, was increasingly compromised by strains and contradictions in the logic of its appeal. Its concern for the disadvantaged had never been universally acceptable to the southern wing of the party: the appeal largely coincided with the viewpoints of southern Democratic populists such as Louisiana's Huey Long, but it ran counter to preferences of southern Democratic patricians such as Virginia's Carter Glass. In one sense the Democratic party in the South was truly classless and unified, however. Its support was rooted in white racial dominance, and the great majority of whites belonged to the party regardless of their class

An earlier version of this paper was presented at the 1990 meeting of the New England Historical Association. We are grateful to Richard Brown of the University of Connecticut and Chandler Davidson of Rice University for their assistance and encouragement.

backgrounds or class loyalties.[1] Thus Roosevelt and the national Democratic party was a bitter pill for conservative southern Democrats to swallow, but swallow it they did: two-party competition among whites was the enemy of white domination and a threat that far exceeded the problems of a coalition with urban ethnics, labor unions, and an increasingly populist national party. Thus the southern wing of the party continued to provide the core of Roosevelt's support in Congress and in the electoral college.[2] In short, continued racial discrimination was the tacit basis for the success of the New Deal coalition—the ugly secret that made Democratic hegemony possible during the 1930s and 1940s.

Such a secret could only be maintained as long as race was avoided as a political issue. And race could be avoided only as long as black citizens could be safely ignored by both major parties. Ignoring blacks was possible in the 1930s because they were still largely concentrated in the rural South. The South, in turn, had perfected the electoral machinery— literacy tests, all-white primaries, and sheer intimidation—to disfranchise blacks and thereby neutralize racial issues as an obstacle to a national Democratic coalition.[3]

But a coalition dependent on white racial supremacy in the South was inherently unstable because it required the demographic concentration and political control of southern blacks, and even as the national Democratic party flourished, these conditions were being undermined. Heavy black migrations to the North had occurred after World War I, and subsequent white race riots in Chicago, Detroit, East St. Louis, and elsewhere provided grim testimony to the hostilities engendered by the population movements.[4] Although the migration radically diminished during the Great Depression, it began again during World War II as renewed economic growth made jobs in the North available once more. As the black population concentrated in northern cities, it also became politically empowered in national electoral politics. Northern cities were certainly not oases of racial harmony, and they developed their own institutions and structures of white domination, but they did not develop the methods of disfran-

---

1. As Alexander Heard recognized in the early 1950s, this classless nature of southern politics, particularly in the urban South, was already changing. See Heard 1952. See also Lewinson 1932; Key 1949; Davidson 1972; Bartley and Graham 1975; Lamis 1984; Black and Black 1987; Huckfeldt and Kohfeld 1989.
2. Ladd with Hadley 1978.
3. Bunche 1973.
4. Judd 1984.

chisement that the South had perfected. Black northern urban residents were able to vote, and politicians, particularly Democratic presidential aspirants, needed the electoral votes of northern industrial states, which meant they needed large majorities in the major northern cities. This further meant that they had to depend on strong support among urban black voters.

Roosevelt had succeeded in attracting black voters not because he championed their interests per se but because he championed the interests of the economically dispossessed.[5] Blacks did not make up a large part of his coalition because they could not vote at sufficiently high rates. But now that they were becoming politically more active and increasingly located in northern cities, they were also becoming crucial to the evolving coalition of the Democratic party. And this meant that Democratic leaders after Roosevelt were no longer able to sidestep or ignore the issue of racial discrimination. Thus they were confronted with an increasingly important strategic problem. How could the party maintain the support of a white and Democratic Solid South, which the coalition badly needed, and still ensure the support of a northern black population, which it also badly needed?[6]

To understand the problem more precisely, it is helpful to look at patterns of postwar political development in the South. In their analysis of the political transformation there during this period, Numan Bartley and Hugh Graham compiled useful data that we have reorganized.[7] Figure 1 shows the average level of support for Democratic presidential candidates in black precincts, working-class white precincts, and higher-status white precincts for a sample of southern cities from 1952 through 1972.[8] Class voting in white precincts during the 1950s and early 1960s had become significant: the Democratic vote in working-class white precincts was

5. Weiss 1983.
6. Petrocik 1981, 1987.
7. Bartley and Graham 1978.
8. The cities and the presidential election years we included are Montgomery, Ala. (1952–68); Greensboro, N.C. (1952–68); Birmingham, Ala. (1952–68); Charlotte, N.C. (1960–72); Little Rock, Ark. (1952–68); Charleston, S.C. (1952–72); Miami, Fla. (1952–72); Columbia, S.C. (1952–72); Jacksonville, Fla. (1952–72); Nashville, Tenn. (1956–72); Atlanta, Ga. (1952–72); Memphis, Tenn. (1960–72); Macon, Ga. (1952–72); Fort Worth, Tex. (1952–72); Baton Rouge, La. (1952–72); Houston, Tex. (1960–68); New Orleans, La. (1952–72); Waco, Tex. (1952–72); Shreveport, La. (1952–72); Norfolk, Va. (1952–68); Jackson, Miss. (1958–68); Richmond, Va. (1952–68); Raleigh, N.C. (1952–68); Roanoke, Va. (1952–68).

FIGURE I. Average Share of Vote for Democratic Presidential
Candidates, by Race and Socioeconomic Status of Precinct, 1952–72

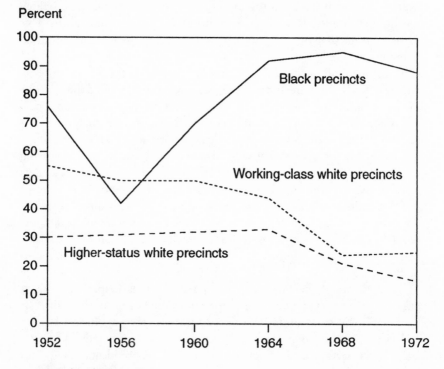

SOURCE: Bartley and Graham 1978.

considerably higher than it was in higher-status white precincts. Mirror-
ing the expectations of Alexander Heard, two-party politics was emerging
in the urban South, and it was organized along class lines.[9] At the same
time, Democratic support among black voters was endangered during
the mid-1950s: black support in 1956 for Adlai Stevenson, particularly,
fell below the level of support he received among voters in working-class
white precincts.

Within this context, John Kennedy's call to Coretta King during the
1960 presidential campaign, made while her husband sat in a Birmingham
jail, takes on political as well as moral relevance. Kennedy, whose position
on civil rights in the campaign was similar to Richard Nixon's, was
attempting to attract blacks without alienating southern whites, and figure

9. Heard 1952.

1 shows that he was relatively successful: black support increased and white support was maintained.

Racial Issues and the 1964 Election

Kennedy was the last Democratic presidential candidate who pursued such a balancing strategy successfully. Four years later Lyndon Johnson tied the future of the Democratic party to the black electorate and racial liberalism. Indeed, the 1964 election marked a restructuring of American political parties around racial issues. Not only did Johnson and Barry Goldwater choose opposite sides of the issue, but in doing so they redefined the positions of their respective parties. This is clearly evident for all elements of the party system. Figure 2 shows the roll call voting scores on racial issues for members of the Senate and House since World War II.[10] In the 1940s and 1950s the Republicans—then the "party of Lincoln"— were clearly more liberal than the Democrats in both houses. The interparty difference in the Senate began to narrow after the Democratic triumph in the 1958 congressional elections but increased moderately during the early 1960s. The turning point was 1964; after Johnson's election, Senate Democrats were not only considerably more liberal in the aggregate on racial matters, they were more liberal in all regions of the country. Today even southern Democrats are less conservative on matters of race than the Senate Republican party as a whole. The pattern is similar in the House. Again, Republicans were more liberal on race throughout the 1940s and 1950s. Although the gap between the parties did not narrow until 1964, since then, as in the Senate, Democrats have become increasingly more liberal than their Republican colleagues. In short, figure 2 demonstrates clearly the extent to which the congressional parties revised their positions on race after 1964.

An examination of party platforms leads to the same conclusion. From the beginning of the New Deal in 1932 until 1964, Republicans not only devoted more attention than Democrats to racial matters in their platforms, but they also consistently discussed these matters earlier in their programs. Since 1964, Democrats have given more space to racial concerns in their

10. These scores are derived from a principal components analysis of all roll call votes focusing on race cast by all members of both houses of Congress from 1945 through 1980. For a detailed discussion of the construction of these racial scales, see Carmines and Stimson 1989, 84–88.

FIGURE 2. Racial Liberalism in Senate and House Roll Call Votes, by Party, 1945–80

Index of liberalism

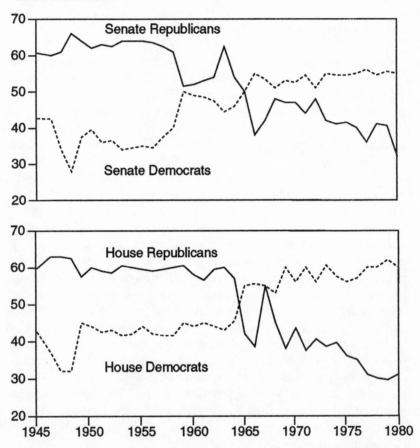

SOURCE: Carmines and Stimson 1989, figure 7.2.

platforms, and they have placed the racial plank in a more prominent location.[11]

Just as party elites and activists have altered their positions on racial matters since 1964, so the public has revised its assessment of the parties'

11. For an extended analysis of the racial content of the party platforms, see Carmines and Stimson 1989, 55–57.

positions. Before 1964 when citizens were asked about the positions of the parties—specifically whether Democrats or Republicans were more liberal on racial issues—they failed to distinguish between the two. For example, when the 1960 National Election Study asked survey respondents which party was "more likely to see to it that Negroes get fair treatment in jobs and housing," 23 percent said Democrats, 21 percent Republicans, and 56 percent no difference.[12] In 1964 the same question evoked responses of 61 percent Democrats, 7 percent Republicans, and 32 percent no difference. Similarly, when the 1960 National Election Study asked which party was more likely to "stay out of the question of whether white and colored children go to the same school," the public responded 20 percent Democrats, 16 percent Republicans, and 64 percent no difference. By 1964, however, 56 percent identified the Democrats as the party "more likely to want the government to see to it that white and Negro children go to the same schools," and only 7 percent identified the Republicans.[13] In sum, by 1964 the Democrats were being seen as the party of racial liberalism and the Republicans as the party of racial conservatism.

A less direct but equally revealing indication of the transformation of public perceptions of racial matters can be obtained by simply dividing the public into groups based on racial attitudes—racial liberals and racial conservatives. Racial liberals and racial conservatives had similar assessments of the parties throughout the 1950s and early 1960s. However, beginning in 1964, racial liberals substantially preferred the Democrats and racial conservatives the Republicans.[14]

All the evidence so far points in the same direction: 1964 was a crucial year in the redefinition of party positions on racial matters. A final piece of evidence, and one that perhaps sheds the most light on the transformation, is the change in attitudes of the members of the party coalitions themselves. From 1945 to 1963 the differences between self-identified Democrats and Republicans were relatively small: Republicans had somewhat more liberal racial attitudes than Democrats (figure 3). However, a sharp polarization occurred in 1964 and continued through the 1970s.[15]

12. Carmines and Stimson 1989, 165–66.
13. Institute for Social Research 1961; Institute for Social Research 1965.
14. For further discussion of the measurement of the effect of parties' racial positions on the public perceptions of the parties, see Carmines and Stimson 1989, 166–67.
15. Figure is based on the National Election Studies series for even-numbered years from 1956 to 1980 and a Harris poll of November 1963. Racial attitudes, an equally

FIGURE 3. Racial Liberalism of Self-Identified Democrats and
Republicans, 1945–80

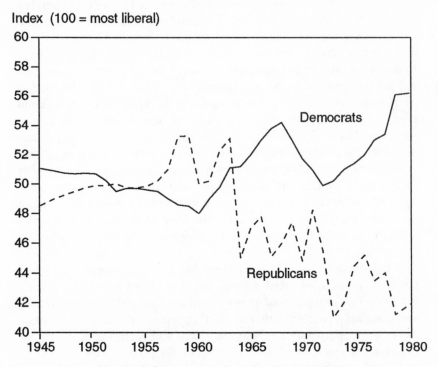

SOURCE: Carmines and Stimson 1989, figure 7.4.

Democrats became increasingly liberal on racial issues and Republicans
increasingly conservative. The relatively small differences that existed
between partisans not only became large differences, but the new reality
of racially liberal Democrats and racially conservative Republicans became
a permanent feature of contemporary American politics.

The 1964 presidential election, to repeat, was a watershed event. As
figure 1 shows, for southern cities Democratic support among blacks
increased in that election to an extraordinarily high level at the same

---

weighted summation of the survey items available in each cross section, are scaled with a
common metric for all cross sections and reconstructed backward in time to create a
continuous annual series. For further information on the construction of this time series,
see Carmines and Stimson 1989, 168–69.

time that it deteriorated among whites, particularly among working-class whites. As a result, class voting among southern whites has virtually disappeared, and the racial basis for party support has increased dramatically. As we shall see, this same basic pattern is mirrored in the national electorate.

Democratic Party Strategy and the Voting Rights Act

Where does the Voting Rights Act fit into this transformation and what was the political basis for Johnson's decision to support it? First, it is important to recognize that in many areas the massive gains in black voter participation occurred before the Voting Rights Act was adopted. Figure 4 compares the turnout levels of whites and blacks, in the same southern cities used for figure 1, as a proportion of turnout levels in 1952. Turnout among blacks accelerated in 1960, increased dramatically in 1964, and declined in 1968, the first presidential election after passage of the act. The same general pattern appears in the national election data: self-reported nonvoting among blacks decreased rapidly between 1956 and 1964 but only slightly from 1964 to 1968 (figure 5).

These observations are not intended to diminish the importance of the Voting Rights Act. Rather, as an element of political strategy the act must be seen in two contexts. First, for those blacks who had already been mobilized in 1960 and 1964, the act provided insurance against any later effort to deny them the vote once again. Second, and perhaps more important, bastions of white domination still remained in the 1960s, and legal and political impediments to voting were still being felt by many prospective black voters.

The location and political significance of the opponents of equal voting rights are not inconsequential. Table 1 shows the percentages of blacks registered to vote in 1960, 1964, and 1970 in the eleven former Confederate states. The states carried by Barry Goldwater were also the states that kept blacks off the registration rolls. Just as important, these states realized the most significant increases in black registration after the Voting Rights Act was passed. The revolution in black voting rights had already occurred in many parts of the South by the time the act was adopted. In other places, federal registrars and the force of federal law accomplished

FIGURE 4. Relative Turnout for Presidential Elections in White and
Black Precincts, Selected Southern Cities, 1952–72

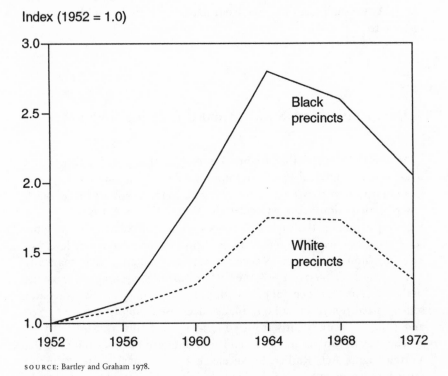

SOURCE: Bartley and Graham 1978.

what had not been possible previously—the full implementation of voting
rights in the hard core of the white supremacist South.[16]

Considering these demographic and political realities, the impossibility
of maintaining a political balance between the interests of the white South
and the increasingly black urban North had become apparent by the time
Johnson became president. Ironically, this loyal son of the South became
a champion of civil rights when he took the dramatic step of endorsing
the Civil Rights Act of 1964 at the same time that Goldwater was opposing
it. Through his support of civil rights Johnson resolved the crisis of the
Democratic party but alienated most white southerners.

It is in this light that the Voting Rights Act must be understood. If
white southern voters would no longer provide the solid core of the

16. Wright 1976, 200–15; Matthews and Prothro 1963, 24–44.

FIGURE 5. Share of Whites and Blacks Who Reported Not Voting in Presidential Election, 1948–88

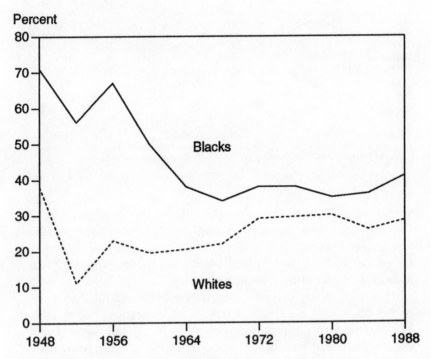

SOURCE: National Election Studies 1948–88 (University of Michigan, Institute for Social Research).

national coalition, it became crucial that black voters take their place. The Voting Rights Act was not only morally correct but also politically expedient. A Democratic administration and a Democratic Congress empowered themselves to mobilize black voters, more than 90 percent of whom would vote Democratic.

Political Consequences

Fewer than 1,000 people voted in Birmingham's black precincts in the 1952 presidential election. In 1963 Birmingham's police chief turned dogs and fire hoses on black demonstrators. By 1968 nearly 10,000 people voted in the black precincts. Today Birmingham has a black mayor.[17]

17. Birmingham's black population increased from 40 percent of the city's total in

TABLE I. Percentage of Blacks Registered to Vote in Eleven Southern States, 1960, 1964, 1970, and State Presidential Majority, 1964

Carried by Johnson in 1964				Carried by Goldwater in 1964			
State	1960	1964	1970	State	1960	1964	1970
Arkansas	37.7	54.4	71.6	Alabama	13.7	23.0	64.0
Florida	39.0	63.7	67.0	Georgia	n.a.	44.0	63.6
North Carolina	38.2	46.8	54.8	Louisiana	30.9	32.0	61.8
Tennessee[a]	64.1	69.4	76.5	Mississippi	6.1	6.7	67.5
Texas[a]	33.7	57.7	84.7	South Carolina	n.a.	38.8	57.3
Virginia	23.0	45.7	60.7				
Mean	39.3	56.3	69.2	Mean	16.9	28.9	62.8

SOURCES: Congressional Quarterly Service 1967, 43, 74; Congressional Quarterly Service 1970.
n.a. Not available.
  a. Data for Tennessee and Texas for 1960 are incomplete. For Tennessee, percentage reflects data for 63 counties; for Texas, 213 counties.

Similar changes have occurred throughout the South. Lily-white city councils and state legislatures have become integrated. Georgia, Mississippi, Texas, and Tennessee have black congressmen. Virginia has a black governor. Enormous strides have been made following the civil rights movement and the adoption of the Voting Rights Act.

This is not to say that all the hurdles to black and minority political participation have been cleared nor all the contentious issues resolved, and thus the Voting Rights Act continues to be a political focal point for demands of equal treatment. But our concern is with more subtle but equally profound effects arising from the political mobilization of black citizens, in particular the responses of the party system to black mobilization. First, the party system has responded in terms of individual voters and their behavior. Second and equally important, it has responded in terms of the racial composition of the major party coalitions. While these two responses are interdependent, they are not the same, and each helps explain the current state of American politics.

The growth in black support for the Democratic party is startling (figure 6). In 1948 less than 20 percent of the black population reported voting for the Democratic presidential candidate, a level that was primarily a reflection of the high rates of nonvoting among blacks: more than

---

1950 and 1960 to 42 percent in 1970 and 56 percent in 1980. Thus shifting demographics must be given substantial credit for the most recent transformation of Birmingham politics. But without the revolution in black voting rights, changing demographics would have had no electoral consequence.

FIGURE 6. Share of Voting-Age Respondents Voting for Democratic Presidential Candidates, by Race, 1948–88

Percent

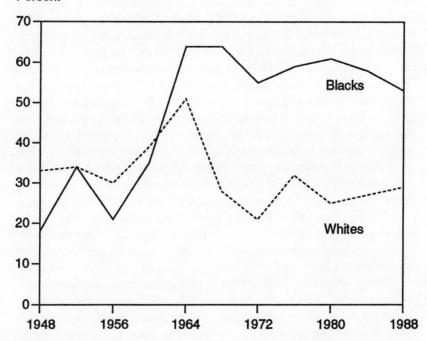

SOURCE: National Election Studies 1948–88 (University of Michigan, Institute for Social Research). The percentages represent all respondents to the surveys who reported voting Democratic. The remainder either voted for another candidate or did not vote.

70 percent of blacks reported not voting. The growth of black support for the Democrats did not come at the direct expense of the Republicans. Rather, it reflects the mobilization of nonvoters into the ranks of Democratic voters. And as figure 6 shows, the greatest-change occurred in 1964.

But Lyndon Johnson's mobilization of black citizens did not come without political costs. White support for the Democratic party peaked in 1964 and has since steadily deteriorated. Indeed, 1964 was the last election in which the Democratic presidential candidate received a majority of his support among voting whites. The only subsequent Democratic victor, Jimmy Carter, won the election in 1976 with a minority of support among voting whites but with overwhelming and offsetting support among blacks.

To understand the source of Democratic difficulties among whites, it is also important to consider the aggregate, coalitional response of the party system to the mobilization of black citizens. First, it would have been possible to mobilize blacks in a bipartisan manner, with higher turnouts benefiting both Democrats and Republicans. If, during the crucial days of the 1964 election campaign, Barry Goldwater had given his wholehearted support to the federal effort to ensure equal treatment of black citizens, the future of the party system might have been very different. Political precedent certainly would have been on his side: the civil rights record of the Republican party was at least as progressive as that of the Democratic party through most of the 1950s. Indeed, nearly one-third of voting blacks supported Richard Nixon in the 1960 presidential election. But in fact, 1964 marks the point at which race becomes an explicitly partisan issue. The party of Lincoln became the party of white racial disaffection, and the party of the Solid South replaced its old white core support with new black core support (figure 7). At least 20 percent of total Democratic support in presidential elections after 1964 came from black voters, except for the Carter victory in 1976. And the revolution was even more extreme in the South, where black voters accounted for 35 to 40 percent and more of Democratic support in every presidential election except in 1976.[18]

What are the political consequences of the Democratic party's reliance on black voters? White voters are frequently unwilling to support a party that depends heavily upon black support, and the decline in white support for Democratic presidential candidates has been most pronounced among working-class whites. Thus class differences in party support among whites have narrowed as racial differences have increased.[19] Furthermore class differences in voting behavior among whites tend to be larger where the Democratic party is less reliant upon black support.[20] In short, it is not only the white South whose support of the Democratic party has been compromised, but the support of the northern white working class as well. This is perhaps most obvious in the large urban areas of the North where blacks and working-class whites often represent competing elements in local Democratic party politics. Thus the mobilization of blacks by the Democratic party has fundamentally altered its status as the working-

18. As Huckfeldt and Kohfeld 1989, chap. 3, document using exit poll data, the situation is even more extreme in particular states and locales. Approximately 70 percent of Walter Mondale's Mississippi support in the 1984 presidential election came from black voters.

19. Abramson, Aldrich, and Rohde 1986; Huckfeldt and Kohfeld 1989, chap. 1.

20. Huckfeldt and Kohfeld 1989, chap. 3.

FIGURE 7. Share of Republican and Democratic Presidential Votes
Cast by Blacks, Nationwide and South Only, 1948–88

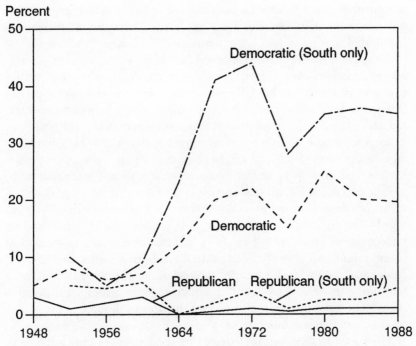

Percent

SOURCE: National Election Studies, 1948–88 (University of Michigan, Institute for Social Research).

class party in American politics. And at least in this regard, the New
Deal party system has been significantly transformed.

The New Strategic Environment

When Lyndon Johnson decided that the Democratic party should turn
its back on the solid white Democratic South and embrace the black
electorate, he ushered in the transformation of the electoral environment
of American politics. The result has been a continuing tension within the
party among the blacks, working-class whites, and white liberals upon
whom the party depends.[21]

The party's dependence on solid support among blacks is clear: the
levels of black support have been equaled only by the level of support

21. Huckfeldt and Kohfeld 1989.

given by southern whites during an earlier era. In this sense, the political mobilization of blacks by the Democratic party has been a remarkable success. But the Democratic party as well as American blacks have paid an enormous price in national politics. Since 1964, white support for the party has seriously deteriorated, and blacks have found themselves committed to a party that cannot win the presidency.

The genius of the New Deal party lay in its ability to unite liberals and the working class. Given the issues of the depression years, such a feat was possible. To be a liberal in the 1930s meant that a person supported legislation favoring labor—establishing a minimum wage, regulating working conditions, creating social security. Liberalism was nearly synonymous with support for programs designed to help disadvantaged Americans. Such an agenda obviously found favor among labor leaders, and thus the New Deal coalition of liberals and labor was born.

One part of the Democrats' current electoral problems is that the focus of liberalism has shifted in a way that frequently ignores the disadvantaged. The contemporary liberal agenda is increasingly dominated by noneconomic issues as well as new social movements and new political issues: support for environmental protection, abortion rights, civil liberties, feminism.[22] Many disadvantaged whites are hostile to or unconcerned with these matters. As a result, attention to these issues often disrupts the white Democratic party, much as it disrupts traditional leftist parties in other industrial democracies.[23]

How are black Americans affected by these issues? Many are able to embrace major elements within both the old and the new liberal agendas. Much of the black population is disadvantaged, and thus possesses interests that are well served by an explicit focus on the traditional economic and social welfare agenda. Postindustrial affluence has bypassed major portions of black America, thereby maintaining the appeal of an emphasis on an adequate minimum wage, national health insurance, job creation, and so forth. At the same time, elements of the newer liberal agenda, particularly civil liberties and the extension of political access, are also relevant to their needs and aspirations. In short, because black Americans might be allies of either the old or the new liberal agendas, the challenge to Democratic party strategists is to combine these interests in ways that appeal to white voters and win elections.

One option is to combine blacks and new liberals into a single coalition.

22. Inglehart 1977; Lipset 1981, 503–21.
23. Koelble 1991.

This strategy has already achieved notable successes in urban politics, electing several black mayors, in particular Tom Bradley of Los Angeles.[24] The strategy has been especially successful because the crucial issues of local politics do not typically bring the interests of blacks and white liberals into conflict.[25] White liberals are usually middle class, and thus they do not fear competition from blacks for a place to live or for most public services because they are segregated and protected from such a challenge. Indeed, many analysts have become so accustomed to the coalition of blacks and white liberals that they frequently view it as the only possible biracial coalition that might incorporate black Americans within the power structure of urban politics.[26]

The black–new liberal coalition creates several problems, however. First, while it can produce some victories in local politics, it can seldom produce victories in nationwide or even statewide contests. The coalition simply does not generate enough votes because there are not enough white liberals. Thus Tom Bradley regularly wins elections in Los Angeles, but he was defeated twice when he ran for governor of California. Second, the coalition is poorly equipped to address the social welfare concerns of black Americans because finally, fundamentally, the new white liberals tend to be affluent, and the economic needs of disadvantaged Americans can only be served by their good intentions and altruism. But it is mutual interests, rather than good intentions and altruism, that cement durable political coalitions.

A second option for the Democratic party is to construct an appeal that combines the interests of blacks with the interests of working-class whites. Such a populist coalition, committed to improving social welfare, might be capable of generating sufficient votes to win state and national elections. But the potential is limited by the perennial Achilles heel of populism in America—racial hostility between blacks and working-class whites.[27] This problem is especially serious in local politics, where the disputes over residential space and shared public facilities, especially schools, are particularly severe.

Thus the Democratic party has found itself faced with a new strategic

24. Browning, Marshall, and Tabb 1984; Browning and Marshall 1986.

25. Davidson 1972, 205–07, argues that creating a coalition of blacks and new liberals is more difficult in nonpartisan local elections because the focus tends to be directed away from issues related to economics and class.

26. Compare, for example, the work of Davidson 1972 with the argument of Browning, Marshall, and Tabb 1984.

27. Woodward 1966; Huckfeldt and Kohfeld 1989.

dilemma in the years since the Voting Rights Act was passed. The coalition of blacks and new white liberals that is often able to win elections in local politics is doomed to failure in national politics because there are not enough white liberals. The coalition that might conceivably win elections in national politics, that of blacks and working-class whites, harbors too many racial tensions to be successful, especially in local politics. And thus the party stumbles along in a strategic schizophrenia created by the contradictions of its own coalition and unable to focus its vision for American society. Until the Democrats can confront and solve their own racial divide in a creative manner, the party will be unable to articulate a vision for the future of the republic.

The Voting Rights Act and the Two Reconstructions

J. MORGAN KOUSSER

In 1895, WHEN THE FIFTEENTH AMENDMENT turned twenty-five years old, nobody celebrated. In South Carolina, Ben Tillman's faction passed a temporary registration law to prevent blacks from voting in a referendum on calling a disfranchising convention, ensured that the convention would be called by stuffing the ballot box, struck a deal with the faction's "upper class" opponents to disfranchise many poor whites along with nearly all blacks, and proclaimed the new state constitution without offering the voters a chance to reject it. Five years earlier, the Democratic leadership of Mississippi had jammed through a similar disfranchising scheme. By 1895 Georgia, Florida, Tennessee, and Arkansas had buttressed white Democratic supremacy with poll taxes, while every other former Confederate state except North Carolina had enacted some direct restriction on voting with the basic intent and effect of disfranchising African Americans.[1]

Ninety-five years later, on the twenty-fifth anniversary of the passage of the 1965 Voting Rights Act, Virginia had a black governor, 24 blacks and 10 Hispanics sat in Congress, 417 blacks and 124 Hispanics were state legislators, 4,388 blacks and 1,425 Hispanics held offices in city or county governments, and 6 of the 10 largest cities in the country had elected black mayors. In the 11 former Confederate states, 61 percent of blacks and 70 percent of whites were registered to vote.[2] South Carolina's nomination of a black American for governor in 1990 was hardly considered worthy of national remark. No one, even in the Reagan administration, the most reactionary since Calvin Coolidge's, had proposed openly to restrict the suffrage of nonwhites.

Why the contrast? A comparison of certain aspects of the two Reconstructions will help us understand both more adequately. On the one hand, by making us more conscious about the nature of facts that

For comments and references, I thank Luis Fraga, Hugh Davis Graham, David Mayhew, and Rick Valelly, who are not, of course, responsible for the substance of the paper.

1. Kousser 1974.
2. As of 1986. See Department of Commerce 1990, 257, 260–61, 264.

are too often taken for granted, the comparison provides a new approach to the classic question of why the first Reconstruction failed. On the other hand, the analogy throws a new light on controversies over the intent, development, consequences, and desirability of the 1965 Voting Rights Act, its interpretations, amendments, and proposed relaxation.

In 1989, C. Vann Woodward, who invented the term *second Reconstruction* to describe the period since 1954, and who almost single-handedly initiated the comparative history of America's first Reconstruction, confessed, in his typically ironic tone, to failure. Not only had the first Reconstruction failed, but he personally had failed "to find a satisfactory explanation" for its failure.[3] In contrast, Eric Foner, no doubt constrained by the textbook format of his recent masterwork on Reconstruction, could not afford Woodward's coy reticence. Foner enumerated six reasons for the demise of Reconstruction: violence, the weakening of northern resolve, the inability of southern Republicans to develop a long-term appeal to whites, factionalism and corruption within the Republican party, the rejection of land reform, and changing patterns in the national and international economic system.[4]

As much as I admire the work of both Woodward and Foner, I suggest that rather different and perhaps more satisfying answers to the question may be obtained by simultaneously narrowing and lengthening the inquiry. To render the problem tractable, I will concentrate solely on politics. Instead of comparing the politics of race relations in post–Civil War America to that in other postemancipation societies, I will compare it to politics in post–World War II America. And instead of truncating the first period at 1877, when the revolution was not only unfinished but not even clearly over, I will carry my analysis through the turn of the nineteenth century.

The centerpiece of Reconstruction, Radical Republicans thought, was the vote. "A man with a ballot in his hand," the abolitionist Wendell Phillips declaimed, "is the master of the situation. He defines all his other rights. What is not already given him, he takes. . . . The ballot is opportunity, education, fair play, right to office, and elbow-room."[5] But Republicans were not, even as they celebrated passage of the Fifteenth Amendment in 1870, so naive as to believe that the right to vote was self-executing,

---

3. Woodward 1989, 199.
4. Foner 1988, 603.
5. Quoted in Gillette 1979, 23.

as Phillips's and other similar statements might seem to imply.[6] All too aware of the difficulty of struggles over black enfranchisement even in the North, where blacks were largely disfranchised in 1865 and where white voters rejected racially equal suffrage in eight of eleven referendums from 1865 to 1869, Radical Republicans fully realized that enfranchisement required practical safeguards against evasions of the law and retrogression. From the first drafts introduced into Congress of what were to become the Fourteenth and Fifteenth Amendments, therefore, proponents of racially impartial suffrage banned abridgement as well as outright denial of the right to vote of any loyal, noncriminal, adult male citizen.[7] Although they never specified in reports or floor debates from 1866 to 1869 exactly what practices the term *abridgement* covered, members of Congress probably had in mind the widely known example of New York, where in 1821 Martin Van Buren and his allies in the Albany Regency had imposed a $250 property requirement on blacks but not on whites and where attempts to repeal the discriminatory standard had failed, though by ever closer margins, in referendums in 1846, 1860, and 1869.[8]

The meaning of *abridgement* was not the only ambiguity in the deceptively simple Fifteenth Amendment. After Congress enfranchised blacks in ten southern states through the 1867 Military Reconstruction Act, white Democrats in Georgia, reasoning that the right to vote did not imply the right to hold office, expelled all the blacks elected to the subsequent state legislature.[9] When, in 1869, Congress first explicitly guaranteed the right of African Americans to hold office, then deleted that provision from the Fifteenth Amendment, was it done, as historian William Gillette has claimed, with the intent of allowing racial restrictions on officeholding? Or, as prominent Radical congressmen and senators

6. And as some scholars carelessly charge. See Gillette 1965, 161–62.

7. Section 2 of the Fourteenth Amendment requires reduction of the congressional representation of any state in which the suffrage "is denied to any of the male inhabitants of such State, being twenty-one years of age, and citizens of the United States, or *in any way abridged,* except for participation in rebellion, or other crime" (italics added). According to Blaine 1886, vol. 2, 418–19, this language barred states from passing even property, literacy, or religious tests that were on their face neutral. Repeated attempts in the first quarter of the twentieth century to enforce this section failed in Congress.

8. Field 1982, 199 and throughout; Mathews 1971 [1909], 14–15, 25, 34, 38–39. That they had a particular instance in mind, of course, does not mean that they would have opposed the application of the amendment to other examples of abridgement. They were, after all, enacting a broad constitutional principle rather than a minor statute that aimed to correct a transient situation.

9. Drago 1982, 48–49, 55–56.

asserted at the time, was the connection between voting and officeholding so obviously close as to make formal protection of the latter superfluous, and might mentioning it explicitly be taken to imply that other restrictions were allowed?[10] Similarly, did the deletion of bans against literacy and property tests, initially included in the Fifteenth Amendment, indicate that such qualifications, which everyone recognized would have a disproportionate impact on blacks, were constitutional?[11] Or, as the Radicals' position on the controversy over officeholding suggested, did the broad statement of the Fifteenth Amendment, together with the equal protection clause of the Fourteenth, outlaw literacy, property, and all other similar qualifications?

How wide was congressional power under section 2 of the Fifteenth Amendment? Did the section grant Congress almost unlimited control over local, state, and federal elections, as Democrats and many Radicals agreed during the 1869 debates?[12] In particular, did it authorize Congress to prohibit individuals from interfering with other individuals' right to vote, and could Congress regulate elections in an attempt to eliminate fraud? Or was section 2 essentially meaningless, as Democrats claimed whenever Congress considered bills to implement the Fifteenth Amendment after it had passed?[13] To what degree did the Fifteenth Amendment, combined with the Fourteenth, constitute a national guarantee of fundamental rights, including the right to be protected by state governments against violence, that might be enforced by courts as well as by Congress?

Acting within two months of the ratification of the Fifteenth Amendment, Republicans in Congress sought to protect every male citizen's voting right against interference through violence, intimidation, or bribery by any persons or groups, official or unofficial.[14] The far-reaching law, which still forms the basis of national protective legislation, undercuts the arguments of those historians who claim that Reconstructionists were

---

10. Gillette 1965, 64–71; Mathews 1971 [1909], 47–48.

11. For the bare-bones narrative of these and other roll call votes on the Fifteenth Amendment, see McPherson 1972 [1871], 399–406.

12. Mathews 1971 [1909], 47–50.

13. Mathews 1971 [1909], 76–77, 90–96.

14. Compare Belknap 1987, 10: "It was only with great reluctance that the Republican majority in Congress moved beyond the sort of negative intervention represented by statutory and constitutional prohibitions limiting what states could do to the enactment of legislation authorizing the federal government itself to prosecute wrongdoers who otherwise would have evaded punishment." Whatever reluctance congressmen felt did not slow them down appreciably.

constitutional conservatives, seriously constrained by traditional theories of federalism.[15] Within a year, Congress had passed two more election acts, one enabling supervision of congressional elections from registration through the counting of ballots and the other granting the president extensive powers to suppress the Ku Klux Klan and similar conspiracies.[16] In 1875 the House passed an even stronger "Force Bill," providing more severe penalties, increasing the number of violent offenses that were federal crimes, and prohibiting excessive poll taxes (an indication that Republicans believed the Fifteenth Amendment at least allowed *Congress* to forbid tests that did not explicitly mention race). Defiance from Democrats and the disillusionment of some Republicans prevented the Senate from acting on the bill.[17] In the next Congress in which they were in the majority in both houses, that of 1890, the Republicans came within a single vote of passing the most extensive bill in American history aimed at preventing corruption in elections.[18]

The Fifteenth Amendment and the Enforcement Acts were more effective than many scholars contend, and extensive black voting continued long after 1877.[19] Table 1 gives an incomplete and inadequate glimpse of the situation. In the early part of Reconstruction, blacks elected from 264 to 324 state legislators and congressmen each election—about a sixth of the total—in the eleven states that had joined the Confederacy.[20] Blacks also made up a quarter of the delegates to the ten state conventions that reshaped the southern constitutional order between 1867 and 1869.[21] In the mid-1870s the number of elected black officeholders plunged, but thereafter the total shrank gradually. At the end of the 1880s, as more southern states began to adopt laws restricting suffrage, the number of black legislators was about the same as in 1970, five years after the passage of the Voting Rights Act.

15. The most careful and qualified of these arguments is by Benedict 1974 and 1978.
16. Gillette 1979, 25–27; Foner 1988, 454–59.
17. Gillette 1979, 283–84; McPherson 1876, 13–18.
18. McPherson 1974 [1890], 207–19; Kousser 1974, 29–33.
19. For charges of ineffectiveness see, for example, Gillette 1979, 292–99.
20. There is no central source for the figures in table 1, which was put together from numerous books and articles about each state. Because many of the Reconstruction state legislators were very obscure, and because Democrats later made considerable efforts to blot out evidence about Reconstructionists from published and unpublished records, the race of some legislators is unknown. Statistics for later years are generally more reliable, when they exist. The scanty histories of Florida give very incomplete lists, and this is the state for which the data is listed as missing in table 1. The composition of the 1870 Georgia legislature is also unclear from published sources.
21. Hume 1982, 133.

TABLE I. Blacks Elected to State Legislatures and Congress in Eleven
Former Confederate States, 1868–1900, 1970–88

Year	Number[a]	Year	Number
1868	300(11)	1970	40
1870	264(9)	1972	63
1872	324(11)	1974	97
1874	281(11)	1976	106
1876	162(10)	1978	113
1878	74(10)	1980	129
1880	75(10)	1982	129
1882	71(10)	1984	167
		1986	186
1884	66(11)	1988	192
1886	56(10)		
1888	45(10)		
1890	35(10)		
1892	15(10)		
1894	10(11)		
1896	11(11)		
1898	10(11)		
1900	5(11)		

SOURCES:
Congress (1870–1901): Smith 1940.
State legislatures, first Reconstruction (years in parentheses). Alabama: Wiggins 1977, 147–51 (1868–78); Taylor 1949 (1880–1900). Arkansas: Perman 1984, 138 (1872); Arkansas House Journal 1889, 1044 (1889); Gatewood 1972, 220–23 (1890); Graves 1967, 208 (1894–1900). Florida: Richardson 1965, 188 (1868–69, 1871–75); Jacksonville Times–Union, November 18, 1884, 1; May 6, 1887, 1 (1885–87). Georgia: Conway 1966, 161 (1868); Bacote 1955, 524–25 (1880–1900); Shadgett 1964, 28, 52 (1872–74); Work 1920, 63–119 (1876–78). Louisiana: Vincent 1976, 228–38 (1868–76); Uzee 1950, 203–04 (1878–1900). Mississippi: Harris 1979, 264, 428, 479 (1870–74); Wharton 1947, 202 (1876–92). North Carolina: Padgett 1937, 483–84 (1868–88); Work 1920, 63–119 (1890–92, 1900); Edmonds 1951, 116 (1894–98). South Carolina: Holt 1977, 97 (1868–76); Tindall 1952, 309–10 (1878–1900). Tennessee: Cartwright 1976, 20, 66, 103, 105, (1871–83, 1889–1900); Work 1920, 63–119 (1885–87). Texas: Barr 1986, 340–52 (1870); Smallwood 1974, 406–11 (1872–74); Barr 1971, 27 (1876); Rice 1971, 100–11 (1878, 1894–1900); Brewer 1935, (1876; 1894–1900). Virginia: Blake 1935, 137, 182, 232, 252, (1869–71, 1879, 1891); Buni 1967, 4, 8 (1881); Wynes 1961, 45, 49 (1889); Jackson 1945, 1–43 (1873–77, 1883–87).
    Congress and state legislatures, all states (since 1970): Bureau of the Census, Statistical Abstract of the United States (annual).
    a. Number of states with no missing data is in parentheses.

Perhaps most interestingly, the series of elections beginning in 1868 is almost a mirror image of the series a century later, the pattern of decay in the first inversely reflecting that of growth in the second, with relatively flat periods of little change in the middle of each. Because the Fifteenth Amendment and the Voting Rights Act were roughly analogous laws and because each was followed by enforcing and strengthening acts, the stark divergence in the trends in officeholding demands explanation.

Although blacks' first preference, then as now, was to be represented by people of their own race, other things being equal they continued to vote in large percentages even after widespread black officeholding became infeasible. In the 1880 presidential election, three years after Rutherford B. Hayes symbolically confined U.S. troops in the South to their barracks, an estimated two-thirds of the adult male blacks were recorded as voting, and two-thirds of those managed to have their votes recorded for James A. Garfield, whom they nearly all no doubt supported. The high black turnout, which would be very respectable a century later, was no fluke. Nor was it the situation that Democrats allowed the turnout only because national elections were less important to them than those closer to home. An average of estimates for one gubernatorial contest in each of the eleven states during the 1880s shows that 60 percent of blacks voted, even though none of these elections took place on the same day as voters balloted for president. A similar percentage supported the Republican, Greenback, or other anti-Democratic candidate.[22] Even in the 1890s, after several states had restricted suffrage, nearly half the blacks are estimated to have voted in key gubernatorial contests, although the Populist-Democratic battles were sufficiently severe that Democrats pushed fraud to new levels, and only a third of black votes for anti-Democratic parties were counted.

What accounts for the trend in the nineteenth century figures and for the differences between the nineteenth and twentieth century patterns? The late nineteenth century counterrevolution took time, and its mechanisms were complex. There were five elements in the reversal of political Reconstruction—none sufficient by itself—all working together, but roughly following a predictable developmental sequence: violence, fraud, structural discrimination, statutory suffrage restriction, and constitutional disfranchisement.[23]

Violence was important, not only because it killed off or scared off southern Republican leaders, as is often noted, but also because it transfixed northern Republicans. The extent of Reconstruction violence and its political nature have been rightly stressed. Between the gubernatorial election in April 1868 and the presidential election in November, for instance, Louisiana Democrats, according to a congressional investigation, killed 1,081 persons, mostly black. In St. Landry Parish alone in that six-month period, as many as 200 African Americans fell to the

<hr/>

22. Kousser 1974, 15, 28. In these instances there was probably not as much fraudulent counting as in the presidential race. Several Democratic candidates openly appealed for black votes, while some independents had such bad civil rights records that many black voters deserted their tickets.

23. For evidence on the existence of this developmental sequence, see Kousser 1974.

Knights of the White Camelia, about four times as many as died in the whole South during the civil rights movement of the 1950s and 1960s.[24] Forty-six blacks were massacred in Memphis and 34 in New Orleans in 1866; 25 to 30 at Meridian, Mississippi in 1871, and 35 at Vicksburg in 1874; and 105 at the tiny hamlet of Colfax, Louisiana, on Easter Sunday, 1873, including 40 or so after they had laid down their arms and surrendered.[25] This extensive, systematic political terrorism has had no parallel in the modern civil rights movement, and in sheer extent it far surpassed the lynching spree of the 1890s.[26] Reconstruction violence astonished, mesmerized, and sometimes paralyzed the national Republican leaders, who devoted much—too much—of their legislative attention and a great many "Bloody Shirt" speeches to the topic.

The attention was excessive because violence was relatively ineffective politically as well as a dangerous weapon for a conservative, upper-class-dominated group such as the southern Democrats to employ. If violence had permanently inhibited the political opposition, one would expect presidential returns from counties where there were well-known violent incidents in the 1860s and 1870s to show a once-and-for-all destruction of the Republican vote. Table 2 demonstrates that this was not the case. In nine of twelve southern counties in which there were major "riots" or extensive assassinations, Republicans received approximately the same proportion of the votes as there were blacks in the population in the election after the incidents. Even in the remaining three, the Republicans polled *some* votes.[27] Furthermore, establishment violence is costly, because those who own and control property and power have much to lose if the labor force leaves or fights back by sabotaging property.[28] And outside the region the southern whites' reputation for violent oppression of blacks fueled campaigns for national intervention.[29] In sum, the direct political

24. Trelease 1971, 129–35. Belknap 1987, 29, notes only six murders connected with civil rights matters in the four years beginning in 1955 in the eleven states of the former Confederacy.
25. Trelease 1971, xliv; Wharton 1947, 189–90; Tunnell 1984, 192.
26. I do not mean to belittle the violence of the 1950s and 1960s nor the suffering it caused. My point is that the violence in the first Reconstruction claimed perhaps a hundred times as many victims.
27. In six of the nine counties in which meaningful comparisons can be made, the Republican percentage of the two-party vote in the election after the violence was lower than in the election before the violence, though in two of these six the decline was less than 10 percent. Violence, especially if accompanied by fraud, could certainly have an important effect. My point is that the effect was not unlimited.
28. Belknap 1987, 23.
29. See, for example, Senate 1879. As Republican Congressman Jonathan Rowell of

TABLE 2. Republican Share of Vote in Presidential Elections
Following Violent Racial Incidents, Selected Southern Counties,
1866–76

Town	County	Year of incident	Black population, 1880 (percent)	Republican vote[a] (percent)
Memphis	Shelby, Tenn.	1866	56	64(1868)
Orleans	Orleans, La.	1866, 1868	27	38(1872)
Camilla	Mitchell, Ga.	1868	55	51(1872)
(None)	St. Landry, La.	1868	49	45(1872)
Laurens	Laurens, S.C.	1870	60	72(1872)
Eutaw	Greene, Ala.	1870	82	68(1872)
Meridian	Lauderdale, Miss.	1872	54	54(1872)
Colfax	Grant, La.	1873	46	43(1876)
Vicksburg	Warren, Miss.	1874	72	23(1876)
Coushatta	Red River, La.	1874	71	67(1876)
Clinton	Hinds, Miss.	1875	73	25(1876)
Hamburg	Edgefield, S.C.	1876	65	14(1880)

SOURCES: Trelease 1971, xliv, 129; Tunnel 1984, 173–209. Data on black population are in Census Office 1883. Data on Republican vote are in Burnham 1955.
a. Year of election is in parentheses.

effect of violence, though significant, cannot by itself account for the decline of black voting in the nineteenth century.

Fraud was probably more significant than violence, as composing election returns became a recognized art form and excuses for the loss of official ballots stretched even the southern capacity for hyperbole. Mississippi officials, for instance, reported that horses and mules had developed a taste for ballot boxes.[30] Governor Samuel D. McEnery of Louisiana, a zealous enforcer of the legislative will, said that his state's election law "was intended to make it the duty of the governor to treat the law as a formality and count in the Democrats." Virginia elections, according to the author of the state's chief election statute, were "crimes against popular government and treason against liberty." A delegate to the Alabama Constitutional Convention of 1901 reported that "any time it was necessary" whites who controlled the Black Belt "could put in ten, fifteen, twenty or thirty thousand Negro votes." And a leader of the 1890

Illinois said during the debates on the Lodge Fair Elections Bill in 1890, "It is everywhere in Northern circles believed that the black vote of the Southern States is suppressed. It is everywhere believed that the Fifteenth Amendment to the Constitution of the United States is nullified." *Congressional Record*, 51 Cong., 1 sess., 6555.
    30. Wharton 1947, 204.

Mississippi Constitutional Convention admitted, "It is no secret that there has not been a full vote and a fair count in Mississippi since 1875."[31] But Congress often unseated counted-in candidates, and Republicans twice almost succeeded in strengthening laws against electoral chicanery.[32] Like violence, moreover, fraud was a dangerous device for a government of the "best men," one whose propagandistic staple, especially in the North, was the charge that Reconstructionists had been corrupt.[33]

The third means of accomplishing the counterrevolution, structural discrimination, involved such tactics as gerrymandering, annexations, the substitution of at-large for single-member-district elections and appointive for elective means of filling offices, and the adoption of nonstatutory white primaries. By severely limiting the number of offices that anti-Democratic parties could hope to capture even in a fair election, structural changes reduced the amount of overall violence and fraud necessary for the Democrats to carry elections, concentrated the opposition's attention on a few potentially winnable seats, dispirited the Democrats' adversaries, especially in districts where they had no chance to win, and increased the number of legislators willing to support further attacks on ethnic and political minorities.[34]

Gerrymanders were the paradigm of this strategy. Two of the most impressive ones were the congressional monstrosities perpetuated in South Carolina and Mississippi. (See figures 1 and 2 and tables 3 and 4.) In the 1860s and early 1870s, Radical Republicans drew roughly equipopulous and compact districts that, with the exception of Mississippi's First District after 1873, did not outrageously concentrate the white population. Democrats played by no such rules, constructing the bizarre South Carolina Seventh District, which contained the homes of two Republican incumbents and sliced across county lines in order to pack in every possible black voter, and the notorious Mississippi "shoestring" Sixth District, which tracked the river for the length of the state and contained so much of the black population as to make the other five districts easy to carry with a modicum of violence and fraud. The outcomes in the districts, as table 4 shows, were entirely as predicted. Well-known gerrymanders reduced the chances of electing black congressional candidates or sympathetic white candidates in other states.[35] Similar discriminatory

31. All quoted in Kousser 1974, 46–47.
32. Kousser 1974, 45–47.
33. The best-known examples of such propaganda are Pike 1874 and Herbert 1890.
34. Kousser 1984.
35. Anderson 1981; Wiggins 1980, 68–69; Foner 1988, 590–91.

actions no doubt took place on the local and state legislative levels.[36]

Although violence, fraud, and restructuring could usually keep political dissent in check, they could not eliminate it. Before legal disfranchisement nineteenth century Democrats rightly feared national antiviolence and anticorruption bills, for there was a core of black political strength to build on if southern Democrats could be forced to allow "a free ballot and a fair count."[37] The final solution to the problems of political dissent was to adopt statutory restrictions, such as registration and secret ballot laws (which often served as de facto literacy tests), and constitutional provisions such as poll taxes and literacy or property qualifications. The statutory restrictions often shrank dissent so that constitutional restrictions could be imposed.[38] It is these latter laws, along with the formal white primary that often attended them, that first attracted national legislative and judicial attention after 1930.

To recapitulate the argument briefly, each nineteenth century tactic became more effective as it allowed others to be employed. Violence and intimidation enabled Democrats to take over the polls, after which they could fabricate election returns. Fraudulently elected state and local government officials could then gerrymander election districts, switch from ward to at-large elections, or impose other structurally discriminatory devices. Because their numbers were decreased, Republican, independent, or populist representatives on governing bodies were thereafter even less able to block the passage of direct legislative and, ultimately, state constitutional restrictions on the suffrage. By itself, no stage except the last made the South safe for the white supremacist Democratic party. Effectively enforced national legislation could have blocked this process at one point or another, and in the second Reconstruction national laws and court decisions attacked every one of these five stages. If there is one element that explains the contrast between the two Reconstructions, it is the Voting Rights Act of 1965.

Why, then, was there no move to attack the discriminatory southern electoral structures, which were widely known and condemned in the late nineteenth century, and why were congressional efforts to punish violence and prevent fraud much less successful than they have been since

36. For instance, in Jacksonville, Florida, a poll tax and a multiple ballot box law failed to rid the city council of all black members, so in 1907 the council constructed a blatant racial gerrymander. No black was elected to the council from then until the 1970s. Akin 1974.

37. This argument is developed at much greater length in Kousser 1974.

38. The sequences and much detail are provided in Kousser 1974.

FIGURE 1. South Carolina Congressional Apportionments, 1867–93

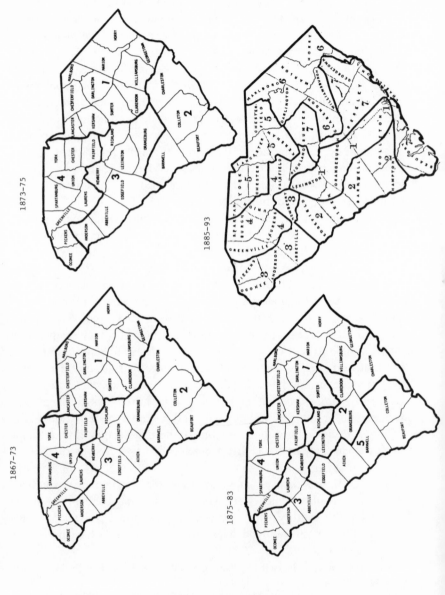

1867–73

1873–75

1875–83

1885–93

FIGURE 2. Mississippi Congressional Apportionments, 1869–93

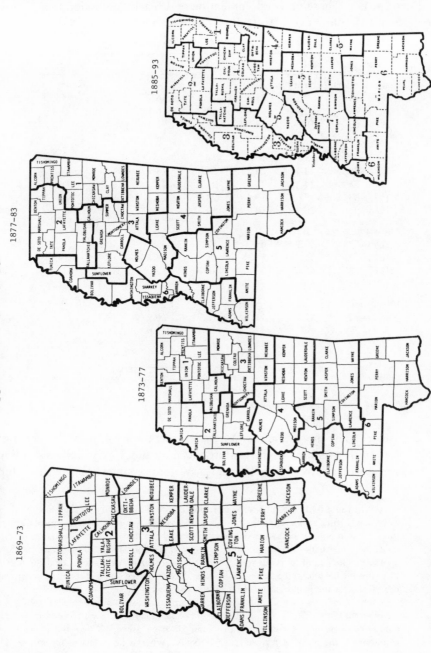

SOURCES: Parsons, Beach, and Durbin 1986, 121, 185, 187; "Some Mississippi Plans" 1882, 5.

TABLE 3. Share of Total Population and Black Population in
South Carolina and Mississippi Congressional Districts, 1867–93

	District						
Year	1	2	3	4	5	6	7
South Carolina, percent black							
1867–73	59.9	68.4	58.3	46.7	...	...	...
1873–75[a]	60.6	69.6	59.0	46.1	...	...	...
1875–83	59.6	64.5	51.6	51.1	67.5	...	...
1885–93	[b]	63.0	52.3	56.9	57.1	56.6	81.7
South Carolina, percent of state population							
1867–73	24.5	26.0	24.8	24.7	...	...	...
1873–75[a]	24.2	25.3	26.8	23.8	...	...	...
1875–83	19.6	18.8	20.2	21.8	19.6	...	...
1885–93	20.1	14.2	13.7	12.6	12.6	13.4	13.3
Mississippi, percent black							
1869–73	47.9	49.0	52.9	63.3	58.2	...	...
1873–77	21.9	56.1	59.4	57.1	56.4	54.4	...
1877–83	45.0	52.5	40.9	52.0	52.0	77.5	...
1885–94	49.2	53.7	80.4	53.8	51.6	52.6	64.5
Mississippi, percent of state population							
1869–73	17.7	16.1	18.7	26.9	20.5	...	...
1873–77	16.3	17.8	16.1	17.6	15.2	17.1	...
1877–83	20.8	15.5	15.2	15.4	15.9	17.2	...
1885–93	12.3	14.9	11.5	17.3	17.0	11.1	15.9

SOURCES: Parsons, Beach, and Durbin 1986, 121, 136, 184, 186, 212–13; Parsons, Durbin, and Parsons 1990, 228–29, 273–74.
a. Also one at-large district.
b. Figure unavailable because county lines crossed.

1957?[39] The most common answer to this question, a marked liberal-
ization in twentieth century white racial attitudes, is at best misleading
and at worst flatly wrong. The real answers are congressional partisanship

39. In 1890, Radical Republican Harrison Kelley of Kansas did introduce a bill drafted
by former North Carolina carpetbagger Albion Tourgée that required congressional districts
to be equal in population and gave Congress the right to draw district boundaries. It also
made the secret ballot mandatory in congressional elections and required states to allow
all adult males except felons to vote. Tourgée appeared before a congressional committee
to testify for his bill, and Speaker Thomas B. Reed endorsed some parts of it, but it was
too radical for the Republican caucus. Crofts 1968, 252–61.
    On the condemnation of southern electoral structures, see for example, "Flaws in the
Solid South," July 13, 1882, 5, and "Some Mississippi Plans," July 27, 1882, 5. In his first
annual message in 1889, President Benjamin Harrison asked, "When and under what
conditions is the black man to have a free ballot? When is he in fact to have those full
civil rights which have so long been his in law? When is that equality of influence which

TABLE 4. Party and Race of Members of Congress in South Carolina and Mississippi, 1868–86

Year took office	South Carolina			Mississippi		
	Republicans		Democrats (all white)	Republicans		Democrats (all white)
	White	Black		White	Black	
1868	4	0	0	...	...	...
1869	3	1	0	5	0	0
1871	1	3	0	5	0	0
1873	1	4	0	4	1	1
1875	3	2	0	2	1	3
1877	0	3	2	0	0	6
1879	0	0	5	0	0	6
1881	1	1	3	0	1	6
1883	1	0	6	1	0	5[a]
1885	0	1	6	0	0	7

SOURCE: U.S. Congress 1989.
a. There was also one Greenback party member in 1883.

and judicial perfidy in the last quarter of the nineteenth century.

Civil rights was an entirely partisan issue in the nineteenth century (table 5). But in the North at least, voting rights has enjoyed nearly unanimous support since 1957 (table 6). It has often been noted that partisanship helped consolidate Republican support for civil rights after the Civil War, and Republicans have repeatedly been derided for it.[40] Many Republicans did not "really" support black rights, the line goes, but only "expediently" endorsed bills under the party whip.

Whatever the validity of this argument, its converse surely holds for the Democrats.[41] From 1866 to the turn of the century, not a *single* Democrat in the House or Senate *ever* voted in favor of a piece of civil rights legislation. Northern Democrats repeatedly defended southern violence and fraud or denied their obvious existence, and they staunchly supported the endless filibusters—including one lasting a month in the Senate in 1890—against civil rights laws.[42] This was true even though

---

our form of government was intended to secure to the electors to be restored?" In his second annual message in 1890, he remarked that "Equality of representation and the parity of the electors must be maintained or everything that is valuable in our system of government is lost." Richardson 1900, vol. 9, 56, 127–29.

40. Gillette 1965 is perhaps the most strident modern example of these accusations.

41. I find, somewhat to my chagrin, that C. Vann Woodward 1960, 97, anticipated this argument long ago.

42. Grossman 1976, 48–49, 143–55. Thus Democrat Roswell P. Flower of New York

TABLE 5. Partisan Lineups in House and Senate Votes on
Civil Rights Laws, 1866–90

		House vote		Senate vote	
Year	Law	Republican	Democrat	Republican	Democrat
1866	Civil Rights Bill	111–5	0–33	33–2	0–10
1866	Fourteenth Amendment	138–0	0–36	33–4	0–7
1869	Fifteenth Amendment	144–3	0–41	39–2	0–11
1870	Enforcement Act	133–0	0–58	48–1	0–10
1871	Ku Klux Klan Act	93–0	0–74	36–2	0–11
1872	Enforcement Act	102–0	0–79	39–4	0–13
1875	Civil Rights Bill	147–14	0–79	38–7	0–19
1875	Enforcement Act	135–31	0–78	No vote	
1890	Lodge Bill	155–2	0–147	34–8	0–27

SOURCES: Civil Rights Bill (1866): *Congressional Globe*, 39 Cong., 1 sess., 606–07. Fourteenth Amendment (1866), Fifteenth Amendment (1869), Enforcement Act (1870): McPherson 1972 [1870], 102, 399, 550. Ku Klux Klan Act (1871), Enforcement Act (1872): McPherson 1872, 85, 91. Civil Rights Bill (1875), Enforcement Act (1875): McPherson 1876, 3, 8, 18. Lodge Bill (1890): For House vote, McPherson 1974 [1890], 218–19, 1368; for Senate vote to consider, *Congressional Record*, 51 Cong., 2 sess., 1740.

a considerable number of Democrats defected from their party's racist tradition from time to time on local issues in the North. As governor of New York, for instance, Grover Cleveland signed a school integration measure that applied to Manhattan in 1883; and Governor George Hoadly of Ohio convinced some Democrats to vote for school integration bills in that state's legislature in 1884. Democrats all over the North either supported or acquiesced in the passage of state laws requiring integrated public accommodations after the Supreme Court's abrogation of the 1875 national Civil Rights Bill in 1883.[43] It was neither constituency pressure nor personal racist belief that kept Democrats from backing voting rights bills in the nineteenth century, for at home some were willing to defect from the party's traditional racism.

---

condemned the 1890 supervisory bill as an attempt to "revolutionize the Government and set up on the ruins of our free institutions a government by fear, force, and fraud." Democrat Richard Vaux of Pennsylvania thought the authors of the bill were aiming at the "overturning of the Constitution of the United States and destroying our form of government." Democrat William McAdoo of New Jersey denounced the effort as "drastic and revolutionary," and Democrat William J. Stone of Missouri referred to proponents of the bill as "damned, odious traitors." See *Congressional Record* 51 Cong., 1 sess., 6601, 6603, 6672–75, 6848. Democratic bills to repeal the Reconstruction Supervisory Act passed both houses of Congress, on strict party-line votes, in 1878 and 1894. President Hayes vetoed the 1878 bill, even though it was a rider to an army appropriations act. President Cleveland signed the 1894 bill. DeSantis 1959, 85; Hirshson 1962, 56–57; Richardson 1940, 461–64.

43. Grossman 1976, 66–67, 82–106.

TABLE 6. Partisan Lineups in House and Senate Votes on Civil
Rights Laws, 1957–82

Year	Northern Democrat	Northern Republican	Southern Democrat[a]	Southern Republican[a]	Vote number
House					
1957	118–8	167–16	0–99	1–3	42
1960	174–12	130–12	5–82	2–3	15
1964	145–8	136–24	8–83	0–11	63
1965	199–2	111–9	22–59	1–15	87
1970	145–7	97–55	27–49	3–21	97
1975	198–4	84–26	49–23	10–17	192
1981–82	167–1	137–4	62–6	23–13	228
Senate					
1957	26–1	43–0	5–17	0	75
1960	38–0	29–0	4–18	0	69
1964	45–1	27–5	1–20	0–1	180
1965	44–0	30–0	3–17	0–2	78
1970	28–2	32–0	3–9	1–1	97
1975	40–1	26–1	9–5	2–5	329
1981–82	31–1	37–3	11–0	6–4	190

SOURCE: *Congressional Quarterly Almanac*, relevant years.
a. Eleven former Confederate states.

Support for voting rights has been overwhelming since 1957 (table 6) and constant for northern Democrats in both houses of Congress, and for northern Republicans in the Senate.[44] There was a substantial movement against the Voting Rights Act among House Republicans during the Nixon administration, but that "southern strategy" quickly faded. The southern pattern is one of a dramatic shift toward supporting civil rights, most strikingly among House Democrats, who opposed the extremely weak 1957 law unanimously but backed the much more stringent 1982 act by a ten-to-one ratio. At the height of the Reagan administration's power, six out of ten southern Republicans supported the Voting Rights Act on final passage.

Why was there such unanimity within and such division between the parties on this issue in the nineteenth century, and why did the two centuries' patterns contrast so starkly? Before presenting evidence, let me

44. This fact has either gone unnoticed or been treated as unimportant. Huckfeldt and Kohfeld 1989, 179, comment, "To the extent that both major parties depend upon black votes, they would both be forced to become parties of civil rights." As they show, blacks are overwhelmingly Democratic, yet on voting rights issues the two parties are already parties of civil rights.

summarize my argument. Competition for Congress and the presidency was much closer and more heated in the late nineteenth century than in the late twentieth. The composition of Congress in the nineteenth century repeatedly shifted violently, and few members had secure seats. Instead, and in stark contrast to the safe and relatively autonomous members of the recent era, nineteenth century members were almost wholly dependent on their parties for their brief tenures. Congressional elections were considerably more volatile, and margins in presidential contests were sufficiently narrow as to encourage each party to strain for every vote. If blacks voted freely, Republicans would be able to carry at least some southern states and, almost certainly, the presidency. It was not differences in racial attitudes alone, or perhaps even primarily, that drove Democrats to abandon democratic ideals in the nineteenth century and induced Republican allegiance to those ideals; it was the drive for national political power. Since World War II, however, the South has seldom been a swing region in presidential elections, and incumbents have been safe enough to be willing to vote for democracy.

Statistics on the delegations from Illinois, Indiana, and Ohio, the homes of four presidents in the late nineteenth century, suggest the greater volatility of membership in Congress then.[45] On average, 45 percent of the members from those three states in the 40th through 57th Congresses had not served in the previous Congress; in the 86th through 101st the average of new members was only 16 percent (table 7). Only in the 1898 and 1900 elections was the turnover as small as in the 1958 election, which had the highest replacement rate in the contemporary period.

Midwestern members of Congress in the nineteenth century had, then, very little congressional experience compared with their post-1956 counterparts: 65 percent of the time in the nineteenth century but only 15 percent in the twentieth, congressional seats from Illinois, Indiana, and Ohio were filled by people who sat for three terms or fewer (table 8). Eighty-five percent of all those who held seats from these three states between 1865 and 1902 served for three or fewer terms; only 46 percent were as inexperienced from 1957 to 1990. The prospect of repeated interaction in the future gives careerist twentieth century members more reason to compromise and to develop policy incrementally. Congressmen

45. Few historians have yet studied the nature and degree of competition for congressional seats in the nineteenth century. Political scientists' time series, which focus on the incumbency advantage and often leave out crucial elections, such as those immediately after decadal reapportionments, are also inappropriate for my purposes. See, for example, Garand and Gross 1984; Alford and Brady 1989.

TABLE 7. New Members in Congress from Illinois, Indiana, and
Ohio, 1866–1900, 1958–88

Year elected	New members	Total delegation	Percent new[a]	Year elected	New members	Total delegation	Percent new[a]
1866	15	43[b]	35	1958	18	59	31
1868	18	43	42	1960	12	59	20
1870	17	43	40	1962	9	58	16
1872	26	43	60	1964	11	58	19
1874	23	43	53	1966	9	59	15
1876	26	52	50	1968	4	59	7
1878	26	52	50	1970	11	59	19
1880	22	52	42	1972	8	58	14
1882	25	52	48	1974	14	58	24
1884	22	54	41	1976	9	58	16
1886	20	54	37	1978	5	58	9
1888	18	54	33	1980	11	58	19
1890	29	54	54	1982	11	53	21
1892	22	54	41	1984	7	53	13
1894	40	56	71	1986	5	53	9
1896	26	56	46	1988	4	53	8
1898	17	56	30	Mean[c]	...	...	16(6)
1900	16	56	29				
Mean[c]	...	...	45(11)				

SOURCES: Author's calculations based on Congressional Quarterly 1975; Congressional Quarterly 1985.
a. Percentage who did not serve in immediately preceding Congresses.
b. At-large contests excluded.
c. Unweighted mean, with standard deviation in parentheses.

in the nineteenth century, who could not expect to sit long enough to
benefit from a "tit-for-tat" strategy, had less reason to compromise and
less stake in the incremental development of policy.[46]

The career of the nineteenth century member of Congress was more
evanescent because elections were more closely contested. In Ohio, Indiana,
and Illinois there were landslide margins (more than 55 percent for the
winning major-party candidate) in only two-fifths of the districts from
1864 to 1900; four-fifths of the elections were landslides from 1956 to
1988 (table 9). More than a quarter of the contests were decided by two
percentage points or less in the earlier period but by less than one-twelfth
since 1956.

46. Axelrod 1984.

TABLE 8. Longevity of Members in Congress from Illinois, Indiana, and Ohio, 1865–1902, 1957–90

Terms served	Percent of all terms served by members who served stated number of terms[a]		Percent serving stated number of terms[a]	
	1865–1902	1957–90	1865–1902	1957–90
1	18	5	40	24
2	27	4	30	11
3	20	6	15	11
4	13	9	7	11
5	8	7	3	7
6	1	4	*	4
7	4	8	1	6
8	3	11	1	7
9	0	7	0	4
10	3	9	1	5
11	0	6	0	3
12	0	10	0	4
13	1	4	*	2
14–17	1	8	*	3

SOURCE: See table 7.
* Less than 0.5 percent.
a. Totals may not equal 100 percent because of rounding.

With such small margins of victory, the shift of comparatively few votes could produce a huge alteration in a party's congressional seats. In 1890, for example, Republican congressional candidates in the three states polled only 2.4 percentage points less of the two-party vote than they had in 1888 but won fewer than half the seats they had won in 1888 (table 10). Democrats enjoyed a seats-to-votes ratio of 1.41 (72.2 / 51.2) in 1890, receiving 1.41 percent of the congressional seats for every 1 percent of the vote they won, and a swing ratio of 13.13 (27.8 / 2.4). The higher seats-to-votes ratios in the nineteenth century, and the elevated and erratic swing ratios in the nineteenth but not the twentieth, suggest that the volatility induced by the electoral structure itself rather than the volatility of the electorate accounted for the instability of congressional membership during the first Reconstruction. In fact, popular voting for Congress varied less from election to election in the nineteenth century. The mean change in the statewide Republican percentage from one election to the next was 2.1 percent between 1864 and 1900 but 3.6 percent between 1956 and 1988 in these three states.

Partisan instability in Congress also differed strikingly from period to period. In the nineteenth century no party majority, no matter how large,

TABLE 9. Margin of Victory in Congressional Elections in Illinois, Indiana, and Ohio, 1864–1900, 1956–88
Percent of congressional districts

	Nineteenth century margin of victory[a]			Twentieth century margin of victory[a]	
Year	55 percent or more	52 percent or less	Year	55 percent or more	52 percent or less
1864	44.2	18.6	1956	18.6	3.4
1866	65.1	20.9	1958	33.9	15.3
1868	67.4	39.5	1960	30.5	16.9
1870	69.8	32.6	1962	25.9	8.6
1872	56.0	24.0	1964	32.8	6.9
1874	69.2	32.7	1966	16.9	6.8
1876	59.6	34.6	1968	18.6	3.4
1878	11.5	3.8	1970	10.2	5.1
1880	63.5	36.5	1972	13.8	6.9
1882	59.3	44.4	1974	34.5	6.9
1884	64.8	33.3	1976	13.8	8.6
1886	64.8	35.2	1978	12.1	5.2
1888	75.9	35.2	1980	12.1	2.6
1890	59.3	31.5	1982	15.4	9.6
1892	68.5	37.0	1984	11.5	3.8
1894	48.1	14.8	1986	17.3	7.7
1896	58.9	28.6	1988	9.6	1.9
1898	66.1	23.2	Mean	19.3	7.0
1900	51.8	28.6			
Mean	59.1	27.4			
Mean excluding 1878	61.8	30.6			

SOURCES: See table 7.
a. Winner of major-party vote. At-large contests have been excluded from these tallies, as have votes for minor parties. No minor-party candidate won a seat from these states in either period. The Greenback party in 1878 apparently drew votes from minority parties in a large number of districts, increasing the margin of the two-party vote for the winners.

was safe for long. The standard deviation of the Republican percentage of House members in the nineteen sessions from 1865 through 1901 was more than four times as high as that for the seventeen sessions from 1957 through 1989. The standard deviation for Senate members was nearly twice as high (table 11). Politicians, of course, took note; James G. Blaine, for instance, remarked in his memoirs that new members composed majorities in nine of the ten sessions of the House from 1861 to 1881.[47]

It was not the fickleness of the nineteenth century electorate that led

47. Blaine 1886, vol. 2, 675.

TABLE 10. Volatility in Congressional Elections in Illinois, Indiana, and Ohio, 1864–1900, 1956–88

Year	Percent Republican of two-party vote statewide	Percent of seats won by Republicans	Ratio of seats to votes (for winner)[a]	Swing ratio (2 elections)[b]
		1864–1900		
1864	55.3	83.7	1.51	. . .
1866	54.7	79.1	1.45	7.67
1868	52.3	67.4	1.29	4.88
1870	50.9	62.8	1.23	3.29
1872	52.3	68.0	1.30	3.71
1874	47.8	36.5	1.22	7.00
1876	50.1	61.5	1.23	10.87
1878	53.8	55.8	1.04	−1.54
1880	51.9	69.2	1.33	−7.05
1882	49.4	44.4	1.11	9.92
1884	50.6	44.4	0.88	0
1886	51.3	66.7	1.30	31.86
1888	51.2	59.3	1.16	74.00
1890	48.8	27.8	1.41	13.13
1892	49.0	42.6	1.13	74.00
1894	58.0	92.9	1.60	5.59
1896	53.9	73.2	1.36	4.80
1898	53.0	67.9	1.28	5.89
1900	53.0	67.9	1.28	0
Mean	52.0	61.6	1.27	. . .

to the more extreme fluctuations in congressional representation. In presidential elections, the recent period is the unstable one; the earlier period was comparatively immobile (table 12). In the percentage of the popular vote and of the electoral vote, the standard deviation in the nine presidential contests from 1956 through 1988 has been more than twice that in the nine elections from 1868 through 1900.

If changes in the behavior of the electorate do not account for the pattern of outcomes of elections, what does? Historians have just begun to examine such structural questions as how unequal and how partisan congressional and legislative apportionments were in nineteenth century politics outside the South.[48] For the years since 1946 the most recent work rejects structural explanations in favor of political ones. "Divided party control," Gary Jacobson contends, "reflects, rather than thwarts,

48. Argersinger 1989.

TABLE 10. (*Continued*)

Year	Percent Republican of two-party vote statewide	Percent of seats won by Republicans	Ratio of seats to votes (for winner)[a]	Swing ratio (2 elections)[b]
		1956–88		
1956	55.4	67.8	1.22	. . .
1958	47.1	47.5	0.99	2.45
1960	51.5	57.6	1.12	2.40
1962	52.4	62.1	1.19	5.00
1964	47.3	51.7	0.92	2.04
1966	55.1	62.7	1.14	1.41
1968	55.4	62.7	1.13	0
1970	51.6	59.3	1.15	0.89
1972	52.9	63.8	1.21	3.46
1974	46.6	48.3	0.97	2.46
1976	48.7	48.3	1.01	0
1978	51.6	51.7	1.00	1.17
1980	53.4	55.2	1.03	2.51
1982	44.8	50.0	0.91	0.60
1984	49.9	46.2	1.07	− 0.75
1986	48.4	44.2	1.08	1.33
1988	48.2	42.3	1.11	9.50
Mean	50.6	54.2	1.07	. . .

SOURCE: See table 7.
    a. The proportion of congressional seats won by the victorious party divided by that party's proportion of the two-party vote.
    b. The change in the proportion of seats won from one election to the next by the Republicans divided by the change in the proportion of the two-party popular vote won by Republican candidates.

popular preferences."[49] Although certainly not decisive, the evidence I have presented suggests that structural or institutional explanations might better account for such large changes as those between the nineteenth century and twentieth century patterns than they apparently do for the slowly fading marginals after 1960.

Whatever the causes of the differences in patterns in the two centuries, the consequences seem clear. When members of Congress arrived in Washington in the nineteenth century, they had little identity apart from their political party, and few remained long enough to develop one. They therefore naturally adopted their party's dominant view: as the Senate leader of the fight for the Fair Elections Bill of 1890 said, a free ballot

49. Jacobson 1990, xv. The debate and references to the "vanishing marginals" literature may be followed through references in Jacobson's book.

TABLE 11. Party Balance in Congress, 1865–1901, 1957–89

	House			Senate		
Year	Republican	Democrat	Percent Republican	Republican	Democrat	Percent Republican
			1865–1901			
1865	149	42	78	42	10	81
1867	143	49	74	42	11	79
1869	149	63	70	56	11	84
1871	134	104	56	52	17	75
1873	194	92	68	49	19	72
1875	109	169	39	45	29	61
1877	140	153	48	39	36	52
1879	130	149	47	33	42	44
1881	147	135	52	37	37	50
1883	118	197	37	38	36	51
1885	140	183	43	43	34	56
1887	152	169	47	39	37	51
1889	166	159	51	39	37	51
1891	88	235	27	47	39	55
1893	127	218	37	38	44	46
1895	244	105	70	43	39	52
1897	204	113	64	47	34	58
1899	185	163	53	53	26	67
1901	197	151	57	55	31	64
Mean[a]	...	...	53(14)	...	...	60(12)
			1957–89			
1957	200	233	46	47	49	49
1959	154	283	35	34	66	34
1961	174	263	40	35	65	35
1963	176	258	41	33	67	33
1965	140	295	32	32	68	32
1967	187	247	43	36	64	36
1969	192	243	44	43	57	43
1971	180	254	41	44	54	45
1973	192	239	45	42	56	43
1975	144	291	33	37	60	38
1977	143	292	33	38	61	38
1979	159	273	37	41	58	41
1981	192	243	44	53	46	54
1983	165	267	38	54	46	54
1985	182	252	42	53	47	53
1987	177	258	41	45	55	45
1989	175	260	40	45	55	45
Mean[a]	...	...	39(4)	...	...	42(7)

SOURCES: Congressional Quarterly 1981, 1148–49; *Congressional Quarterly Almanacs* 1983–88.
a. Standard deviations in parentheses.

TABLE 12. Percentage of Popular and Electoral Vote for Republicans in Presidential Elections, 1868–1900, 1956–88

Year	Percent of electoral vote	Percent of popular vote	Year	Percent of electoral vote	Percent of popular vote
1868	73	53	1956	86	58
1872	78	56	1960	42	50
1876	50	48	1964	10	39
1880	58	50	1968	61	50
1884	45	50	1972	97	62
1888	58	50	1976	45	49
1892	34	48	1980	91	55
1896	61	52	1984	98	59
1900	65	53	1988	79	54
Mean[a]	58(14)	51(3)	Mean[a]	63(30)	53(7)

SOURCES: Congressional Quarterly 1976; Scammon and McGillivray 1976–88.
a. Standard deviations in parentheses.

was the "very definition of Republicanism."[50] The only way party identity changed was when parties experienced whipsawing elections, such as those from 1890 through 1894, that first leveled Republican incumbents then did the same thing to the Democrats, resulting in the retirement of many core members of each party.

As for presidential elections in the late nineteenth century, they were so close and candidates before civil service reform so dependent on party activists and so independent of nonpartisan special-interest groups compared with their counterparts today, that they had to enliven the faithful with appeals to traditional issues—the Civil War and its associated racial issues, as well as tariff and monetary policy. Furthermore, since Republicans realistically believed that with anything approaching a fair count they could carry some southern states, and since Democrats needed every southern electoral vote to win the presidency, control of the southern ballot box was crucial to both parties. By contrast, only in 1960, 1976, and 1980 in recent years have the two parties closely contested southern electoral votes. Usually the Republicans have been able to count on them, even when blacks voted overwhelmingly for the Democrats. Republican presidents therefore have had little incentive to oppose even a strengthened Voting Rights Act, and Democrats, heavily dependent on their black constituents if they were to have a chance of carrying a national election, have had no choice but to support civil rights enthusiastically.

50. Hoar 1891.

As far as minority voting rights are concerned, in the nineteenth century the parties were too competitive, too "responsible," too dependably committed to a program, and the voters were too civically conscious to let elites stray from orthodoxy. Black votes counted for too much nationally. In this view, the presidential landslides of the past generation, the durability of congressional incumbents, the decline of party loyalty among voters and elites, and the inattention of the public explain the consensus supporting voting rights for blacks and other minorities. The first Reconstruction died, I am suggesting, from too much democracy; the second has thrived precisely because competition has shriveled.

Even if political conditions had favored congressional action on civil rights after 1874, the Supreme Court would probably have invalidated or undermined any resulting laws. During the 1880s, to be sure, in *Ex parte Siebold, Ex parte Clarke,* and *Ex parte Yarbrough* the high court interpreted the plenary power of Congress under Article I, section 4, of the Constitution to regulate the "times, places and manner of holding elections" to Congress broadly enough to allow it to guarantee peaceable assembly and restrict fraud and violence.[51] These decisions encouraged the sponsors of the 1890 Fair Elections Bill.

But two disastrous opinions of 1876, *United States* v. *Reese* and *United States* v. *Cruikshank,* had ruled unconstitutional or largely unenforceable those sections of the 1870 and 1872 Enforcement Acts that attempted to protect all citizens against violence or fraud, state-sponsored or private, in connection with state or local elections.[52] Kentucky officials had refused to accept the ballots of citizens because they were black, and Louisiana had neither protected the victims of the "Colfax riot" nor indicted the perpetrators of that largest murder of African Americans in American history. Yet according to Chief Justice Morrison Waite, convictions for these actions in federal courts had to be overturned. In each case, the key to the ruling was Waite's insistence that laws and indictments focus on racial intent.

The Enforcement Act at issue in *Reese* had four relevant sections: the first two mentioned race; the second two did not but referred, for instance, to the "wrongful act or omission as aforesaid," that is, the act by which

51. *Ex parte Siebold,* 100 U.S. 371 (1880); *Ex parte Clarke,* 100 U.S. 339 (1880); *Ex parte Yarbrough,* 110 U.S. 651 (1884).
52. *United States* v. *Reese,* 92 U.S. 214 (1876); *United States* v. *Cruikshank,* 92 U.S. 542 (1876).

blacks, on account of their race, were denied the right to become legally qualified to vote.[53] Waite ruled that sections 3 and 4 were unconstitutional because they did not directly mention race and that the only national power to protect a citizen's right to vote in a state or local election derived from the Fifteenth Amendment. Likewise, in *Cruikshank*, after a preliminary disquisition on federalism that echoed Democratic rhetoric during the "Force Bill" debates, Waite dismissed the case not on grounds that the law was unconstitutional but on grounds that the indictment did not aver that the blacks were murdered or denied the right to vote *because* they were black.

The decisions were deeply disturbing. First, the Lexington blacks were admittedly denied the right to vote on account of their race, all the victims at Colfax were black, the laws perfectly fit the situations in each instance, and indictments were filed and southern juries convicted the malefactors. Yet the Republican Supreme Court overruled the verdicts. The attempt to use the normal instrumentalities of government to protect the new citizens had failed at the top. Second, the Fourteenth Amendment, which sought, without explicitly mentioning race, to protect all citizens against discrimination and deprivation of liberty, was significantly weakened.[54] Waite might have severed sections 3 and 4 from sections 1 and 2 and still sustained them as protections of citizens' rights to enjoy suffrage impartially under the equal protection or privileges or immunities clauses of the Fourteenth Amendment. He might then have ruled that the rights of peaceable assembly and life were guaranteed by the nation under the Fourteenth Amendment and the rights applied to all citizens.[55] Third, by insisting on proof of a racist intent, perhaps even of racial hostility, Waite

53. For a trenchant analysis of the act, see the dissent of Justice Ward Hunt, 23 L.Ed. 563 at 572 (1876).

54. Unlike the Fifteenth Amendment, which bans discrimination in voting "on account of race, color, or previous condition of servitude," the Fourteenth Amendment does not mention race (it was used extensively before 1937 to guarantee the rights of corporations, which have no race). Zuckert 1986 demonstrates conclusively that in the debate over the Ku Klux Klan Act, Congress relied on the Fourteenth Amendment, adopting the "state failure" rather than the "state action" interpretation of it. In other words, if Congress anticipated that a state would fail to protect its citizens against other individuals, Congress could provide that protection directly.

55. To consider merely one fact, extensive reports from the South emphasizing persecution not only of blacks, but of southern ex-Unionists were crucial in building support for Radical Reconstruction after 1865; see, for example, Foner 1988, 225–26. That the Fourteenth Amendment was meant to protect the rights of all citizens is argued most forcefully in Curtis 1986.

made it much more difficult to obtain convictions. If 105 black bodies did not prove racial animosity, what would? Finally, these two decisions severely constrained the potential of congressional action.[56]

Whatever potential the Waite Court left, the Court under Chief Justice Melville W. Fuller destroyed.[57] In *Williams* v. *Mississippi* in 1898, the Court denied disfranchised blacks a remedy by very strictly construing its earlier decision in *Yick Wo* v. *Hopkins,* in which the counsel for the Chinese laundrymen had shown that a San Francisco ordinance was adopted with both the intent and effect of discriminating against Chinese.[58] The African American lawyer, Cornelius J. Jones, represented Henry Williams, a black man who had been convicted of murder by an all-white jury. Jones quoted extensively from the Mississippi disfranchising convention of 1890 to demonstrate its racist intent, apparently taking the exclusion of blacks from the Greenville voter rolls, and therefore jury rolls, to be proof enough of the state constitution's discriminatory impact. The Court's crabbed reading of *Yick Wo* cost Williams his life. But when yet another African American attorney, Wilford H. Smith, who represented disfranchised Alabama blacks, presented extensive evidence of discriminatory effect as well as intent, the Court, in a decision written by the "liberal" Oliver Wendell Holmes, declared that judges could do nothing because suffrage was a "political question."[59] Thus blacks never abandoned

56. Warren 1922, vol. 3, 324–30; Benedict 1978; Kaczorowski 1985, 199–229; Braeman 1988, 65–66. The Republican majority in the Senate did pass a bill restoring the provisions of the Enforcement Act that the Court had voided in *United States* v. *Reese,* this time unmistakably limiting their scope to denials based on race, but the Democratic-controlled House, naturally, did not act on the bill; Magrath 1963, 131.

57. As a Copperhead state legislator in Illinois during the Civil War, Melville W. Fuller had, after the Emancipation Proclamation, introduced a bill to endorse a constitutional amendment guaranteeing slavery against legislative or executive action by the national government; King 1950, 116.

58. *Williams* v. *Mississippi,* 170 U.S. 213 (1898); *Yick Wo* v. *Hopkins,* 118 U.S. 356 (1886).

59. *Giles* v. *Harris,* 189 U.S. 475 (1903). In *Guinn and Beal* v. *United States,* 238 U.S. 347 (1915), which struck down the Oklahoma grandfather clause, Chief Justice Edward Douglass White entirely ignored *Williams* and *Giles.* But invalidating the grandfather clause enfranchised no blacks because that patently unconstitutional device merely allowed illiterate whites to register legally. Throwing out *Giles,* however, would have allowed blacks to vote, since *Giles* was a challenge to the administration of the Alabama constitution. A former member of the "conservative" faction of the Democratic party in Louisiana, which had opposed the grandfather clause in that state's constitutional convention in 1898, White wished to rule it unconstitutional, but he did not want to endanger white Democratic supremacy in the South. Consequently, he paid no attention whatsoever to the most obvious precedents. For a more extensive discussion of these cases, see Kousser 1991.

the struggle for the vote; instead, a racist Supreme Court overrode the clear intent of Congress and the framers of the Reconstruction amendments in order to deny African Americans an effective vote.

How did justices who made the decisions get appointed to the Supreme Court? Some were Democrats: Stephen J. Field and Nathan Clifford at the time of *Reese* and *Cruikshank;* Melville Westin Fuller, Edward Douglass White, and Rufus W. Peckham at the time of *Williams* and *Giles.* As in Congress, no Democratic member of the U.S. Supreme Court before 1913 ever voted for black civil rights. But all the other justices in the four most crucial voting rights cases were, nominally at least, Republicans. Thus, partisanship as a motive or an index of racial attitudes does not by itself explain the decisions. Nor will a second potential reason, changes in public attitudes. In Congress, few Republicans abandoned the voting rights issue until after 1890. Almost all state legislatures outside the South passed public accommodations integration bills between 1866 and 1890, and at least fourteen mandated school integration. White racial opinion made its major shift only after 1890, long after the Supreme Court signaled a change in its collective mind.

A third possible explanation is chance occurrences and ambition. Chief Justice Salmon P. Chase, a brilliant lawyer and stalwart racial egalitarian, died at the age of sixty-five, after only eight and one-half years on the bench. His two immediate predecessors, John Marshall and Roger B. Taney, had served three decades apiece. Had Chase's tenure been as long as Marshall's, he would have retired in 1899, and it is impossible to imagine him acceding to *United States* v. *Reese, Williams* v. *Mississippi,* or *Plessy* v. *Ferguson.* Since even on a Court filled with strong-willed judges, Chase was able to prevail on the issues he cared most about— those involving Reconstruction—he would probably have commanded much more than his own vote in support of civil rights had he lived longer.[60] Two other strong personalities and staunch advocates of civil rights, Roscoe Conkling and George F. Edmunds, were each twice offered Supreme Court appointments, which they refused out of ambitions for higher office and higher salary.[61] Waite, whose civil rights views were

60. On Chase, see Friedman 1969; Blue 1987, 40, 49, 53–54, 196, 248–49, 258–59, 300–02, 306–07, 321. Of Chief Justice Fred Vinson's death just before the reargument in *Brown* v. *Board of Education* in 1953, Justice Felix Frankfurter remarked, "This is the first indication I have ever had that there is a God." Quoted in Kluger 1977, 656.

61. Abraham 1974, 121, 129. On Edmunds, see *Cincinnati Daily Gazette,* Dec. 15, 1879, 1; Mar. 8, 1882, 1, 4; Adler 1934. Conkling called Justice John Marshall Harlan's racially liberal dissent in *The Civil Rights Cases,* 3 S.Ct. 18 (1883), the "noblest opinion in history." Quoted in Maddocks 1959, 57.

as unknown before his appointment as he himself was, was Grant's *seventh* choice for chief justice.[62] The civil rights stances of some justices, such as Joseph P. Bradley, changed while they were on the Court, while other justices, such as William Strong, sometimes seemed loyal advocates of civil rights and sometimes silently concurred in reactionary opinions.[63] Furthermore, some, such as David J. Brewer, were chosen by presidents primarily for their views on economic issues, and others, such as Henry B. Brown, an admiralty law expert, for their special knowledge. These turned out to be relatively conservative on civil rights.[64]

In sum, the reasons for the shift by the Supreme Court in the late nineteenth century included the relatively small numbers of men involved, the anomalies of the judicial nomination process with its emphasis on seats held by justices from certain states, the very low salaries that kept some of the best candidates off the bench, and the dearth of organized interest groups to vet nominees and to push for and against specific candidates. These conditions made members of the Court less predictable and less easily influenced than elective officeholders. That popularly elected Republicans stayed loyal to civil rights long after the Supreme Court deserted the cause is evidence of the liberalism, not the conservatism, of white racial opinion in the nineteenth century.

If one line on the tombstone of the first Reconstruction should read "died of democracy," the next should be chiseled "and of an undemocratic institution's failure to protect democracy."[65] The contrast between the actions of the Waite and Fuller Courts and those of the Courts under Earl Warren and even Warren Burger and William Rehnquist could hardly be stronger.

During the second Reconstruction, not only did Congress pass and

62. Abraham 1974, 122.

63. Whiteside 1981; Kutler 1969.

64. Abraham 1974, 136–39; Paul 1969; Goldfarb 1969. Brewer and Brown did dissent in *Giles*.

65. What of Foner's six causes of the failure of the first Reconstruction? Violence and land reform are of fairly small relevance to politics: the same violence that kept blacks from the ballot box could have deprived them of their property. Northern resolve did not weaken uniformly or decisively until much later in the century. Republican factionalism and inability to appeal to whites could have been overcome if Republican voters could have been adequately protected and their votes counted. The depressions of the 1870s and 1890s were critical because they removed from office Republican elites who were committed, in varying degrees, to black rights. Foner's list is, in sum, not so much wrong as it is incomplete. I would put much more stress on political self-interest and on the actions of politicians (including judges) who controlled major political institutions.

repeatedly strengthen its protections of minority voting rights, but the Supreme Court, with the exception of the decision in *City of Mobile* v. *Bolden,* supported the law with considerable vigor.[66] Indeed, *Gomillion* v. *Lightfoot,* the Tuskegee, Alabama, gerrymander case, ran the film of the decisions from *Reese* to *Giles* backward, as it were.[67] Despite brute intransigence and ingenious subterfuges by white officials in the nation's most heavily black county, enough African Americans managed to register to vote to threaten white control of the town of Tuskegee. Macon County Representative Sam Englehardt therefore pushed through the Alabama legislature a bill redefining the boundaries of Tuskegee to make it an almost wholly white town.[68]

Justice Felix Frankfurter's opinion smashed the "political question" or "justiciability" roadblock. Even Frankfurter, who had held up consideration of rotten borough cases in *Colegrove* v. *Green,* was shocked by the "strangely irregular 28-sided-figure" drawn to "fence out" blacks from Tuskegee.[69] The decision also reunited the Fourteenth and Fifteenth Amendments, sundered in *Reese* and *Cruikshank,* ruling that a lack of equal protection through a racially discriminatory electoral structure was also a denial of the right to vote guaranteed by the Fifteenth Amendment, and resting its holding on both grounds. Finally, the Court implicitly ruled that a racially discriminatory intent could be proven on the basis of its effect alone. Robert Carter of the NAACP began his oral argument before the Supreme Court, "Your Honors, our position is simple. This is purely a case of racial discrimination. The *purpose* of this legislation— Alabama Act 140—was discriminatory." When Justice William O. Douglas asked Carter whether purpose was "the central aspect of your case," Carter replied, "purpose and effect—the effect reveals the purpose."[70] Although the NAACP introduced no direct evidence of intent, no "smoking gun" statements, for instance, the Supreme Court ruled in its favor, declaring that "Acts generally lawful may become unlawful when done to accomplish an unlawful *end.*"[71] The nineteenth century decisions were tacitly buried.

The Court continued in the *Gomillion* tradition in *Allen* v. *State Board*

66. *City of Mobile* v. *Bolden,* 446 U.S. 55 (1980).
67. *Gomillion* v. *Lightfoot,* 364 U.S. 339 (1960).
68. The best treatment of these events is Norrell 1985, 79–110.
69. *Colegrove* v. *Green,* 328 U.S. 549 (1946).
70. Quoted in Taper 1962, 86, 88–89 (italics added).
71. *Gomillion,* v. *Lightfoot,* 364 U.S. at 347, quoting *United States* v. *Reading Co.,* 226 U.S. 324 at 357 (1912) (italics added).

of Elections. Chief Justice Earl Warren held that under section 5 of the 1965 Voting Rights Act, the Department of Justice could refuse to allow election laws in Virginia and Mississippi to go into effect even if those laws had no direct connection with voter registration but instead changed the structure of elections, for example, from single-member to at-large districts.[72] In 1973 in *White* v. *Regester,* Justice Byron White introduced the "totality of the circumstances" test and enumerated factors that were to be taken into account for an electoral structure to be ruled racially discriminatory.[73] The Supreme Court briefly departed from this line of decisions in *City of Mobile* v. *Bolden,* in which a plurality endorsed Justice Potter Stewart's opinion that the Fifteenth Amendment and section 2 of the Voting Rights Act required proof of purpose and that, piece by piece, the objective evidence presented by the plaintiffs did not satisfy that standard. The case's troubled life, however, was cut short after less than twenty-seven months. In *Rogers* v. *Lodge* in 1982, Justice White merged the effect-based standards of *Regester* with the intent ideas of a series of Fourteenth Amendment cases, and gingerly sidestepped the *Bolden* plurality ruling.[74] Four years later, Justice William Brennan, in *Thornburg* v. *Gingles,* focused judicial attention on three particularly important factors for determining a voting rights violation and rejected the attempt to make it much more difficult to prove that voting was racially polarized.[75] Plaintiffs did not have to demonstrate that racism was the sole or most important cause of differences in voting patterns but only that the electorate did, as a matter of fact, split along racial lines.

Most lawyers and academics who have studied these developments have approved the five leading Supreme Court decisions and criticized *Bolden.* If the decisions had gone the other way, or if Congress had not continued and expanded its protective acts, progress toward political equality would not only have been stopped but might well have been reversed, as it was a century earlier. Among the few scholarly dissenters, the most comprehensive case has been offered by Abigail Thernstrom. What is Thernstrom's argument, and how well does it hold up, especially in light of the events of the first Reconstruction?

"The aim of the Voting Rights Act—the *single* aim," she asserts, "was black enfranchisement in the South." Four years later, in *Allen* v. *State Board of Elections,* the Court went well beyond the original intent of

72. *Allen* v. *State Board of Elections,* 393 U.S. 544 (1969).
73. *White* v. *Regester,* 412 U.S. 755 (1973).
74. *Rogers* v. *Lodge,* 458 U.S. 613 (1982).
75. *Thornburg* v. *Gingles,* 478 U.S. 30 (1986).

the law when it "turned a minor provision of the act—Section 5—into a major tool with which to combat white resistance to black power." Nevertheless, presumably because of Mississippi's notorious record of discrimination and because its attempt to counteract increased black registration was so blatant, Thernstrom grudgingly approves *Allen,* calling the decision "both correct and inevitable." However, she finds its consequences for other jurisdictions troubling. By implicitly enlarging the definition of enfranchisement, the Court made "proportionate ethnic and racial representation . . . an entitlement," which requires "gerrymandering to maximize minority officeholding." These "large and unanticipated results" brought the nation to "a point no one envisioned in 1965."[76] Marveling that minority electoral rights have enjoyed overwhelming congressional support since 1965 while efforts to combat racial and ethnic discrimination in housing and employment have been bitterly opposed and those in education completely stalled, Thernstrom seeks to eliminate the anomaly by convincing her readers that the Voting Rights Act is now only another affirmative action program.[77]

Allen is not the only Supreme Court case she criticizes. *White* v. *Regester's* judgment was "abstruse," its findings of fact "unexplained assertions of indeterminate weight" that "lacked coherence." Without a complete definition of a fair democratic process, which she apparently thinks it was the Court's duty to provide, the list of factors in *Regester* was arbitrary, and therefore unconstitutional, because "arbitrary federal interference with local and state electoral arrangements is in clear violation of the Constitution." Yet the attempt to codify the decision "simplifies what cannot be simplified; makes orderly a process that is inherently disorderly."[78] *Regester* was a "Chinese menu approach," a formula that never worked, in which factors could be chosen at random to prove tautologically the existence of racial discrimination.[79] *Rogers* v. *Lodge* she condemns as unfaithful to *Mobile* v. *Bolden,* a decision that she terms "principled, simple, and tight" at one point and condemns as vague at another.[80] Nor does she like *Thornburg* v. *Gingles* because of its rejection of the "multicausal" attack on the statistical methods commonly used

76. Thernstrom 1987, 3–9, 30. Although Thernstrom surely does not disagree with *Gomillion,* she barely mentions it (at pages 176–77) and misrepresents its findings when she does. The connection between disfranchisement and dilution, so obvious in *Gomillion,* would no doubt interfere with the argument she wants to make.
77. Thernstrom 1987, 6, 233.
78. Thernstrom 1987, 73–75, 227.
79. Thernstrom 1987, 127, 136.
80. Thernstrom 1987, 75–76, 133.

to determine racially polarized voting and because it "distorts the meaning of electoral opportunity." If blacks are a minority in a jurisdiction, she asserts, they have no right to any representation at all.[81]

Nor are judges the only ones to feel Thernstrom's wrath. Almost all members of Congress are blind, gullible, unobservant, incompetent, or Machiavellian. The mention of discriminatory "effect" in section 5 of the original 1965 Voting Rights Act was "unnoticed." The 1970 amendments "reinforced the act in unintended and unforeseen ways." In 1981 "slapdash, inattentive" House members cast merely "symbolic votes," while the strategy of the leading prospective opponent of the Voting Rights Act, Representative Henry Hyde, was so inept that it presented "a gift" to the bill's supporters, and the Reagan administration's indecisiveness robbed it of any influence whatsoever in the struggle. Senator Orrin Hatch, the book's only heroic figure, was a man of considerable "political acumen," who had, she thinks, the best of all the arguments but commanded almost no votes, betrayed as he was by Senator Robert Dole and other ambitious opportunists. By contrast, Representative Don Edwards and the "diehards," a "determined minority hewing to a hard line" within the voting rights lobby, were insidiously crafty, seeking to "deflect scrutiny" of changes in section 2 that aimed at overruling *Bolden,* harassing potential congressional witnesses who disagreed with them, and, with their "self-proclaimed moral superiority" and deplorable perseverance, overwhelming moderates who had "soft hearts and weak stomachs." Even before 1981, members of Congress, as well as lobbyists, had deliberately obfuscated the voting rights issue by conflating disfranchisement and dilution. The black and brown masses, she thinks, were in no danger of losing their votes, but by charging that they were, the civil rights forces could create safe seats for black and Mexican-American politicians.[82]

During the 1981–82 battle over renewal, Thernstrom charges, the media, "with few exceptions, functioned as part of" the civil rights lobby and "often . . . suppressed information" that might hurt The Cause. Judges on the District Court for the District of Columbia, along with officials of the Department of Justice, wantonly ignored decisions of the Supreme Court. Instead of administering the Voting Rights Act honestly, the Justice Department has created "detours around the law" in an effort to protect and extend the influence, not of minority voters, but of minority

81. Thernstrom 1987, 206.
82. Thernstrom 1987, 26, 38, 101–02, 84, 107, 114–16, 135–36, 83, 87, 98–99, 41, 45–46, 53, 58, 104, 118–19.

officeholders. Those who support the Voting Rights Act as it exists today, she proclaims, are "promoting racial separation" and "inhibit[ing] political integration."[83] One who makes so many harsh accusations against so many people can hardly complain when her own work is subjected to scrutiny.

Although Thernstrom never explicitly describes the world as she would like it to be, her critique implies a vision. Section 5, the preclearance clause of the Voting Rights Act, should have been allowed to lapse, perhaps as early as 1970, because it was proposed only to meet a temporary emergency. Once discrimination against southern blacks in the administration of literacy tests had been eliminated and any southern white efforts to prevent blacks from registering through some other subterfuge had been restrained, there was no further need for section 5. Consequently that provision, which has been distorted through "radical" decisions such as the one in *Allen,* should be repealed, because, as applied, it represents an "extraordinary usurpation of traditional local prerogatives by federal authorities," by which "the career attorneys who roam the halls of the Department of Justice, but seldom the streets of a southern town" can "override decisions arrived at democratically."[84]

Section 4 of the law, which bans literacy tests, would presumably remain, although one who shares the "optimism about American society and its political process" of the opponents of the 1982 amendments, as Thernstrom manifestly does, would not expect a reimposition of such tests even if the proviso were scrapped. Section 2 should be amended to return it to what she thinks was its original meaning, a mere restatement of the Fifteenth Amendment containing an implicit intent test.[85] Library floors would be littered with Supreme Court opinions that would be reversed or made irrelevant—*Allen, Regester, Lodge, Gingles.* Among major voting rights decisions, only Justice Potter Stewart's plurality opinion in *Bolden,* which even Thernstrom admits offers little guidance on how to determine intent, would survive.

In the *Civil Rights Cases,* which overturned the 1875 law mandating

83. Thernstrom 1987, 107, 118, 138, 157, 187, 242.

84. Thernstrom 1987, 25, 31, 46, 78, 104, 168, 237. In her concluding chapter, Thernstrom denies this implication of her earlier argument, saying that she would keep section 5 to guard against intentional discrimination (which she proposes no standards for proving) and backsliding from the previous proportion of minority seats (which, in using an implicit proportional representation standard, contradicts arguments that she makes throughout the book). Because of the inconsistency between this isolated paragraph on page 236 and the burden of her rationale, I have emphasized what seems to me the main line of her case.

85. Thernstrom 1987, 81, 132.

equality of access to national public accommodations, Justice Joseph Bradley announced that after slavery and its "concomitants" had been abolished, "there must be some stage in the progress of [the African American's] elevation when he takes the rank of a mere citizen, and ceases to be the special favorite of the laws, and when his rights as a citizen, or a man, are to be protected in the ordinary modes by which other men's rights are protected."[86] In an eerie echo of Bradley, Thernstrom asks rhetorically "how much special protection from white competition are black candidates entitled to?" Civil rights advocates, she says, should "trust in the political process left substantially to its own devices."[87] Like Bradley during the first Reconstruction, she would remove most of the legislative and judicial protections of the most recent Reconstruction.

Thernstrom's argument suffers from her failure to set out explicit models for the determination of intent, of the normal course of policy development, and of the consequences of policy changes. At key points, she distorts the historical and factual record, most often by omission or by ripping facts from their larger context. Most if not all of these difficulties would have been avoided had she explicitly compared experiences in the two Reconstructions, especially the unraveling of the first.

One of the primary reasons for the length and heat of the scholarly controversy over the original intent of the Fourteenth Amendment is that Republican members of Congress and of the state legislatures that ratified the amendment devoted comparatively few words to explaining what they meant by "privileges or immunities," "equal protection," and "due process." Frustratingly to modern scholars, they spent much more time discussing Confederate disfranchisement and debt.[88] But the amount of attention devoted in floor debate to one provision of a law may not be a good guide to its later or even immediate importance. The lack of attention may represent instead a strategic decision on the part of each side to focus its rhetoric on what unites its forces and divides its opponents. Radical Republicans might disagree on whether the rights of corporations should be protected or whether schools or public places in the South ought to be integrated, but there was no division over their refusal to pay the debts of the secessionist traitors. In other instances, legislators may stress what they perceive to be the strongest or weakest facets of the bill, depending on whether they generally support or oppose it, and

86. *Civil Rights Cases,* 3 S.Ct. 18 at 31 (1883).
87. Thernstrom 1987, 5, 240.
88. Kelly 1956, 1077, 1084; Kaczorowski 1972–73, 379; Curtis 1986, 6.

each side may respond to the other's attacks. In the controversy over the Fair Elections Bill of 1890, Republicans concentrated on the corruption of southern elections and Democrats on the threat that national regulation posed to states' rights; but each did from time to time refer to the other's position. Often, as in the controversies over the proposed provisions on officeholding and on banning literacy and property tests in the Fifteenth Amendment, members' actions and statements were subject to more than one interpretation.

Applied to the question of the intent of the 1965 Voting Rights Act and the subsequent amendments, these historical reflections suggest that expectations about the importance of section 5 cannot be gauged by the comparatively small amount of attention paid to it in the published committee hearings and reports or in floor debate. Southerners brayed incessantly about states' rights, while Yankees recounted lurid tales of the blatantly discriminatory administration of literacy tests and harshly condemned the inequity of requiring poor people to pay for the privilege of voting.

The very nature of section 5 militated against clear definition, for it was an administrative remedy designed to prevent southern states from using new as well as familiar means of inhibiting black voting power. The few discussions of what it was meant to cover, therefore, were necessarily vague. In his opening statement in the House hearings, for instance, Attorney General Nicholas Katzenbach, the Johnson administration's most important witness, noted that "The tests and devices with which the bill deals include the usual literacy, understanding, and interpretation tests that are easily susceptible to manipulation, *as well as a variety of other repressive schemes*," and he prominently mentioned *Gomillion*.[89] Inviting an even broader interpretation, Assistant Attorney General Burke Marshall declared that the changes in election laws that would be disallowed under section 5 were not limited to "tests and devices" but included such measures as poll taxes. Katzenbach declined to enumerate the sorts of changes that might be legitimate, "because there are an awful lot of things that could be started for purposes of evading the Fifteenth Amendment if there is the desire to do so."[90] Within the Justice Department in 1965, the expansive potential of section 5 was clearly recognized and hotly debated.[91] Even as originally introduced,

89. House of Representatives 1965a, 9, 15 (italics added).
90. House of Representatives 1965a, 72, 95. What became section 5 of the bill was originally section 8. I refer to it as section 5 to minimize confusion.
91. Graham 1990, 169.

therefore, section 5 seems easily open-ended enough to have covered structural changes in voting systems.

The section was amended in the House in 1965 to prohibit not only "qualifications or procedures for voting" but any "standard, practice, or procedure with respect to voting," and section 2 was similarly expanded.[92] This final language was arguably as broad as the proposal made by the ever-prescient Don Edwards, which would have prohibited any covered jurisdiction from enacting "any election law or ordinance" different from those in effect on November 1, 1964, a suggestion that Edwards said was offered in an attempt "to preclude other devices which might be used to discriminate, such as changing the boundaries of voting districts or qualifications for holding office."[93] Thus the nature of the remedy established by section 5, its language, and authoritative comments at the relevant hearings strongly support Chief Justice Warren's opinion in *Allen*. Combined with the cautions drawn from the example of the framers' discussions of the Fourteenth Amendment on how to interpret evidence about the weight that Congress intends to place on different parts of laws, this evidence seriously undermines Thernstrom's case about the initial insignificance of section 5 and the *exclusive* concern of Congress and the Johnson administration with getting blacks registered.[94]

Suppose for a moment, however, that these considerations were irrelevant and that an unruly Justice Department and an ideologically committed Supreme Court had overstepped the clear bounds that Congress had meant to impose in 1965. Would one not expect to have seen an attempt in 1970 to rein in section 5, if it could not be repealed altogether, to confine its language so clearly to pure registration and ballot casting that *Allen* would be reduced to a curiosity? Politically, conditions would have seemed primed for such a move, with Richard Nixon's "southern strategy" having paid such large recent dividends, George Wallace's segregationist following ripe for Republican harvest, John Mitchell and Jerris Leonard in place of Nicholas Katzenbach and Burke Marshall at the Department of Justice, and James Eastland still potent in the Senate. A decade later, when the Supreme Court, according to civil rights supporters, distorted the original intent of section 2 in *Bolden,* there was a tremendous outcry and a massive and effective campaign to amend section 2 to reinstate the pre-*Bolden* understanding of the law. But although the Nixon adminis-

92. House of Representatives 1965b, 3; House of Representatives 1965a, 864.
93. House of Representatives 1965a, 767.
94. Of course, no one doubts that that was their *chief* concern. Thernstrom's claim goes much farther.

tration and the Deep South members of Congress sought outright repeal of section 5 in 1970, no one seems to have proposed merely confining the bureaucracy and the Court to banning nonstructural electoral changes, as they would have if Thernstrom's interpretation were correct.[95] And, of course, Congress implicitly accepted the decision in *Allen* by renewing the temporary part of the law for another five years. One of the principal Republican spokesmen on voting rights, Representative William McCulloch of Ohio, commented during the 1970 debate that the Supreme Court's decision in *Allen* guaranteed that "at long last after 4 years Section 5 will become effective."[96] In her analysis of the intent of section 5 then, Thernstrom does not take into account what did *not* happen, or even what *was* said, despite the obvious relevance of such facts to her contentions.

No sins loom as large in Thernstrom's jeremiad as the linguistic dishonesty of the liberals. They twisted the meaning of voting rights deliberately, she charges, substituting a complex and controversial policy of proportional representation and guaranteed minority officeholding for a simple and consensually supported one of ensuring that each individual has a chance to vote.

This indictment is misguided for three reasons. First, nothing in morals or law prohibits the originators of a policy from monitoring its success and changing the means of attaining their goals, or even those goals themselves, as they gain experience. Indeed, this is just what Congress and the Justice Department did in their efforts to expand black voting rights in the 1957, 1960, and 1964 civil rights laws, and what an earlier Congress had done or tried to do in 1866 with the Fourteenth Amendment, in 1867 with the Military Reconstruction Acts, in 1868–69 with the southern state constitutions and the Fifteenth Amendment, in 1870–72 with the Enforcement Acts, in 1875 with the "Force Bill," and in 1890 with the Fair Elections Bill. Unless a legislative policy emerges full-grown from some Jovian legislator's brow, that is just how policy is always set. Voting rights policy, then, provides no occasion for special denunciation on that ground.

Second, civil rights lobbyists were not so sinful as Thernstrom charges. Far from attempting to "deflect scrutiny" from the *Bolden* decision in 1981–82, for instance, they spotlighted it from the first day of hearings in the House, when the first witness, Vernon Jordan, pointed to the

95. The most extensive treatments of the 1970 renewal battle are Lawson 1985, 121–57; and Graham 1990, 346–65.

96. Quoted in Graham 1990, 359.

reversal of *Bolden* as one of the purposes of the proposed amendments to the Voting Rights Act. The Senate report on the amended act devoted at least seventy-three pages to the matter.[97] Although the members of Congress may not have understood every nuance of every amendment, the hearings in 1965 and 1981–82 were extensive, the debates were informative compared with those on more technical issues that are more foreign to politicians than the familiar and easily grasped issues of ethnic politics and electoral rules, and the printed reports and dissenting statements were generally clear and well argued. It is difficult to imagine many other matters on which Congress has acted in a more considered fashion.

Third and most important, disfranchisement and vote dilution are not pure concepts. They not only merge into each other, they are complementary, each increasing the other's force, as Thernstrom would have had to admit if she had confronted the lengthier historical record.

It is in fact her radically foreshortened perspective, not, as she claims, a difference in disposition between her optimism about America and the civil rights community's pessimism that accounts most deeply for the differences in judgment between her and her critics.[98] Two pages on the experiences of litigators bring her from 1957 to 1965. There is nothing on Reconstruction, on nineteenth century attempts to guarantee the right to vote, on disfranchisement at the turn of the century, or on the struggles against the white primary and the poll tax, even though the literature on all these subjects was extensive long before Thernstrom began writing and every one of the topics demonstrates connections and overlaps between dilution and disfranchisement.

The white primary, for instance, formally disfranchised no one. Blacks could, under its rules, register and vote freely in the general election. What it did was to debase their suffrage, to dilute it, by banning them from having a chance to influence the outcome in the only election that mattered, just as at-large elections in areas with racially polarized voting patterns do. Nor did the poll tax by itself preclude people from voting. Instead, it made them pay for the privilege, and groups such as blacks that had fewer members who could afford to pay lost influence. The poll tax, in other words, affected the worth of an individual black's vote by diminishing the power of the principal group to which he or she belonged. In this sense, of course, Thernstrom's vague and unsupported statement

97. House of Representatives 1981b, 18–19; Senate 1982b, 15–43, 127–58, 169–73, 177–87.
98. Thernstrom 1987, 9–10, 240–41.

that "In the American constitutional tradition, it is often said, there are no group rights to representation" is misleading.[99] To discourage from voting a significant proportion of members of a group that others treat as distinct reduces the value of the vote for every individual member of that group, and vice versa. For members of such groups, individual and group rights, disfranchisement and dilution, are integrally connected.

In brief, history, even the fairly recent history of the 1930s, 1940s, and 1950s, undermines Thernstrom's absolute distinction between disfranchisement and dilution, and once this distinction collapses, her chief thesis erodes and her moralistic indictment of the civil rights proponents collapses.

What of the consequences of policy change? What if, as Thernstrom's critique suggests, the Justice Department mostly got out of the business of preclearing changes in electoral rules? What if section 2 and the Fourteenth and Fifteenth Amendments were interpreted to impose an intent criterion that, Thernstrom says approvingly, "made cases harder to win"? What if dilution of the Latino vote were not illegal, as dilution of Italian or Polish votes is not illegal, on the ground that Mexican Americans and Puerto Rican Americans have, in Thernstrom's view, "no legacy of disfranchisement comparable to that experienced by southern blacks"?[100]

The nineteenth century lessons, as well as the more recent aftermaths of the destruction of the white primary in the 1940s and the literacy test in the 1960s, give one little reason to be sanguine—certainly not as sanguine as Thernstrom, who has a tendency to ignore evidence to the contrary.[101] As records of voting rights cases before and since the 1987 publication of *Whose Votes Count?* have shown repeatedly, racially polarized voting continues to be a fact of political life in the United States, particularly in the South.[102] Appeals to racial prejudice continue to appear in every election year, most recently in the Willie Horton ads run by George Bush's 1988 presidential campaign and Jesse Helms's ads against affirmative action. Even in pluralistic, liberal Los Angeles, intentional ethnic gerrymandering and racially polarized voting kept Latinos off the most important county governing board in the country until a legal suit, brought under the Voting Rights Act and the Fourteenth and Fifteenth

99. Thernstrom 1987, 7.
100. Thernstrom 1987, 81, 55.
101. Karlan and McCrary 1988. Similarly, see Parker 1990.
102. McCrary 1990. For evidence outside the South see, for example, Pettigrew and Alston 1988.

Amendments, required districts to be drawn in 1990 to give them a fair opportunity to elect a candidate of their choice.[103]

Perhaps even more fundamentally, Thernstrom mistakes the causes for racial discrimination in electoral affairs. As the record of the northern Democrats on civil rights roll calls in the nineteenth century shows, it was not simple racism or racial hostility that undermined support for black voting rights. And as a more detailed look at the history of disfranchisement and the Jim Crow laws in the late nineteenth and early twentieth centuries would demonstrate, it was not so much that southern whites hated blacks or found contact with them distasteful. Black voting rights and even legalized segregation were more matters of racial *power* than of unthinking racial *animosity*. Consequently, a decline in the overall level of white racism, which has obviously occurred since 1960, does not guarantee the fair treatment of racial minorities if, as in the nineteenth century, national legal and judicial safeguards were to be removed.[104] Indeed, the first Reconstruction provides a realistic counterfactual example with which the period since 1965 can be usefully compared. Replace *Allen* with *Reese* or *Cruikshank,* emasculating congressional protections of the right to vote in a fair electoral structure, or repeal section 5, as Democrats repealed the Supervisory Law in 1894, or fail to overthrow the murky intent-based *Bolden* decision, as 1890 Republicans barely failed to pass the Lodge Fair Elections Bill, and the second Reconstruction might also have begun to unravel.

Ninety-five years ago, on the twenty-fifth anniversary of an earlier minority voting rights act, there were few reasons for congratulations or joy among civil rights supporters. Today, drugs, dropouts, and disease may plague the ghettos and barrios, the growing disparity between the economic and physical health of the rich and the poor would embarrass a properly sensitive nation, and social reform is as unpopular as fiscal responsibility. But the second Reconstruction can boast of one success, at least: minority-group members can often choose candidates who are their first preferences. They can do so, as their great-grandfathers could not, because the national legislature and judiciary have been willing to guard not only the exercise of the right to cast a ballot, but also the right not to have their votes submerged by discriminatory electoral structures. Those who would remove or weaken those protections had best hesitate, while they relearn or reflect upon the nation's earlier history.

103. See Kousser 1991.
104. For the decline in white racism see, for example, Schuman, Steeh, and Bobo 1985.

Voting Rights and the American Regulatory State

HUGH DAVIS GRAHAM

IN THE QUARTER CENTURY since its passage, the Voting Rights Act of 1965 has been one of the most effective instruments of social legislation in the modern era of American reform. In Mississippi the proportion of blacks registered to vote increased from 6.7 percent in 1964 to 67.5 percent in 1970. Throughout the South by 1970 nearly a million new black voters had been added to the rolls, and more than 400 black officials had been elected. Within a decade the law transformed the South's historic pattern of racist politics beyond recognition. Congressional renewals and expansions of the act in 1970, 1975, and 1982 reflected a growing consensus that support for the act was politically essential. By 1990 Virginia had a black governor, 24 blacks and 10 Hispanics sat in Congress, 417 black and 124 Hispanic representatives held seats in state legislatures, and 4,338 blacks and 1,425 Hispanics held office in city or county governments.[1] Indeed, the political mobilization of African Americans since 1965 has transformed their historic marginality in political life: since the 1970s their participation has equaled and often exceeded that of whites of similar socioeconomic status.[2]

There has been little disagreement that the act has been effective and beneficial. And unlike the issues generated by affirmative action in employment or higher education, which have precipitated sharp disputes in election campaigns and courtrooms, and on talk shows and college campuses, voting rights policy has seemed immune from widespread public distemper. Public opinion surveys in 1990 showed that although white respondents increasingly believed affirmative action policies unfairly discriminated against them, they did not generally object to voting rights policy.[3]

Against this context of public acceptance, however, debates on the direction of voting rights policy among legislators, career civil servants,

1. See Morgan Kousser's chapter in this volume.
2. Jaynes and Williams 1989, 230–38.
3. Edsall 1991, A6; Berke 1991b, E5.

agency consultants, interest-group lobbyists, social science researchers, and legal experts have crackled with acrimony. Conferences on voting rights have been so charged with emotion and hostility that some potential participants have declined to attend. Disagreements over policy have revealed a depth of bitterness that seems ill-matched to the magnitude of the social problem. Scholarly literature has featured accusations of malfeasance in research methodology that have reached considerably beyond the normal canons of social science debate: in 1987, for instance, Abigail Thernstrom's *Whose Votes Count?*, which criticized parallels between minority preferences in affirmative action policy and the model of proportional representation that governed many enforcement policies under the Voting Rights Act, drew an unusually hostile reception.[4]

That the literature is argumentive and polarized can in part be explained by the writers and the context. As the editors of *Publius* conceded in a special 1986 issue on voting rights, "Almost without exception, students of the VRA are partisans of the act and its goals."[5] For a generation, defenders of the act, mostly lawyers and political scientists, have provided the scholarship as well as the expert courtroom testimony — an impressive corpus by any standard — and revisionists have not been welcome. Too much of the writing by these experts, however, has been suffused with a testimonial tone, usually favoring minority plaintiffs, that weakens its credibility.[6] Their articles in law reviews and social science journals, while richly documentary, often mirror the attributes of the adversary process they describe. As a consequence, discussions of voting rights issues have been somewhat isolated from discussions of the broader issues of civil rights enforcement.

In the controversies surrounding the enforcement of civil rights policy since 1964, the importance of historical context in determining legislative intent has brought history and historians into the courtroom in unprecedented numbers. But the adversarial format has narrowed the vision of

4. For example, Karlan and McCrary 1988, 751, assert that Thernstrom's book "so distorts the evidence that it cannot be taken seriously as scholarship." A similar tone is reflected in Morgan Kousser's attack in this book on Thernstrom's scholarship. Scholarly discourse over voting rights has taken on some of the attributes of the debate over "political correctness," and to its detriment has come to resemble the volatile dispute of the 1980s over bilingual education.

5. Elazar and Kinkaid 1986, 3.

6. See, for example, Ball, Krane, and Lauth, *Compromised Compliance: Implementation of the 1965 Voting Rights Act*, 1982. The authors' usually judicious analysis of the evidence is contradicted by the book's partisan thesis and title.

historical analysis to case studies.[7] Such studies of electoral behavior in Mobile and Houston and other communities are essential building blocks of policy history, but their compass is narrow and they give historical analysis too little room to maneuver.[8]

This chapter interprets the Voting Rights Act as a special component of a broader movement in social policy that radically transformed the American state during the 1960s. The civil rights movement was at the forefront of a vast shift in the relationship of American citizens and their national government.[9] By the end of the 1960s the struggle for civil rights had combined with other social movements—those to protect citizens from air and water pollution, unsafe products, and dangerous highways and workplaces. Together they created a new model of social regulation. But the model has rested on a paradox. The structure of civil rights regulation, grounded in the breakthrough laws of 1964 and 1965, was built on legal and administrative foundations laid during the Progressive and New Deal eras of economic regulation. This tradition was based on a tort model that enumerated harmful acts and policed violators through courtlike orders to stop. After 1965, however, the implementation process led civil rights policy, and with it voting rights policy, into a new matrix of social regulation. The emphasis shifted from intentional tort and equal treatment to no-fault standards and equal results. Civil rights implementation was caught between the shifting focus and created tensions that were not shared by the movements to protect consumers and the environment.

The similarities between civil rights regulation and the new social regulation are important. Their common origins, structures, and processes have provided a source of legitimacy for the civil rights coalition and for enforcement agencies, especially when their affirmative action requirements have been attacked for violating the Civil Rights Act itself. The differences, however, are perhaps more important. They are the source of a troublesome schizophrenia that has fueled the acrimony that surrounds the contemporary debate.

7. An effective example is McCrary 1984, 47–63. McCrary is a historian with extensive experience as an expert witness for plaintiffs in voting rights litigation.

8. A notable exception is Steven F. Lawson's landmark two-volume study (1976, 1985) of the evolution of voting rights policy from 1944 through 1982. The study concentrates on the link between federal policy and black electoral politics in the South but does not attempt to assess the Voting Rights Act systematically within the larger context of the American administrative state.

9. Graham 1990a.

Civil Rights Policy and the New Social Regulation

On the eve of the "rights revolution" of the 1960s, the Progressive–New Deal tradition of economic regulation had matured into a coherent, time-tested model of national administration. The civil rights movement, forced to build its enforcement apparatus on the foundations laid by economic regulation, inherited a poor fit that plagued new agencies such as the Equal Employment Opportunity Commission and heightened the tensions that would mark the debates over affirmative action in the 1970s and later. To understand how this occurred, one must first understand the structural origins of the economic model that undergirded the civil rights laws of 1964 and 1965.

Economic regulation was created to police the evils of monopoly control, anticompetitive pricing, rate fixing, and the abuse of labor. The federal economic regulatory agencies were typically independent commissions and boards created by Congress in two bursts of reform. The Progressive era had contributed the Federal Reserve Board (1913), and the Federal Trade Commission (1914). The New Deal added the Federal Communications Commission (1934), the Securities and Exchange Commission (1934), the National Labor Relations Board (1935), and the Civil Aeronautics Board (1938).[10]

These were quasi-judicial bodies whose administrative model was adjudicatory. Rooted in the civil law of tort, they inherited the standard of Anglo-American law based on intent. Their regulatory structure was vertical, presiding top to bottom over relatively coherent sectors of the American economy (railroads, trucking and shipping, energy, communications, securities, airlines). Their quasi-judicial processes were "retail," with case-by-case hearings in courtlike proceedings, followed by panel rulings enforced by orders to cease and desist from anticompetitive or unfair practices. Remedies for violations could include make-whole relief (for example, requiring the reinstatement of fired union organizers with back pay), but generally the impact of economic regulation on citizens was indirect and diffuse. The quasi-judicial model was basically reactive and complaint-driven, and its remedies tended to correct specific abuses. This summary does little justice to the system's complexity, but it posits

---

10. There were others, of course, and the granddaddy of them all, the Interstate Commerce Commission (1887). Reagan 1987, 45–71; Breyer 1982, part 1.

a model that the civil rights reformers of the 1960s would find increasingly ill-suited to the needs of modern social regulation.[11]

A new machinery of social regulation emerged during the 1960s in response to a convergence of the black civil rights movement, the new feminist movement, and a host of others that confronted such social threats as environmental pollution, dangerous consumer products and services, unsafe transportation and workplaces, discrimination in jobs and housing and schooling, and even death and maiming in foreign wars. The denominator of the new social regulation was a demand that citizens be protected from being harmed or put at risk by private or governmental behavior. Between 1900 and 1964, Congress had established only one regulatory agency with such a primary responsibility: the Food and Drug Administration (1938). Between 1964 and 1972, however, it created seven new federal agencies with social regulation as their mandate: the Equal Employment Opportunity Commission (1964), the National Transportation Safety Board (1966), the Council on Environmental Quality (1969), the Environmental Protection Agency, National Highway Traffic Safety Administration, and Occupational Safety and Health Administration (1970), and the Consumer Product Safety Commission (1972).

This new social model of regulation differed from the economic model in several fundamental respects. Social regulators were concerned more with reducing future risk than with punishing past behavior, even if there was intent to harm. The Environmental Protection Agency, for example, concentrated on tougher emissions requirements for new automobile engines, not on punishment for the inefficient gas-guzzlers of the past. The regulators' mode of enforcement was therefore "wholesale" rather than "retail"; they issued blanket new requirements—for automotive emissions, waterway discharges, workshop safety, pharmaceutical toxicity—covering entire industrial sectors instead of pursuing violators case by case in response to complaints. The administrative style of the social regulators was thus more legislative and policymaking than adjudicatory. These differences led not to orders that firms stop this price-fixing practice or that union-busting practice, but rather to a detailed process of rulemaking based on future standards of compliance that were often technical and statistically verifiable. These numerical standards and their no-fault rationale tended to sever the old direct link between intent and harm. Quantitative evidence of damage to lungs in Pittsburgh, for example,

11. Graham 1990a, 3–24, 456–72.

was sufficient to warrant remedial action, and evidence of steel industry intent was irrelevant. Proof of a polluter's evil designs need not be adduced by social regulators in order to prevent future harm.

Civil Rights Policy: Precursor to Social Regulation

The movement for black civil rights during the 1960s provided the instigation for the transition from economic to social regulation. The conservative coalition, fearing the government bureaucracy's expansion of regulatory responsibility, sought to limit federal government control of civil rights regulation by channeling its enforcement through the traditionally more conservative courts rather than through administrative agencies. This strategy shaped the court-centered enforcement of the Civil Rights Act of 1957, which concentrated on protecting voting rights as a private rather than a public right. Instead of providing government prosecutors or administrative relief, the law required that citizens bring suit and prove violation in the tradition of the civil law. Guided by traditional Republican opposition to New Dealish economic regulation, Everett Dirksen of Illinois, the Senate minority leader, then engineered a compromise in the Civil Rights Act of 1964, as the price of delivering the Republican votes needed to break the southern filibuster, that hamstrung the new Equal Employment Opportunity Commission even as a model of economic regulation. The EEOC was thus deprived by the Dirksen compromise of the cease-and-desist authority normally enjoyed by the economic regulatory commissions, such as the National Labor Relations Board and the state fair employment commissions pioneered by New York, which had provided the model for the EEOC. The compromise of 1964 was designed to prohibit the EEOC from aggressively enforcing nondiscrimination as a public right in the workplace.[12]

In frustration the almost toothless EEOC in the late 1960s launched a campaign of subversion against its own founding charter. Isolated from Congress and weakly represented in the upper reaches of the executive branch, the commission turned for support to the protected classes that formed its major constituencies—chiefly the black, feminist, and Hispanic rights organizations. In response to demands from these groups that the EEOC produce more dramatic results, the agency moved toward rulemaking. Against a backdrop of riots and burning cities, between 1966

12. Graham 1990a, 125–52.

and 1970 it developed guidelines on employee testing, for example, that required equal passing rates for minorities and whites. By 1970 the agency had developed a proportional model of minority representation in the workforce that the Dirksen compromise had explicitly prohibited in the Civil Rights Act. The federal courts subsequently approved the EEOC's interpretation, most notably in *Griggs* v. *Duke Power Company* in 1971, as consistent with the broader purposes of the 1964 law.[13]

During its first decade of enforcing title 7 of the Civil Rights Act, the EEOC successfully shifted from an equal-treatment to an equal-results standard of enforcement, and thus from a test of civil rights compliance based on intent to one based on effects. The *Griggs* decision upheld the EEOC's "disparate impact" standard for private employers, which presumed that in the absence of discrimination, minority groups would be proportionally represented in the workforce. In 1972 when Congress extended EEOC authority to cover employees of government and educational institutions nationwide, the agency began enforcing a proportional model of representation at all levels of government employment, with provisions made for differing levels of skill and training. A similar shift occurred in the array of new executive agencies created under title 6 of the Civil Rights Act to enforce contract compliance in federally assisted programs. The new agencies and subagencies included the Office of Federal Contract Compliance (OFCC) in the Labor Department, the Office of Civil Rights (OCR) in the Department of Health, Education, and Welfare, and similar offices in most mission agencies, including the Civil Rights Division of the Justice Department and the Office of Minority Business Enterprise (OMBE) that President Richard Nixon created in the Commerce Department in 1969. The OFCC pioneered the Philadelphia plan, which under the Nixon administration won court approval for rules requiring that the composition of work crews at all skill levels on federally aided construction projects reflect the minority population ratios of their metropolitan areas. By the early 1970s, most enforcement agencies in civil rights were requiring "hard" affirmative action plans that gave preferential consideration to minority job applicants. Their procedures were much the same as those of the Environmental Protection Agency, the Office of Safety and Health Administration (OSHA), and other agencies

13. Chief Justice Warren Burger, speaking for a unanimous Court, observed that the administrative interpretation of title 7 by the enforcing agency is "entitled to great deference," and concluded that the guidelines issued by the EEOC should be regarded "as expressing the will of Congress." *Griggs* v. *Duke Power Company*, 401 U.S. 424 at 434 (1971).

in social regulation. They published proposed technical standards of compliance in the *Federal Register,* held hearings, promulgated rules, and threatened to cut off federal funding to those who did not comply and to bar them from bidding on federal contracts.

The Voting Rights Act as Social Regulation

The evolution of the Voting Rights Act and its enforcement activities generally fits the pattern established by the Civil Rights Act. At the core of both laws lies classic American liberalism's bedrock principle of nondiscrimination, the commitment that animated the triumphant reformers of 1964–65. Equal treatment for minorities, so long observed in the breach, meant a color-blind Constitution (and to supporters of the Equal Rights Amendment, a sex-blind Constitution as well) and therefore equal access to hotels, restaurants, parks, schools, jobs, and ballot booths. The most striking similarities are between title 2 of the Civil Rights Act, which desegregated public accommodations and facilities throughout the South with unanticipated speed and ease, and section 4 of the Voting Rights Act, which enfranchised the mass of southern blacks with remarkable thoroughness. Section 4, as radical and effective an innovation as title 2, represented an unprecedented intrusion by federal authority on local prerogatives, an intrusion quickly sustained by the Supreme Court under Chief Justice Earl Warren. Abandoning judicial enforcement through private suits, the enforcement of the Voting Rights Act statistically identified areas of systematic disfranchisement and automatically triggered the intervention of federal officials to guarantee unfettered registration and voting. In its initial five years, section 4 eliminated virtually all barriers to black registration and voting in the seven southern states where literacy tests and similar devices had reduced black voting to a trickle.

In the 1990s we too easily forget that the greatest achievement of the act (which was formally color-blind and enfranchised masses of white voters also) was accomplished by section 4 before the end of the 1960s. Both the 1964 and the 1965 laws asserted centralized federal authority over areas of policy (customer choice, job discrimination, voting requirements) that had hitherto remained under local control. To administer this new authority, both the Civil Rights Act and the Voting Rights Act produced novel machinery. The EEOC was established by title 7 itself. The OFCC and its baker's dozen of subagencies under title 6, however, were created administratively, as was the Voting Section of the Justice

Department, formed within the Civil Rights Division in 1969 by Nixon's attorney general, John Mitchell.[14]

These developments signaled the emergence of new structures and methods of enforcement not contemplated in the founding statutes, but they evolved in a parallel fashion. During the debate over the Civil Rights Act, most attention was devoted to title 2 on public accommodations and to title 7 and the EEOC. Surprisingly little attention was devoted to title 6 by the media, by members of Congress, or by the civil rights groups themselves, including the AFL-CIO, which liberally funded and strongly supported the civil rights reforms of 1964–65. Yet enforcement through contract compliance has proved by far the most powerful and pervasive instrument of government coercion in equal employment policy. Similarly, most debate on the Voting Rights Act focused on the novel statistical trigger in section 4, which was designed to function automatically in the face of years of embarrassing failure under the traditional court-centered approach. Section 5 was added to the 1965 law as a cautionary hedge against backsliding, a necessary but secondary supplement to the teeth of section 4, to protect black voters against the kind of racist, electoral dirty tricks, such as transforming elective into appointive offices and switching from district to at-large elections, that were expected from die-hard white officials in southern areas with large black populations.

Like title 6 of the Civil Rights Act, section 5 provided agency officials in Washington the rationale for expanding their regulatory reach. In the late 1960s this expansion was challenged in court as a violation of the language and intent of the statutes. Construction contractors sued the OFCC for requiring minority preferences in the Philadelphia plan. In Alabama and Mississippi, officials sued the Justice Department for using section 5 to deny preclearance approval to electoral changes that did not directly concern the processes of registration and voting that the Voting Rights Act was designed to reform. The federal courts, however, sustained the regulatory expansion under section 5, much as the decision in *Contractors Association of Eastern Pennsylvania v. Hudgson, Secretary of Labor* (1971) had affirmed the minority preferences required by the Philadelphia plan and the *Griggs* decision had affirmed the disparate impact standard of the EEOC.[15]

---

14. Lawson 1985, 162–63; Graham 1990a, 360–62.

15. The Philadelphia plan was upheld in *Contractors Association of Eastern Pennsylvania* v. *Hudgson, Secretary of Labor,* 442 F.2d 159 (3d Cir. 1971), *cert. denied,* 404 U.S. 854 (1971). The Supreme Court affirmed the section 5 authority of the Department of Justice in *South Carolina* v. *Katzenbach,* 383 U.S. 301 (1966).

Following these victories in the federal courts, the civil rights enforcement agencies consolidated their rulemaking authority. Congress declined to overturn the Philadelphia plan in 1969 (in rare alliance, the Nixon administration and the civil rights organizations defeated the southerners and organized labor). In 1970 Congress rejected Nixon's proposal for a nationwide, sixth-grade-education voting standard and extended the Voting Rights Act for five more years. In 1972 it rejected cease-and-desist power for the EEOC but extended the agency's authority to cover state and local government employees and educational institutions. Also in 1972 Congress affirmed the full application of title 6 enforcement for women and sent the Equal Rights Amendment to the states for ratification. In 1975 it extended to selected language minorities the protections of the Voting Rights Act. The effect of the 1975 law was primarily to add Hispanics to blacks as a protected class and to expand covered jurisdictions by adding areas of heavy Hispanic population in the Southwest to the southeastern states originally covered in 1965. The 1975 legislation expanded Voting Rights Act coverage to all or parts of twenty-two states.

Clientele "Capture" and the Civil Rights Movement

Under the Carter administration in the late 1970s, the civil rights enforcement agencies were following a pattern common in many of the mission agencies: they had become increasingly influenced by their chief clientele groups. For the EEOC and the title 6 agencies, this meant adding political weight through an expanding list of client blocs as the rights revolution spread to new constituencies—women, Asians, American Indians, the elderly, the physically and mentally disabled, gays and lesbians. For voting rights enforcement under section 5 this had come to mean increasing the electoral power of blacks and Hispanics, the two principal minorities that remained residentially segregated. This reality somewhat isolated the two constituencies from the accumulating ranks of title 6 beneficiaries, especially women. In 1988 women constituted just 2 percent of the Senate, 5 percent of the House, and held 15.5 percent of seats in state legislatures. Proportional representation in electoral policy, taking account of both historic discrimination and current patterns of electoral success, would enormously increase their officeholding. But women did not live in identifiably female voting districts.

Clientele "capture" was an old tradition in the American administrative state and its politics of bureaucracy. Farm interests dominated the

Department of Agriculture, as did business interests at Commerce, the military-industrial complex at the Pentagon, veterans at the Veterans Administration, educators at the Department of Education. But with the brief exception of the Freedmen's Bureau and the persistent anomaly of the Bureau of Indian Affairs, minority interests had historically been excluded from the politics of agency capture. Before the 1960s they had not been part of the "iron triangle" coalitions based on bonds of mutual interest, such as one that linked the Army Corps of Engineers, the public works committees in Congress, and the economic interests that profited from damming rivers and dredging harbors. But the civil rights revolution of the 1960s created new constituencies to join the traditional practices of mutual backscratching in pluralistic, Madisonian America.

After 1965 the proliferating constituencies of civil rights regulation found effective political coordination through the Leadership Conference on Civil Rights, which by the 1980s included more than 180 member organizations. In the voting rights coalition, the black and Hispanic organizations coexisted somewhat uneasily under the umbrella of the Leadership Conference but generally submerged their differences in a united front that paid handsome bipartisan dividends in Congress. When the Reagan administration attacked the regulatory legacy of the New Deal and the Great Society, the civil rights coalition successfully deflected most of the sorties in Congress. The growing clout of the voting rights coalition was demonstrated impressively in 1982, when section 5 was strengthened and extended for twenty-five years.[16]

By the early 1990s, when the accumulation of Republican-appointed federal judges had produced a judicial reaction against hard affirmative action programs such as minority set-asides in government contracting and proportional requirements in minority hiring, the equivalent requirements of the voting rights regulators seemed to remain largely immune from judicial attack. In 1980 the Supreme Court in *City of Mobile* v. *Bolden* narrowed the scope of section 5 enforcement by holding that the Fourteenth Amendment required a finding of intentional discrimination in voting rights challenges.[17] In 1982, reacting sharply against the *Mobile* ruling, Congress revised section 2 of the Voting Rights Act to require challengers to demonstrate not discriminatory intent but only the unequal effects of electoral districting on potential minority power. This was the equivalent of the "disparate impact" standard that the EEOC had pioneered

16. Pertschuk 1986, 155–56; Thernstrom 1987, 79–136.
17. *City of Mobile* v. *Bolden* 446 U.S. 55 (1980).

under title 7 and, like the affirmative action requirements for proportionate minority hiring that had evolved from the Philadelphia plan in title 6 enforcement, it was based on an implicit model of proportional representation.

The core of the affirmative action rationale that evolved after 1965 was historical: past discrimination had excluded minority groups from equal participation in American life, and the resultant unequal distribution of power and benefits had become institutionally frozen. Because equal treatment alone was deemed insufficient to compensate, minority preference was required to produce the proportionally equal results that would have been expected in the absence of discrimination. In voting rights law, affirmative action policy has taken the form of giving preference to selected minorities in electoral districting arrangements. The potential power of these minorities, most notably blacks and Hispanics, is protected from dilution, while all other groups and interests are denied such protection.

During the 1980s the federal courts, reflecting the more conservative judicial appointments of Republican presidents, generally tightened the judicial scrutiny of minority preferences under title 6 and title 7. But during the same period the federal bench generally supported the broader interpretation of section 5 that Congress reaffirmed in 1982. Indeed, under the Bush administration the Justice Department quickened its support for black and Hispanic challenges under sections 2 and 5. Despite Republican denials of partisan motives, it seems likely in the 1990s that a proliferation in urban areas of single-member electoral districts, where federal policy requires that boundaries be drawn to maximize the electoral chances of blacks and Hispanics, would displace white voters into suburban districts where Republican prospects would brighten.[18]

Affirmative Action in Voting Rights as Social Regulation

Proponents of vigorous affirmative action policies draw support from the model of social regulation that posits a system of administrative regulation that is modern, forward looking, and results oriented. The system is driven by empirical standards that permit scientific verification, and its administrative procedures remain largely unencumbered by the delays of the judicial process. EPA thresholds of permissible toxic chemicals

18. Skerry 1989, 86–102.

in industrial emissions, which can vary according to regional accumulations of pollution, have performed the same standard-setting and compensatory functions as the OFCC's requirements that black workers in Philadelphia's skilled construction industry, only 12 percent in 1970, be increased within five years to reach 30 percent, the black proportion of Philadelphia's metropolitan workforce. By analogy, the logic of affirmative action in voting rights would seem to extend beyond equal access to the ballot box and reach toward minority representation in elective office that approximates the demographic profile of protected classes.

The share of elected minority officials in 1990, of course, was far from proportional to the minority population. Blacks were 11.2 percent of the population, but held no seats in the Senate, 5.5 percent of House seats, and 5.9 percent of the state legislative seats (440 of 7,466). Hispanics held only 2 percent of congressional seats and 1.5 percent of state legislative seats, although the Hispanic population had reached 8 percent of the U.S. total.[19] In electoral politics the historical barriers and the advantages of incumbency have forced black and Hispanic aspirants for elective office to swim upstream. In Mobile, which was one-third black in 1980, no blacks had been elected to the city commission since the city's at-large election system was created in 1911. In Los Angeles, 35 percent of the 8.5 million residents were Hispanic in 1990, but none had held office on the powerful five-man board of supervisors. Heavy Hispanic immigration and high minority birthrates promise to increase both the number of challenged districts and the number of smaller new districts created to make progress toward proportional minority targets. In the sixteen states covered entirely or in part by the Voting Rights Act since 1982, a goal of proportional representation promises to generate a heavy workload for the voting rights bar. From that perspective, voting rights protection would seem to share with environmental and consumer protection a common evolution toward a structure of social regulation that is nationwide, grounded in scientific standards, and governed by empirical results.

Civil Rights and the Politics of Regulation

The equation of civil rights and social regulation, however, does not take into account one fundamental difference. It hinges on the distribution of costs and benefits, a relationship that heavily determines public attitudes toward fairness. In the 1960s, civil rights enforcement and consumer,

19. Graham 1990b, 43–58.

environmental, and safety regulation, reflected the response of government to demands made by newly mobilized African Americans, feminists,
environmentalists, Hispanics, consumers, and other campaigners. The
new regulatory agencies drew political support from these strongly
motivated and politically organized constituencies. A crucial difference
between the two varieties of social regulation, however, flowed from who
benefited from the regulations and who was excluded. On the one hand
the civil rights constituencies sought to advance the interests of such
discrete population subgroups as blacks, Hispanics, women, and the
disabled. The consumer-environment groups, on the other hand, sought
to protect all citizens equally. The one gravitated toward preferential
policies, the other toward equal protection. As protected classes prolif-
erated, the rights of citizens were fragmented into a confusing variety of
conflicting claims based on race, sex, ethnicity, religion, language, culture,
age, physical or mental handicap, and sexual orientation.[20]

The difference between civil rights regulation and social regulation of
consumer, environment, and safety matters is most apparent when one
compares the distribution of costs and benefits. Social regulation to protect
consumers and the environment has often found wide public approval
because the costs of compliance tend to be narrowly distributed (auto
manufacturers must invest billions to develop more efficient engines),
while benefits are widely distributed (all citizens breathe cleaner air).
James Q. Wilson calls this the entrepreneurial pattern of regulatory politics,
a pattern common in regulating air and water pollution, promoting
workplace and highway safety, and protecting consumers from unsafe
products. In an era of proliferating public interest groups, the cost-benefit
ratio of this kind of regulation favors consumers over producers.
Entrepreneurial regulation is generally resented by power companies,
extractive industries, pharmaceutical firms, motor vehicle manufacturers,
and other regulated industries, but it has remained popular with voters
and hence with politicians.[21]

Conversely, civil rights regulation with its affirmative action requirements remains controversial in part because the cost-benefit ratio is reversed.
Enforcement costs are widely distributed (all nonminority citizens compete
for a proportionally reduced number of jobs, promotions, admissions),
and benefits are narrowly distributed (the beneficiaries are designated
protected-class minorities), a pattern Wilson calls the client model.[22]

20. Horowitz 1977; Glendon 1991. But see also Sunstein 1990.
21. Wilson 1989, 72–83.
22. The other two categories of regulation in Wilson's four-cell, cost-benefit analysis

Popular with beneficiary groups, this pattern is resented by others, who feel penalized by the state for immutable characteristics even though they are accused of no wrongdoing.[23]

The Benefits and Liabilities of Voting Rights Regulation

A quarter century of political compromise on voting rights regulation has left the American polity in an awkward state of tension. Supporters of aggressive enforcement have enjoyed impressive advantages while pressing legitimate claims. Rapid growth in the numbers of minority officeholders since 1965 has given their communities a psychological as well as a patronage stake in the American polity, much as it did for the Irish immigrants in the nineteenth century and the immigrants from southern and eastern Europe in the twentieth.[24] Moreover, the statistical criteria and results-driven standards of voting rights enforcement are consistent with the model of the new social regulation. Administrative enforcement of the Civil Rights Act and the Voting Rights Act has come to resemble the rule making and standard setting of the EPA, OSHA, and other agencies in modern social regulation. The congressional consensus behind the Voting Rights Act has grown stronger since the 1960s, and by 1982 was strong enough not only to reject as insufficient the Reagan administration's proposal for a ten-year extension of the act, but also to reverse *Mobile* by substituting an effects test for the intent requirement and to shield the achievement from future threats by moving the act's expiration date ahead twenty-five years. The federal courts, increasingly critical of preferential treatment of minorities in civil rights enforcement generally, have continued to uphold most nondilution protections for blacks and Hispanics in redistricting challenges. Republican presidential administrations, whatever their mix of principled and partisan motives, have

---

are *majoritarian* politics, where both costs and benefits are widely distributed (antitrust regulation), and *interest-group* politics, where both costs and benefits are narrowly distributed (collective bargaining, shipper regulation); Wilson 1980, 364–72.

23. A study commissioned in 1990 by the Leadership Conference on Civil Rights found that white voters typically saw civil rights as pressing the narrow concerns of particularized groups instead of promoting a broad policy opposing all forms of discrimination. Using a national poll and focus groups, the investigators did not find intensified racism but did find strong opposition to discriminatory practices based on race, gender, age, or disability. Edsall 1991, A6.

24. Erie 1988.

192 HUGH DAVIS GRAHAM

warmed to the prospect of redistricting arrangements that concentrate black and Hispanic Democrats in urban jurisdictions.

Furthermore, under both Democratic and Republican administrations, the Justice Department has scarcely enforced the Voting Rights Act with the draconian measures that could have created widespread public concern. Between 1965 and 1982 the department objected to only 815 of about 35,000 electoral changes submitted for section 5 preclearance.[25] The local and episodic nature of voting rights challenges and the intangible nature of political representation have limited public resentment of enforcement. When district boundaries are redrawn to favor protected minorities, nonminority voters and nonprotected minorities are never deprived of their vote and always retain some indeterminate measure of constituent voice. The proliferation of electoral districts, while fragmenting the electorate if carried to extremes of racial and ethnic Balkanization, counterbalances the political tendency of incumbents to freeze the status quo. And unlike the Civil Rights Act, the Voting Rights Act affects only public decisions in the narrow field of electoral policy, not private decisions or the competition of hiring and promotion in business. Finally, public resentment of preferences accorded minorities in enforcing the Voting Rights Act is limited by the low value the electorate places on the franchise. Public participation in the electoral process remains abysmally low in the United States, and in such an environment, disputes over electoral procedures and technicalities are unlikely to arouse strong public feelings.[26]

The combination of relative indifference from the public and intense engagement by policy elites suggests that the politics of voting rights regulation, unlike the client patterns found in the more controversial affirmative action programs, more closely resembles Wilson's interest-group model. In interest-group regulation (publishers versus printers' unions, railroads versus trucking lobbies), both costs and benefits are narrowly distributed. Under the minority preferences of voting rights districting, the tangible costs are borne by a few white incumbent office-holders, and the benefits are enjoyed by an equally small number of black and Hispanic (and more rarely, Asian) candidates and by the lawyers and experts involved in voting rights litigation. Unlike interest-group contests, however, voting rights contests over districting have produced unusually one-sided public debates. Charges of racism by minority interest groups have proven effective in muzzling opponents.

25. Davidson 1984, 16.
26. Ginsberg and Shefter 1990.

For all these reasons, public opinion surveys have not identified a tide of popular resentment against electoral benefits for minorities that is equivalent to the growth of opposition to preferences shown minorities in other areas.[27] The very narrowness of voting rights issues has helped to insulate the law's enforcers from the storms of controversy that surround other affirmative action issues. Voting Rights Act enforcement, like Civil Rights Act enforcement, draws its political strength primarily from the "iron triangles" that connect the civil rights lobbying groups to legislative committees and regulatory agencies. But voting rights enforcement draws much of its moral strength, and its tactical leverage, from the persistence of residential segregation. Were American society not so residentially segregated a full generation after the passage of the Open Housing Act of 1968, conservative critics would have a stronger hand in complaining about the growth of racial gerrymandering in favor of blacks and Hispanics. There have been no complaints, for example (excluding some experiments within the Democratic party), about heavy-handed enforcement of proportional representation for women.

Still, a quarter century of political compromise has created awkward contradictions in voting rights law and policy. In 1965, sections 4 and 5, the operative components of the Voting Rights Act, were designed as temporary emergency measures to root out institutionalized racism in southern electoral procedures and thereby permit a return to federalism's norm of local but nondiscriminatory electoral autonomy. The normative model of local electoral determination in the United States still has not changed, and it applies to most political jurisdictions. But in the de facto world of policy applications, temporary measures have tended to become permanent. Local elective control has increasingly yielded to centralized and appointive control. Bailout provisions in the Voting Rights Act continue to stipulate procedures for covered jurisdictions to return to the norm, free from the obligations to seek approval for every local modification from appointed officials in Washington. But in practice, as Timothy O'Rourke observes elsewhere in this volume, bailout for most covered jurisdictions has been impossible. Although statutory language continues to disclaim any goal of proportional representation for protected minori-

27. Voting rights issues have received little attention in the standard surveys on racial attitudes. In a comprehensive 1985 review of the literature and the polling data on racial attitudes, the trend-revealing questions covered residential and school integration, job discrimination, minority economic aid, personal relations, and racial intelligence, but electoral issues were confined to white voter support for a black presidential candidate. See Schuman, Steeh, and Bobo 1985.

ties, enforcement practices tend to affirm it. Hispanic immigrants are protected, but Russian immigrants are not. Minority rights leaders claim a right to vote for candidates of their "first choice," but it is not clear from what principle this right derives, or how it is defined, or whether nonminority voters (or women) also possess it. Protected classes are given rights to nondilution, but other voters, including women and many minorities, possess no such rights.

Indeed, the theory of nondilution is so tactically selective that it risks incoherence as a general proposition. It does not apply to women, whose history of political discrimination and electoral underrepresentation equals and arguably exceeds that of blacks and Hispanics. Furthermore, it is not clear upon what principle the right of nondilution rests. If redistricting in contiguous neighborhoods of black and Hispanic voters brings competing claims to protection against nondilution in newly drawn districts, as is increasingly likely between blacks and Hispanics in Miami, Houston, and Los Angeles, then whose claims should be vindicated and why? Will blacks, as the target beneficiaries of the Voting Rights Act during its first decade, have a superior claim to nondilution in the coming electoral clashes with neighboring Hispanics? Upon what principles are federal judges to award nondilution preference?

Such thorny questions have not troubled the agencies that protect people from foul air, toxic water, and dangerous workplaces. Their claims to protection apply to all citizens. Thus, while environmental regulation remains politically popular, civil rights regulation has produced growing public resentment. When a *New York Times* poll asked a national sample of respondents in May 1985 if they favored preference in hiring or promotion for blacks in areas where there has been discrimination in the past, 42 percent said yes and 46 percent said no. Asked the same question in December 1990, 32 percent said yes and 52 percent said no.[28] When a 1990 survey by Times-Mirror Corporation asked a national sample of more than 3,000 people whether they agreed that "we should make every possible effort to improve the position of blacks and other minorities, even if it means giving them preferential treatment," white men disagreed by a margin of 81 to 16 percent. White women, who comprise 40 percent of the U.S. voting population, and who have benefited greatly from nondiscrimination and very little from the group preferences of affirmative action, agreed with the opinion of white men.[29]

28. Applebome 1991, A18.
29. Brown 1991, 18–19. Among white women, 17 percent agreed and 79 percent

The Voting Rights Act and the Politics of Redistricting

Nevertheless Voting Rights Act enforcement, unlike Civil Rights Act enforcement, has thus far navigated a relatively safe political passage through the shoals of public opinion. How then do we account for the paradox that in a relatively benign environment of public opinion for voting rights issues the policy community boils with renewed controversy? One reason may be found in the 1990 census, which showed unprecedented growth in the Hispanic and Asian populations. Legislative districts were redrawn for the 1992 elections under circumstances that increasingly strained the fragile alliance between Hispanics and blacks. According to Raul Yzaguirre, president of the National Council of La Raza, relations between the two "have not been particularly wholesome or happy" in the past twenty years.[30] Redistricting under these circumstances threatens to split the alliance and further fragment the Democratic coalition. Republicans, determined to accelerate this process, have pressed for strict voting rights enforcement with the zeal of new converts. Under these circumstances it is no surprise that tensions within the voting rights policy community should rise, especially at its Democratic core among party professionals, committee staff, and practitioner academics.

Two states illustrate the dilemma for the Democratic coalition. Population shifts required Illinois to lose two of its 22 congressional seats in 1992. Three of the existing Illinois districts were largely black and protected by the Voting Rights Act. In Chicago, Republicans, eager to dilute white ethnic Democrats out of potential new minority districts and into Republican suburban districts, joined with traditionally Hispanic and black groups in a battle to redraw the districts of three white Democratic incumbents to create a new Hispanic district. The redistricting forced one Democratic retirement and two races between Democratic incumbents. Hispanic residential dispersion in Chicago required the new Hispanic-majority district to assume a bizarre snakelike configuration.

In California, population growth added seven new House seats to the forty-five existing in 1990. California contains 34.4 percent of the nation's Hispanics, 39.1 percent of its Asians, and 7.4 percent of its blacks. Yet blacks in 1990 occupied four of California's congressional seats, while Hispanics, a quarter of the state's population, held only three and demanded

---

disagreed, a response that within the margin of error was indistinguishable from that of white men.

30. Parsons 1991, 4A.

four more Hispanic districts. In addition to Illinois and California, incumbent white Democrats are threatened by proposals to add minority districts in Florida, Texas, New Jersey, Virginia, Georgia, Arkansas, and Alabama.[31] In North Carolina, voting rights enforcement by the Bush administration to create a black-majority congressional seat led to a serpentine district that promised to concentrate Democratic voters in the piedmont cities and solidify Republican control in the surrounding districts. In the new cartography of voting rights, the salamander-shaped district drawn by Massachusetts Governor Elbridge Gerry in 1811 looked innocent by comparison.

We should be sobered by the Republican discovery in the 1990s of the moral grandeur of granting minority preferences in electoral districting. It should remind us not that Republicans are more hypocritical than Democrats but that regulation in voting rights policy has become deeply entangled in the political thicket. These developments should not however, be surprising. The evolution of minority preferences in civil rights policy has been defended with eloquence and power on theoretical grounds.[32] But the practical consequence of this shift in the politics of regulation has been to align civil rights regulation with the characteristic attributes of widely shared costs and narrowly focused benefits of the client model. Historically, this type of regulation brought American society the classic abuses of clientele capture and special-interest triangles, and in economic regulation it produced the deregulation movement of the Carter and Reagan years. In civil rights regulation the client model has also grown more controversial as the political process has institutionalized practices of minority preference that were originally defended as temporary. In voting rights regulation, advocates of aggressive federal pressure to increase the number of minority officeholders have brought mixed motives to an enterprise that combines worthy targets (concentrations of power and privilege like those in Mobile and Los Angeles) with cynical partisanship (Republican-minority redistricting coalitions in Chicago and other cities). In the face of such complexities, students of politics should welcome critical dissent rather than rally in defense of orthodoxy. This volume of essays attests, in part, to the vigor of renewed debate.

31. Berke 1991, A1, A11.
32. Rawls 1971; Dworkin 1977.

Expert Witness Testimony and the Evolution of Voting Rights Case Law

BERNARD GROFMAN

TESTIMONY FROM SOCIAL SCIENTISTS on the concept of vote dilution and the elements from which it is made has played a major role in shaping the way the provisions of the Voting Rights Act of 1965 and its amendments have been interpreted by courts and by the Department of Justice. The focus of this chapter is on the role of the expert witness in the evolution of voting rights case law and on criteria for evaluating such testimony in the light of conflicts among experts testifying for opposing sides. Initially, courts looked to the seven factors of what has been called the "totality of circumstances" test for voting rights violations. Then in *Thornburg* v. *Gingles* (1986) the Supreme Court provided a set of sufficient (and, in certain contexts, necessary) conditions for when a multimember or at-large election plan would be held to have diluted minority voting strength under the strictures of section 2. I pay particular attention to issues of definition and measurement involving one of the three prongs of the *Thornburg* test—whether a pattern of racially polarized voting exists—which has become the linchpin of many voting rights cases and the subject of great dispute. As an expert witness for black plaintiffs in *Thornburg* v. *Gingles,* I write about these matters from both a professional and a personal perspective.

Once, the test for the existence of vote dilution rested on factors such as a history of state-sanctioned discriminatory practices, the existence of racially polarized voting, the use of electoral practices that enhanced the opportunity for discrimination against a minority group, the exclusion of minorities from any slating process, lingering effects of past discrim-

This research was partially supported by NSF grant SES 88-09392 to Chandler Davidson and me and draws on earlier work supported by NSF grant SES 81-07754, as well as on my testimony in numerous voting rights cases in the past decade, including *Gingles* v. *Edmisten,* 590 F.Supp. 345 (E.D.N.C. 1984), heard *sub nom Thornburg* v. *Gingles* 478 U.S. 30 (1986). Part of this paper is an update of material contained in Grofman, Migalski, and Noviello 1985. I am indebted to many helpful conversations with attorneys and other expert witnesses over the years. Bibliographic assistance on this paper was provided by Dorothy Gormick. The original inspiration was Cotrell 1981, and I have especially benefited from the discussion of racial bloc voting in McCrary 1990.

ination that may have affected the ability of minorities to participate effectively in the political process, the presence of racial campaign appeals, and the record of minority electoral success.[1] These factors, generally referred to as *Zimmer* factors, were the basis of the constitutional test for vote dilution used by lower courts from 1973 when, in *White v. Regester,* the Supreme Court first struck down a multimember district plan as an unconstitutional denial of equal protection, until 1980 when, in *City of Mobile v. Bolden,* the Court imposed a requirement that discriminatory purpose be shown.[2] After the extension of the Voting Rights Act in 1982, the seven totality of circumstances factors formed the basis of virtually all court decisions under the amended section 2 language, until in 1986 the Supreme Court in *Thornburg v. Gingles* provided a new and simplified three-pronged test. Even after *Thornburg* the factors of the totality of circumstances test that were not incorporated into the three prongs of the *Thornburg* test remained of some subsidiary importance.

With respect to establishing these factors, the testimony of social scientists has been indispensable. In vote dilution cases, experts for opposing sides have squared off against one another, sometimes one on one, sometimes in conflicts resembling tag-team wrestling on late-night television.[3] In some voting rights cases, the outcome of the litigation has been decided largely by the credibility of expert witness testimony as to the factors in the totality of circumstances or *Thornburg* tests. However, most of the disputes among experts have dealt with only one of the seven factors listed above, measurement of racially polarized voting. Assessing the extent of racially polarized voting is arguably now the most important of the empirical questions investigated in the course of an inquiry into vote dilution, at least in the context of challenges to multimember or at-large elections.[4]

1. See the discussion in Grofman, Migalski, and Noviello 1985; McDonald in this volume.

2. Before 1982, the factors were derived from *Zimmer* v. *McKeithen,* 485 F.2d 1297 (5th Cir. 1973) (en banc) aff'd on other grounds *sub nom East Carroll Parish School Board* v. *Marshall,* 424 U.S. 636 (1976); see also *White* v. *Regester,* 412 U.S. 766 (1973); *City of Mobile* v. *Bolden,* 246 U.S. 55 (1980), *remanded.*

3. As in *Garza* v. *Los Angeles County Board of Supervisors* (D. Cal. 1990), 90 C.D.O.S. 8138 (9th Cir. 1990), *cert. denied* January 1990.

4. Courts have generally used "racial bloc voting" synonymously with "racially polarized voting." I will do so here. Testimony by historians as to discriminatory purpose underlying a statute or plan has also played an important role in voting rights litigation.

Although racially polarized voting was not mentioned in either *White* v. *Regester* or *Zimmer* v. *McKeithen*, by the mid-1970s it was an important evidentiary element in challenges to at-large elections and other districting schemes based on the Fourteenth Amendment.[5] Moreover, in *Beer* v. *United States*, the 1976 case that developed the nonretrogression test applied to cases arising under section 5 of the Voting Rights Act, the Supreme Court projected outcomes in a proposed plan based on the assumption that voting was racially polarized, where that term was used synonymously with whites voting for white candidates and blacks voting for black candidates.[6] Indeed, even before *White* v. *Regester*, testimony about racially polarized voting played a prominent role in some vote dilution cases before lower courts.[7]

Although a Senate report in 1982 treated racially polarized voting as only one of the seven primary factors that could be used to prove vote dilution, with no single factor or even any particular combination of factors being either necessary or sufficient to prove a violation, in a number of cases alleging racial gerrymandering or submergence of minority voting strength brought under the new 1982 language of section 2 of the act, proof of racially polarized voting was assigned much greater weight than other factors.[8] For example, in *United States* v. *Marengo County*

For example, it is often forgotten that, after *City of Mobile* v. *Bolden,* the lower court's reconsideration of the case on remand led it to find intentional vote dilution even though essentially no blacks were voting at the time the at-large plan was adopted. But historical evidence showed that the plan's proponents saw its at-large election feature as a safeguard against a later time when blacks might possess an effective franchise. Although the section 2 effects standard has minimized the importance of a showing of intentional discrimination, evidence about intent is still put forward by plaintiffs in a number of cases. Indeed, in *Garza* v. *Los Angeles County Board of Supervisors,* a historian gave extensive testimony showing a pattern of discrimination against Hispanics by reconstructing four decades of evidence about the redistricting options that were chosen as compared to those that were rejected. Basing its decision on this testimony, the district court found discriminatory purpose as well as discriminatory effects of racial gerrymandering.

5. See *Lipscomb* v. *Wise,* 399 F.Supp. 782 (N.D. Texas 1975); *Wallace* v. *House,* 515 F.2d 619 (5th Cir. 1975); *Kirksey* v. *Board of Supervisors of Hinds County,* 554 F.2d 139 (1977). See also other references in McCrary 1990.

6. *Beer* v. *United States,* 425 U.S. 130 at 142 (1976).

7. For example, in *City of Petersburg* v. *United States,* a 1972 annexation case, the district court found "a dramatic polarization of the races in Petersburg with respect to voting" and presented a chart showing votes for white and black city council candidates in the heavily white and heavily black areas of the city (354 F.Supp. 1021 at 1025–26).

8. Senate 1982b.

Commissioners racially polarized voting was identified as "the keystone of a dilution case."[9] But the apogee of the importance of considerations of racial vote dilution was yet to come.

In *Thornburg* v. *Gingles* (1986) the Supreme Court identified a requisite level of racial bloc voting as one of the basic factors under the 1982 language of section 2 for proving minority vote dilution in an at-large or multimember district system. According to Justice William Brennan, who delivered the opinion of the Court, "The purpose of inquiring into the existence of racially polarized voting is twofold: to ascertain whether minority group members constitute a politically cohesive unit and to determine whether whites vote sufficiently as a bloc usually to defeat the minority's preferred candidates." Each of these two inquiries forms one of the elements of what has come to be called the *Thornburg* three-pronged test. The third key element of proof in the *Thornburg* section 2 test is the requirement that the minority group be shown to be "sufficiently large and geographically compact to constitute a majority in a single-member district."[10]

Thornburg is a landmark case that continues to define how the 1982 amended language of section 2 of the act is to be interpreted. The Supreme Court has so far refused to hear cases disputing the proper interpretation of the *Thornburg* three-pronged test that have been brought to it on appeal. The *Thornburg* test has affected the outcomes of scores of voting rights cases. Virtually all challenges to election practices as racially discriminatory are now brought under either section 2 or section 5 of the act. The chief purpose of this chapter is to analyze from the perspective of social science the dispute over the issues involved in making the concept of vote dilution usable; it focuses on the elements of the *Thornburg* test, especially racially polarized voting.

Factors Relevant to the Totality of Circumstances Test

The seven typical factors that may be used to establish a violation of section 2 that were identified in the 1982 Senate report are listed below.[11]
Factor 1. The extent of any history of official discrimination in the

9. *United States* v. *Marengo County Commissioners*, 731 F.2d 1546 (11th Cir. 1984).

10. *Thornburg* v. *Gingles*, 478 U.S. 30 at 56, 50 (1986). Heard in the lower court *sub nom Gingles* v. *Edmisten*, 590 F.Supp. 345 (1984), *aff'd in part rev in part sub nom, Thornburg* v. *Gingles*.

11. Senate 1982b, 28–29. The report identifies two additional factors that in some cases have had probative value: "whether there is a significant lack of responsiveness on

state or political subdivision that touched the right of the members of the minority group to register, to vote, or otherwise to participate in the democratic process.

Factor 2. The extent to which voting in the elections of the state or political subdivision is racially polarized.

Factor 3. The extent to which the state or political subdivision has used unusually large election districts, majority vote requirements, anti-single-shot provisions, or other voting practices or procedures that may enhance the opportunity for discrimination against the minority group.

Factor 4. The extent to which, if there is candidate slating, the members of the minority group have been denied access to that process.

Factor 5. The extent to which members of the minority group in the state or political subdivision bear the effects of discrimination in education, employment, health, and other matters that hinder their ability to participate effectively in the political process.

Factor 6. The extent to which political campaigns have been characterized by overt or subtle racial appeals.

Factor 7. The extent to which members of the minority group have been elected to public office in the jurisdiction.

I now turn to proposed operationalizations of five of the seven factors in the totality of circumstances test. Discussion of two of the seven—factor 2, the extent of racially polarized voting, and factor 7, the extent of minority electoral success—I reserve until later, when I analyze the *Thornburg* three-pronged test of which they are an integral part.

At minimum, as I have argued elsewhere, there are four criteria that any particular concept must satisfy if it is to be of use to courts.[12]

—The definition of variables must be unambiguously operationalizable in an objective fashion.

—The necessary data can be generated within the time frame

---

the part of elected officials to the particularized needs of the members of the minority group," and "whether the policy underlying the state or political subdivision's use of such voting qualification, prerequisite to voting, or standard, practice or procedure is tenuous." But the report makes clear that "unresponsiveness is not an essential part of plaintiff's case" and that "even a consistently applied practice premised on a racially neutral policy would not negate a plaintiff's showing through other factors that the challenged practice denies minorities fair access to the process" (127, notes 116, 117). I shall neglect these factors in my discussion because they seem to have had little practical importance in any of the section 2 litigation since the 1982 amendments.

12. Grofman, Migalski, and Noviello 1985, 201, with a slight change in wording.

of a court case and without imposing unreasonable burdens on the litigants.

— The definitions and their operationalization can be explained clearly and simply to lawyers.

— There is a prima facie link between terms as defined by the social scientist and the ways in which statutory or constitutional language has been (or might reasonably be) interpreted by the courts.

For each of the five factors discussed below I provide information bearing on how well the proposed operationalization fares under each of the first three criteria of the above test. Since all are factors identified by the Senate report as directly relevant to determining compliance with section 2 of the Voting Rights Act, and the operationalizations described below are based in large part on what types of evidence courts have found persuasive, we may take for granted that the fourth criterion above is satisfied.

Of course, the four criteria for evaluating operationalizations of the social science concepts I have identified are far from the whole story. Even for a concept to which social science expertise is clearly legally applicable, when one looks at what social scientists actually rely on to reach their conclusions, one must still distinguish good social science from sloppy social science.[13] Also, for some concepts there may be alternative plausible operationalizations, choice among which has important substantive implications. Nonetheless, for each of the various factors that courts and expert witnesses have proposed or relied on in evaluating compliance with the Voting Rights Act of 1965 as amended, asking whether that factor can be operationalized in a way that satisfies the above four criteria is a useful beginning.

Factor 1. History of Official Discrimination

Proving a history of official discrimination is in most cases not difficult. The social science expertise that is most relevant is, of course, that of the historian. In most southern states a statewide history of official discrimination against blacks can readily be established from standard sources by any competent historian; the same is true in the Southwest for Hispan-

---

13. One must also distinguish honest social science from the performance of hired guns who deliberately distort their testimony in the interests of the side on which they are testifying.

ics or native Americans.[14] It is useful, however, to take the history as close to the present as possible. Because de jure segregation will have ended some time ago, this can be done in part by tracing official positions or legal resistance to various race-related situations that have resulted in court-imposed solutions, such as affirmative action hiring for police and fire departments, simplified procedures for voter registration in the minority community, school busing, denial of preclearance under section 5, location of public housing, and so forth. Evidence of statewide policies of discrimination, while often sufficient, has frequently been supplemented with evidence specific to a given polity—segregated private clubs and other forms of social segregation participated in by local political officials, for example, or segregated housing patterns buttressed by red lining, or historical use of restrictive covenants. Of particular relevance is evidence on barriers to voting participation and registration (for example, few bilingual registrars, few minority poll watchers and election officials, or polling precincts located disproportionally in white Anglo areas). Some of this data can be established from polling maps, property deeds, litigation dockets, court records, and census data, but some can be introduced only through the testimony of knowledgeable local citizens.[15]

Factor 3. Election Practices that Increase the Likelihood of Vote Dilution

Federal courts have repeatedly accepted the claim that majority vote requirements, anti-single-shot voting rules (or ones that, for multimember district elections, specify numbered places or staggered elections or both), and unusually large multimember districts are practices that make the

14. For official discrimination against blacks, see, for example, Kousser 1974. Extensive evidence about discrimination against Hispanics in California is reviewed in the first appellate decision in *Gomez* v. *City of Watsonville*, 863 F.2d 1407 (9th Cir. 1988), *cert. denied* (1989). A New Mexico constitutional provision adopted in 1912 that was used to deny native Americans the right to vote in state elections until a successful challenge was brought in federal court in 1948 illustrates their treatment in the Southwest (Garcia and Hain 1981, 171).

15. In section 2 cases, as in other civil rights litigation, hard data that is comprehensive in scope, if available, is to be preferred to personal reports, which can too easily be dismissed as idiosyncratic or biased. However, testimony by those with direct experience of local politics can be important in providing flesh and substance to the rather bloodless and abstract reports commonly provided by social scientists and in reminding the court that judicial decisions will affect the lives of real people.

dilution of minority voting strength more likely.[16] The existence or past use of majority runoff requirements, numbered places, or staggered elections is clearly a matter of record; but the meaning of "unusually large election district" is not so clear. In testimony in *Gingles* v. *Edmisten* the reference was to the number of representatives elected from a particular multimember district. That number, eight, was compared to the average number of legislators per district in the North Carolina legislature as well as to the average number of legislators per district in the state houses and the state senates in each state as of 1980, but that testimony was not discussed in the opinion.[17] In *Garza* v. *Los Angeles County Board of Supervisors*, in which a single-member-district plan was challenged, testimony by plaintiffs' experts had to do with the population in each of the supervisorial districts; at roughly 1.7 million persons per district, each was at least as populous as any of the sixteen smallest states and twice the size of any other county supervisorial district in the country. The Court specifically acknowledged that the small size of the board of supervisors (five) that led to the creation of such populous districts—in which the costs of running a successful campaign are huge—could make it harder for minority candidates to compete successfully, given the limited financial resources of the minority community. Also potentially relevant to a claim that a particular district was unusually large would be data on the sheer physical size of the district and the transportation difficulties in gaining access to its remotest parts or data on the number of different media serving the district.

Factor 4. Candidate Slating Process

In many jurisdictions there is no formal slating process (especially for nonpartisan elections), although groups of candidates may band together to run as an informal slate. In other jurisdictions, party organizations

16. For definitions of these terms, see Davidson in this volume. In section 2 cases involving at-large elections, showing that such practices exist or have been used has generally been all that is needed; the causal link between such practices and minority vote dilution in the particular case at issue need not be demonstrated. However, in challenges to majority runoffs, evidence that minority candidates who were plurality (but not majority) winners of an election were more frequently defeated in a subsequent runoff than was true for plurality winners who were not minority members is likely to be necessary. Whether (in conjunction with racially polarized voting and perhaps other elements of the totality of the circumstances test) such evidence is also legally sufficient remains an open question (Grofman, Handley, and Niemi, forthcoming).

17. The data are reproduced in Grofman, Migalski, and Noviello 1985, table 2.

may designate certain candidates as having official endorsement, even though the actual nomination may take place in a party primary. In still other jurisdictions, most commonly ones with a nonpartisan ballot, business and civic groups may endorse slates. In expert witness testimony in *United States* v. *City of Augusta,* a case settled out of court, it was argued that the endorsement of the major newspaper in the city was a type of slating process.[18]

If there is a slating process, and slated candidates are more likely to win than nonendorsed candidates, the number of minority candidates who are interviewed or nominated by it is, of course, the single most important piece of information bearing on the fairness of the process. However, of almost equal importance is information on the composition of the slating group itself. For example, in *Alonzo* v. *Jones,* a successful section 2 challenge in 1983 to at-large city council elections in Corpus Christi, Texas, the district court judge noted in his finding of facts that, although Mexican-American candidates had been slated and successful in their election campaigns, all who won had done so by "being members of a slate basically assembled by Anglo . . . leaders."[19]

Factor 5. Lingering Effects of Discrimination

Lower levels of education, employment, income, health, and longevity have been taken by courts to be indicators of the extent to which minority group members bear the burden of previous discrimination. Such data are published at the county level and for at least the larger cities in each state and can be obtained from census tapes for any desired unit of aggregation. Customarily, sociologists or demographers present such data as a routine part of section 2 litigation. The data are rarely subject to dispute.

Lower levels of minority voter registration and election turnout relative to the eligible population have also been taken as indicators of lingering effects of discrimination. For the handful of states where registration or sign-in data are available by race, the basic facts on comparative levels of minority and nonminority registration or turnout are readily available. However, because of inadequacies in recordkeeping or systematic biases in purging the rolls of deadwood, such data may be suspect. In *Push* v.

18. *United States* v. *City of Augusta* (S.D. Ga., 1987), settled out of court.

19. Indeed, slate-endorsed Hispanic candidates, in winning, defeated non-slate-endorsed Hispanic candidates who had greater support from the Hispanic community. *Alonzo* v. *Jones,* No. C-81-227 (S.D. Texas, February 3, 1983).

Allain Mississippi registration information was held to provide an inaccurate picture of relative rates of black and white registration in the state.[20] For states, and for other jurisdictions large enough to be reasonably coterminous with standard metropolitan areas (SMAs), the current population surveys of the census permit an estimate of registration rates and turnout in federal elections of eligible voters by race and by Spanish origin. In *Push* v. *Allain* the accuracy of that data for Mississippi was challenged because of claimed differential misreporting of registration by whites and blacks, but there were factors idiosyncratic to Mississippi involved as well. In *Garza* v. *Los Angeles County Board of Supervisors,* current population survey data for Los Angeles County were accepted by the court as a check on the accuracy of the county's own population projections. For cases involving Hispanics, a matchup of registrar lists with the census list of Spanish surnames has been accepted by courts as a proxy for Spanish-origin registration.[21] Although the accuracy of that matchup was subject to extensive challenge in *Garza,* the court accepted testimony by a demographer on its general accuracy that was based on a detailed look at type I and type II error rates at the census tract level in Los Angeles County.

For jurisdictions (or smaller units such as districts) where data of the above sorts are unavailable, estimates of registration and turnout by race or Spanish origin can be generated by combining census, registration, and election data and making use of the ecological and homogeneous precinct analysis techniques that have become standard in the analysis of racially polarized voting.[22]

Factor 6. Racial Campaign Appeals

It would appear that a racial campaign appeal, like pornography, is in the category of "I know it when I see it." The only two definitions in court cases or the social science literature I have been able to locate are ones offered by two sociologists, Paul Luebke and Jerry Himelstein. Luebke's definition, offered as testimony in *Gingles* v. *Edmisten,* is that racial appeals occur in a campaign if one candidate calls attention to the race of his opponent or his opponent's supporters, or if media covering a

20. *Mississippi State Chapter, Operation PUSH* v. *Allain,* 674 F. Supp. 1245 (N.D. Miss. 1987).

21. For example, in *Gomez* v. *City of Watsonville* (1988).

22. Grofman, Migalski, and Noviello 1985.

campaign disproportionally call attention to the race of one candidate or of that candidate's supporters. I believe that Luebke's definition satisfies the fourfold usefulness test presented earlier. It is clear and is as unambiguously operationalizable as one can hope, given the inherent fuzziness of the term. One instance of a racial campaign appeal that fits the definition perfectly would be when a white candidate uses a picture of his black opponent in his own campaign material. Except as a notice to white voters of his opponent's race, no candidate would give such free photographic publicity. Luebke provided such an example from the 1982 Michaux-Valentine Democratic congressional primary in North Carolina in his testimony in *Gingles*.[23]

Himelstein has shown how themes identified as racist in earlier historical contexts are still being invoked during political campaigns in the South in sanitized forms that avoid overt references to race by using code words and other concealed messages that appeal to lingering feelings of white antiblack sentiment. As Himelstein points out (in remarks directed to Mississippi politics but applicable in the South and elsewhere), "overt appeals to segregationist sentiments are no longer practiced by politicians who expect to win. . . . Black voter strength and perhaps some degree of cultural change in the etiquette of race relations seems to have sanitized the language of political rhetoric. However, segregationist sentiments and political action continue among a large portion of the white population. . . . In a society so recently and so dominantly obsessed with race . . . one important way political leaders have walked the line between divergent audiences is through the use of code words," also known as racial telegraphing.

A code word . . . is a word or phrase which communicates a well understood but implicit meaning to part of a public audience while preserving for the speaker deniability of that meaning by reference to its denotative explicit meaning. As for example, in 1968 presidential candidate Hubert Humphrey accused his Republican opponents of using the phrase "law and order" as a code word for repression of blacks in reaction to riots in black ghettoes. Another presidential campaign example is Jimmy Carter's

---

23. Other Luebke illustrations included the use by Senator Jesse Helms's reelection campaign committee of a picture of Jesse Jackson, identifying him as a Hunt supporter in a 1983 advertisement attacking Governor Hunt of North Carolina (Helms's probable opponent), and a Helms reelection campaign committee ad accusing Hunt of using taxpayer funds to register black voters.

1976 awkward attempt to pacify residents in a Polish neighborhood who were worried about desegregation in housing. He endorsed the preservation of "ethnic purity" in residential patterns. But blacks quickly identified this phase as a code word for segregation, and Carter spent some time trying to explain it away. Code words are intended as rhetorical winks, and if they are too easily detected they lose their deniability and thus their effectiveness.[24]

Luebke's definition of racial appeal is easier to measure objectively than Himelstein's definition of code words. As Himelstein notes, "identification of code words is an enterprise akin to the interpretation of symbols in literary criticism."[25] For code words, such identification requires careful sociological and historical analysis. Nonetheless, because overt racial appeals may be absent, testimony about more subtle and covert forms of racial appeal such as the use of code words and of themes associated with white supremacy and antiblack sentiment may be required if this element of the totality of circumstances test is to be proved. Luebke presented such testimony in *Gingles,* and the trial court gave it considerable credibility. For example, in the Michaux-Valentine runoff primary, one advertisement accused Valentine's black opponent of "planning on bussing his supporters" to the polls—with "bussing" emphasized—and attacked the bloc vote in the previous election. According to Luebke terms like "bussing" and "bloc vote" were used to trigger white fears.[26]

The *Thornburg* Three-Pronged Test

Since the mid-1970s virtually no vote dilution case has lacked an analysis of racial vote dilution by one or more witnesses expert in social science. And almost invariably there has been conflicting testimony by experts, usually political scientists or sociologists, but also historians and, more recently, economists and statisticians. Bloc voting has been too important to cases of voting rights violations for plaintiffs not to give evidence as to its presence, and proof of racially polarized voting has made defeat too likely for defendant jurisdictions not to hire their own

24. Himelstein 1983, 155–56. For the previous quotation see p. 155.
25. Himelstein 1983, 157.
26. Also see Luebke 1990, 118. It does not appear that anything beyond the mere existence of racial appeals needs to be demonstrated. In particular, the effectiveness of the racial appeals need not be shown. If voting is racially polarized, that fact provides indirect support for the probable impact of any observed racial appeals.

experts to seek to rebut the claims of the plaintiffs' experts. In addition to statistical disputes about the accuracy of estimated levels of polarization, fundamental questions of definition have been at issue.

Defining Racial Bloc Voting in Thornburg

Much of the expert witness testimony in voting rights cases, especially that offered between 1982 and 1986 when it became clear that proving racial bloc voting was critical but the Supreme Court had not yet provided solid guidelines to lower courts as to how the term was to be defined and the conditions measured, could be seen as part of an ongoing struggle to control the legal meaning to be attached to the term "racially polarized voting." The outcome of that struggle would have critical consequences for whether plaintiffs or defendants were to prevail in voting rights litigation.

There were three not necessarily mutually exclusive choices open to the courts.

First, they could focus on the correlation coefficient obtained when the support rate for minority candidates was regressed against the minority percentage in the voting precinct. Experts in some cases had done just that, treating correlation levels of .7 or so as prima facie evidence of polarization. Some experts who made use of the correlational approach also testified about the statistical significance of the evidence for polarization, with t statistics and similar measures being offered in evidence.

Second, courts could focus on the difference between the levels of support for minority candidates from minority voters and the support those candidates were receiving from nonminority voters to see if the nature of the differences was important. If courts took this tack, the obvious next question was what level of differences in support proved polarization. Many experts proposed to look at the sum of "own race" voting—the percentage of minority voters who voted for the minority candidate added to the percentage of nonminority voters who voted for the nonminority candidate. Some experts for plaintiffs argued that an own-race voting percentage that summed greater than 160 percent was evidence of strong polarization; others proposed lower figures, arguing for example that, in American politics, landslide proportions meant a 60–40 split, and thus a cutoff of 120 percent was appropriate. In my testimony in *Gingles* v. *Edmisten,* I proposed that *substantively significant* racially polarized voting be defined as that which occurs when the candidate or set of candidates chosen by voters of one race differs from the candidate or candidates chosen by voters of the other race. In contrast, some experts for the defendants argued that unless the own-race voting percentage exceeded 180 percent, voting should not be considered polarized.

Third, courts could require that experts look at more than just the simple pattern of observed election results to try to determine whether racial animus was driving the choices of nonminority voters. There were two ways that witnesses for plaintiffs proposed this be done. One was to require evidence for indicators of racial backlash such as racial campaign appeals or especially high levels of majority turnout in elections involving minority candidates. Essentially this approach was accepted by a federal district court in *Collins* v. *City of Norfolk*. The second approach involved using multivariate methods to determine whether race made an independent contribution to explaining patterns of voting once other factors such as newspaper endorsements, incumbency, campaign spending, socioeconomic characteristics of the voters, and so forth were controlled. This approach was argued for by a court of appeals judge in an obiter dictum in his concurring opinion in *Jones* v. *City of Lubbock* and accepted by a federal district court in *McCord* v. *City of Fort Lauderdale*.[27]

In *Thornburg* the Supreme Court chose the commonsense idea that racially polarized voting reflected the differences in the voting behavior of groups that had characterized the early cases, including *Beer* v. *United States*. The approach to racially polarized voting taken in *Thornburg*, however, reflected the Court's unique synthesis of the expert witness testimony in *Gingles* v. *Edmisten* (which in turn drew on the approaches using data and statistical methodology) and the analytical framework for understanding vote dilution presented in a 1982 law review article by James Blacksher and Lawrence Menefee that the Court found highly persuasive.[28]

In *Thornburg* the Court codified the definition of racially polarized voting that was henceforth to govern vote dilution cases by accepting the definition offered by the plaintiffs' expert witness in that case (me), a definition also adopted by the lower court, that voting was polarized when there is "'a consistent relationship between race of the voter and the way in which the voter votes,' or to put it differently, where 'black voters and white voters vote differently.'" *Thornburg* asserted that racial

27. *Collins* v. *City of Norfolk*, 883 F.2d 1232 (4th Cir. 1989); *Jones* v. *City of Lubbock*, 730 F.2d 233 (5th Cir. 1989); *McCord* v. *City of Fort Lauderdale*, 83-6182-CIV-NCR (S.D. Fla. 1985), remanded 1986 (settled out of court).
28. Blacksher and Menefee 1982.

polarization can be established in terms of observed correlations between the racial composition of election districts and candidate choices in those units, at least insofar as a correlation between the race of the voter and the way in which the voter votes implies differences in the voting behavior of minority and nonminority voters.[29]

But for the Supreme Court, as for the lower court, the inquiry into racial polarization did not stop with a finding that voting was racially polarized. The Court also accepted the distinction between the existence of racial polarization per se and the nature of that polarization being of practical or legal significance. In particular, the Court recognized that racially polarized voting was neither a necessary nor a sufficient condition for minority electoral loss.[30] It held that for racially polarized voting to rise to the level of legal significance it must be shown, on the one hand, that "the white majority votes sufficiently as a bloc" to enable it in the absence of special circumstances "usually to defeat the minority's preferred candidate." On the other hand, the minority group must be shown to be "politically cohesive"; that a "significant number of minority group members usually vote for the same candidates is one way of proving the political cohesiveness necessary to a vote dilution claim."[31]

In *Thornburg* the inquiry into polarization was thus effectively bifurcated. The first part was the judgment of whether polarization existed. The second part was whether it was legally significant. Moreover, this second inquiry was itself bifurcated. It required two "discrete inquiries," the first into minority voting practices, the second into white voting practices.[32]

29. *Thornburg* v. *Gingles,* 478 U.S. at 53, note 21; and at 62–63.

30. For example, on the one hand, a minority group's candidate might win even if voting was racially polarized as long as the minority population was large enough (given the relative levels of minority and nonminority crossover for the candidate of the other group) to elect its candidate of choice; and on the other hand, the lack of success of minority candidates could occur in the absence of racially polarized voting.

31. *Thornburg* v. *Gingles,* 478 U.S. at 51, 56. The inquiry into racially polarized voting was thus a multipart inquiry. In principle, therefore, situations could occur in which racially polarized voting existed and the evidence of polarization was of statistical significance *but not* of legal significance.

32. 478 U.S. at 56. The Court stated that "the usual predictability of the majority's success distinguishes structural dilution from the mere loss of an occasional election." Thus the Court did not accept "substantive significance" (as I had defined that term in my *Gingles* testimony and in Grofman, Migalski, and Noviello 1985) as being synonymous with legal significance. Rather, substantive significance, as I had defined that term, was found necessary but not sufficient for the evidence for a pattern of racial bloc voting to rise to the level of legal significance, since without it there could not be either minority political cohesion or minority losses that could be attributed to the lack of support for minority candidates given by nonminority members.

Of course, in expert witness testimony at trial, the two halves of racial bloc voting are often presented together.

In *Thornburg* Justice Brennan also decisively rejected the claim, made by the defendant jurisdiction and supported by the United States as amicus curiae, that race must be shown to be the "primary determinant of voting behavior" for voting to be found to be racially polarized. He specifically rejected approaches to racially polarized voting of the sort that had been accepted by lower courts in the *Norfolk* and *Fort Lauderdale* cases. His opinion asserted that "the legal concept of racially polarized voting incorporates neither causation nor intent. It means simply that the race of voters correlates with the selection of a certain candidate or candidates, that is, it refers to the situation where different races (or minority language groups) vote in blocs for different candidates."[33]

The *Thornburg* opinion provided considerable additional legitimacy to the use of homogeneous precinct and ecological regression as appropriate techniques to estimate the levels of white and black support for particular candidates in the absence of reliable survey data for the elections under analysis. Justice Brennan repeated the lower court's characterization of these as standard techniques for the analysis of racially polarized voting and then added references to published articles by social scientists — Richard Engstrom and Michael McDonald and Bernard Grofman, Michael Migalski, and Nicholas Noviello — that also so characterize them.[34] And in judging the statistical significance of the correlation coefficients obtained in regressions of support levels for minority candidates versus the percentage of minority residents in the voting precinct, the Court accepted the accuracy of the conclusion that had been offered in my testimony in *Gingles* that the data "reflected positive relationships and that the correla-

33. 478 U.S. at 62. The quoted material ends with a reference to Grofman, Migalski, and Noviello 1985, 203. Shortly thereafter Brennan similarly asserted that "it is the difference between the choices made by blacks and whites — not the reasons for that difference — that results in blacks having less opportunity than whites to elect their preferred representatives. Consequently, we conclude that under the 'results test' of Section 2, only the correlation between the race of the voter and selection of certain candidates, not the causes of the correlation, matter." Brennan spoke directly only for a plurality in the particular section of his opinion from which these quotations come. But because Justice Byron White's concurring opinion expressed no disagreement with the plurality position on this point, the rejection of multivariate and related approaches to bloc voting in the Brennan opinion is the governing case law.

34. Engstrom and McDonald 1985; Grofman, Migalski, and Noviello 1985.

tions did not happen by chance."[35] Thus the specific thresholds for statistical significance that I offered in *Gingles* v. *Edmisten* and that were accepted by the *Gingles* court in effect became incorporated into the voting rights case law.

Another measurement question discussed in *Thornburg* had to do with whether the terms "minority candidate of choice" or "minority preferred candidate" mean simply the candidate who has received majority or plurality support from the minority group's voters regardless of the race of that candidate. The answer given by Justice Brennan was that, "under Section 2, it is the *status* of the candidate as the *chosen representative of a particular racial group,* not the race of the candidate that is important."[36] However, his position on this point did not reflect a majority; other justices took the position that the race of the candidate could or should be relevant, especially to a judgment of political cohesiveness. Moreover in *Gingles* the only elections that were examined by experts for either side were ones involving black candidates, but no Supreme Court justice required information on any elections other than those reviewed by the lower court to reach conclusions about whether voting in any given North Carolina legislative district was polarized. The relevance of the race of a candidate to judgments about polarized voting continues to be debated in the courts and by expert witnesses.

Issues in Racial Bloc Voting after Thornburg

Although the Court's decision in *Thornburg* effectively decided the question of how, for voting rights purposes, racially polarized voting was to be defined, and provided considerable legitimacy to the use of homogeneous precinct and ecological regression techniques for measuring bloc voting, it certainly did not end the disputations in court about racial bloc voting.[37] Not all these questions have yet been definitively resolved, but some appear to be near resolution.

One set of related questions that has arisen since *Thornburg* has to do with which elections are appropriate to examine to test for a pattern of racially polarized voting. For example, are the only relevant elections those that were for the office under litigation? What weight, if any, is to

35. 478 U.S. at 53, note 22.
36. 478 U.S. at 68.
37. Especially the double-equation approach; see Grofman, Migalski, and Noviello 1985; Loewen and Grofman 1989.

be given to patterns of polarization in other types of elections? How many elections must there be data from to establish a pattern of polarization? Are there some minority candidates who are so minor in terms of their campaign efforts that lack of minority support for them should not count as evidence for lack of minority political cohesion?

In a situation where the only minority candidates for supervisorial positions were minor ones as judged by campaign expenditures (with most spending less than $500 on their campaigns for an office in which a $1 million war chest was the sign of a viable candidate), the district court in *Garza* v. *Los Angeles Board of Supervisors* paid little attention to the evidence for racially polarized voting in supervisorial elections, relying instead on other types of evidence for polarization and minority cohesion, including the fact that the only Hispanic congressional and legislative officeholders in the county were elected from heavily Hispanic areas and that these areas elected Hispanic candidates with virtual certainty. However, the court noted that the relatively high levels of support from Hispanic voters for minor Hispanic candidates indicated a potential for political cohesion in contests where viable Hispanic candidates were running. In *Garza,* I testified that in the absence of special factors such as the absence of viable minority candidates, results in elections involving minority candidates of the same or similar type as were at issue in the lawsuit and relatively proximate to the present were the most relevant. Elections that satisfied only some of these conditions were informative to a lesser degree, depending on case-specific circumstances. These three criteria for selecting the most relevant elections are also found in my testimony in *Gingles.* Generally, however, courts have adopted considerable case-specific flexibility in judging the relevance of other elections.[38]

Other questions have arisen concerning the meaning of minority candidate of choice. What kinds of inferences about polarization, if any, can be drawn from elections without any minority candidates? Are there some minority candidates who could be identified as not supporting the minority group's particular interests, and thus for whom lack of minority support should not be taken as lack of minority cohesion? Is there a test to determine which nonminority candidates, if any, actually reflect the minority group's own particular interests?

In *Citizens for a Better Gretna* v. *City of Gretna* a Louisiana dis-

---

38. See, for example, *Citizens for a Better Gretna* v. *City of Gretna,* 834 F.2d 496 at 502–03 (1987).

trict court rejected as spurious the claim made by defendants that "black citizens have elected candidates of their choice to the Board of Aldermen with regularity because Gretna's white officials have always received a significant portion of the black vote and the support of Gretna's political organization."[39] The Fifth Circuit Court, on appeal, stated its test for the relevance of the race of the candidate by holding that "the race of the candidate is in general of less significance than the race of the voter—but only within the context of an election that offers the choice of supporting a viable minority candidate. . . . Implicit in the [Thornburg] holding is the notion that black preference is determined from elections which offer the choice of a black candidate. The various . . . concurring and dissenting opinions do not consider evidence of elections in which only whites were candidates. Hence, neither do we."[40] The Supreme Court denied certiorari of this case. Another district court decision, Chisom v. Roemer, took the opposite position, that black support of successful white candidates in contests in which only white candidates are running can be used to demonstrate absence of racial polarization, but that feature of the Chisom opinion is unlikely to stand up on appeal because it is before the same circuit that decided Citizens for a Better Gretna.

Another question has arisen with respect to whether polarized voting is sufficient evidence for cohesiveness. If voting is polarized, can socioeconomic differences among the members of the protected class be taken as evidence for lack of cohesion? If voting is polarized, can low minority turnout be taken as evidence for lack of minority cohesion? In Gomez v. City of Watsonville a demographer testifying for the city pointed out that Hispanics in the wealthier parts of the city were better educated and earned higher incomes than did Anglos citywide and were much better off than Hispanics in the heavily Hispanic areas of the city. He also testified that low levels of minority turnout vitiated any claim that Hispanics were cohesive. Both arguments were accepted by the district court; both were rejected by the Court of Appeals, which reversed the lower court's

39. Slip opinion at p. 20. The Court ventured that this argument recalled an anecdote once attributed to Henry Ford: "Any customer can have a car painted any color he wants so long as it is black." As I stated in my testimony in a subsequent case in Louisiana, Chisom v. Roemer, 853 F.Ed 1186 (5th Cir. 1988), now on appeal: "In like manner, if blacks are able to elect any candidate they want, but only as long as that candidate is white, we cannot say that blacks have an equal opportunity to elect candidates of their choice."

40. Citizens for a Better Gretna v. City of Gretna, 834 F.2d 496 at 503 (1987).

finding that there was no section 2 violation. The appellate decision said that the behavior of minority voters was a litmus test of cohesion and that there was unrebutted testimony in the trial record, based on standard ecological regression methods, that Hispanic voters overwhelmingly supported Hispanic candidates for city council.

Perhaps the single most important measurement issue that has arisen in cases since *Thornburg* has to do with how to judge the probable reliability of ecological regression and homogeneous precinct methods in particular circumstances. In the *Thornburg* decision the Supreme Court required expert witnesses to do far more than produce correlations; they must also estimate levels of candidate support among minority and nonminority voters.

A defense to a section 2 claim based on allegations about the unreliability of the methodology used in plaintiffs' expert testimony about bloc voting is becoming increasingly common in court. Jerome Sacks, one of the expert witnesses for Los Angeles County in *Garza*, in his depositions in some previous cases, took the position that none of the statistical analyses of racial voting patterns that he had ever seen (including the one accepted by the Supreme Court in *Thornburg*) was statistically valid. In his testimony in *Garza*, however, he tempered his remarks about the accuracy of at least the *Thornburg* analysis. He continues to attack the standard methods for proving polarization as unreliable except in circumstances where housing patterns are almost completely segregated. *Garza v. Los Angeles County Board of Supervisors* has the most extensive attack on the reliability of methodology to determine bloc voting of any court case to date. In it Sacks, another statistician, and social scientists testified that it was impossible to reliably estimate the voting behavior of blacks or Hispanics in Los Angeles County elections in the absence of exit poll or other survey data. According to these experts, no conclusions could be drawn about whether voting in the county was polarized along Hispanic versus non-Hispanic lines in a fashion that would affect the ability of Hispanics to elect a candidate of choice to the county board of supervisors. The district court found otherwise. "While in theory there exists a possibility that ecological regression could overestimate the [degree of polarization], experts for defendants have failed to demonstrate there is in fact any substantial bias."[41]

How can there can be so much dispute about what should be a relatively

41. *Garza* v. *Los Angeles County Board of Supervisors* (D.Cal. 1990), 90 C.D.O.S. 8138 (9th Cir. 1990), *cert. denied* January 1990.

straightforward measurement problem? In a nutshell, the answer is that estimates of racial polarization are often the targets of attack for three reasons. First, exit poll or survey data for the elections most relevant to a finding of racial polarization (those that involve minority candidates, those of the same type that are at issue in the lawsuit, and those that are relatively proximate to the present, with data from all three types highly desirable) are almost never available. Thus inferences about the voting behavior of individuals of each race must normally be based on evidence from aggregate (precinct-level) data, and courts must be convinced that such inferences can validly be drawn, even though no one can penetrate the secrecy of the ballot box to know how any given person voted. Second, estimates of racial polarization are attacked because the statistical techniques used to generate inferences about racial bloc voting are likely to be unfamiliar to courts and involve esoteric terminology such as "correlation coefficient," or "regression slope." Explaining results intelligibly can be difficult. Third, explanations of how estimates are derived can be subject to claims that problems of nonlinearity, such as those that may arise from contextual effects, invalidate the reliability of the statistical and descriptive techniques that were used, especially if only a small number of precincts are racially homogeneous.

My own view, quite simply, is that in most instances statistical issues raised to challenge the accuracy of bloc voting estimates are esoteric quibbles that lack any practical importance and that serve mostly to prolong trials and to increase the incomes of expert witnesses for both sides. Nonetheless, a mechanical application of regression methodology without an understanding of its basic logic and without attention to any accuracy checks can lead to error in some special circumstances, such as situations in which there is more than one covered minority of substantial size and in which minority populations are heavily intermingled without any single-minority homogeneous precincts.[42]

The Third Prong of the Thornburg Test

Although in most recent voting rights cases, most of the testimony by defendants' experts has been about alleged flaws in the testimony on purported measurements of polarization by the plaintiffs' experts, in

42. Accuracy checks are described in Grofman, Migalski, and Noviello 1985; Grofman and Migalski 1988; Loewen and Grofman 1989.

several recent cases a crucial matter of dispute has been whether the minority is large enough and geographically compact enough to constitute a majority in one or more districts. There are three aspects of this prong of the *Thornburg* test that have been subject to dispute.

First, what constitutes a minority group? In jurisdictions with more than one covered minority, the question has arisen as to whether distinct covered groups (blacks and Hispanics, for example) could be combined to determine if they passed *Thornburg*'s threshold size test. Most courts that have looked at this question have held that blacks and Hispanics could, in principle, be treated as a combined group, but to do so would require proof of electoral coalitions between them. In several California cities where this issue has arisen and in Boston, courts have rejected as inadequate the evidence of such coalitions offered by plaintiffs' witnesses. But in some Texas jurisdictions the evidence presented has been held to be sufficient.

While the question of whether distinct minority groups can be combined has been the focus of some litigation, there has also been at least one case in which experts for the defendant jurisdiction have claimed that a group covered under the Voting Rights Act should have its size reduced because it actually consists of disparate subgroupings that should not be combined for purposes of voting rights analysis. In *Garza* v. *Los Angeles County Board of Supervisors,* expert witnesses testified that not all those who identified themselves as of Spanish origin in the census should be regarded as falling under the covered rubric of "persons of Spanish heritage." In particular it was argued that persons born in Spain were not covered under the Voting Rights Act and that the portion of the Filipino population who identified themselves as of Spanish origin ought not to be counted as being of Spanish heritage. This issue was important in the litigation because removing these and some other categories from the protected class would reduce to below 50 percent the proportion of Hispanic citizens of voting age in the most heavily Hispanic district. The court followed the precedents of earlier decisions involving Hispanics by taking a response of Spanish origin on the census questionnaire as the defining characteristic of the covered population.

A second matter of dispute has been what constitutes geographic compactness. The use of the phrase in the *Thornburg* test raises the possibility that some sort of compactness analysis is called for.[43] Courts

43. See, for example, Niemi and others 1990.

generally have taken this language, however, to mean nothing more than indicating the existence of a minority population sufficiently geographically concentrated so that a district could be created in which the minority is a majority. This is certainly my view of how the phrase is to be interpreted in the context of section 2, and it is an interpretation consistent with the discussion by Blacksher and Menefee that Justice Brennan cited when he outlined the *Thornburg* three-pronged test.[44] Even more important, it is what the language of Justice Brennan's own discussion of the phrase suggests was intended.[45]

In *Gomez v. City of Watsonville* the demographer Peter Morrison, testifying on behalf of the city, pointed out that most of the Hispanic voters were located outside either of the two Hispanic-majority districts that were created as part of the plaintiffs' proposed seven-district replacement for the at-large elections then being used to elect city council members. As a consequence, the district court held that the city's Hispanics were not sufficiently geographically concentrated to have a claim under *Thornburg*. The appellate opinion, in reversing the lower court, held this finding erroneous as a matter of law. It called attention to the undisputed fact that two city council districts could be drawn, in each of which a majority of the population, the voting age population, and the estimated voting age citizen population was Hispanic.

A final difficulty involving the third prong of the *Thornburg* test has been how to resolve ambiguities in the phrase "constituting a majority in at least one district." The phrase is ambiguous without further specification. What is it that the minority is to constitute a majority of? Population? Voting age population? Voting age citizen population? Registrants? Actual voters?

Justice Brennan's discussion in *Thornburg* suggests a test based on potentially eligible voters, that is voting age population or citizen voting age population: "Unless minority members possess the *potential* to elect representatives in the absence of the challenged structure or practice, they cannot claim to have been injured by that structure or practice."[46] In *Romero v. City of Pomona* the appellate court required that the minority be numerous enough to constitute a citizen voting age majority in at least one district.[47] A majority of voting age population was the threshold

44. Blacksher and Menefee 1982.
45. 478 U.S. at 50–51, note 17.
46. 478 U.S. at 50–51, note 17.
47. *Romero v. City of Pomona*, 883 F.2d 527 (5th Cir. 1989).

used in an Illinois case. However, in that case, citizenship was not an important consideration.

In *Garza* v. *Los Angeles County Board of Supervisors* the district court rejected a rigid application of a bright-line test and harkened instead to the functional approach advocated by Justice Brennan in *Thornburg*. Judge David Kenyon noted that the Hispanic population in Los Angeles County was steadily growing, and the non-Hispanic white population was declining. In the light of this and other considerations a supervisorial district that almost met a 50 percent citizen voting age population test and that had roughly a 65 percent minority population and a Hispanic registration percentage comparable to that in other districts that had regularly elected Hispanic candidates was held to be adequate to create a realistic opportunity for Hispanics to elect a candidate of choice during the decade.[48] Judge Kenyon also found purposeful discrimination in the form of racial gerrymandering to fragment the Hispanic core population in the eastern and central part of the county. When the Eleventh Circuit Court considered *Garza* on appeal, it held that a bright-line test of minority population concentration was not a prerequisite to a voting rights violation in a situation where intentional discrimination had been shown. It upheld unanimously the trial court's finding of purposeful discrimination. The Supreme Court subsequently denied certiorari.

All but one court since *Thornburg* has treated the "ability to elect candidates of choice" as the right to be protected, although the Brennan opinion in *Thornburg* was explicit on the point that the decision did not address the question of "what standards should pertain to a claim brought by a minority group that is not sufficiently large and compact to constitute a majority in a single-member district, alleging that the use of a multimember district impairs its ability to influence elections."[49] The sole exception

48. Judge Kenyon also noted a fact pointed out by an expert witness in the Los Angeles County case, and not raised in earlier litigation, that citizen voting age population by race and Spanish origin was not available at the time of the postcensal redistricting in 1981 and would not be available in time for redistricting in 1991 or even 1992. Thus a threshold test that requires use of citizen voting age population data makes it effectively impossible for Hispanic plaintiffs to challenge 1990s redistricting plans until 1993 or so, and in some instances makes it impossible for jurisdictions to know whether they have drawn plans that will satisfy the provisions of the Voting Rights Act. Also, a number of Hispanics who are not citizens may be naturalized in the 1990s as a result of the special amnesty provisions passed by Congress several years ago, suggesting that the proportion in 1990, even if it could be known, may be a poor indicator of Hispanic potential to elect candidates of choice during the decade.

49. 478 U.S. at 46, note 12. The court in *Gingles* v. *Edmisten*, considering a remedy

is a recent opinion in *Armour* v. *Ohio* holding that racial concentrations of any size that constitute communities of interest cannot be unnecessarily fragmented.[50] However, that case is presently on appeal.

Social Science in the Courtroom

In the 1980s a number of social scientists whose testimony on bloc voting had been accepted by trial courts wrote journal articles explaining the nature of the methodology they had used, sometimes also arguing against alternative approaches. Some of these articles were cited in *Thornburg*, a few extensively. Indeed, one of the more remarkable features of the *Thornburg* opinion is its frequent citation of articles by social scientists, seventeen references in all. Moreover, unlike the common lawyerly practice of drawing only on social science materials that had been given the imprimatur of acceptance by a law review, many of the Court's citations were to articles in social science journals. These materials were used in the opinions, especially that of Justice Brennan, to support or to critique the expert testimony that was being reviewed. While many of the citations were no doubt window dressing, some of the articles proved influential in informing Justice Brennan (or perhaps it would be better to say, his clerk) about the methodological problems involved in defining and measuring racial bloc voting. No doubt in part because they believe their views may influence future decisions, expert witnesses who have lost in court and seek vindication are now also beginning to attack ecological regression and homogeneous precinct methodology in social science and law journals.[51]

The debate in the federal courts as to the measurement of racially polarized voting and the interpretation of the data is important because once racial bloc voting became the linchpin of any vote dilution case, how racially polarized voting was to be defined often had critical implica-

---

to the dilution it found occurring under multimember district elections, rejected the need to combine minority populations that were not large enough to form the majority within a single district.

50. *Armour* v. *Ohio*, 895 F.2d 1078 (6th Cir. 1990).

51. For example, Freedman and others 1991 repeat nearly verbatim the testimony offered by Freedman, Klein, and Sacks that was rebutted by the district court in *Garza* v. *Los Angeles County Board of Supervisors*. Their views are in turn rebutted by social scientists who testified for the plaintiffs in *Garza* (see Grofman 1991; Lichtman 1991).

tions for whether plaintiffs or defendants prevailed in the now hundreds of jurisdictions that have had their election mechanisms challenged. Moreover, the remarkable success rate of plaintiffs in section 2 litigation has affected outcomes in scores of other jurisdictions that have now shifted to single-member districts because of the fear, or the actual threat, of a voting rights lawsuit. Once the Supreme Court picked a definition of racial polarization, social scientists offering definitions that were incompatible would not be listened to by the courts.[52]

The definitions of racially polarized voting favored by expert witnesses for plaintiffs have considered correlations between race of the voter and race of the candidate and levels of own-race voting in elections involving minority candidates. Given the realities of own-race voting patterns in the jurisdictions being sued, an acceptance of definitions of this sort would almost certainly guarantee that courts would find voting to be racially polarized.

In contrast, the definitions of polarized voting offered by many experts for defendants before *Thornburg* made it almost impossible to prove polarization. Under the requirement that at least 90 percent of each minority group had to have voted for candidates of its own minority, for example, few elections anywhere would be found to be polarized. Requiring evidence of racial campaign appeals or turnout surge to prove polarization meant that business-as-usual voting by whites against black candidates would not count as polarization. Requiring that race be shown to have a major independent causal effect, after controlling for a laundry list of factors that were highly collinear with race, was to set a virtually impossible hurdle—as well as to ask the wrong question, as Justice Brennan's opinion in *Thornburg* made clear.

After *Thornburg* racially polarized voting became an even more important determinant of the outcomes of voting rights litigation, and the legal battle over racial bloc voting intensified as defendant jurisdictions sought loopholes in the definition of bloc voting in *Thornburg* and tried to force a reconsideration of the reliability of the techniques customarily used to estimate it. After *Thornburg*, if a case did go to trial, the defendant jurisdiction was apt to spend rather lavishly on expert testimony (mostly about alleged flaws in the testimony of plaintiffs' experts' measurements of polarization), and plaintiffs responded in kind—a litigious arms race in terms of the number of expert witnesses and the length of

52. See, for example, the trial court decision in *McNeil v. City of Springfield,* 658 F.Supp. 1015 (C.D. Ill. 1987).

their testimony. There has also been an escalation in the desirable length of the resumé of an expert witness. In many early cases, locally knowledgeable social scientists provided testimony about polarization that was sometimes little more than a look at election outcomes in racially homogeneous precincts. Now experts testifying about racial bloc voting who are not intimately familiar with heteroscedasticity and contextual effects may find themselves at a severe disadvantage.

In one 1987 vote dilution case in Peoria, Illinois, six experts were brought in, three of whom were from out of state. The plaintiffs' lead expert was a quantitative historian and author of the only statistical textbook devoted exclusively to ecological regression. The former chair of the Statistics Department at the University of Illinois and the former chair of the Statistics Department at Stanford were brought in by Peoria to rebut his testimony and that of another expert witness, a political scientist, that voting in the city was racially polarized. Plaintiffs, in turn, brought in as a rebuttal witness to these statisticians the political scientist who was the principal expert in *Thornburg*. Teams of experts on bloc voting also appeared on each side in *McNeil* v. *City of Springfield* and in several other cases since. In 1990 the ultimate battle of the experts occurred in *Garza* v. *Los Angeles County Board of Supervisors*. At one point, nearly two dozen were on the potential witness list, and eleven or more actually testified, five of them (three for defendants and two for plaintiffs) primarily on racial bloc voting. (It is hard to find better evidence for the importance attached by litigants in voting rights cases to social science testimony, especially that concerning racially polarized voting, than the amount of money litigants, especially defendant jurisdictions, are willing to pay for it.)[53]

The history of the debate over racially polarized voting shows that there has been a complex interaction between social science terminology and legal definitions, to the point that it is virtually impossible to distinguish where the former leaves off and the latter begins. For example, "racially polarized voting" is a term originating in social science that has come to be given a precise legal meaning whose relevance is supported in the Supreme Court's reading of the language of the Voting Rights Act and its legislative history. Still, it is impossible to imagine the Court's definition of "legally significant" polarization in *Thornburg* apart from the social science definition of polarization on which it rests. Similarly,

53. Several of the expert witnesses testifying for the County of Los Angeles in *Garza* received nearly $100,000.

questions about specification of the elections relevant to a polarization analysis and about the definition of "minority preferred candidate" that have been the topic of litigation in cases since *Thornburg* also have the characteristic that social science testimony is helping to shape legal conclusions in a fashion analogous to the way it shaped the standards for the definition and measurement of racially polarized voting in *Thornburg* itself. Moreover, the testimony of experts in voting rights cases sometimes is allowed to deal directly with the ultimate question of law, the finding of vote dilution in violation of the Voting Rights Act or the Constitution or both.

Also, most expert witnesses build upon both earlier expert testimony and earlier legal decisions in crafting their testimony. It is particularly important to recognize the continuities between the Supreme Court's approach to racial polarization in *Thornburg* and the way that previous lower court decisions had approached the matter. Much as I would like to take all the credit, the definitions I offered in my testimony in *Gingles* v. *Edmisten* were not really original with me. They built upon the earlier testimony of experts such as Charles Cotrell, James Loewen, Richard Engstrom, Chandler Davidson, and others, and the ways in which previous courts had looked at polarized voting.[54]

The *Thornburg* Test and the "Totality of Circumstances"

In *Gingles* v. *Edmisten,* both the expert testifying on behalf of North Carolina (Thomas Hofeller) and I offered virtually identical definitions of submergence of minority voting strength in an at-large or multimember district system. We each defined submergence as occurring if the minority group did not comprise a voting majority of the multimember district, but the minority population was large enough and concentrated enough

---

54. As I see it, my original contributions in *Gingles* to the analysis of racial bloc voting were threefold. First, I codified, in something approaching a logically exhaustive fashion, the questions that needed to be answered and helped reconcile conflicts in the earlier testimony between experts who sought to rely primarily on the correlation coefficient and those who had focused on the actual level of differences in minority and nonminority voting. Second, I invented (or, as I later learned from James Loewen and Alan Lichtman, reinvented) the double-equation regression methodology designed to cope with the problem that minorities often do not vote at the same rates (relative to voting-age population or even relative to registration) as those who are members of the majority—a methodology

to form at least one single-member district in which its members would constitute an effective voting majority, *and* voting was significantly racially polarized. If this test were to be used, the standards for a section 2 violation for multimember districts could be dramatically simplified.[55]

The three-judge federal district court in *Gingles,* having found evidence of six of the seven factors of the totality of circumstances test, did not discuss whether submergence, as defined here, had occurred. Justice Brennan, writing the opinion of the Supreme Court in *Thornburg,* cited my coauthored 1985 article but did not adopt the two-pronged test suggested there. Instead, following an approach suggested by Blacksher and Menefee, the Court majority adopted a three-pronged test that combined the two-pronged test of submergence with factor 7 of the totality of the circumstances test, the history of minority electoral success. With the advantage of hindsight, I prefer the Supreme Court's three-pronged test of vote dilution in a situation involving at-large or multimember district elections to the two-pronged test I offered. I also believe that, from the standpoint of social science, the *Thornburg* three-pronged test scores far better marks than does the old totality of circumstances test.

From the perspective of both law and social science, one of the greatest potential difficulties with court intervention into any legislated policy is the problem of developing manageable standards that are plausibly related to the relevant statutory and constitutional provisions. The test for manageable standards is similar to my earlier discussion of criteria for evaluating proposed use of social science variables. For standards to be manageable they must be clear, workable, explainable, and capable of developing the necessary evidence within the realistic time frame of litigation. With respect both to manageable standards and to relevance, the merits of the *Thornburg* test are considerable, especially when compared to its totality of circumstances predecessor.

that has now become standard in voting rights cases. Third, I worked out the statistical refinements to this regression methodology that were needed to cope with North Carolina multimember districts without head-to-head contests (see Grofman and Migalski 1988). (In some of these districts, voters could cast as many as eight votes. Moreover, voters varied considerably in how close they came to using all the votes to which they were entitled, and black and white voters did not on average cast the same number of ballots.)

When I testified in *Gingles* I was a relative novice. *Gingles* was my third voting rights case. Leslie Winner and Lani Guinier, the two lead attorneys with whom I worked on *Gingles,* had a thorough knowledge of the voting rights case law and previous expert witness testimony. I learned a great deal from them by "osmosis" and by having my ideas subject to mock (and not so mock) cross-examination.

55. Grofman, Migalski, and Noviello 1985.

First, while each of the elements of that test may be subject to dispute among competing expert witnesses, each can be related to objective indicators of the potential for and previous success of members of the minority group (and of those nonminority candidates who share the particular interests of the minority) who are the minority's candidates of choice, based on electoral data.

Second, each of the factors in the test is directly related to the definition of racial vote dilution offered in *Fortson v. Dorsey,* and repeated in subsequent cases, in which the Court alluded to practices that minimized or canceled out the voting strength of racial (or political) groups.[56] For there to be a violation under *Thornburg* there must first be a group that is sufficiently politically cohesive in its voting patterns (in the relevant elections) so that it is sensible to talk about that group's voting strength being minimized or canceled out. Next, given this level of minority cohesion, the general lack of minority success must be attributable to the unwillingness of the majority to support minority candidates. Finally, there must be an alternative to the challenged practice in which fairer representation would have been possible. In marked contrast, most of the factors in the totality of circumstances test bear only an indirect relationship to the concepts of vote dilution or submergence.[57] Thus although the *Thornburg* test deemphasizes the importance of factors highlighted by the 1982 Senate report and by previous court cases, this is not a failing. As I wrote in 1985, "Given the nature of the definition of vote dilution in Section 2 of the Voting Rights Act, it seems reasonable to look for factors which may impact the ability of a protected class to . . . translate its voting strength into representation of its choice."[58]

Third, the critical factors to be looked at under *Thornburg* are both few and close-ended, at least for cases involving the potential submergence of a single protected group's voting strength in an at-large or multimember district plan. (In *Thornburg* the Supreme Court clearly recognized that other types of factors might be relevant in other types of cases.)[59]

Fourth, unlike the totality of circumstances test, the three-pronged *Thornburg* test provides a clearly specified set of conditions sufficient to prove a voting rights violation, rather than a grab bag of factors whose exact relevance to a vote dilution claim is very much left to the vagaries

56. *Fortson v. Dorsey,* 379 U.S. 433 at 439 (1965).
57. See Grofman 1985, 144.
58. Grofman, Migalski, and Noviello 1985, 216.
59. 478 U.S. at 46–47, note 12.

of the trial court. The 1982 Senate report makes clear that there is no intent that any particular number of factors must be proved, nor that a majority of factors must point one way or another, and warns against using the factors in a mechanical point-counting fashion.[60] In the totality of circumstances test, identical factual conditions could, in principle, be interpreted in quite different ways by different judges. As one noted civil rights attorney characterized the test, it was "Throw mud against the wall. If enough of it sticks, you win."[61] However, some courts may have teflon-coated walls.

Fifth, despite what appears to have been the aims of the *Thornburg* test both to simplify the criteria for establishing a voting rights violation and to make them more precise and more relevant to the underlying concept of vote dilution, the Court also recognized that an inquiry into vote dilution is very much a fact-intense and a case-specific one. Thus while in most instances involving at-large or multimember jurisdictions the *Thornburg* three-pronged test specifies factors that are necessary as well as sufficient to establish vote dilution, the decision permits lower courts a flexibility in appraising particular facts in the light of common sense and local knowledge that has proved to be important in subsequent cases. Thus the Court has retained one of the most attractive features of the totality of circumstances approach without most of its drawbacks.

Sixth, the three-pronged test sets standards for minority vote dilution that allow litigants to anticipate the probable outcome of any litigation. In particular, jurisdictions for which no single-member remedy is feasible, or those in which voting is not racially polarized, or those in which minorities regularly succeed despite the presence of patterns of racially polarized voting (at levels comparable to what might be expected from a fairly drawn single-member-district plan), cannot be successfully challenged. This has meant that scores of jurisdictions now settle cases out of court once they review the relevant *Thornburg* factors and that plaintiffs prosecute only those cases with a high probability of success. Indeed, plaintiffs lose relatively few cases that they bring, with those few mostly on the cutting edge of voting rights case law—for example, cases in jurisdictions with more than one covered minority such as *Romero* v. *City of Pomona* or *Badillo* v. *City of Stockton*.[62]

60. Senate, 1982b.

61. Frank Parker, personal communication, 1986.

62. *Romero* v. *City of Pomona*, 883 F.2d 527 (5th Cir. 1989); *Badillo* v. *City of Stockton* (D. Cal. 1989), appeal pending.

Discussion

There are many avenues of further research that an examination of the testimony by experts in racial vote dilution cases might explore. For example, detailed examination of courtroom testimony and of depositions and other supporting documents could illuminate the dynamics of complex litigation and the ways in which the adversarial process reveals and conceals truth. Courtroom testimony is an almost unexplored source for comparative analysis of state and local election practices, comparisons of levels of polarization over time or across jurisdictions, and evidence about racial discrimination more generally. The specific topics of expert testimony in voting rights matters also raise important methodological issues that are of very general relevance to social science, as was suggested by the discussion earlier of the uses of ecological regression. Important issues worthy of inquiry include criteria to detect and measure racial gerrymandering in the context of single-member districts and standards for deciding when a district contains a minority population sufficient to give minorities a realistic opportunity to elect candidates of choice.[63] Another matter is to decide on methods for estimating the Hispanic share of registration using Spanish surname data and other population data, given the fact that not all people with a Hispanic surname are of Spanish origin, and some who lack a Hispanic surname nonetheless consider themselves of Spanish origin, and given the fact that Spanish origin is not a racial category and thus whites as well as blacks and Asians may be Hispanic. All these issues and many more were the subject of expert witness testimony in *Garza* v. *Los Angeles County Board of Supervisors*.[64] Racial gerrymandering and deciding the viability of a minority population, at least, can be expected to be important in voting rights litigation in the 1990s.

---

63. On racial gerrymandering, see Engstrom and Wildgen 1977; Grofman 1990; Grofman and Handley, forthcoming. On deciding when a district contains a significant minority population, see Brace and others 1988.

64. In *Garza* experts for plaintiffs introduced an alternative measure of Spanish origin based on corrections at the level of the census tract for type I and type II errors in surname-to-origin matchups. The two measures were shown to yield highly similar conclusions about minority registration percentages at the district level and virtually identical conclusions about levels of polarization in voting.

Other important questions for social scientists and other scholars to consider involve the normative implications of the *Thornburg* test and other recent developments in voting rights case law (see Cain in this volume). My views on that topic must be left to another paper.

I would however not wish to leave the reader with an overestimate of the importance of social science testimony in voting rights litigation. As in other civil rights domains, the nature of the case law is critical in determining who is likely to win and who to lose.[65] Given that case law, it is the facts—not attorneys and not expert witnesses—that almost always prove dispositive.[66] Here the *Thornburg* test offers a clear and manageable standard for vote dilution, and American politics is the better for the gains in minority representation it has brought.

65. Compare with Chesler, Sanders, and Kalmuss 1988. Success has many parents, failure is parthenogenic. The Voting Rights Act has been a marvelous success and there is plenty of credit to go around. The act would not have come to be without courageous black Americans willing to risk their lives to gain justice and the leadership of Lyndon Johnson and a Congress that provided bipartisan support for the act and then to its several extensions. It would never have had the success it had without the actions of the Supreme Court, the Department of Justice, and the many attorneys who litigated to make its provisions meaningful. Credit also must go to foundations such as Rockefeller, Ford, and Carnegie that helped finance and bring into being groups such as the Lawyers' Committee for Civil Rights Under Law, the Southwest Voter Registration Institute, and the Mexican American Legal Defense and Educational Fund.

66. As one prominent civil rights attorney, James Blacksher, once put it: "the job of the expert witness is to put the hay down where the goats can get at it" (as quoted by Peyton McCrary, personal communication, October 19, 1990).

Litigation, Lobbying, and the Voting Rights Bar

GREGORY A. CALDEIRA

THE MERITS OF MOST LEGISLATION initiated in the mid-1960s under the rubric of the Great Society have continued to be the focus of controversy. But few citizens, policy analysts, or public officials doubt the success of the reforms initiated by the Voting Rights Act or its continued vitality as an instrument of political power. Indeed, the act seems to have transformed southern politics and altered the structure of all American politics. Blacks have taken part in electoral politics in large and increasing numbers since the late 1960s. And politicians have taken notice. No longer can conservatives in the North count on Democrats in the South as faithful allies. In several important legislative campaigns of the 1980s, southern Democrats contributed the margin of victory for the cause of a liberal coalition: in response to strong pressure from blacks, for example, southern Democrats sealed the defeat of Robert Bork's nomination to the Supreme Court in 1987.[1] Former segregationists now unabashedly court the votes of black constituents. It is particularly ironic to witness in the past few years the organizational apparatuses of both parties cultivating litigators for minorities as the reapportionments of the 1990s begin.

Litigation has played a crucial part in the successful implementation of the Voting Rights Act. Indeed, litigation on voting rights has developed into something of a cottage industry, and I would argue that a "voting rights bar" has sprung into being.[2] This bar encompasses private attorneys, interest groups, attorneys for the federal government, expert witnesses, and consultants. It has enjoyed an impressive record of success, even in the face of federal courts that can be unreceptive to liberal causes. The

I would like to acknowledge the expert assistance of William Swinford, a doctoral candidate at Ohio State University, the help of Michael Banish, a senior at Ohio State, and conversations with John R. Wright, University of Iowa.

1. Pertschuk and Schaetzel 1989; McGuigan and Weyrich 1990.
2. Of course, a bar exists in many other areas of law. Bars have grown up around the law of patents, civil rights, energy, the rights of consumers, and other issues. Social scientists have long recognized the role of specialization and expertise in the practice of law (see, for example, Heinz and Lauman 1982). But to my knowledge no one has focused on the policy consequences of the development of these cadres of lawyers and their adjuncts.

development and institutionalization of groups of policymakers and satellites should surprise no one: numerous subgovernments of this sort have flourished in a similar fashion in the past twenty years. Here I shall sketch briefly the rise of the voting rights bar as a political phenomenon, a development few scholars have treated as of importance and interest in itself.[3]

I also want to emphasize the growing importance of legislative lobbying for blacks and other minorities. The passage of the Voting Rights Act, together with scores of successes in the courts, has translated into greater political clout for blacks and Hispanics in Congress as well as in legislatures around the nation. Black and Hispanic leaders would not, of course, express much satisfaction with the success achieved so far; but there is little doubt that these groups can boast of greater access and influence in the legislatures. Before the Voting Rights Act, minorities relied heavily on the federal courts to achieve their goals. Since the 1980s, lobbying in the legislature has become a potent weapon in the hands of minorities, especially blacks. Indeed, as the political makeup of the federal courts becomes overwhelmingly conservative, legislative lobbying may very well become the strongest armament in the arsenal of blacks and Hispanics. And although aggressive litigation has contributed much to successes in legislative lobbying, the goals of lobbyists and litigators for blacks and other minorities are not always in synchronization. Successful litigation can make the lives of lobbyists more difficult, and what a lobbyist may view as an achievement may not satisfy a litigator.[4]

The Evolution of Interest-Group Litigation on Voting Rights

Several of the authors in this volume trace the development of the law on voting rights, statutory and judicial, in great detail, and others have done so even more elaborately elsewhere. I will review some of this history to remind readers of the intricate involvement of interest groups—at the

3. But see Graham 1990, 362–65, for a brief discussion of the Voting Rights Act as having created an "iron triangle" by the early 1970s. Although many scholars have studied the critical role of interest groups in the expansion of the franchise for blacks and Hispanics, no one seems to have analyzed the development of voting rights activism as a business.
4. For tensions between lobbyists and litigators in the negotiations over the amendments to the Voting Rights Act in 1982, see Thernstrom 1987, 105–36, and Pertschuk 1986, 148–80. This is not an issue on which I have seen any discussion in the relevant literature, and yet if an organized interest hopes to influence policymaking, effective lobbying and litigation are important.

outset, principally the National Association for the Advancement of Colored People and the NAACP Legal Defense and Education Fund; later, more diverse organizations—in litigation on racial discrimination in voting. The participation of the NAACP in the earliest lawsuits stands as a classic example of interest-group litigation, the intentional and often opportunistic use of the courts by an organized interest to pursue well-defined political goals. To provide a context for understanding the development, characteristics, and consequences of the voting rights bar, it is important to illustrate the distinctive stages in the history of litigation on the franchise.

Litigation on voting rights began as an essential, perhaps the most important, part of the movement for the civil rights of black Americans. Leaders of the black community saw the franchise as the linchpin of civil and political freedom. Few people disputed the fundamental right to vote—after all, the Fifteenth Amendment explicitly prohibited racial discrimination in the franchise. It was thus much easier to construct a consensus among whites on this right than around efforts to achieve racial integration in housing, schools, and public accommodations, which stood on much more controversial grounds, both constitutionally and as a matter of practical politics. So when black leaders came together in 1909 to found the National Association for the Advancement of Colored People, extension of the franchise became the organization's major political commitment. For the next sixty years, challenges to official and unofficial discrimination in voting invariably involved the NAACP. No other organization had the skills or resources to mount such efforts, and similar organizations representing other minorities did not appear until the 1960s. In the absence of statutory mechanisms, campaigns to enfranchise blacks emphasized litigation, mostly to abolish grandfather clauses and white primaries.

The NAACP's efforts in litigation were initially limited to small steps. In 1910 Oklahoma had amended its constitution to excuse all those who had a right to vote in 1866 or "anyone who was a lineal descendant of such persons" from taking a literacy test to qualify to vote. On the surface this grandfather clause did not discriminate on account of race, but, of course, its intent was clear. Accordingly, the Department of Justice, acting on the basis of the Enforcement Acts of 1870, charged several registrars with racial discrimination in congressional elections. *Guinn and Beal* v. *United States* duly came before the Supreme Court on certification from a conviction and an affirmance in the circuit court of appeals.[5] Moorfield

5. *Guinn and Beal* v. *United States,* 238 U.S. 347 (1915).

Storey, president of the NAACP, filed an amicus curiae brief in which he did not challenge the constitutionality of the literacy test but rather the racially motivated exemption. The NAACP seems to have joined the fray late in the battle; in the earlier stages, the Republican and Socialist parties and several black organizations, including the Constitutional League, the Protective League, and the Fourth and Fifth Congressional League, had resisted the grandfather clause in Oklahoma.[6]

In the litigation over white primaries in the 1920s the NAACP, together with its chapters and other organizations, began to take a leading role in planning, staffing, and providing resources. Various leaders in Texas, the main theater of action, created difficulties for the national leaders of the NAACP. R. D. Evans of Waco, Texas, a Democrat and president of the Independent Colored Voters' League, fought the decision of the Democratic Executive Committee in Houston to exclude all black voters in the next primary and carried the challenge all the way to the Supreme Court, which denied the claim for lack of a remedy.[7] This dramatized the dangers of unmanaged litigation for the long-term success of the NAACP's efforts in the courts. Even though the issues in the case held significant implications for the campaign of litigation on voting rights, Evans did not, apparently, communicate with or receive assistance from the NAACP. A few years later, *Nixon v. Herndon,* a product of the thriving El Paso branch of the NAACP, marked a shift in the pattern of litigation on voting rights.[8] The leaders of this branch "offered the national office in New York a case, money, local lawyers, and responsibility for carrying the action to the higher courts."[9] Local lawyers, advised by the national office, carried the suit to the doors of the Supreme Court and then turned it over to the counsel on which the NAACP relied, Moorfield Storey and James A. Cobb. The justices invalidated the law in 1927.

Changes in the leadership and structure of the NAACP in the late 1920s and early 1930s brought different litigators and modes of operation. Storey, Louis Marshall, Clarence Darrow, and other eminences died or left the organization; and the success in *Nixon v. Herndon,* apart from bringing in money, drew other distinguished lawyers to the National Legal Committee of the NAACP and helped to recruit young attorneys.

6. Vose 1972, 21–46.
7. *Love* v. *Griffith,* 266 U.S. 32 (1924).
8. *Nixon* v. *Herndon,* 273 U.S. 536 (1927). This case involved a challenge to a statute that said in part: "in no event shall a Negro be eligible to participate in a Democratic primary election held in the state of Texas" (Vose 1972, 293).
9. Vose 1972, 294.

Nathan Margold, a high-powered graduate of Harvard Law School, joined the organization in 1930 as special counsel to construct a plan of litigation for constitutional change. Clement E. Vose characterized Margold's plan as a "perceptive and ambitious blueprint of how an organization might cope with social disadvantage and legal invidiousness by planning and conducting test cases."[10] The emergence of Charles Houston, a leader of the civil rights bar in the 1930s, signaled another change in the NAACP: the increasingly important role of black lawyers. In 1934 he became the first general counsel.

Yet even as the NAACP became better organized and staffed and black lawyers began to take larger roles in litigation, the national office had to deal with disputes among rival chapters in Texas—in the prelude to *Nixon v. Condon,* a successful venture—and with members of the black civil rights bar who did not cooperate or submit to the authority of Houston, Margold, and others as leaders of the campaign to enfranchise black Americans, as in *Grovey v. Townsend.*[11] There was in the *Grovey* litigation a streak of independence, in large part the result of resentment among members of the black civil rights bar toward the NAACP's past dependence on white lawyers.[12] In the middle and late 1930s, black lawyers—Houston, Thurgood Marshall, James Nabrit, Jr.—became the dominant forces in the NAACP. The creation of the Legal Defense and Education Fund in 1939 represented a response not only to the installation of a full-time staff and the substantial overhead of a program of litigation but also to an increasing differentiation of the goals and styles of litigators and others in the NAACP. Gradually, and based on a wealth of experience in dealing with lawyers and local NAACP branches, Thurgood Marshall pressed for control of litigation. He devised policies and procedures to fend off interference from the national office and Walter White of the Washington Bureau and to discipline the state and local chapters to a national strategy. Litigation on voting rights in the 1940s accordingly followed a more orderly path than it had in the previous twenty years.[13] From time to time, of course, the Legal Defense Fund had strong allies in voting rights cases from among organized white liberals, including

10. Vose 1972, 308.
11. *Nixon v. Condon,* 286 U.S. 73 (1932); *Grovey v. Townsend,* 295 U.S. 45 (1935).
12. Vose 1972, 316; Meier and Rudwick 1976.
13. For helpful discussions of litigation on the voting rights of blacks before the 1950s, most of which involved the NAACP, see Vose 1972, 287–326, and Lawson 1976, 18–54.

the American Civil Liberties Union, American Jewish Committee, and the National Lawyers' Committee, but it did the bulk of the work.

In the 1950s and early 1960s the civil rights movement expanded the push for enfranchisement of blacks to include the national legislative process; the civil rights acts of 1957 and 1960 followed. The NAACP Legal Defense and Education Fund of course continued to litigate on voting rights and to have an extraordinary record of success in other areas.[14] But the Civil Rights Division of the Department of Justice, especially after 1957, controlled the flow of much of the essential judicial agenda on the franchise. "Beginning about 1960," Frank Parker of the Lawyers' Committee for Civil Rights Under Law has commented, "the civil rights movement switched its emphasis from a litigation strategy to a mass-based protest strategy" to overcome the remaining restrictions on the franchise.[15] Litigators adopted a defensive strategy, protecting the organizational activities of workers in the movement from various legal and illegal barriers.

The political ferment in the early 1960s and especially the passage of the Voting Rights Act of 1965 provided the environment for a vigorous expansion in the number, size, and specialization of organizations concerned with civil rights and in the business of voting rights litigation.[16] These new organizations included the Mexican American Legal Defense and Educational Fund, the Puerto Rican Legal Defense and Education Fund, the Lawyers' Committee for Civil Rights Under Law, and the Lawyers' Constitutional Defense Committee.[17] No longer did the NAACP Legal Defense Fund occupy the field alone. In fact, in some parts of the nation, the Lawyers' Committee for Civil Rights Under Law, the Southern Regional Office of the ACLU in Atlanta, and the Lawyers' Constitutional Defense Committee (in existence briefly) dominated litigation on voting rights while the NAACP litigated on other issues. In some states such as Alabama, a handful of lawyers handled most of the cases. And, of course, the Legal Defense Fund and NAACP had split apart and the NAACP had established its own litigating arm in 1964.[18]

14. One example of voting rights litigation in these years is *Gomillion* v. *Lightfoot*, 364 U.S. 399 (1960).

15. Parker 1990, 9.

16. Heck and Stewart 1982; Stewart and Heck 1983.

17. O'Connor and Epstein 1984; O'Connor and Epstein 1989.

18. In the mid-1950s, the Legal Defense Fund became "completely independent of the NAACP, primarily to protect the tax-deductibility of LDF's contributions; the sharing of

As the cast of characters changed, so did the strategy of litigation. The Voting Rights Act had eliminated the main restrictions on the franchise, and accordingly the voting rights bar refocused on challenging the final barriers—subtle and not-so-subtle dilutions of the electoral strength of newly enfranchised black voters. Many of the jurisdictions that had invented and then defended the grandfather clause, the poll tax, and the literacy test were not sitting still for implementation of the act, and in the ensuing years blacks faced substantial, at times massive, resistance to their attempts to vote.[19] Until the appearance of the new civil rights organizations, the Department of Justice controlled the pace of litigation, but despite devoting substantial resources to threats to voting rights, it never moved as quickly or forcefully as the victims would have liked. The amplified voting rights bar litigated hundreds of cases, primarily in the South, and sought to remove not only mechanisms *intended* to discriminate against minorities but also those with the *effect* of disadvantaging these groups. It made a particular target of at-large elections and other modes of districting that diluted the power of black voters. The ultimate aim was to permit minorities to elect candidates of their own choice—often, presumably, minorities. In the past twenty-five years, with certain important exceptions, the Supreme Court and lower federal courts have rewarded the efforts by expanding the rights of minorities and protections against discrimination.[20] Amendments to the Voting Rights Act in 1982—criticized in some quarters as affirmative action in electoral affairs—provided legal standards designed to prevent electoral mechanisms that would deny minorities a fair chance of electing candidates of choice and enshrined as the criterion the discriminatory effect rather than the intent of the mechanisms.[21] These statutes have strengthened the hand of the voting rights bar in the courts,

---

staff and the interlocking of the boards of directors were eliminated" (Wasby 1985, 342). Tensions over credit for victories and competition for financial support resulted in a lawsuit in which the NAACP sought to prohibit the Legal Defense Fund from using NAACP in its name but lost on appeal in the Circuit Court of the District of Columbia in 1985 (O'Connor and Epstein 1989, 129).

19. See Parker 1990 for vivid descriptions from one who experienced these episodes of political chicanery.

20. This is no place to provide a detailed account of the ins and outs of voting rights litigation before the Supreme Court since 1965. Besides, no one would agree with the details of anything but an exhaustive review, and those who disagree on the crucial issues do not agree on what the Supreme Court has said in the various landmark decisions. Nevertheless the Court does seem to have responded favorably to much of the agenda of the voting rights bar.

21. For criticism of the amendments, see Thernstrom 1979; Thernstrom 1987.

and in the years since the 1982 amendments the number of private and federal cases filed has been substantially greater than in the previous decade. Reapportionment in the 1990s will no doubt bring, as it already has brought in many cases, a new wave of challenges from the voting rights bar; and the renewed vigor of statutory protections and the impressive steadfastness of the federal courts in enforcing the rights make the prospects of the voting rights bar relatively bright.

Development and Consequences of the Voting Rights Bar

A large number of individuals and organizations inside and outside the federal government participate in voting rights litigation. These often act in concert, but they have different interests and use different strategies and tactics. To understand the development of voting rights advocacy for blacks and other minorities, one needs to take account of the growth of interest groups founded to represent their rights, for as in many other areas of litigation, individuals in voting rights lawsuits are exemplars of larger social phenomena and organized interests seek to vindicate values much broader than those required to settle a particular suit.[22] One should not assume an identity of interests between the litigant and those who as representatives of an interest group provide legal counsel. And, of course, the goals of mature organizations often displace the original purposes. Indeed, the voting rights bar and litigation on voting rights evince a complex set of relationships.

Voting Rights Litigation and Interest Groups

Those who write on interest-group litigation normally use the phrase loosely. Nonetheless it implies a form of litigation more planned than that in the usual run of cases, for stakes broader than the concerns of the immediate parties, and executed or supported by an organized group or set of people or institutions working in concert.[23] Participation can

22. Organized interests bring or respond to an overwhelming majority of the cases the Supreme Court decides to hear on merit. In some instances an organization participates as party or direct representative; in others it takes part as amicus curiae. If one uses a broad definition of organized interests, then the proportion of cases of this kind on the Court's plenary agenda would be even larger. See Epstein 1991.

23. I prefer to cast the net of "organized interest" very broadly to include trade associations, civic advocacy groups, public interest law firms, labor unions, corporations, state governments, charitable institutions, and peak associations (associations of associations).

be as a party or amicus curiae, direct representative, financial supporter, or consultant.

The great names associated with litigation on voting rights—Moorfield Storey, Louis Marshall, Thurgood Marshall, Charles Houston—exemplify organizational attempts to shape litigation to achieve well-defined policy goals. Two of the campaigns to which I referred earlier, against grandfather clauses and white primaries, often serve as textbook examples of how an interest group, especially if it is an underdog, can go into the courts if no other forum is available.[24] Today, of course, more interest groups participate, so litigation on voting rights is not as organized as during the era of the NAACP's dominance; but the litigation remains a relatively self-conscious campaign.

Litigation of the sort seen in the 1970s and 1980s does not just happen; interest groups encourage and foster these cases. Those who have participated, inside and outside organizations, emphasize coordination and control, and institutions or regimes form around litigation to ensure that coordination and control. Litigation on voting rights, although nominally concerning particular groups or districts or states, articulates a vision of the interests of broad, national classes of people. It is ongoing "public law litigation," to adopt a term coined to describe judicially managed restructuring of social, political, and economic institutions.[25] Finally, many of those who litigate in voting rights cases file lawsuits strategically; lawyers and interest groups take into account the long-range consequences of particular legal battles. This is a natural corollary of the emphasis on broad policy goals rather than the concerns of individuals. I do not wish to overstate the degree of coordination and control or the rationality of the litigators. Much of the time, they do file lawsuits strategically; but it is often hit or miss, and other lawyers, private or from other organizations, may jump into the fray and complicate the situation and the issues.[26] And of course, the plaintiffs themselves drive some of the lawsuits. Some organizations, such as the Southwest Voter Education Project, pay particular attention to minority plaintiffs active in local communities. Such sensitivity naturally makes strategic litigation more difficult.

24. Of course, the campaigns against discrimination in housing, which began around the same time as the litigation on voting rights, and against segregation in education, which started somewhat later, also come in for much praise as organized efforts. For excellent treatments of these instances of interest group litigation, see Vose 1959; Vose 1972; Tushnet 1987; Kluger 1976; and Lawson 1976.

25. Chayes 1976.

26. Wasby 1985.

The Voting Rights Bar and Policy Dominance

In voting rights litigation and politics, as in innumerable other areas of public interest, an identifiable set of individuals and institutions have developed high levels of continuing communication with one another; substantial shared interests, values, and often backgrounds; some degree of coordination—often very loose—as a result of the communication and shared interests; and cooperation in support of an agenda. As is true in any informal organization, not all members share the same political vision or hold views with the same intensity. Many whom I include in the voting rights bar would fall at the periphery of the policy network. For some who litigate on voting rights, I suppose "policy network" will conjure up visions of the military-industrial complex, the construction lobby, and the like, and thereby raise hackles.[27] But I use the term in a descriptive rather than evaluative fashion.

Who belongs to the voting rights bar? Jeremy Bentham referred to "judge and company" to describe the development of common law, and I take a similarly broad view of policymaking on voting rights. The members include lawyers working for or representing a long list of interest groups; cooperating and affiliated attorneys for many of the same groups; private lawyers, many of whom started out in one of these organizations; the Ford and Rockefeller foundations, which sponsor biennial conferences to bring together current and potential members of the voting rights bar and have supported the movement in many other ways; and officials and rank-and-file lawyers in the voting rights section of the Department of Justice.[28] The members also include bureaucrats in the various federal agencies, organized projects in support of voting rights and registration, think tanks, portions of the federal and state bench, members of the academic bar and a few political scientists, interested members of the judiciary committees of the Senate and House, officeholders and potential officeholders who stand to gain or lose from future voting rights litigation, and expert witnesses who provide evidence in case after case.[29]

---

27. These days, conservatives often refer to the members and friends of the Leadership Conference on Civil Rights, the peak association in this area, as the civil rights lobby. This is supposed to label advocates of the civil rights of blacks and other minorities as disproportionately and inappropriately influential in Congress. Meant pejoratively by most opponents and critics, it also indicates the esteem in which Washington holds representatives of minorities and other disadvantaged groups.

28. Graham 1990.

29. See Grofman in this volume.

If the NAACP and the NAACP Legal Defense and Education Fund dominated the first forty years of litigation on voting rights, in the 1960s and 1970s the voting rights bar grew from a few lawyers and groups into a large and thriving industry.[30] It is now not only a broad coalition, but comprises very diverse interest groups and litigators. In the 1960s the Lawyers' Committee for Civil Rights Under Law, created at the behest of President Kennedy and funded by the Ford Foundation, became especially important. For a time the Lawyers' Constitutional Defense Committee, established by a coalition of the chief legal officers of the Congress of Racial Equality (CORE), the ACLU, the NAACP Legal Defense Fund, the American Jewish Congress, the National Council of Churches, and others to defend civil rights activists in the South, litigated a substantial number of cases. Soon new organizations, modeled on the Legal Defense Fund, began to participate in the development of voting rights law. These included the Mexican American Legal Defense and Educational Fund and the Puerto Rican Legal Defense and Education Fund. The American Civil Liberties Union, which had for decades litigated on some facets of racial discrimination, often in alliance with the NAACP Legal Defense Fund, sponsored the Voting Rights Project. From 1972 through 1988 the director of the project, Laughlin McDonald, filed 157 suits against 180 jurisdictions. The project did much of the day-to-day work of private enforcement of the Voting Rights Act, especially during the Nixon and Reagan administrations, years of conflict between the federal government and the civil rights movement.[31]

The campaign of litigation has received aid from many groups, some of which do not litigate. The NAACP, National Urban League, and other well-established organizations have done much of the hard work of registering and mobilizing black voters. But new organizations sprang into being in the 1960s and 1970s for the specific purpose of increasing the political participation of minorities. The Southwest Voter Registration and Education Project attempted to enfranchise Hispanics around the nation, but especially in Texas, New Mexico, Arizona, Colorado, and California.[32] The cause of voting rights has also received assistance

30. Thus far, no one has done a comprehensive census of organizational activity—litigation, lobbying, grass-roots activism, and electoral mobilization—in voting rights matters. Even a cursory glance at the main sources on voting rights suggests an extraordinary amount of organized activity, especially in the past quarter century. Here I mention several organizations and activities by way of illustration.

31. Walker 1990, 355–57.

32. The project also supplies expert witnesses in litigation brought by other Hispanic organizations and private lawyers.

from the Leadership Conference for Civil Rights, a coalition of 185 groups that includes virtually all the national organizations involved in protecting civil rights and liberties. It helped coordinate lobbying in favor of the several statutes on voting rights and provides a regular forum for the exchange of information.

The creation of new organizations and specialized units within established ones thus strongly suggests the institutionalization of the voting rights bar, but there is other evidence. The number of voting rights cases filed in federal district courts has risen from 100 each year in the early 1970s to more than 200 in the late 1980s. Similarly, class actions brought by private litigators in the federal courts have increased from 60 in 1977 to a high of 158 in 1988, although the number varies considerably from year to year. At the behest of the voting rights bar the Supreme Court continues to accept a significant number of cases on their merits, even though one would anticipate a diminution of this activity as more and more issues become settled.[33] Members of the voting rights bar outside the federal government institute perhaps 95 percent of these cases in any particular year. Enforcement of voting rights is, therefore, very much an activity of the private sector.[34]

No well-organized opposition has arisen to challenge the power of the voting rights bar: no one has a strong, direct, long-term interest in defeating those who seek to vindicate claims under the Voting Rights Act.[35] Defendants in particular cases, of course, have a strong interest in winning, but none has set out to pursue the legal issues systematically over an extended period of time. Extension of the franchise features a classic pattern of conflict over policies with distributive consequences; it pits concentrated, organized interests against diffuse, unorganized interests.[36] Some have expressed surprise at the weak opposition to the legislative campaign for amendments to the Voting Rights Act in 1982, but in view

33. In the past five terms the Court has decided five cases on the merits; in the previous five, ten cases.

34. Administrative Office of the United States Courts, various years.

35. There is apparently some evidence of organized opposition on the part of those who insure cities and states for liability, but no one has documented the extent of this development or explored its consequences.

36. In contrast, for example, on issues of employment and benefits, organized labor faces the stiff opposition of trade associations, the National Right to Work Committee, the National Association of Manufacturers, the Chamber of Commerce, and others. And supporting the Civil Rights Act of 1990, lobbyists for the civil rights movement ran into important and respectable opposition from trade associations and major associations for business, which lobbied effectively in the executive branch and strenuously but not very successfully before Congress against certain portions of the act.

of the nature of this policy, precisely this pattern should have been expected.[37]

The voting rights bar has effectively framed the voting rights debate in the courts and in the legislature. It controls the initiative in the courts. In the court of public opinion, those who argue in favor of stringent protection of voting rights have claimed and occupied the high ground; it is understandably difficult for opponents to catch the imagination of the public. The bar decides where and when to strike with a lawsuit, which provides more favorable forums and better evidence.[38] Government units can only respond in a defensive fashion. In part the bar's advantage results from the very nature of the Voting Rights Act; and in significant part it is the result of the large number of egregious situations from which the voting rights bar may choose. The credible threat of a lawsuit places the bar and its allies in a strong bargaining position.

The Success of the Voting Rights Bar

Members of the voting rights bar have been successful because they have litigated many similar cases, which gives them a tremendous edge over "one-shotters."[39] No one in this legal system has the clout of the United States government, which is the ultimate repeat player; but many interest groups and large institutions can come close, and in so doing reap advantages that include the "ability to structure the transaction; expertise, economies of scale, low start-up costs; informal relations with institutional incumbents; bargaining credibility; ability to adopt optimal strategies; ability to play for rules in both political forums and in litigation itself by litigation strategy and settlement policy; and ability to invest to secure penetration of favorable rules."[40]

---

37. Pinderhughes (forthcoming); Pertschuk 1986.

38. Lately the voting rights bar has sought to expand the domain of conflict (for example, black-Hispanic alliances) and has lost more cases on the legal frontiers.

39. Writing of the influx of litigators into Mississippi in the 1960s, Frank Parker of the Lawyers' Committee has remarked, "Now black plaintiffs had their own lawyers who resided in the state and who developed alliances with their clients; who were familiar with local conditions; who developed a certain level of credibility even with hostile local federal judges by repeatedly getting their decisions reversed on appeal; and who, by repeatedly filing the same kinds of cases and exchanging information and litigation techniques among themselves, developed a high level of expertise in civil rights litigation that gave their clients an advantage" (1990, 81–82).

40. Galanter 1975, 347.

Over the years, much of the voting rights bar has, while seeking justice in individual cases, kept an eye peeled for the long-range consequences of judicial decisions. The large number of potential and actual cases permits the bar to trade immediate victories for advantageous changes in the legal rules. It can play for rules changes instead of achieving implementation case by case, although it clearly mixes the two approaches: the first makes the second easier. I do not wish to impute perfect rationality to these litigators, but relative to one-shotters, members of the voting rights bar have shown strategic sensibilities.

Because of the vast and diverse array of "litigators and company," few issues in law and politics can boast such an impressive store of expertise, much of it on one side of the argument. Many advocates, inside interest groups and in private practice, have years of experience in voting rights litigation, and law schools around the nation harbor a ready collection of collaborators and supporters.[41] And although there is a natural tension between the Department of Justice and the private bar, the store of talent in the federal government also constitutes an important resource for the voting rights bar. But if they represent a store of expertise, larger numbers of organizations and litigators do bring complications: organized interests compete with one another for members, supporters, financial assistance, political credit, and prestige. Still, the diversity and specialization have permitted a rough division of labor among interest groups, private litigators, and the Department of Justice. No two organizations do precisely the same thing, although to the uninitiated the field may sometimes look crowded. And so, the voting rights bar rests on a firm and deep infrastructure.

Repeat participants can engage in careful screening of cases. A long-range legal strategy or anything resembling a campaign requires a judicious choice of vehicles. In setting the Supreme Court's agenda, for example, the great success of Office of the Solicitor General may depend not so much on the inherent political clout of the federal government as on the extraordinarily self-conscious process of selection through which it decides what cases to push. The Voting Rights Section of the Department of Justice is extremely careful in the selection of cases and like the Solicitor General rarely loses in the courts. Organized private interests have also

41. To be sure, the defendants in litigation on voting rights can also boast of a large and talented stable of expert witnesses, including Charles Bullock, Susan McManus, John Wilgden, and Harold Stanley, and a smaller number of lawyers such as John McDermott and Katherine Butler who are repeat players.

often, although not always, shown great care not to squander resources on cases of little importance or poor quality.[42] Most have stringent guidelines on case selection, and many use sophisticated networks of people and organizations—often affiliates, chapters, or cooperating attorneys—to help in this task.[43] These networks bring with them all the advantages of information gathering at the grass roots. Coherent strategy and coordinated action has marked litigation on voting rights. Organizations seem to select the different kinds of legal activity from the full range of options, from the filing of briefs amicus curiae prior to certiorari, through sponsorship and representation of parties, to the careful balancing of political forces on briefs.

For the advocates of voting rights, especially since 1965, legislative and judicial victories or losses have complemented and affected one another. If litigators suffer important defeats on the legal rules or see important opportunities in changes, advocates of voting rights can seek assistance in Congress. The very record of the voting rights bar in the federal courts also provides important leverage in bargaining within the legislative process.[44] The voting rights bar has an advantage in negotiating compromises in legislation; its litigators have practical knowledge about how judges and lawyers interpret the legislation and the judicial decisions stemming from it. Minorities can in some circumstances use a similar combination of legislative and judicial action in other areas of policy, but the law of voting rights is peculiar in the breadth of support enjoyed in both Congress and the courts.[45]

42. The diversity of the organizations and individuals involved in voting rights sometimes militates against the best selection of cases, and in hindsight some have seemed poor choices. Even the most sophisticated attempts at organized litigation have their limits.

43. For examples of guidelines for the American Civil Liberties Union and the NAACP Legal Defense Fund, see O'Connor and Epstein 1989, 12, 130–31. Thus in policy 516, the American Civil Liberties Union states that a case "should involve a determination of the civil liberties issue in such a fashion as to have an impact on other cases beyond the particular one in question. . . . Consideration should, of course, always be given to the possible adverse affects should a case be lost. . . ." Policies in other organizations show similar concerns.

44. Until recently, political scientists have tied the use of litigation to the peculiar needs of blacks and other disadvantaged groups (Olson 1990). Before the 1960s these groups could not hope to gain redress in Congress, the state legislatures, or the national or state executive branches, but the structure of courts, together with the ideological makeup of the federal courts until the 1980s, provided a sympathetic environment for those who could not command significant financial resources or a majority of voters. Ideological retrenchment in the federal courts during the past decade, however, suggests that litigation now holds no inherent advantages for minorities or the disadvantaged.

45. Lawson 1976; Lawson 1985; Kousser in this volume.

No set of organized interests ever has sufficient financial resources to engage in all of the litigation it could or should, except, perhaps, for the corporate world, and even there decisionmakers allocate money and effort carefully and tell stories of opportunities missed on account of scarce resources. Financial limitations constitute a major problem for the voting rights bar and the civil rights community in general. Members of the voting rights bar typically face opponents who can muster impressive numbers of personnel and financial backing—the deep pockets of state and local governments and sometimes insurance companies. Still, the bar, like much of the rest of the civil rights community, garners a fair amount of financial support from large foundations, individual contributors, interorganizational transfers, and legal fees. Some organizations can muster impressive budgets and staffs. For example, in 1988 the NAACP Legal Defense and Education Fund estimated a budget of $8.1 million and thirty-eight professional staff members; the Mexican American Legal Defense and Educational Fund, $3.3 million and thirty-eight profession-als.[46] These funds must take care of a wide range of programs and concerns, so the point is not that the voting rights bar is awash with money but that it has significant financial resources. Other advantages of the voting rights bar, including expertise and the ability to do long-range planning, help offset the financial advantage of governmental units.

The voting rights bar, as I remarked earlier, also faces no effective and organized opposition in either the courts or the national or state legislatures. This, I have no doubt, has contributed mightily to its impressive success.

Finally, the voting rights bar has enjoyed the sympathy of the federal courts. In the 1960s federal district judges in the South may have denied the meritorious claims of the Lawyers' Committee, the NAACP Legal Defense Fund, or the ACLU, but advocates could rely on the steadfastness of the Supreme Court under Chief Justice Earl Warren. Even as appointees of Ronald Reagan and George Bush have come to dominate the federal courts, the voting rights bar continues to find a positive response. Litigation on voting rights has fared better in the federal courts in the 1970s and 1980s than that on any other civil rights issues. The question is, how will conservative federal judges balance a general unwillingness to meddle in the affairs of legislatures and elections against the potent symbols and weighty body of voting rights law as well as the arguably positive consequences for the Republican party in some situations?

46. Foundation for Public Affairs 1988, 159, 168.

The Voting Rights Bar and Representation

Litigators and leaders of the voting rights bar seem to exhibit little sensitivity to the representational conundrums in this policy area; and in this respect they resemble lawyers in other areas of policy.[47] Like politicians, litigators are practical people and do not worry much about theory. But because voting rights is a matter rife with questions about representation in legislatures and other political institutions, it is surprising to find no self-consciousness among litigators about their own difficulties. Legislators and executives, sometimes even judges, worry about the relationship between themselves and the represented. Who is represented? Who should be represented? Everyone in the constituency? Supporters? Are the interests of constituents coherent enough to permit effective representation? Leaders of membership organizations fret about these questions all the time; for them it is a matter of organizational life and death. Legislators must define constituencies and interests to represent if they are to be elected and be effective policymakers.

In a bygone era, when lawyers represented individual clients and had no commitment to overarching goals and interests, an ethical code spelled out the duties of good litigators. They should devote all reasonable effort to winning the case at hand. To take into account interests other than those of the client in the presentation and resolution of a case would, by this ethical code, constitute a serious violation of duty. Fifty years ago, a practicing lawyer could define such arcane terms as barratry and champerty, but judges have long since given up on trying to enforce these precepts and have tacitly and sometimes explicitly approved the use of individual litigants as exemplars for underlying social, political, and economic realities.[48] America has left behind the simple world of bipolar

47. For a detailed discussion of the problems of representation in class actions, one of the most important weapons in voting rights litigation, see Rhode 1982.

48. Southern lawyers and courts used these ethical precepts as a means of hampering the efforts of the NAACP Legal Defense Fund. For example, in *NAACP* v. *Button,* 371 U.S. 415 (1963), the Supreme Court reversed a Virginia court's judgment. The lower court had found the NAACP guilty of "fomenting and soliciting legal business in which they are not parties and have no pecuniary right or liability, and which they channel to the enrichment of certain lawyers employed by them, at no cost to the litigants and over which the litigants have no control." See *NAACP* v. *Harrison,* 202 Va. 142 at 155 (1960), quoted in 371 U.S. 415 at 426. Barratry is defined as "the offense of frequently exciting or stirring up quarrels and suits, either at law or otherwise," and champerty as a "species of maintenance, being a bargain made by one called the champertor with a plaintiff or defendant for a portion of the matter involved in a suit in case of a successful termination of the action, which the champertor undertakes to maintain or carry on at his own expense."

conflicts between narrow interests to enter a world of clashes between individuals who stand for broad interests. This change means that advocates must strike some sort of balance among the interests—often in conflict—of the immediate parties, citizens and potential officeholders in a state or district, and the various minorities around the nation, whose fate current litigation will shape. A dilemma of this kind faces almost all those who engage in interest-group litigation, but it is especially sharp for the voting rights bar. Drastic changes in electoral structures, for which the voting rights bar often asks, hold unanticipated consequences, and no one can predict with any confidence the impact on the planned beneficiaries.

No organized interest can escape the Michelian problem of oligarchy; almost as soon as an organization comes into being, distance develops between leaders and those led. Leaders develop interests and ideologies apart from, often in opposition to, the membership or those represented. For example, elites in the Democratic and Republican parties stand ideologically far apart from the rank and file; and leaders of unions and other interest groups hold more extreme political views than do members. Officeholders and activists in an organized interest will dominate its agenda, policies, and actions; members will have little or no voice in these determinations. Membership-based organizations in the voting rights bar, like those in other areas, will fall prey to these oligarchical tendencies and representational failures.

Some of the most vigorous and effective organizations involved in voting rights do not rest on a base of membership. They are essentially public interest law firms, or staff organizations. Public interest law firms, such as the Legal Defense Fund and the Mexican American Legal Defense and Educational Fund (MALDEF) exist to file suits and have a life independent of a membership. Many organizations with memberships will set up and spin off a public interest law firm to derive the benefits of independence and of the more favorable treatment of contributions under the tax code. These firms lack a clear and binding constituency. Their staffs need not answer to a membership, even in the loose sense of most organizations. To whom, then, must they answer? In the broadest sense, they owe a responsibility to the constituency for which the organization claims to provide representation—blacks, Hispanics, Asians, and so on. That, as we shall see, can cause problems. In a narrower sense, they must cultivate current and potential supporters among foundations and the wealthy. Because individuals and foundations do possess ideological agendas, the leaders of public interest law firms cannot venture too far afield from these agendas if they are to continue to receive financial support. For example, in 1988 MALDEF reported the sources of its income as 93 percent from corporations and foundations and 7 percent from individuals and legal fees. Others do not rely quite as heavily on foundations, but the share of income is substantial.[49] Public interest law firms can and do, of course, receive legal fees from the federal courts; but even there funding constitutes a constraint on their actions.

The structure of public interest law firms also makes it difficult to discern and respond to the interests of those they ostensibly represent. To be sure, they often field cooperating attorneys or others who can tap in at the grass roots; but in the absence of affiliates or chapters, public interest law firms will not have access to the kinds of information membership-based groups routinely receive. A membership constrains an organization, but it also generates intelligence, credibility, and support. However, cooperating attorneys can, and presumably often do, develop ties to leaders and activists in local membership organizations and in this way overcome some of the informational difficulties in the structure of public interest law firms.

Twenty-five years ago, representational linkages did not pose much of a practical problem for members of the voting rights bar. The interests of blacks and other minorities seemed clear: they should have the right to register, vote, have their votes counted, and remain safe from physical threats. And the task of litigators was to ensure that this happened. For the past decade, however, the job of litigators and litigation has been more difficult and the solutions to remaining problems more ambiguous. Clear and detectable problems and goals—proportions of groups registered and voting, threats to minorities—have been succeeded by vague and slippery ones such as creating districts in which a black or Hispanic has a reasonable probability of winning. Once the goals and remedies for a problem become complicated, the problem of representation becomes as acute for courts, litigators, and interest groups as it is for legislatures.

Significant changes within and across the various minorities in the United States complicate the job of the voting rights bar still further. It is not as easy to define the interests of blacks and Hispanics as it was in the 1950s and 1960s. Both groups have diversified socially, politically, and economically. The black middle class, for example, has grown substantially, and the distance between middle-class blacks and the poor has increased markedly. There are now thousands of nonwhite office-

49. Foundation for Public Affairs 1988, 124, 160, 164, 169.

holders who may well have interests apart from those of the nonwhite citizenry. Some of the strongest civil rights interest groups have felt the squeeze of these changes: for example, the membership and financial base of the NAACP have declined as it has failed to enlist younger members. On the hard questions at the vanguard of the contemporary agenda of the voting rights bar, the various elements of the black and Hispanic communities may not share an interest. Is it, for example, in the interest of poor blacks to trade strength of numbers in liberal white Democratic representatives for smaller numbers of black representatives?

Representational difficulties of the voting rights bar have come into stark relief as conservatives and the Republican National Committee have attempted to cooperate with the bar in the battles over redistricting that have followed the 1990 census.[50] Blacks, of course, have had strong ties to the Democratic party since the 1930s, and although Hispanics have shown somewhat more independence, they remain loyal to the Democratic coalition. According to Carol Matlack,

> When it comes to redistricting, the interests of minority groups overlap considerably with those of Republicans. Urban districts, where most black and Hispanic voters live, are often represented by white Democrats. Minority groups want district boundaries redrawn to consolidate their voting strength, to increase the likelihood that more blacks and Hispanics will be elected. But Republicans also have an interest in concentrating minority voters in a few districts because the remaining districts will become more heavily white—and, GOP strategists figure, more likely to vote Republican.[51]

This journalist assumes a single set of interests on the part of minorities, but as I said earlier, there is good reason to view this notion skeptically. An implicit coalition between the Republicans and minorities in the 1990s

50. On June 22, 1990, the Democratic National Committee, the NAACP, MALDEF, the Lawyers' Committee for Civil Rights Under Law, the Southwest Voter Registration Education Project, and the Southern Regional Council met in Washington at the invitation of the Lawyers for the Republic, a group of Republican lawyers who with money from the Republican National Committee have created a software package and data base to assist minorities in redrawing legislative maps. Dennis Hayes, a lawyer for the NAACP, remarked on the obvious: "I've heard it described as an unholy alliance. . . . [But] if they've got something they can give that would help, I don't think we should turn our nose up" (Matlack 1990, 1540). For more on the Lawyers for the Republic, see Cohen and Matlack 1989, 2986; and on redistricting and minorities, Barnes 1990.

51. Matlack 1990, 1540.

would, of course, signal a major departure from the minority loyalties of the past fifty years. And it would probably result from divisions among minorities along the lines of social and economic class and degree of political activism. The state of affairs the voting rights bar envisions might or might not be in the interests of poor blacks and Hispanics. If, as a result of litigation and redistricting, the size of the black caucus doubles, then it is questionable whether economic programs of direct benefit to the poor will suffer because of lost Democratic seats.

Internal Tensions of the Voting Rights Bar

Despite unity of purpose, the voting rights bar encompasses diverse political activists, and there is necessarily some tension among them. There is a conflict of interest between the Department of Justice and organized interests outside the government, even during periods in which friends of minorities occupy the White House. And the bitter feud between the NAACP and the NAACP Legal Defense Fund, which ended in a judicial decision in the 1980s, shows how intense organizational rivalries can become. Competition between blacks and Hispanics has also increased. "Demographic shifts have dramatically altered the politics of minority-group advocacy. The nation's Hispanic population is growing more than twice as fast as the black population. . . . With blacks competing against other minorities for jobs, frequently on the lower rungs of the economic ladder, the potential for political division between the groups is intensifying."[52] In 1990 Hispanic groups threatened to leave the Leadership Conference on Civil Rights over a dispute about the conference's unwillingness to take a position against provisions of the Immigration Reform and Control Act of 1986. Finally, the movement of the voting rights bar toward the Republicans, however opportunistic and tactical, raises anxieties among white Democrats, the traditional allies of minorities in Congress, and risks a decrease in support for future initiatives on voting rights and other matters. These Democrats are, after all, officeholders and value political survival.

A Perpetual State of Dissatisfaction

The more often the voting rights bar wins, the worse its members seem to feel. Perhaps in large part the dissatisfaction is an occupational disease. By nature, litigators for organized interests attempt to push back

52. Kirschten 1991, 496–97.

legal frontiers. No court can ever satisfy them, and in this respect the voting rights bar is not peculiar. Organizations as well established and successful as the mainstays of the voting rights bar rarely disappear; and so the policy agenda, if satisfied, expands and business continues. This seems a natural consequence of building organizations to defend interests.

Over the years the voting rights bar and its precursors have won a tremendous number of cases, many of them landmarks. They persuaded the Supreme Court to sweep away grandfather clauses and white primaries, they moved successfully against the last vestiges of official and semi-official barriers to registration, voting, and participation in the parties, and they have sought to dismantle much subtler barriers to minority victories at the polls. But in each phase of litigation on voting rights, victories made the next threshold higher and harder to jump.

Furthermore, most knowledgeable observers would agree that there are some limits to the efficacy and desirability of litigation as a tool for broad-scale social, political, and economic reform. Litigation can work well if the parties can set out clear and verifiable outcomes; it is less useful if lawyers and clients cannot easily define the desired state of affairs and if compliance is difficult to detect. Until quite recently, claims of voting rights violations made these cases ideal for litigation; now the goals sought and the appropriate means are a good deal less clear. All of this is a result of the ambitious program of the voting rights bar.

For minorities the practical problem of the 1980s and 1990s lies in the unwillingness of white legislators to overturn schemes of districting in which blacks and Hispanics seldom come together in sufficient numbers to elect a member of a minority. It is much less a matter of racial animus than of political power. Everyone knows about the messy and unprincipled nature of legislative redistricting. Advocates in these battles have greater difficulty than they once did in offering clear and workable standards for courts to adopt. And even if the federal courts do rule in favor of the voting rights bar in the wake of the 1990 census, victory does not guarantee a large infusion of black and Hispanic officeholders in Congress and the state legislatures.[53] Courts will try to balance the creation of

53. Stewart and Sheffield 1987 show the elusive connection between interest-group litigation and the political success of blacks in Mississippi. They report a strong positive relationship between interest-group litigation and increases in black registration and black candidacies. They find no correlation between litigation and the success of black candidates for office, and little between litigation and the turnout of black voters. But in a study of southern legislatures from 1965 through 1985, Grofman and Handley 1991 show a significant increase in the number of black state legislators—due, they argue, to the creation in response to the Voting Rights Act of more districts with a majority-black population.

districts in which minority candidates have a good chance of winning against packing an excessive number of nonwhites into these districts. The number of opportunities available to black politicians will continue to grow.

Nevertheless scholars of electoral politics have demonstrated the elusiveness of victory in elections. Even though candidates win seats against considerable partisan odds in dozens of congressional districts across the nation, and advantages in partisan registration help, the crucial link between electoral aspirations and victory seems to be the recruitment of good candidates, however one wants to define this concept. No court can build a pool of candidates or produce quality challengers. So no matter how glorious the victories of the voting rights bar in the 1990s, we should anticipate considerable slippage between the courthouse, voting booths, and statehouses and Congress. Last, quite apart from increasing the number of minority members in Congress and statehouses to increase the political clout of blacks and Hispanics, other goals of the voting rights bar, often not articulated, are intangible, and therefore whether they have been achieved is difficult to measure.

The increased number of minorities in legislatures has a tremendous symbolic value for rank-and-file blacks and Hispanics and even greater value for elites. These increases may well lead to the empowerment of minorities and to a heightened sense of political efficacy. For many blacks and Hispanics, behind the push for increased numbers of minorities in legislatures lies a disgruntlement with the current distribution of power and a desire to reap a fair share of society's resources. But although numbers help, legislatures are institutions bound up with rules and procedures, and large numbers of minority members do not necessarily translate into a fair share of political power or economic resources. Here, again, we should expect a shortfall between aspirations and accomplishments, even under the rosiest of scenarios in the courts.

The Voting Rights Bar and the Congressional Lobby

Lobbyists for the interests of various racial and ethnic minorities have become major forces in the halls of Congress, not only on clear-cut issues of civil rights but also on questions of indirect concern to minority constituencies. The coalition in Congress in favor of voting rights, for example, has grown each time the issue has come up for consideration.[54] And the

---

54. Pertschuk 1986, 148–80; and the chapter by Kousser in this volume.

core of supporters for even the more controversial portions of the civil rights agenda, such as affirmative action, has grown to surprising proportions.[55] Thus in the 101st Congress, supporters in the House voted to override a presidential veto of the controversial Civil Rights Act of 1990, and the Senate came within a vote or two of doing so.

Early in this chapter I posited a tension between lobbyists and litigators. Their respective roles mean they have different needs and interests. Michael Pertschuk's essay on the campaign in 1982 to extend the Voting Rights Act highlights one source of tension: because of past experience in court, the litigators wished to avoid compromise on the specific elements and wording of the bill, but the lobbyists knew the importance of ambiguity and compromise in legislation.[56] And there are other disparities. To put the matter simply: litigators seek to increase the chances of office-holding for minorities; lobbyists rely on widespread diffusion of nonwhite voters to muster support in Congress.

In the complexity of discussions on voting rights litigation it is easy to lose sight of the ultimate goals of minorities in American politics. One may safely assume that they want to shape public policy to their liking. That must occur in the legislative process, since legislatures in our society establish the contours of public policy and allocate most of the financial resources. In one sense or another the goal of legislative influence animates the voting rights bar's continuing campaign of litigation, just as it did in the past. Yet it is certainly not the only goal; many leaders and litigators see inherent value in broadening the participation of black and Hispanic voters and increasing the number of minorities in legislatures and other elective posts. The placement of minorities in elective offices may help mobilize and empower rank-and-file blacks and Hispanics.[57] Even in the 1990s, long after the enactment of the Voting Rights Act, victory in elections holds enormous and entirely understandable symbolism for minorities, very much as it once did for other ethnic groups.

Organized interests attempt to shape outcomes in Congress in a variety of ways, and the most successful use multiple methods in a coordinated fashion.[58] These include recruiting and electing like-minded legislators

55. See Black 1978; Black 1979; Bullock 1981; Watson 1990.
56. Pertschuk 1986, 148–80.
57. Bobo and Gilliam 1990.
58. Berry 1989, 140–95; Schlozman and Tierney 1986, 289–321. Of course, I focus on lobbying in Congress. The voting rights bar has devoted a significant amount of attention to state legislatures and other elective offices, and no doubt these campaigns will change the balance of political forces over the next decade, but these consequences are beyond the purview of this chapter.

or their own members, allocating campaign contributions, direct lobbying, grass-roots lobbying, coalition building, and testimony. Most organizations that take part in the electoral phase of legislative politics choose like-minded candidates instead of those from the organization or group itself. Organized labor, for example, has never made a particular point of electing unionists, although some have indeed gone to Congress under the banner of labor. Instead it has cultivated the friendship of politicians from diverse backgrounds and both parties. Perhaps by choice but more probably from lack thereof, blacks and other racial minorities have traditionally pursued a legislative strategy along the same lines. Few members of minorities could, until recently, hope to win a seat in Congress or even in a state legislature. Minorities accordingly supported white legislators on both sides of the aisle. Litigation by the voting rights bar in recent years, together with the 1982 amendments to the 1965 act, marks a shift in the strategy of minorities toward a greater emphasis on representation by minorities.

Few in the voting rights bar have acknowledged a trade-off between increased numbers of elected minorities and loss of overall influence in legislatures. Yet such a trade-off is an unavoidable feature of legislative politics. Research on how to determine the population required for effecting equality of voting has addressed the problem. In one particularly clear example of the costs of litigation, when Georgia's Fifth Congressional District was made 65 percent black as a result of voting rights litigation, "the neighboring fourth district was reduced from 28 percent to 13 percent black. *The result in the fourth district was the defeat of a moderate Democrat by an extreme right-wing Republican.*" The price of minority districts will thus "sometimes be the loss of one or more liberal white representatives."[59] And if reformers create too many safe seats for minorities, they may well reduce the number of districts in which blacks and other nonwhites have a realistic chance of winning.

To create such districts normally requires bunching blacks or Hispanics. For minorities to achieve influence throughout Congress, by contrast, they must be broadly distributed. I would, indeed, attribute much of the success of the civil rights movement in Congress to the geographic distribution of concerned and identifiable constituents. The size of the black and Hispanic populations places a natural limit on the number of minority officials if these groups pursue a pure strategy of virtual representation.[60]

---

59. Brace and others 1988, 55–56; see also Grofman, Griffin, and Glazer 1991.
60. Swain 1992; Grofman and Handley 1989.

Demography clearly constrains blacks; for Hispanics the effect is much less clear. For the foreseeable future, then, if minorities wish to achieve success in Congress, they must be able to mount effective lobbying efforts to sway the votes of white legislators. Lobbying, not officeholding, will remain the hallmark of their influence in Congress.

Efforts to reshape electoral districts and increase significantly the prospects for Hispanic and especially black officeholders in Congress *could* decrease the effectiveness of lobbying by minorities. I emphasize "could" because institutional designs in politics have gone astray too often to speak with great confidence. Why might this happen? It has much to do with the nature of lobbying in Congress. On what bases do organized interests build effective lobbying?

For a long time, conventional wisdom characterized effective lobbying as mobilizing one's friends and supporters; the lobbyist was a "service bureau for those congressmen already agreeing with him, rather than an agent of direct persuasion."[61] More recently, scholars have given greater credence to persuasion, especially in lobbying legislators who have not decided how to vote on a measure.[62] On an important issue a lobbyist for an organization will place legislators into one of usually five categories: correct, leaning correct, undecided, leaning wrong, and wrong. How does a lobbyist decide which legislators to place in which category? Decisions result from subtle, usually unarticulated, considerations of the behavior of both the legislator and the interest group. First the lobbyist will look at voting records on similar issues: generally a legislator's voting record is a product of personal ideology, the preferences of constituents, previous lobbying efforts, and partisanship. Once the lobbyist has identified legislators whose support may be mobilized or the undecideds or those weakly against, he then faces critical choices.

No single organization can mount a credible lobbying campaign, direct or from the grass roots, on all members of either house of Congress. Lobbyists for membership groups rely heavily, if not exclusively, on the strength of their organizations within constituencies. A research report on recent lawmaking in agriculture and energy shows a strong connection between an organization's strength in a district and its lobbying efforts and the expenditures of its political action committee; contributions and direct influence "only supplemented, or reinforced, whatever pressures the group was able to exert through its organizational presence in the

61. Bauer, de Sola Pool, and Dexter 1963, 353.
62. Smith 1984.

representative's district."[63] If an interest group has many members or a strong organizational presence in a legislator's state or district, a lobbyist will very likely make him or her a target. Just as decisions to lobby a legislator are in part a function of organizational strength, so, too, is organizational strength in large part a function of the number of members in a district. As an example of the importance of organizational strength, consider the coalition against Judge Bork's confirmation to the Supreme Court in 1987. The leadership of this large and diverse coalition crafted a strategy of grass-roots lobbying based on the membership and organizational strength of the constituent organizations in the states of the various senators whose views were, one way or the other, in doubt.[64]

Legislators continually monitor the effects of alternative policies on constituents in their electoral coalitions. Accordingly, it is difficult for lobbyists to rally members of Congress in the absence of a significant and identifiable group of concerned constituents. Controversies over civil rights and liberties by and large do not generate large amounts of political campaign contributions, so members of Congress do not for the most part respond to political action committees or other contributors. The comparative lack of financial stakes makes concerned and visible constituents all the more important. To make a difference, these citizens need not constitute a majority or contribute to campaigns; the member bent on reelection takes into account constellations of voters whose defection might prove significant.[65]

These worries will not, of course, halt the efforts of the voting rights bar to create districts in which minorities have a reasonable chance of electoral success. But they should give the leadership of the various communities of minorities good reason to calculate the potential costs of this course of action.

Concluding Remarks

The various constituents in the voting rights bar have become formidable participants in American legal and political processes. In the past sixty years, litigation on voting rights has evolved from a small number of cases in the province of a few people to a major, continuing subject of judicial decisionmaking in the hands of well-established institutions. Few groups can match the voting rights bar in experience, expertise, and

63. Wright 1989, 724.
64. For examples drawn from the House of Representatives, see Pertschuk 1986.
65. There is a significant difference between the responsiveness of Democrats and

commitment. And few can match the Leadership Conference on Civil Rights on which the voting rights bar depends. The coalition has rightly earned a reputation as one of the most potent lobbies in Washington, unrivalled "in mobilizing grass roots; in structuring the media; in formulating and implementing legislative strategy; in substantive expertise and legislative draftsmanship; in building and sustaining a close and trusting relationship with its congressional leaders; in seeking out, packaging, and coaching a knockout array of witnesses at a hearing."[66]

Successes in the renewal and amendment of the Voting Rights Act in 1982 and in litigation throughout the decade since place the voting rights bar in an excellent position to carve out major achievements in the political transitions of the next few years. These opportunities hold potential dangers for the ultimate goal of legislative influence. The voting rights bar will attempt to create districts in which minorities have a high probability of winning office, but if it has too much success in doing so, minorities may risk losing influence in Congress. Scholars and politicians do not agree on the partisan and ideological impact of the Voting Rights Act, so the voting rights bar will have to operate under considerable uncertainty about the consequences of its actions. To maximize influence in Congress will require a shrewd balancing of strategies and tactics in litigation. Of course, legislative influence is but one of the goals of the black and Hispanic communities. Even if the reapportionments in the 1990s should decrease the political clout of blacks and Hispanics in the aggregate, minorities might well harvest other significant gains—movement of black officeholders up the hierarchy, increases in political participation, and subtle changes in the political environment.

Republicans in the House to the demands of black interest groups (Grofman, Griffin, and Glazer 1991). On average, the Republican members show less sympathy for the interests of blacks. One of the chief reasons is the partisan loyalty of blacks: Republican members do not generally have a good reason to fear the defection of these voters since blacks show remarkable loyalty to Democrats.

66. Pertschuk 1986, 150.

Part Three

The Voting Rights Act and the Concept of Voting Rights

Voting Rights and Democratic Theory: Toward a Color-Blind Society?

BRUCE E. CAIN

THE IMPLEMENTATION OF THE Voting Rights Act and related court decisions during the past twenty-five years has changed patterns of voter representation. The actions arising from these changes have given rise to equally significant political reactions. Resentments abound, especially in communities that have been forced to alter their traditional electoral procedures under legal duress. Leaving aside the all-important political fact that changes in electoral rules can lead to significant redistributions of power (which will be favored by those who gain and opposed by those who lose), some observers object to what is happening primarily on grounds of principle. Democratic theory has little to say to those who resist voting rights changes based on calculations of naked self-interest and desire for power (although this is the stuff of analytical and empirical political science). It can, however, shed some light on arguments based on principle.

The most common objection to the evolution of voting rights laws and enforcement is that it has bestowed special representational advantages upon some racial and ethnic groups but not others and has pulled the United States back from its much cherished ideal of a color-blind society. Entitlements to representation based on race and ethnicity, it is argued, are unfair and dangerous, inflaming racial and ethnic tensions. This viewpoint is most commonly identified with Abigail Thernstrom (perhaps to a greater degree than she deserves), but it is also widely held in the American white middle class.[1] I remember the consternation of a senior Los Angeles City councilman of Italian descent when the city attorney explained to him that section 2 of the Voting Rights Act, amended during a Republican administration, might make it illegal to divide the Los Angeles Latino community into six different districts. "Italians never had such protections," he said; "why should Latinos get it? This is un-American."

In fact, the Supreme Court has been quite cautious in its characteri-

---

1. Thernstrom 1987.

262   BRUCE E. CAIN

zation of what voting rights the Constitution and the Voting Rights Act give minorities. It has, for instance, steadfastly denied that there is a right to proportional representation, even while accepting a disproportionality between population and representation as an indicator of a voting rights violation. The court has referred to remedies for situations of political exclusion rather than permanent entitlements to particular kinds of representatives. It requires that underrepresented groups meet the conditions of the criteria set forth in *Thornburg* v. *Gingles* rather than assuming that the groups automatically qualify for protection.[2]

But despite the Court's cautious approach, a serious issue of representation remains, one that reasonable people might disagree over: to what degree should a democracy give special recognition in any form to the rights of disadvantaged minorities? A majoritarian system that ignores minority rights might be formally fair (that is, individuals might have legal equality with respect to the voting franchise or an equally weighted vote) but nonetheless unfair in its operation (for example, if the conjunction of racially biased behavior and majoritarian institutions prevents minorities from electing representatives of their own choice). But a system that awards minority groups too much power might lose legitimacy in the eyes of the majority and foster conditions that undermine stability and governability. In other words, the voting rights controversy is really another variant of a long-standing dilemma in democratic theory: How should minority rights be balanced against the majority will in a system of government that derives its legitimacy from the consent of the governed?

Accordingly, the questions relevant to voting rights include: Have recent trends in voting rights interpretation made the U.S. political system more or less democratic? Do these developments impede the assimilation of minorities and therefore threaten democratic culture? What are the potential costs and limitations of solutions imposed by a court as opposed to political solutions, and how can these costs be minimized?

Voting Rights and the Proportionality Debate

The debate over voting rights is a modern and peculiarly American variant of a long-standing issue in political science—the relative merits of more or less proportional representational systems. The matter is rarely

2. *Thornburg* v. *Gingles*, 478 U.S. 30 (1986). The Supreme Court ruled that six multimember legislative districts in North Carolina violated the Voting Rights Act of 1982 because they impermissibly diluted the strength of black voters. The Court ruled that regardless of the lawmakers' intent, a voting system that has the effect of discriminating against minorities is in violation of the law.

stated that way, especially by proponents of expanded voting rights legislation, because proportionality is something of a dirty word in the Anglo-American tradition. Americans prefer to use terms such as *fairness* and *nondilution* of minority votes without explicitly defining them, which causes significant confusion because electoral fairness could in fact mean something other than proportionality.[3] For instance, fairness could mean that parties receiving a given share of the vote receive the same share of the seats (also called symmetry), or it could refer to the rate at which changes in vote share translate into changes in seat share (responsiveness). In fact, nonproportional measures of fairness have been proposed in cases of political gerrymandering, but to my knowledge they have never been discussed in cases of racial vote dilution nor for that matter ever actually been adopted by the Court in gerrymandering decisions.

The debate over the relative merits of systems of greater or lesser proportionality goes as follows. Proportional systems award representation in relation to electoral or population shares, thereby minimizing the number of wasted votes (a vote is defined as wasted when it is cast for a losing candidate or in excess of the minimum needed to win a seat). Although it is possible in a plurality or majority system to get no seats with 49 percent of the vote, any system of proportional representation with a reasonable threshold requirement will yield a given party a proportion of seats roughly equal to its proportion of votes, thus wasting the fewest possible. Systems with majoritarian biases exaggerate the larger party's share of seats and increase the number of minority votes cast in a losing cause.[4] This undercuts the system's legitimacy because minority groups do not feel that their votes have as much impact as the majority's and because their representation tends to be less than their share of the population. Decisions emanating from a polity that uses majoritarian rules, it is argued, have less legitimacy for excluded or underrepresented groups because these minorities are unable to give their consent to the government's action through their own elected officials. The argument for proportionality, in other words, relies heavily on considerations of legitimacy—proportional representation makes more people feel that they have a voice in the legislature and that what the legislature does derives more solidly from consent.

The argument against proportionality emphasizes efficiency and stability more than legitimacy. Anglo-American observers point to the experi-

3. King and Browning 1987.
4. Duverger 1964; Rae 1971.

ences of the Fourth Republic in France, in which the fragmentation of the legislature induced by proportional rules caused perpetual stalemate. Crisis was necessary to shock the system into compromise. The French coalition governments lacked the tools of control—powers over nomination, electoral resources, and ultimately the use of a party label—possessed by majority parties in the British parliamentary system. Governments that need crises to force them into action are less efficient than those with the means to head off or mitigate crises. Proportional-representation governments are also purportedly less stable. In Italy and Israel, which employ proportional representation, changes in government occur frequently, and extremist parties flourish. This dampens confidence in the government's ability to govern and gives legitimacy to parties with ideologies that would destroy the system.

Proponents of majoritarian systems thus weigh the trade-offs between legitimacy, efficiency, and stability differently from the proponents of proportional representation. Groups can be excluded from representation for the sake of governability, they contend, without much sacrifice of the legitimacy of the system. As long as conditions of voting eligibility are not biased or arbitrary, and as long as everyone's vote is equally weighted, every person has a fair chance to influence the outcome of the election. Groups have no right to an undiluted or unwasted bloc vote because the only legitimate rights in a democracy are individual not group rights. Since people can be thought of as bundles of many potentially politically relevant attributes, why should some of these attributes get political or legal recognition but not others? An electoral outcome might be unfair to a middle-aged male Latino in his identity as Latino, but perfectly fair in his identities as a male or a middle-aged person. Which is the relevant criterion by which we assess fairness and why? It is morally less complicated to ignore the group attributes of individuals and give them only individual rights (such as the right to vote and the right to an equally weighted vote).

Proponents also argue that governments employing majoritarian rules do not suffer any more often from crises of legitimacy than do those employing rules of proportional representation and that, for the reasons previously discussed, majoritarian or pluralist systems tend to be more governable, that is, more efficient and stable. Because the larger party's share of the vote is exaggerated, it is more likely to have the legislative votes it needs to achieve its program. Extremist groups are also more easily denied a forum, and the median voter effect induces moderation in candidates.

Such then are the terms of the debate over the relative merits of proportional and majoritarian systems. But how is the voting rights controversy related to this classical dispute? Section 2 of the Voting Rights Act prohibits any rule, institution, or procedure that has the effect of diminishing the opportunity of a community to elect a representative of its own choice. Drawing on the Senate's voting rights report and the criteria used by the courts in previous decisions, the Supreme Court in 1986 enunciated a test for the legitimacy of a section 2 claim in *Thornburg v. Gingles.*[5] Is a group sufficiently large and located in a sufficiently compact area to elect a representative if grouped in a single-member district? Is the group politically cohesive? Is there racially polarized voting by the white majority against candidates from that group?

What this test amounts to is a requirement for some degree of greater proportionality (or at least that minority preferences will not be excluded) in majoritarian-pluralistic rules, given the historical exclusion of particular groups and the sociological facts of white voting behavior. The premise is not that multimember districts or at-large elections or runoff elections are always unfair but that under certain conditions they contribute to unfair treatment of historically disadvantaged groups. This is a narrower, more specialized claim than the one usually posed in the classical political science debate on proportional representation because it accepts the general validity of majoritarian rules and only seeks to make a special exemption from their effects.

But even though plaintiffs frequently aspire to nonexclusion as opposed to exact proportionality, the underlying logic of their argument remains more akin to the logic of proportionality than to other ideas of political fairness such as symmetry or responsiveness. In voting rights litigation against Los Angeles City and County, no one suggested that the seats-vote curve needed to be made more symmetric or sloped differently. Rather the argument was that Latinos constituted a third of the city's population and a quarter of the county's, but at the time the litigation was initiated by the Justice Department, there were no Latinos on either body.

As with agreements offered in litigation to enforce the act, the arguments offered against implementation are also variations of classical themes. Consider a few commonly voiced objections. Minorities, some maintain, do not have to be represented by their own kind to be well represented. White people can represent blacks and Latinos as well as blacks and

5. Senate 1982b.

Latinos can (which is, in essence, another way of reiterating the old argument that legitimacy does not require descriptive representation). Drawing minority single-member districts, others say, will increase factionalism and racial tension (which is a variation of the classical concern about democratic stability). Finally, some defend the use of at-large and multimember mechanisms because they produce a less parochial perspective of city or county affairs. Mandating district elections for the sake of racial justice, they contend, will only lead to a narrower representational focus (which amounts to saying that these changes will produce less governability and efficiency). Each argument has a slightly different slant from the usual because instead of focusing on the standard question— proportional representation versus single-member, simple plurality rules— each concerns the merits of a relatively minor perturbation from a fundamentally majoritarian system. Thus the American voting rights controversy focuses on a very small movement toward the proportional end of the spectrum from a point very near the majoritarian end. This may seem terribly important in the United States, but from the grander perspective of democratic theory, the proposed shift is not very great.

Are Color-Conscious Voting Rights Policies Undemocratic?

In the very specific sense that recent trends in American voting rights policy have tried to create a small degree of greater proportionality for blacks and Latinos, one can call them color-conscious as opposed to color-blind. Are they undemocratic? The argument that they are says that democracy rests on two principal tenets: popular sovereignty and relative equality.[6] Popular sovereignty means that options that have more popular support should generally prevail over those that do not. Related to this is the idea that the greater the level of support for a choice, option, or decision, the greater its inherent legitimacy. Relative equality requires that when preferences are aggregated into a collective choice, individual preferences should be weighted as equally as possible.

Does the Voting Rights Act violate either of these two conditions of democracy? Critics would say that if the act is used to strike down at-large and multimember mechanisms under conditions governed by the criteria of *Thornburg* v. *Gingles*, communities are denied the use of voting mechanisms that better support the ideals of popular sovereignty. If a

6. Dahl 1956.

district system elects a member of a minority but an at-large system does not, then mandating the district system favors choices with diminished legitimacy in the sense that winning candidates have less overall popular support. Moreover, since some groups (blacks and Latinos) are given voting rights protection but others (Irish, say, or Italians) are not, the system does not rest on equality. If there is a right to an unwasted vote, it should be granted to everyone, not just disadvantaged minority groups.

I do not believe either objection has much force. True, a majoritarian system is more democratic in that it favors choices with the highest general level of support, but there have always been a number of good reasons for modifying or abridging the principle of popular sovereignty in practice. To begin with, what we mean by popular sovereignty without unanimity of preferences rests on morally arbitrary differences in procedures. The principle of popular sovereignty can lead to vastly different outcomes depending on the sequence of choices and the rules for making them. Particular sequences can lead to different winners, and under certain configurations of preference to no winner at all. For instance, the decision to use plurality rules instead of simple majority or supermajority rules can influence the outcome of collective decisions. Forty-five percent of the vote can win in plurality systems but lose in majority or supermajority systems. In this sense, whether the electorate should be subdivided (as in district elections) or not (as in at-large elections) is simply another example of the varied, acceptable ways that popular sovereignty can be interpreted. Unless one wants to dispute the assignment of the term democracy to many European countries, one must accept what is true in practice: the strongest versions of popular sovereignty are not required in order to have a democracy.

In addition, democratic theory has long been concerned with how popular sovereignty should be balanced against minority rights. James Madison, for instance, was as much concerned about majority tyranny as minority tyranny. Robert Dahl elaborates this concern in some detail in *A Preface to Democratic Theory*.[7] Should an indifferent majority prevail over an intense minority? Are some individual rights in a democracy inviolable whatever the majority thinks? Political science research reveals that many segments of the U.S. electorate are surprisingly intolerant of individual liberties, but the courts protect these liberties nonetheless.[8] Protecting the voting rights of minority groups that have suffered much

7. Dahl 1956.
8. On intolerance see Sniderman 1981.

discrimination historically by the white majority is very much in the Madisonian tradition of offsetting majority tyranny.

However, doing this means that protected groups receive considerations not bestowed upon others. Abigail Thernstrom and other critics do not object to the initial applications of the Voting Rights Act when the purpose was to give blacks the right to vote per se. After all, that was a right the majority already enjoyed. Rather, what disturbs them is the later focus, especially after the mid-1970s, on the right of blacks or Latinos to an undiluted vote, because that is not a right (until *Davis* v. *Bandemer* in 1986) the Court had recognized or protected for other political groups and individuals.[9] If Republicans, Democrats, those identifying with small parties, and independents have no right to claim vote dilution, and if the system has worked for years on the premise that disproportionate outcomes were the price of single-member districts and simple plurality winners, then why should this right be given to blacks and Latinos? In short, critics believe racial and ethnic minorities are getting a special new right, thereby violating the second principle of democracy, political equality.

We shall discover during the next decade whether the right to an undiluted vote will be extended to other groups in the electorate. The opaque decision in *Davis* v. *Bandemer* had a phrase, clause, or section for nearly everyone on all sides of this issue. However, assuming for the moment that this right remains stillborn for all but a few racial and ethnic groups, does this situation violate democratic principles? It does if it makes the right to an undiluted vote permanent, if it associates that right with some demographic characteristic without regard for changing historical and sociological circumstances, and if it prescribes descriptive representation for some groups but not others. I hasten to say that Congress and the courts have tried not to violate these three conditions, although opponents of the Voting Rights Act may disagree. The 1982 Senate report and the decision in *Thornburg* v. *Gingles* refer to remedies, not permanent rights; they specify conditions that have to be met—the "totality of circumstances" test, or the *Gingles* criteria—to qualify for protection, and they have said explicitly that there is no right to proportional representation. Opponents reply that, de facto, the Court has made this a permanent right, that it tends to accept weak evidence on discrimination and racially polarized voting, and that the Voting Rights Act is slipping

9. *Davis* v. *Bandemer*, 478 U.S. 109 (1986). Although the Supreme Court decided that the Republican-drawn legislative map in Indiana did not constitute a partisan gerrymander, it declared that partisan gerrymanders were legally challengeable.

away from its initial goal of preventing exclusion to a new goal of achieving near or exact proportional representation. From my perspective in California, I just do not see this trend. The California district courts have ruled against minority plaintiffs in several instances—Latinos and blacks in Pomona, Koreans in Los Angeles—but in the much publicized litigation against Los Angeles City and County, where there had been blatant ethnic gerrymandering that had led to political exclusion, the plaintiffs prevailed.

In the future, the courts could go in either of two directions without seriously violating the principle of political equality. First, they could continue to deny the general right to an undiluted vote but still grant it as a special exception in cases where serious exclusion, discrimination, and gross underrepresentation have occurred against a minority group. This violates the principle of political equality, but in a temporary, contingent manner that promotes a balance between majority and minority voices. Second, the courts could extend the right to an undiluted vote to all groups, which would seriously undermine the current electoral system and possibly lead us down a path we might ultimately regret. If we decide to adopt proportional representation or semiproportional representation, we should do so in a manner that allows us to abandon those rules if we do not like them or if they no longer serve any need. It makes no sense to say that proportional representation is constitutionally required or that it is in some sense fundamental to the meaning of democracy. It might be the right political choice in certain circumstances, but America should not set a rigid legal course in that direction.

Is the Voting Rights Act Anti-Assimilationist?

A second question asks whether the Voting Rights Act and associated trends in representation are pulling us away from the goal of an assimilated and color-blind society. Even if sections 2 and 5 do not seriously violate democratic principles, they might still undermine the operation of U.S. democracy if their effect is to create permanent, destabilizing racial and ethnic divisions.

The argument that this trend is destabilizing goes as follows. Madison and others in the pluralist tradition warned that a democracy cannot thrive under the wrong socioeconomic conditions. Maintaining a stable democracy is particularly troublesome in large societies in which friendship, propinquity, likeness of thought, pressures to conform, and other informal mechanisms of social restraint and control are attenuated or nonexistent. The Madisonian solution, as outlined in the *Federalist Papers,* was that a large, extended republic would permit interests to play off against one another. Recent pluralist theorists have amended this proposition slightly by adding the condition that memberships in multiple groups and flexible coalitions prevent potentially destabilizing situations in which there are permanent policymaking winners and losers.[10] In addition, they have found correlations between democratic stability, higher levels of income and education, and favorable evolutionary paths in the early stages of nationhood (it has been better, for instance, to evolve from a situation in which power was dispersed than from a long history of despotism). The crucial lesson is that there are important links between a democracy's formal structure and the informal social and economic relations that underlie it.[11]

Laws and rights that treat racial and ethnic groups unequally, say those who fear compromising the movement toward assimilation, could promote excessive factionalism by further encouraging racial and ethnic group identities. As Daniel Patrick Moynihan and Nathan Glazer have argued, if laws bestow political or material advantages upon people because they belong to a particular demographic group, the mere condition of belonging may acquire greater political significance than it would otherwise.[12] The effects of formal recognition might be such that otherwise politically dormant groups could come to emphasize and preserve their political identities for the first time. So, if the Voting Rights Act gives special privileges to certain groups, it might unintentionally promote stronger racial and ethnic factions.

The effects of these incentives to stronger racial or ethnic identity may be particularly critical in the United States. For a society that has at various times absorbed large numbers of immigrants, assimilation may be more important than in more insular and racially homogenous countries. It is, one might argue, one thing for a democracy with small numbers of immigrants and relatively stable populations to allow special arrangements for minority populations—for example, arrangements in the United Kingdom that give Scotland special treatment—but it is quite another for the United States to do so. Race and ethnicity may be particularly troublesome categories because unlike membership in groups based on issues, belonging to a racial or ethnic group tends to define a person's social relations at many different levels and, of course, there is no open

10. Dahl 1961.
11. Dahl 1971.
12. Moynihan and Glazer 1975.

membership. Racial and ethnic groups tend therefore to conform less well to the pluralist ideal of multiple, transient group memberships. Finally, one should not overlook the historical context of these concerns. Perceptions among whites about voting rights for blacks and Latinos have been influenced by debates over inner-city problems and affirmative action and civil rights controversies. Resistance to the implementation of the Voting Rights Act must be seen in the context of similar reactions against set-aside programs, remedial preferential hiring, or special admissions policies for nonwhites. Many of those who oppose affirmative action in other realms tend to oppose it in voting rights as well.

Are these fears warranted? Is there a point at which racial and ethnic group loyalties (or indeed any group loyalties) become too strong for the good of democracy? It is hard to say, since much of this argument rests on assertions for which there is little or no systematic evidence. Have black and Latino identities been hardened by the political advantages and incentives of voting rights protections? In the absence of reliable data (as opposed to casual observation), one cannot know with certainty.

I do not regard the fear of excessive racial and ethnic factionalism as irrational. There are too many examples of nations with severe and sometimes violent divisions of this nature to dismiss the problem. However, the effects of incentives for factionalism stemming from a remedial voting rights policy seem relatively weak and, in any event, must be balanced against the need to bolster minority voices in a society in which the majority has numerous advantages. One reason is that for disadvantaged minorities, as for the white majority, politics is a relatively peripheral concern, and all leaders must struggle to mobilize their communities. Turnout in the Latino Fourteenth Council District in Los Angeles, for example, rose during the campaigns to recall Art Snyder, when the community had gone for so many years without a representative of their own, but has since subsided to normal levels. Throughout the U.S. electorate apathy and indifference are more prevalent than intense politicization.

Apart from the issue of identity, do ethnically and racially conscious voting rights policies per se promote increased voting along racial and ethnic lines? There has been a sorting out along party lines by race during the past twenty-five years. The Republicans continue to become the party of whites and Democrats the party of nonwhites. Some of that movement is clearly related to white resentment over affirmative action and other perceived unfair advantages given to nonwhites. However, since this polarization has taken place along party lines, it is hard to say how much is purely racial or ethnic and how much is due to other factors such as class and ideology. There is not much evidence of ethnic chauvinism among black and Latino voters outside their normal partisan attachments: they usually give white Democrats running against Republican opponents about the same level of support they give black and Latino Democratic candidates. Still, when districts are drawn to empower black and Latino communities, they tend to produce black and Latino incumbents, and in Democratic primaries and nonpartisan races, there is racial polarization among both whites and nonwhites. But, and this is critical, the polarization existed before section 2 could be invoked. Voting along racial and ethnic lines in these instances is the result of much larger social and historical forces. To blame the Voting Rights Act for racial polarization in areas where it has been implemented would be putting the cart before the horse.

A second reason to think that anti-assimilationalist incentives are relatively minor is that there are more powerful countervailing forces at work. Social mobility is one example. My own studies have shown that upwardly mobile Latinos in Los Angeles tend to move out of inner-city barrios and into the suburbs (as did previous generations of immigrants) and are more likely to change their party identification to Republican as they do so. In addition, the importance of ethnic identity as a shaper of views on issues begins to wane significantly by the third generation.

The career incentives of minority politicians provide another countervailing force. Blacks and Latinos who aspire to run for state or national offices must broaden their electoral appeal to include voters who do not belong to their racial or ethnic group. Even those elected to a local council or legislature must obtain the working cooperation of other legislators if they are to secure approval for their programs and policies. In short, the structure of politics in most situations in which the Voting Rights Act might be implemented (that is, where a particular nonwhite group is in a minority) creates pressure for coalitional strategies. Anticoalitional behavior and single-group chauvinism are more likely in situations in which one group is so dominant as not to need coalition partners.[13]

In sum, drawing districts that respect racial and ethnic communities may increase racial and ethnic consciousness, but I suspect that the effects are far from being any danger and are weaker among the public than among political elites and social activists. In addition, these effects may be offset by social mobility, political career incentives, and coalitional

13. McClain and Karnig 1990.

needs. But even if I am wrong, the effects must be weighed against the losses in system legitimacy and stability when minority voices are not well represented. This is a judgment call well within the range of normal democratic choices.

The Irony of Voting Rights Achievements

The real problem in the 1990s may very well not be that the effects of empowering minorities through the Voting Rights Act are too strong, but that the majoritarian predisposition of American political culture will ultimately prevail over those gains and that minorities will continue to feel politically marginalized. Foremost of my concerns is that at the same time the act is being used to remedy gross underrepresentation in legislative bodies at various levels of government, representative institutions are being weakened.

Consider the following. The emphasis of the Voting Rights Act is to prevent unfair electoral arrangements from diluting the voice of minorities that have been historically discriminated against. At-large electoral mechanisms have been challenged because they permit white voter majorities to elect representatives of their choice and to exclude or nearly exclude representatives of minority communities. The strongly majoritarian skew of at-large arrangements under certain conditions of electoral behavior, such as racially polarized voting, can produce consistently unfair results that contribute to a larger pattern of discrimination. Similarly, multimember districts can be manipulated to use majoritarian tendencies to mute the voice of a minority—for instance, by strategically combining areas that might each by themselves elect a minority representative. Gerrymandered lines also employ the logic of dilution by mixing white and nonwhite neighborhoods in a manner that is disadvantageous for the minority community (although in theory lines could be gerrymandered in a manner disadvantageous for the majority).

The effect of litigating against majoritarian mechanisms when they contribute to discrimination against racial or ethnic minorities has been to promote the electoral success of black and Latino candidates (and some white representatives with close ties to minority communities). However, while federal, state, and local legislative bodies are becoming more racially and ethnically representative, the electoral majority is reasserting its power by undercutting and constraining the power of representative government. This phenomenon is what I call the *new populism*.

New populism expresses the frustrations and concerns of the white middle and working classes. It may constrain by constitutional amendment the amount of money a state legislature can spend or restrict the sources of government revenue as did California's Propositions 13. It may tell the legislature how to spend its budget (Proposition 98 in California requires that 41 percent of the state budget go to public schools). Or it may mandate special taxes to pay for specific public services rather than raising general revenues and letting representatives decide how to spend, or make public policy in insurance reform, toxics regulation, or other matters that were previously in the realm of the legislature.

The critical voting rights feature of new populism is that the majority can do all this through the increased use of referendum, initiative, and recall. New populism is most pronounced in California, but the trend toward direct democracy is also evident nationwide. Although the point has not been made very often, referendums and initiatives are essentially forms of at-large elections. As such, they tend to produce outcomes with a majoritarian skew. Indeed, the problem may actually be worse if the subjects of the mechanisms are highly technical, if the ballot is long and confusing, or if the measures appear on ballots during special elections or primaries. People with less education (which will of course include many of the disadvantaged) will have more trouble making choices if the first two of these conditions hold. The electorate in special elections tends to have a higher socioeconomic status than in general elections, and primaries can produce different kinds of skew in partisan turnout depending on which party has more contested races.

Is this trend intentionally discriminatory? Probably not, at least not in California, but the effects are increasingly clear, and there are definite racial overtones. For the past decade the California Assembly has been controlled by a powerful black speaker, Willie Brown, and many of the key people in his political circle are Latino and black legislators from safe inner-city seats. As such they are in much the same position that rural southern congressmen were before the decision in *Baker* v. *Carr* in 1986 and the reform of the seniority system in Congress—that is, these minority representatives have the experience and electoral freedom that allows them to take on important committee and leadership responsibilities.[14] Since their districts are poor and needy, their political orienta-

14. *Baker* v. *Carr*, 369 U.S. 186 (1962). In a landmark 6–2 decision, the Supreme Court decided the federal judiciary had the power to review the apportionment of state legislatures and thus by implication congressional redistricting. The case involved the apportionment of the Tennessee General Assembly.

tions are liberal. Thus to many moderate and conservative white voters, the California legislature looks unrepresentatively liberal, and they see the need to take action via direct democracy to constrain what the legislature can do.

I do not mean to imply that legislative liberalism is the only important cause of new populism in California. The power of special interests over the legislature due to the costs of political campaigns is also critical. But whatever the driving motive, the increasing use of direct-democracy mechanisms undercuts the power of representative mechanisms. Thus the hard-fought gains of minority groups are partially negated because the very institutions that have been made more diverse are now less powerful, particularly at state and local levels (fortunately, the country does not have a national referendum). There seems to be a kind of logic of equilibrium at work. When the voting franchise was extended in 1965 to southern blacks, multimember districts and at-large elections were used to dilute the political impact of the new minority voters. Now that the Voting Rights Act has been amended to permit legal scrutiny of majoritarian institutions when there is evidence that they are being used unfairly, this effort may be undercut by the majoritarian techniques of new populism. Every adjustment to give greater weight to minority voices can be offset by new methods of majoritarianism. This is part of the irony of voting rights achievements. It will be hard to counter the trend toward direct democracy (the Supreme Court will only very reluctantly curb or abridge the right to initiative). But even if that succeeds, the majoritarian biases will emerge in a new form. Purely legal strategies can only make a small dent in the system's majoritarian bias. In the end, minority groups have to learn how best to operate in this environment.

Toward a More Political Focus on Minority Power

I have a second and related concern about the evolution of voting rights in the United States. To force the political system to be fairer, people may try to define some things as voting rights that are not rights at all. There is a limit to how far we can litigate our way to better government. Legal intervention into matters of representation may be necessary, but it is distinctly a second-best strategy. It would have been better if the political system had been able to correct itself, because that would have preserved the diversity, richness, and flexibility of the early representative system in the United States. Different areas of the country have different representational needs, and in an ideal world it would be nice to preserve the option of varied electoral arrangements (within some broad democratic range) to meet these varied conditions. That diversity has been ploughed under by the evolution of the Supreme Court's thinking about voting rights. The doctrine of one person, one vote, for instance, has ruled out upper houses in state legislatures that are malapportioned by county or region. This affects not only old rurally biased arrangements, which one could say were no longer serving a useful modern purpose, but also the prospects of solutions to new problems.

In a recent case involving the New York City Board of Estimate, an arrangement that gave the ex officio representatives from boroughs of New York equal votes in board decisions was ruled to be in violation of the Court's one person, one vote principle.[15] This ruling will deprive local governments of the use of compromise, transitional schemes that might be used to consolidate cities, counties, and special agencies into some more rational and effective regional government structure. Political goals such as nonthreatening merger, consolidation, and rationalization would be easier to realize without tight constitutional limits. I do not mean to take issue with the Court's thinking in *Board of Estimate* v. *Morris* but only to point out that something is lost when it begins to define representational rights very specifically.

To be sure, the litigating-our-way-to-fair-representation approach was necessary because the political system had produced gross malapportionment, exclusion of minorities, and other intolerable abuses. So whatever the opportunity costs, the legal strategy must be credited for remedying injustices that the political system could not or did not want to fix. However, we will reach a point when the next stage in the revolution in political fairness increasingly means meeting more than the threshold of exclusion and aiming for proportional or roughly proportional representation. There is nothing wrong with this as a political goal. But it is not a fundamental right of democracy. The choice between more or less proportional systems is a trade-off between the competing democratic concerns of legitimacy, stability, and efficiency. The Supreme Court is correct in holding that there is no right in the Constitution to proportional representation. Some types of political fairness such as the right to vote can reasonably be defined as matters of right, but others such as the right

15. *Board of Estimates of New York* v. *Morris*, 489 U.S. 688 (1989). The Supreme Court ruled New York City's complicated scheme for selecting the powerful Board of Estimate was unconstitutional. Among other things, the process provided for one member from each of the city's boroughs regardless of their population and also provided for a weighted voting system, giving some members more power than others.

to descriptive representation cannot. They may be good ideas, and they may fit the representational needs of a given community, but they are not democratic rights per se.

I am not denying that there is a role for voting rights litigation in the future. It will no doubt be possible, for instance, to prod communities into more proportional outcomes by proving retrogression in areas covered by section 5 or by securing institutional remedies in the course of section 2 cases that tend to produce semiproportional vote systems, increased size of representative bodies, or other more proportional outcomes.

In spite of this, I foresee the underrepresentation of Latinos and blacks at all levels of American government as a continuing problem in the 1990s. Demographic disadvantages, such as the presence of many noncitizens or a higher-than-average fraction of persons under the voting age; socioeconomic liabilities, such as inadequate education and participation; and systemic hurdles, such as a relatively onerous registration system as compared with those in other democracies and the increasing importance of money and media exposure in campaigns, will continue to hinder minority electoral power. The problem of securing minority political power is broader and more profound than that of securing voting rights.

I fear that too much hope is placed on legal solutions to these political problems. Many other political changes could be made that would have as much or more effect on black and Latino political power, but they do not receive their proper share of attention. For instance, the naturalization process for Latinos and Asians could be speeded up, voter registration could be made easier, and mail-in and absentee ballots could be used more widely. In addition, campaign finance reform could be scrutinized more closely to assess its effects on minorities, political parties could be strengthened, and coalition partners could be found who might support institutional changes that yield more proportional results. More attention should be given to these broader political challenges and to structural changes that move beyond voting rights per se.

Comments

THE EDITORS believe that the matters raised in Bruce Cain's chapter deserve further consideration. The following comments, from four distinct and disparate points of view, consider the continuing implications of the Voting Rights Act for American society and democracy.

Latino Political Incorporation and the Voting Rights Act
Luis R. Fraga

Any knowledgeable student of the Voting Rights Act, advocate or critic, understands that the crucial fact of minority politics—whether that of African Americans, Latinos, or other groups—is their exclusion from the mainstream of American political affairs in spite of their desire to be full participants in it. They want representation by candidates of their choice, and they want policy benefits in proportion to their needs. Their goals are basically to be assimilated into the body politic, and the Voting Rights Act has been a most effective means to that end. But as Bruce Cain's essay makes clear, these goals and the ways to achieve them have engendered considerable debate.

Latino politics provides a good example of one aspect of the controversy. There is no doubt that Latinos aspire to assimilation, much as have other ethnic groups. As an avowedly ethnic politics, however, Latino politics has very often focused on maintaining a distinct cultural community marked by the Spanish language, a pride in distinctive origins, special family relationships, distinctive public celebrations, and, to an extent, Catholicism. The appeal of cultural distinctiveness has been used by Latino politicians to increase popular political mobilization, establish candidate credibility, and even question assimilation as an unexamined goal in politics.[1] So, paradoxically, as the Latino community struggles

---

1. Rendón 1971, 191–215, 241–325; Acuña 1981, 299–349, 384–427.

toward assimilation, its political leaders often trade on the community's distinctiveness to rally it behind political causes.

The very success of the Voting Rights Act is now forcing the Latino community to confront this conflict and attempt to resolve it. The community's leaders should be aware that Latino political successes threaten the maintenance of a cultural community with distinct political interests. Ironically, the act, in offering greater opportunities for self-determination through the election of Latino officials, threatens cultural distinctiveness, perhaps more than exclusion and exploitation ever did.

This disjunction between the goals of political incorporation and cultural maintenance can be resolved. It will require, however, a recognition of the limits of interest-group politics with its focus on parity of benefits, as well as a much broader understanding of *community* defined in terms of the overall public interest. The reconciliation will require the achievement by the nation as a whole of what I shall term *informed public interest*. To suggest what I mean by this, I shall focus on two major criticisms of Latino politics, criticisms that will probably become even more severe as the 1990s progress. Each criticizes the success of the act in increasing Latino representation in legislatures at all levels of government.

Abigail Thernstrom and some other critics of the act have made an impassioned argument that by adopting a strategy of increasing the number of minority officeholders through the creation of safe single-member seats, the act institutionalized and made permanent ethnic and racial conflict that would not otherwise exist.[2] An incentive, they argue, has been built into the system to reward appeals to racial and ethnic exclusivity. Cooperation and compromise, when they occur, represent aberrations in the structured legislative process. As a result, both legislators and the public evaluate public policy in an intensely racially or ethnically conscious way. Thus the elimination of ethnocentrism and racism in American society becomes even less likely.

This argument, which laments the structural changes that have led to greater representational equity for Latinos and African Americans, is misguided in a key respect. The changes simply reflect already existing cleavages within the polity: the cleavages are not necessarily a function of the changes. It is not true that Latino voters, for example, continue to think ethnic simply because they are represented by Latino officials. Whatever the heritage of their representatives, Latino voters will make

2. Thernstrom 1987, 192–244; Bullock 1989, 97–98.

decisions based on ethnicity so long as ethnicity is relevant in assessing the costs and benefits of public policy. Undoubtedly, it will be relevant for some time to come, especially in light of the continued immigration from parts of Latin America. Making it more difficult for Latino candidates to win office will not eliminate ethnic thinking at the voting booth. The same applies to African Americans.

A second line of criticism, put forward by Adolph Reed and others, maintains that the election of minority officeholders made possible by the act has had largely symbolic payoffs to minority voters, who have received few material benefits.[3] There are three disadvantages to this state of affairs, they argue. First, minority communities develop a false sense of hope that the mere presence of minority representatives will be sufficient to provide them benefits from policies, when in fact the benefits go primarily to the middle class through public employment, appointments to boards and commissions, more favorable minority-firm contracting, or capital investments premised on a trickle-down effect that may or may not materialize. Second, the Anglo community mistakenly believes that real progress has been made when they see minority officeholders elected, and it becomes complacent about minority advancement. Third, too much concern with drawing districts that are safe for ethnic minority candidates precludes the creation of districts that bring different ethnic groups—including whites—of the same social class together and thus discourages interethnic class alliances that many observers believe are necessary if minority interests are to be well served in the future.

These arguments make two errors. First, they understate the benefits to minority communities resulting from the act. They focus primarily on material benefits, measured proportionally. But while these benefits must be considered in assessing minority success, a proportional shares-of-the-pie or zero-sum attitude is encouraged at the expense of an equally important concept of informed public interest. This extends beyond the particular interests of the minority and majority communities to include the interests of the whole. Merely obtaining parity in material benefits is insufficient justification for a group's demanding a particular policy.

The Anglo majority, of course, has long invoked precisely this idea of the public interest in justification of policies designed primarily to benefit its group. Indeed, it is so natural to identify one's interest with that of the larger community that it is difficult to know whether this approach

3. Reed 1988.

has been taken strategically or unconsciously. But there is no doubt that the conflation of the public interest with that of the Anglo majority has all too often been the normal one made by Anglo officials. What makes this identification particularly easy is the absence of minority officials who can sharply dispute it in rational and—when necessary—dramatic ways on the public stage. African American and Latino officials, as the elected representatives of the emerging minority voters' choices, are now strategically placed to do this in a manner that their fellow Anglo liberals seldom are.

A second problem with the argument that benefits to minorities are largely symbolic stems from its proponents' failure to understand the nature of community within ethnic and racial groups. The Latino political community, like Latino culture, is not static. And how could it be, if it reciprocates in its expectations that mainstream politics will change to accommodate to Latino interests? The 1990s will be a time when a reconsideration of that community, and in particular its purpose, will be possible for the first time in American history. The development of the idea of an informed public interest can provide that purpose by requiring Latino representatives, intellectuals, and scholars to ground their calls for policy benefits in terms consistent not only with their own needs but with those of the entire polity.

The 1990s will be a time when Latino communities, largely through their elected representatives, will begin to outline the dimensions of a new public interest in a way that, on the one hand, goes beyond the narrow self-interest of traditional minority-group politics but on the other also goes beyond the "public interest" that the Anglo majority has long invoked as a screen for its narrow self-interest. Representatives of Latino communities, like representatives of many African American communities, operate within a system of majoritarian legislative decisionmaking that demands they not simply try to substitute their own disguised self-interest for a more comprehensive public interest. Unlike representatives of most Anglo communities, representatives of communities of color do not constitute the majority of legislators. If Latino and African American representatives are to serve their constituencies, if they are to provide the types of policy benefits needed, they must convince those who represent Anglo constituencies that these communities will also benefit from policies designed to serve minority communities. Stated differently, representatives of communities of color can no longer rely on white sympathizers to be moved by righteous indignation. A much more precise language of mutual benefit based on the larger informed public interest must be developed.

Some of the dimensions of this informed public interest can be specified. It must be premised upon a principle of access in which both electoral participation and influence in public policymaking are as great as possible for all segments of the community. It must allow many opportunities for self-determination by Latinos, African Americans, Anglos, and all other groups of citizens. Other dimensions might include a concern for long-term social stability, economic security, and the continued acceptance of the state's legitimacy by all groups.

Such an informed public interest will not appear without conflict, controversy, and considerable compromise. It will not be easy to achieve, nor will its dimensions, once established, be unchanging. For Latino communities its attainment will require that their representatives begin to renegotiate the terms of the political incorporation of these communities, that is, not just their access to the political process but their pursuit of properly informed self-interest. This will require that the representatives understand their communities in ways that are largely new.

This new conception must be developed in large measure through self-determination, in which Latino officials, freely and fairly elected by Latino voters and in constant contact with them, redefine their relation to the American polity on terms that all groups can accept as fair. This redefinition will take place, I believe, in any event. If it does not come about with full participation by Latinos through their elected representatives, it is likely that others will speak for them; and the resultant conception of the new informed public interest in that case will not have been made democratically.

In summary, the improved representation of Latino communities brought about by the Voting Rights Act will provide the crucial opportunity for Latino, African American, and Anglo communities, and the rest of the polity, to create together a new version of the public interest. It will supersede past versions because it will be based not simply on claims for proportional material benefits nor on a false, if tacit, premise that what is good for the Anglo majority is good for the polity as a whole, but instead on a realistic understanding of how the particularized needs of Latino and other minority groups can be met in ways that are beneficial to all groups. This achievement, I reiterate, cannot come about without the active participation of large numbers of officials elected by Latino voters. And we have the Voting Rights Act to thank for this necessary precondition's being met.

Voting Rights and Democratic Theory:
Where Do We Go From Here?
Lani Guinier

I propose to reexamine the goals and methods of voting rights litigation using the question first posed twenty-five years ago by Dr. Martin Luther King, Jr.: "Where do we go from here?" The strategy of voting rights litigation, preoccupied as it has been with creating districts in which black representatives can be elected, has traded genuine protection of minority rights for a claim of fairness based on electing a few minorities simply to promote an ideal of descriptive representation.[4] To overcome white bloc voting that consistently defeats the choices of black voters, voting rights activists have endorsed as a remedial strategy the creation within the larger electorate of some majority-black election districts. The exclusive remedial focus, however, ignores the broad-based participatory and transformative politics implicit in the original vision of the civil rights movement that led to passage of the Voting Rights Act in the first place. Even at its most impressive, the remedial focus has failed to produce real transfers of power. The main beneficiaries have been individual candidates and the middle-class blacks occasionally included in white-dominated governing coalitions. Such victories too often are little more than political and psychological symbols for poor and working-class blacks.[5]

4. Descriptive representation physically mirrors relevant characteristics of the electorate. Elsewhere I characterize these related propositions as "the theory of black electoral success." See Guinier 1991b, which describes the theory as an attempt to define descriptively—physically and culturally—black representation as a meaningful empowerment goal for a minority group engaged in structural reform legislation and litigation. The theory has four basic assumptions: authenticity of the representative, mobilization and electoral control of the electorate, racial polarization, and responsiveness and reform action by the representative. District-based electoral ratification by black voters is the primary enforcement mechanism.

The theory of black electoral success is an inchoate set of assumptions and goals that emerged from the civil rights movement's vision of minority empowerment and was then modified by the pressures of litigation to enforce the 1965 Voting Rights Act. By virtue of voting and election opportunities, black electoral success attempts to advance the black political agenda of civil rights enforcement, government intervention on behalf of the poor, and the development of black role models (the litigation model romanticizes black elected officials as empowerment role models). Ignoring problems of tokenism and false consciousness, voting rights litigation thus tends to promote a marginal kind of black legislative leadership, focused primarily on opportunities for electoral ratification and reelection through the mechanism of majority-black, single-member districts.

5. See generally Guinier 1991b. See also Scavo 1990, a study of the relevance of the

Bruce Cain defends the current approach to enforcing the Voting Rights Act in large measure by understating its goals and strategy. He perceives the act as balanced temporarily on a historically compelled equilibrium point that permits limited judicial intervention to cure blatant disfranchisement. The act's appeal for him lies in the modesty of its success. Black plaintiffs do not always prevail, which he attributes to rigorous judicial construction of limitations on proportional representation. Moreover, he cites assimilationist and other coopting effects that counteract any tendency for "racial hardening of identity among blacks." He argues that critics have overstated the act's propensity to inflame race consciousness and have supplied no empirical support for their concern that enforcement of the act is slipping toward achieving near or exact proportional representation. To other critics, who charge that the act has failed to achieve more than cosmetic changes in the makeup of elected bodies, he responds that litigation is inherently circumscribed as a strategy for reform. The ultimate problem of black political power, he argues, is essentially political, not legal.

Cain's statements are both accurate and fatalistic. He is accurate that the act has achieved very limited objectives; he is fatalistic in endorsing those objectives as representing the full measure of black voters' legitimate and achievable goals. I agree that the problem of achieving black political power is broader and more profound than current legal views assume, but for reasons other than those Cain supplies. Many factors, including economic and structural causes of racism, geographic isolation, poverty, and a retreat by the federal government from addressing issues critical to minorities, are indeed beyond the manipulations of any single strategy of litigation. But even within the achievable objectives of a legal agenda to ensure voting rights, the reasons for and the consequences of the failure of litigation to mobilize the black community or to achieve the reforms voting once promised are different from what Cain supposes.

First, Cain and I differ on the nature of the vision that informs the act. The act is premised on a broad vision of political equality and

---

increase in the number of local-level black elected officials in seven small cities in rural North Carolina, equity relevance for the black middle class, and symbolic success and role models for black youths. In terms of unaddressed issues of concern to black citizens— economic development, poverty, and unemployment—the black political agenda is more encompassing and less successful than the white political agenda. Black politicians see the problem of severity and government effectiveness differently from whites. Of the five problems blacks rate as serious, they rate four as showing little evidence of effective government action.

empowerment. The vision of empowerment anticipated an electorate actively participating in policy reform, not merely reconfigured districts that ensure legislative voting privileges for a few black elected officials. The vision imagined a transformative politics that would value political participation for its own sake in order to recognize the autonomy and dignity of black voters. Participation would affirm their status as first-class citizens in a democracy. A transformative politics would also ensure government legitimacy because it would give disadvantaged groups a substantive basis for lending their consent to government decisions.

In a transformative politics, empowerment means the ability to make government more responsive to minority interests, not just the ability to integrate legislative bodies. Yet, focused primarily on such limited integration and uncoupled from the original vision of the civil rights movement, litigation to subdivide at-large jurisdictions into majority-black districts has settled for a principle of physical inclusion. White majority rule in the majority's self-interest remains legitimate as long as some minority representatives are physically present when the majority makes its decisions.

As Cain points out, even within black single-member districts, politics may remain a peripheral concern for most people. Although he cites this result as an example of the inherent limitation of a legal approach, I would argue that the single-member-district model is simply one remedial focus, and it is that focus, not the fact of litigation itself, that unnecessarily constrains current enforcement strategies. Litigation may be self-limiting, but it is an especially impoverished strategy when limited to ensuring fair election day voting opportunities in majority-black, single-member districts. Such districts, which create important election opportunities for black officials, do not invigorate the electorate beyond first-time election opportunities, do not mobilize the electorate to ensure accountable, effective representation, and consequently do not realize the basic empowerment objectives of voting reform.[6]

Cain and I also differ about the value of proportional representation to measure political equality. Cain uses "proportional representation" to mean "the modern and peculiarly American variant" of descriptive representation or a relation between the characteristics of the population and the physiognomy or cultural attributes of representatives. The classic view, however, refers to nonmajoritarian or consensus representation based on voluntary constituencies with the same interests. The American variant focuses instead on the narrow, specialized exception to majori-

6. See Guinier 1991a.

tarian rules claimed by minority proponents of descriptive representation. The American view thus contracts the classic definition of proportionality to measure what Jennifer Smith has called a proportion of "like bodies, not like minds."

Cain writes in response to those conservative critics who worry that the act's tilt toward this version of proportional representation will heighten race consciousness among blacks. Neither he nor those critics, however, discuss the problem of race consciousness or racial privilege among whites who are now disproportionately overrepresented. As identified by Cain, the act's conservative critics are proponents of majoritarian systems who define political equality as electoral fairness guaranteeing nonbiased conditions of voting eligibility and equally weighted votes. These critics challenge the right of minority groups to representative or responsive government because the right to vote is individual, not group-based. Special protection for the rights of minority groups is unnecessary as long as individual members have a fair chance to participate formally in an election.

In this debate Cain sides with demands of voting rights plaintiffs not to be excluded. The remedy of race-conscious districting for specially protected groups is a necessary but special exception to political equality. He endorses this narrow remedy because it is temporary and contingent on evidence of gross underrepresentation. Since redistricting to create majority-black districts represents only a small movement toward proportionality in the American sense, Cain justifies this relatively minor perturbance from a fundamentally majoritarian system.

Preoccupied with the conservative critique, Cain does not explore the failure of proportional representation to realize the full dimension of political equality. Political equality also has an implicit component of equal influence, of an equal opportunity to influence legislative outcomes.[7] Proportional descriptive representation, or simply counting the number of black elected officials, does not necessarily address this component. Although majority-black, single-member districts provide legislative seats for black representatives, legislative seats alone do not enfranchise.

As a result of voting rights lawsuits, some jurisdictions now have proportionate black representation in their governing bodies. Yet even proportionately represented blacks may not enjoy effective representation in legislative deliberation and coalition building. Black legislators, not just black voters, may be the victims of prejudice, especially if they represent

---

7. I develop the argument for this component in Guinier 1991a.

a geographically isolated constituency in a racially polarized environment, and may have little influence over the policy choices made by representatives of majority-white, single-member districts. Especially where blacks have a more encompassing political agenda than whites, district-based black electoral success may ensure more representative but not necessarily more responsive government.

Cain accurately portrays the debate between conservative critics and voting rights advocates over competing claims to democratic legitimacy based on the value of integrated government. Distracted by this debate, however, he fails to explore other critical aspects of the act's original visions of political empowerment and political equality. It is to these missing conditions of political equality that I now turn.

In these comments I simply assume the first condition: a transformative, insurgency model of political empowerment. Black voters would be empowered to participate energetically and continuously throughout the political process. The statutory language enforcing a right to participate and a right to elect representatives of choice would be interpreted broadly to protect black voters' dignity, autonomy, and interest in self-government as citizens in a democracy.

The second condition of political equality is legislative influence, not just legislative presence. I limit my comments to the failure of black single-member districts to ensure legislative responsiveness to black interests because of prejudice in a polarized environment. I focus here only on the enduring effect of prejudice, through first-, second-, and third-generation legal remedies, on black political opportunity.[8]

Essentially, voting rights litigation developed a cramped version of the equality principle in response to the racially polarized voting that prevented blacks from electing representatives of their choice. Fairness was defined as equal electoral opportunities for minorities in a majoritarian system. But this principle has proven inadequate. Equal prospects of electoral success do not necessarily lead to equal prospects of political satisfaction. Indeed, in a racially polarized environment, particular systems that improve the prospects of black electoral success, such as those that include majority-black, single-member districts, may perpetuate inequalities. They may

---

8. The first-generation cases directly challenged obstacles to the access of the voter to the ballot. Second-generation cases involved qualitative vote dilution that challenged the weight of a voter's vote. Third-generation cases must now consider the legislative or deliberative gerrymander in which black representatives, elected as a result of second-generation lawsuits, are excluded from meaningful participation in the decisionmaking body. Third-generation cases reflect the transfer of electoral polarization to the legislature.

undermine the prospect of achieving policies responsive to minority needs by isolating black constituents from the white majority, from other blacks who do not reside in the black district, and from potential legislative allies.

Thus litigation on voting rights misses the point of its own polarization hypothesis. In a racially polarized environment, simple representation achieves some but not all that is necessary for political equality. It cannot ensure a fair chance to influence policy or a chance to win a fair number of contested policy decisions. Political equality requires both a standard for evaluating legislative influence and explicit mechanisms for overcoming inequality within the governing policymaking body.

To realize political equality, two previously overlooked elements are crucial. First, voting rights activists and litigators should begin to worry more about the fundamental fairness of permanent legislative hegemony of the majority in a political system that derives its legitimacy from the consent of a simple, racially homogenous majority. The original vision of the civil rights movement was one of fundamentally different trade-offs between majority rule and minority rights, consistent with concepts of fairness, equality, and legitimacy.[9]

Second, voting rights activists and litigators should think about the problem of voting rights in the context of what Kathy Abrams calls "the extended political process."[10] I recommend extending the inquiry from opportunities to vote on election day to issues of legislative decision-making for politically marginalized groups. This focus must be based on the idea that the values for which our society stands are defined by what we do for the dispossessed. A theory of representation that derives its authority from the original civil rights vision must address concerns of equal status for minorities as full participants in the broad range of political decisionmaking in order to bring about fair results.[11] For those at the bottom, it is not enough that a representation system give everyone an equal chance of having policy preferences physically represented. A fair system of political representation should include mechanisms to ensure

9. See Guinier 1991b. Cain considers competing concepts on which some democratic theorists rest their case for majoritarian principles—concerns for stability and efficiency.

10. Abrams 1988.

11. This is essentially a claim for qualitative fairness involving equal recognition (equal status as full participants in politics) and just results. Beitz 1988 argues that any satisfactory doctrine of political equality must simultaneously address three concerns of democratic decisionmaking about public policy: its value by virtue of public cooperative enterprise, the content of legislation it produces, and its contribution to the political education of its citizens.

that a disadvantaged and stigmatized minority group also has a fair chance of having its needs and desires satisfied.

To achieve these dual objectives, I propose a concept, tentatively called proportionate interest representation, to address the failure of the model of black electoral success to develop substantive standards or a realistic enforcement mechanism for achieving legislative influence or responsiveness.[12] At one level an inquiry based on proportionate interest representation might explore basic issues of democratic principle. My purpose here is necessarily more limited. My object is to invite voting rights activists and litigators to adopt a different approach to the immediate problem of legislative influence yet remain within the statutory framework of the Voting Rights Act, especially as amended in 1982.

Proportionate interest representation challenges three aspects of the prevailing assumptions about institutional reform. First, it challenges the assumption, accepted somewhat uncritically by the theory that black electoral success is an ultimate goal, that minorities have the right to representation but majorities hostile to them should always govern. Second, it challenges the assumption that access to the decisionmaking process through district-based electoral control adequately ensures representation of minority interests. Finally the concept challenges the assumption that it is unnecessary or undesirable to develop substantive or procedural standards to describe the way a just society would distribute political satisfaction in the absence of racism.

To restate these challenged assumptions affirmatively, proportionate interest representation has three interrelated goals: to give dignity and satisfaction to the strongly held sentiments of minorities, to make black representatives necessary participants in the governing process, and to disaggregate a majority faction that is permanently self-constituted based on prejudice. Proportionate interest representation challenges the entitlement of such a 51 percent majority to exercise 100 percent of the power. It focuses on requirements of structured election and legislative decisionmaking mechanisms to enforce fairness in policymaking. Proportionate interest representation takes the idea of democracy by consensus and

12. In proportional representation systems, losers (those with less than a plurality) as well as winners are elected; see Riker 1984, 183–84 and note 10. Others use different terms to refer to a similar concept: see Young 1990, who argues for a communicative theory of democracy based on specific group representation. The term "interest" in proportionate interest legislation refers to self-identified interests, meaning those prominent needs, wants, and interests articulated by any politically cohesive group of voters. Interests are not necessarily descriptive of an essential group identity but are fluid and dynamic articulations of group preferences.

compromise and structures it in a deliberative, collective decisionmaking body in which the prejudiced white majority is disaggregated.

It begins with the proposition that a consensus model of power sharing is preferable to a majoritarian model of centralized, winner-take-all accountability and popular sovereignty. By definition, majority preferences enjoy greater popular support; yet from the minority perspective, centralized authority is neither legitimate nor stabilizing if the majority is permanent and racially fixed. In this sense, American majoritarianism, including the tradition of direct election of single executives, unnecessarily marginalizes the minority perspective in a society deeply riven by race.[13]

Proportionate interest representation disaggregates the white majority by minimizing the threshold of exclusion, the number of votes necessary to win under the most adverse possible circumstances. It lowers the threshold for participation and representation to something less than 51 percent to neutralize any existing prejudice.[14]

Proportionate interest representation attempts to move the process of governmental decisionmaking away from a majoritarian model toward one of proportional power.[15] In particular, efforts to centralize authority in a single executive would be discouraged in favor of power-sharing alternatives that emphasize collective decisionmaking. Within the legislature itself, rules would be preferred that require supermajorities for the enactment of certain decisions so that minority groups have an effective veto, thus forcing the majority to bargain with them and include them in any winning coalition. Other devices for minority incorporation might include rotation in legislative office. And still other electoral and legislative decisionmaking alternatives, such as legislative cumulative voting, also exist that are fair and legitimate and that preserve representational authenticity yet are more likely than current practices to promote just results.[16]

---

13. In this sense proportionate interest representation builds on contemporary pluralist analyses that emphasize the importance of multiple group memberships and flexible coalitions to prevent the destabilizing situation of permanent winners and losers. Lijphart, Rogowski, and Weaver, forthcoming, for example, write about alternative, consensual approaches to managing deep racial cleavages in a democracy.

14. Such "democratic" enforcement occurs not simply by putting limits on majoritarian democracy in the form of a constitutional or statutory right to group representation but by inviting specific challenges to discredit the idea that a fair voting process alone supplies majoritarian legitimacy.

15. See Lijphart, Rogowski, and Weaver, forthcoming.

16. Guinier 1991a. Legislative cumulative voting presents legislative alternatives in multiples of three or more. By aggregating voting choices, individual representatives may

The concept of proportionate interest representation is molded by the hope that a more cooperative political style of deliberation and ultimately a more equal basis for satisfying constituents is possible when authentic minority representatives are reinforced by structures to empower them at every stage of the political process. In this sense, proportionate interest representation is a liberal view of strategic political interaction framed and modified by firm procedural rules.[17]

Ultimately, however, proportionate interest representation is also an attempt to hypothesize about the reconstruction of political equality.[18] It recognizes that simply changing the way voting preferences are weighted cannot rid a society of racism. A normative directive to reinvigorate the basic motivation for the Voting Rights Act, it begins the work of designing a political process without racism, a project that is necessarily speculative and specific to each situation.[19]

I recognize that this task, though relatively easy to describe, may be harder to implement, especially in a context in which a strategy based

---

express the intensity of preferences and forge coalitions in which they trade votes on matters of relative indifference. Representational authenticity describes the value of community-based leadership. Representatives are authentic if sponsored or elected by voters who have a full range of leadership options. In addition to electoral ratification, authenticity subsumes the cultural or psychological value of descriptive representation.

17. Proportionate interest representation is not a system of electoral quotas. As a system of like minds, not like bodies, it is based on subjective preferences, not physically descriptive characteristics. It is also consistent with "one person, one vote" because each voter casts the same number of ballots or votes on the same number of choices. Compare Michelman 1989, 449: liberalism may "valorize strategic political action" in contesting a certain range of governmental spoils but regulate that strategic interaction by well-crafted procedural rules and firm substantive limits.

18. Proportionate interest representation may be relevant to other bases of inequality, but here I confine my speculations to the situation of blacks in general and to black political empowerment within the context of Voting Rights Act enforcement in particular.

19. To be judicially manageable, litigation based on proportionate interest representation must offer a plausible rationale for objecting to the types of irregularities in effective representation, just as it now challenges irregularities in electoral representation through litigation over vote dilution. It must also suggest a judicially manageable standard of evidence, an outcome-oriented attempt to develop a measure of what the normal baseline would be. One such possibility, for example, might be to compare what a legislature with black elected officials produces to what it produced in their absence. See Guinier 1991a. In response to my critique of the theory of black electoral success, therefore, I plan to develop what are now merely tentative suggestions for a different approach to voting rights reform based on the concept of proportionate interest representation for self-identified communities of interest. Guinier 1991a examines this concept and attempts to show how its application differs both in practice and potential results from current district-based electoral structure reform.

on litigation heads the agenda. But I remain confident in its objective: to reorient voting litigation away from the chimera of achieving a physically integrated legislature in a color-blind society toward a clearer vision of a fair and just society. The struggle of the civil rights movement for passage of the Voting Rights Act has been transformed by contemporary views of integration to justify a majority-white society with a racially neutered legislature exercising its power consistently in the majority's self-interest, sometimes to freeze out minority representatives, other times simply to outvote minority preferences. We need to redefine effective empowerment to break down majority hegemony. The Voting Rights Act should be used to monitor all aspects of the political process to challenge the right of the majority to its monopoly of power at the executive and legislative, not just the electoral, level. The act should also be enforced to challenge the right of the majority to wield its power on the basis of its prejudices. To do so, the act must use a substantive measure of political equality, not merely a process-based measure of minority group protection and access.

Black legislative visibility, while it is an important measure of electoral fairness, by itself represents an anemic approach to political fairness and justice. A vision of fairness and justice must begin to imagine a full and effective voice for disadvantaged minorities, a voice that is accountable to self-identified community interests, a voice that persuades, and a voice that dependably produces policy satisfaction through the political process.

Although Bruce Cain may be right that such a project requires sustained political commitment, not merely legal capital, it is a project to which activists, lawyers, and scholars can each contribute. Whatever the merits of my particular vision, I hope at least to revitalize the debate about where we are going, not just how far we have come.

Some Consequences of the Voting Rights Act
Carol M. Swain

African Americans have made substantial progress in getting themselves elected at all levels of government. Rather than rejoicing, however, voting rights advocates—those people who make it their business to testify and litigate for the creation of minority districts—often seem threatened when an election sees no racial polarization or when black voters choose to elect white candidates instead of black. If blacks from local communities testify for defendants in voting rights cases, the advocates may even dismiss that testimony and call the witnesses Uncle Toms and Aunt Janes.

Such attitudes are typified by a voting rights advocate whom I heard say, "Unfortunately for our case, we did not find the expected pattern of racial voting."

No one can deny the remarkable contribution of the Voting Rights Act of 1965 to the empowerment of racial minorities. Not only have minorities been elected at all levels of government since the passage of the act, but white elected officials have shown greater responsiveness to minorities in the South and throughout the nation.[20] Today there are few places where white politicians, especially Democrats, can afford to ignore their black constituents. Even long-time segregationists changed in response to the act. In 1963 Governor George Wallace told the people of Alabama, "I draw the line in the dust and toss the gauntlet before the feet of tyranny, and I say: Segregation now—segregation tomorrow—segregation forever." Ten years later he was actively courting black voters, crowning a black homecoming queen at the University of Alabama, and telling a biracial conference of mayors, "we're all God's children. All God's children are equal."[21] In 1982 Senator Strom Thurmond of South Carolina, the man who led the filibuster against the 1957 Civil Rights Act and who had previously opposed all such legislation, cast votes for extending the Voting Rights Act and making the birthday of Martin Luther King, Jr., a national holiday.[22]

In spite of such positive changes, however, the Voting Rights Act has also brought several unintended consequences that have impeded progress toward a color-blind society. One of these has been an overemphasis on the creation of majority-black political units, which despite evidence to

20. Blacks who have won elections with white support include Douglas Wilder, lieutenant governor and later governor of Virginia; David Dinkins, mayor of New York City; and Norm Rice, mayor of Seattle. Senator Edward Brooke's victory in 1966 was a harbinger for the elections to Congress of other blacks from majority-white constituencies. George Collins was elected in 1970 from a 42 percent black Chicago district and Ronald Dellums was elected from a 70 percent white district. Thereafter, Andrew Young (1972), Harold Ford (1974), Alan Wheat (1982), Katie Hall (1982), and Gary Franks (1990) were elected from majority-white districts, and not from the traditionally liberal constituencies in Massachusetts and Berkeley, California, that sent Brooke and Dellums to Washington. Since the early 1970s a much larger group of black representatives—Barbara Jordan (1972), Julian Dixon (1978), Mickey Leland (1978), Mervyn Dymally (1980), Floyd Flake (1986), and Craig Washington (1989)—have been elected in districts where no racial group constitutes a voting-age majority. Others, such as William Clay (1968) and Charles Rangel (1970) held their seats as their majority-black constituencies became either majority-white or became a plurality. By 1988, 39 percent of the blacks in Congress represented districts that were less than 50 percent black. See Williams 1988, 23–24; Swain 1992, chap. 9.

21. Quoted in Bass and De Vries 1976, 62, 68.

22. Cohodas 1984, 70.

the contrary, many assume are needed to elect black politicians. The drawbacks of this strategy for increasing the number of black elected officials are obvious. Blacks are not concentrated enough geographically to create a significant number of new majority-black political units. Indeed, population losses threaten existing minority enclaves: the 1980 census revealed that thirteen of the seventeen districts represented by blacks in 1980 had lost more than 10 percent of their population in the 1970s, and five had lost more than 20 percent. George Crockett's Detroit-area district lost 37 percent of its population, more than any other in the country.[23] Although population losses in districts represented by blacks were lower between 1980 and 1990, those with the greatest losses were in the Northeast and Midwest, the regions currently producing the most black representatives.[24] Illinois, Michigan, New York, Ohio, and Pennsylvania lost congressional representation after the 1991 redistricting.

Another unfortunate consequence is an overemphasis on creating safe black districts. This strategy has meant redrawing some majority-white districts that had already elected black representatives. Atlanta's Fifth District (1972), Tennessee's Ninth (1974), and Illinois's Seventh (1970) elected blacks to Congress before being redrawn to have black majorities. Increasing the black population in such districts wastes black votes that might have had greater impact in districts not already sending blacks to Congress.[25] The fact of black representatives from majority-white districts flies in the face of the conventional wisdom that majority-black political units, preferably 65 percent black or more, are needed to elect black politicians. As Charles Bullock has pointed out, thresholds lower than that give black candidates a reasonable chance of winning elections without squandering black votes.[26]

For many advocates of voting rights a reasonable chance of winning is not good enough when a minority victor can be guaranteed by the creation of an overwhelmingly minority electoral district, a view supported in effect by a number of court rulings.[27] Such developments led Abigail

23. "Urban Districts Suffer Big Population Losses" 1981, 646–49.
24. "Official 1990 Count by District" 1991, 1309–12; Huckabee 1988; Rich 1988, A21.
25. Some researchers argue that Atlanta became more racist during the 1980s because white voters rejected former Congressman Andrew Young during his mayoral bid in 1981 when he got 8.9 percent of the vote. However, this argument ignores the fact that he was running against a popular liberal white opponent, and white voters may have spurned him because of his highly publicized spats with President Jimmy Carter, a Georgia native. McDonald, Binford, and Johnson 1990.
26. Bullock 1982, 436.
27. For more information on the courts' reasoning see *Kirksey v. Board of Supervisors*

Thernstrom to complain that recent interpretations of the Voting Rights Act have gone beyond the goal of ensuring blacks the right to vote to that of insisting on proportional representation.[28] But proportional representation has serious shortcomings for increasing black political influence. Even if black Americans, who are 12 percent of the population, held 12 percent of the political offices in this country, they would be unable to implement their legislative goals without help. No doubt proportional representation systems could be devised that would increase the number of black officeholders in the short run, but in the long run these electoral arrangements could be a barrier to building black strength: they could hold the proportion of black legislators to the proportion of blacks in the population. Proportional representation could also deprive white legislators of a sense of obligation to blacks. At present many white officials consider representing blacks and other minorities a significant part of their duty. In doing so they may even support controversial minority rights issues opposed by many of their white constituents, something they might not do if the electoral system were changed.

Furthermore, race relations suffer when electoral remedies favor one minority group or create environments in which candidates can engage in racially or ethnically polarizing tactics without fear of defeat. This is true whether one is discussing former Klansman David Duke, whose racist insinuations garnered him 55 percent of the white vote in his 1991 gubernatorial race in Louisiana, or Chicago's Gus Savage, whose stock-in-trade seems to be anti-Semitism.

Political and racial majorities show much ingenuity in resisting unwanted changes. In some areas of the country, for example, states are moving toward deciding important policy questions by referendum on a statewide ballot, that is, toward government by unalloyed majority rule, which can harm minorities if their preferences differ from those of the majority. For example, California's passage by referendum of Proposition 13 (cutting property taxes) and Proposition 98 (stipulating the percentage of state funds to be allocated to public schools) pitted racial and political minorities against majorities. Referendums and government by initiative can doom the coalition building by elected officials that is the essence of compromise and harmony.

---

of Hinds County, Mississippi, 554 F.2d 139 (1977); State of Mississippi v. United States, 490 F.Supp. 569 (1979); United Jewish Organizations v. Carey, 430 U.S. 144 (1977); Major v. Treen, 574 F.Supp. 325 (1983); Thornburg v. Gingles, 478 U.S. 30 (1986).
28. Thernstrom 1987.

Whether to form biracial coalitions has been intensely debated since the 1960s, when Stokely Carmichael and Charles Hamilton wrote *Black Power,* in which they argued that such coalitions would be detrimental until African Americans had developed independent bases of power that would allow them to become equal partners.[29] That time has come. Since the 1960s, African Americans have become far more politically effective. They have shown white politicians that they expect something in return for their votes. As a consequence, more and more white elected officials are responsive to minority concerns.

All of this suggests a number of conclusions. First, proponents of voting rights should acknowledge the growing number of elections in which racial polarization does not occur. Its absence may mean that the laws have done their jobs well. Second, we should not second-guess the choices black voters have made among candidates. Sometimes, white politicians are simply better than their black alternatives. Third, advocates should stop denigrating those blacks who testify for defendants in voting rights cases. No one is in a position to deny the reality of another person's experience. Finally, people must move beyond entrenched positions that require them to resist the logic of opposing arguments.

So, the knowledge of how majority rule works should push America toward greater creativity in finding ways to remove not-so-obvious barriers to minority influences: overly restrictive registration laws, resistance of party leaders to the recruitment of black candidates in majority-white areas, the absence of a system of financing political campaigns that could encourage challengers to incumbents. A focus on removing such barriers is a more efficient use of time and energies than fighting old battles and refusing to recognize the signs of progress.

Case-Specific Implementation of the Voting Rights Act
James P. Turner

In preparing remarks on Bruce Cain's chapter, I read Laughlin McDonald's account of the origins of amended section 2 of the Voting Rights Act in 1982 and had the feeling of having been present at the creation.[30] The Department of Justice supported the challenge to Mobile,

29. Carmichael and Hamilton 1967, 81.
30. The views expressed here do not necessarily represent those of the Department of Justice.

Alabama's, at-large commissioner system in *City of Mobile* v. *Bolden*.[31] Despite two oral arguments that I presented with plaintiff's attorney, James Blacksher, the Court handed down inconsistent opinions that seemed to close the door on the theory of minority vote dilution as a statutory violation. In the long view, however, the shadow cast by the *Bolden* decision led Congress to amend section 2. But for our unsuccessful advocacy in *Bolden,* there probably would be no statutory "results" test, and certainly no scholarly analyses of section 2's reshaping of democratic theory. It is extremely doubtful that the theory of vote dilution would have developed to its present scope had it remained a matter of concern only to the federal courts. However, by losing the case, we set the stage for winning a more important battle in Congress.

From this perspective, Cain's chapter can be seen as an examination of the congressional effort to counter the results of *Mobile* v. *Bolden.* But it is more than that. His thesis is that the nature of politics to favor majoritarian rule must sometimes yield under the constraints of section 2 and section 5 of the Voting Rights Act to correct problems of minority dilution and underrepresentation. He observes that moving toward proportional representation can be justified but recognizes there are some long-range liabilities. Requiring or encouraging proportional representation will discourage the formation of interracial coalitions, encourage racial bloc voting, and create special preferences for selected minorities. Although I generally concur with this analysis, as a lawyer I would prefer to arrange the ideas and emphasis in a slightly different way.

In what has become the most important vote dilution case since the congressional expansion of section 2 in 1982, Justice William Brennan wrote for the majority in *Thornburg* v. *Gingles* on how to focus a vote dilution inquiry: "The essence of a Section 2 claim is that a certain electoral law, practice or structure interacts with social and historical conditions to cause an inequality in the opportunities enjoyed by black and white voters to elect their preferred representatives."[32] Thus from a legal standpoint I must regard the section 2 standard as case-specific: a practice that is legal and proper in one jurisdiction may be illegal and improper in another because of the interaction defined by Justice Brennan. The Supreme Court earlier, in *White* v. *Regester,* referred to the "intensely local appraisal" that a trial judge must make in assessing proof of vote

31. *City of Mobile* v. *Bolden,* 446 U.S. 55 (1980).
32. *Thornburg* v. *Gingles,* 478 U.S. 30 at 47 (1986).

dilution.[33] This case-specific analysis can be contrasted perhaps with the approach of the social scientist in identifying the intersection of various trends and models.

For example, under section 5 of the Voting Rights Act, the Department of Justice has approved the adoption of an open primary system in Louisiana while objecting to its adoption in Mississippi because of the department's pragmatic appraisal of differing electoral customs. Similarly, in *Thornburg* v. *Gingles,* while condemning most of the challenged districts, the Supreme Court approved the use of one multimember district after examining the local voting patterns.

Once a violation of section 2 has been identified by the Justice Department and action moves to the remedial stage, the department frequently encounters some of the social science considerations discussed by Cain. Typically, relief may involve replacing a majority electoral system with a plurality system or designing single-member districts to replace an at-large election or eliminating numbered posts. In each case, however, the relief must be tailored to fit the violation and should conform, if possible, to local preferences.

Accordingly, the result may well be susceptible to the criticism that, to comply with the law, a jurisdiction has been required to move away from majoritarian principles toward racial or ethnic proportionality. However, in the eyes of the law, the enforcement scheme is to tailor remedies to fit discrete local problems. It does not perceive any requirement in sections 2 or 5 that adopts or promotes one theory of democratic representation over another.

The object of the voting legislation implementing the Fourteenth and Fifteenth Amendments is to do whatever is required to purge all traces of racial or ethnic discrimination from the conduct of elections. This is done, first, by making sure that everyone who is eligible can participate without discrimination in registration and all the other steps leading to the nomination and election of candidates for public office. Second, these provisions are aimed at making sure that the districts, the method of election, the representational structure, and the entire process are not infected, designedly or otherwise, with racial or ethnic bias. Necessarily, these legislative goals are reached in case-by-case adjudication, with the facts of each case controlling the scope of needed remedies.

I must digress here to deny vigorously the suggestion, which Cain has not made but others have, that the Justice Department's Civil Rights

33. *White* v. *Regester,* 412 U.S. 755 at 469 (1973).

Division has carried out its responsibilities under the Voting Rights Act in pursuit of a political agenda. (Indeed, several journalists and lawyers have made this claim recently in the media.) I have worked in this effort since the act was passed in 1965. With only a few possible exceptions, political considerations have not entered into the application of the provisions of the Voting Rights Act in any national administration. The division has recently completed, for example, the longest and largest dilution case ever tried under the act, successfully challenging the election districts in Los Angeles County. The remedy obtained there has abolished the longstanding conservative Republican control of the county commission in favor of a system in which Hispanics are able to choose one of the five members, a remedy that has had the effect of electing Democrats to three of the five seats.

Returning to Bruce Cain's discussion, in addition to my preferring a case-by-case emphasis, I would have to dissent from some of his broad language implying that section 2 requires "color-conscious voting rights policies" that can generally be labeled "affirmative action." Such labels do not advance the understanding of the purpose behind the act. In administering and enforcing this law, the Justice Department and the courts are not seeking to maximize the number of minority officeholders. Instead the department seeks to analyze individual circumstances to see that the actual operation of a particular election system is not infected by racial bias and that minority voters have a nondiscriminatory opportunity to participate. Cain is right that this may cause some changes in democratic theory. But any such general shift will be based on changes required in many individual cases. Our democratic system will evolve and improve, but it should not be programmed by either lawyers or political scientists to reach certain results.

Postscript: What is the Best Route to a Color-Blind Society?

BERNARD GROFMAN & CHANDLER DAVIDSON

WE BELIEVE THAT MANY of the controversies over minority voting rights are exaggerated and that the positions of disputants are considerably closer than some of them might be prepared to admit. For example, most of the current disputants share certain basic premises, such as the goal of a color-blind society. While there may be some advocates of minority empowerment who desire a world where fixed racially defined groups are awarded a share of the pie (and the power) in proportion to their numbers, that is not, we believe, a widely held vision. It is certainly not our vision—nor the one responsible for the Voting Rights Act.

Like most advocates of minority voting rights, we remain committed integrationists. Like many critics of the act, we see race-conscious remedies as inherently undesirable. Where we differ with these critics is, first, in our view that ours is still a race-conscious world in which there remains a need for race-conscious remedies; second, in our recognition that the requirement of single-member districts as a remedy for vote dilution is in no way incompatible with the fundamentally majoritarian features of American politics; and third, in our belief that the election of minority officeholders from such districts ultimately fosters rather than frustrates minority political integration.

Starting from this premise of the desirability of a color-blind society—one, in Martin Luther King's words, where people, including political candidates, "will not be judged by the color of their skin but by the content of their character"—we do not believe that only blacks can represent blacks or that only whites can represent whites, and our hope is that one day race and ethnicity will not be important factors in electoral choices. Consequently, under normal circumstances the absence of racial bloc voting should be celebrated because it may signal change for the better that obviates the need for federal intervention. A world in which fixed and distinct racial and ethnic groups slice the political pie according to their numbers is as anathema to us as it is to certain critics who see the Voting Rights Act as encouraging such a world.

Thus at the heart of the current debate about voting rights is a disagreement not about ends but about means. We would like to shift the debate away from its present mode of highly abstract normative or constitutional argument and away from polemics to a consideration of the empirical evidence of the actual consequences of the act.[1] If we want to understand whether it has outlived its usefulness and what American electoral and racial politics might have looked like if the act had not been renewed and amended in 1982, we need to know what it has accomplished and what remains to be done. To examine these questions, it is helpful to explain some of our disagreements with various of the act's critics.

Our differences generally have to do with how the Voting Rights Act has actually worked, and with how best to achieve integration in the racially divided world in which we live. There are three principal points of dispute, each of which is amenable to empirical analysis. First, does section 2 (and section 5, which now incorporates section 2 standards) actually require proportional racial representation? Second, are there significant changes in the extent to which politics is now driven by race-conscious voting, changes that indicate the Voting Rights Act has outlived its usefulness? Third, does the act reduce minorities' overall political influence by unduly concentrating them in districts where they are the majority? While these questions may not always have easy answers, focusing on them allows us to eschew rhetoric and look at evidence.

Does Section 2 Require Proportional Representation of Minorities?

The principal criticism of the Voting Rights Act comes from those who argue that it has been turned from its original appropriate aim of ending barriers to black enfranchisement and redirected to destroy barriers to minority officeholding.[2] Yet there is almost no one who disagrees that

1. This volume is part of a larger project funded by the Law and Social Sciences program of the National Science Foundation, SES 88-09392, to the editors. There will be another volume from the project with separate chapters that look at voting rights issues in each of the eight southern states covered by the act. These chapters will provide, in a historical context, a detailed empirical examination of minority representation brought about by the Voting Rights Act. Such analyses will permit an estimate of how much of the dramatic growth in minority representation in the South can be traced to the elimination of at-large election systems and multimember districts.

2. There is considerable disagreement in the scholarly literature about the intent of the framers of the 1965 act and the interpretation given to the amended 1982 language of section 2 by courts and by the Department of Justice. The decision in *Allen* v. *State Board of Elections*, 393 U.S. 544 (1969), in which a Mississippi law that converted the basis of

there are circumstances when vote dilution, as distinct from disfranchisement, is illegal.[3] The issue is how to define dilution.[4]

The 1982 amendments to section 2 include the following language:
"The extent to which members of a protected class have been elected to
office in the State or political subdivision is one circumstance which may
be considered: *Provided,* That nothing in this section establishes a right
to have members of a protected class elected in numbers equal to their
proportion in the population." However, Justice Sandra Day O'Connor's
concurring opinion in *Thornburg* v. *Gingles* asserts that the Court (speaking
through Justice William Brennan) in fact makes "usual, roughly proportional success the sole focus of its vote dilution analysis." This charge,
which seems to imply that section 2 has been converted into a requirement

---

elections for county supervisor from ward to at-large was held to need preclearance under
section 5, legitimated subsequent Justice Department review not just of at-large elections,
but also of redistricting plans and annexations. It also touched off, in Timothy O'Rourke's
words in this volume, "an ongoing debate on the questions of when and under what
circumstances an otherwise legitimate election procedure might be discriminatory." That
debate intensified after the 1982 extension of the act and the development of the new
section 2 standard. O'Rourke and some of the other authors in this volume see the original
act as intended to be limited to disfranchisement issues, with the broader concept of vote
dilution a later graft-on. Others see the decision in *Allen* to include election systems under
the act as a natural and inevitable consequence of the need to deal with southern attempts
to prevent blacks from achieving an effective franchise.

Our own views are like those of Days in this volume. Rebutting the claim that Congress
was simply seeking in 1965 to ensure that blacks had, in the words of Thernstrom 1987,
5, "the right to enter a polling booth and pull the lever," Days asserts that, "on the contrary,
the history of racial discrimination in voting had made clear that Congress could not
anticipate the variety of stratagems that officials in covered jurisdictions might resort to
in order to maintain the status quo." Days considers section 5 to be a "testament to
Congress's view that flexibility should characterize the government's enforcement efforts. . . . The Supreme Court's *Allen* decision correctly captures the spirit of that congressional objective."

3. Even Thernstrom 1987, 238–39, one of the act's severest critics, concedes that
"there is no doubt that where 'racial politics . . . dominates the electoral process' and public
office is largely reserved for whites, the method of voting should be restructured to promote
minority officeholding. Safe black or Hispanic single-member districts hold white racism
in check, limiting its influence."

4. Should any deviation from proportional ethnic representation be sufficient to establish a claim of dilution? Should dilution be measured with respect to a single-member-
district baseline? Should dilution require proof of racial bloc voting? Should it require
proof of intentional discrimination or racial animus on the part of either voters or those
who adopted the plan under challenge? Should dilution be found only if there is retrogression, that is, only if the proposed change leaves minority voters with less chance to elect
their preferred candidates after the change than they did before (as Thernstrom 1987, 236,
argues should be the proper standard for section 5 preclearance)?

of proportional representation for minorities, has been repeated by many authors. We believe it is misleading. To understand why, it is necessary to explicate various meanings of proportional representation.

The first of these meanings refers to a formal set of election rules, called a proportional representation system, to ensure proportionality between each political party's percentage of candidates elected and its percentage of voter support. Such a system, used in many European countries, is familiar to students of comparative election laws.[5] But obviously this is not what O'Connor means. The baseline used in *Thornburg* and subsequent cases to judge vote dilution is that of a single-member-district plan. By definition, such a plan, with winner-take-all plurality-based elections in each district, does not make use of proportional representation of the sort referred to above—one that provides representation to each party according to the number of votes cast for that party.[6]

Nonetheless, one might reply that the single-member-district remedy has the same results as proportional representation. But even this is not really true. As Timothy O'Rourke points out in this volume: "It would be more accurate to say that the operative standard is a qualified proportional representation. . . . It may be impossible, given a fixed number of districts [and a given distribution of minority voters] to draw a proportional number of single-member districts with a majority black or Hispanic electorate. Moreover, minority districts, once drawn, do not guarantee that a minority candidate will win."

One might, however, argue that the distinction is academic. Whatever the remedy mandated by *Gingles* is called, when it is applied it might still accomplish roughly the same end as a system of formal proportional representation. It might seem that amended section 2 pretty much guarantees minority candidates a percentage of seats roughly proportional to minority population. Is this true? We do not think so, for two reasons.

First, we cannot emphasize too strongly the contingent nature of the minority voting rights specified in *Gingles*. Without a showing that white officials established or maintained certain election rules to prevent the election of minority voters' candidates of choice, courts require that all three prongs of the *Gingles* test be met before there can be a finding of vote dilution: residential segregation of the minority group sufficient to

5. See, for example, Lijphart and Grofman 1984.
6. In actuality, even proportional representation systems may not be perfectly proportional in their allocations of seats since there may be thresholds designed to discourage minor parties, such as a 5 percent share of the national vote, below which a party is entitled to no representation.

create a district in which the minority is in the majority; cohesion among that group's voters; and bloc voting by the white majority sufficient usually to defeat the minority group's candidates. There is no presumption that any group that is underrepresented automatically qualifies for protection under section 2.

Second, those who argue that proportional representation is mandated by section 2 often seem to imply that a right is being granted for the election of candidates of a certain race or ethnicity. On this interpretation, the right belongs to the ethnic candidates themselves, once their ethnic group is regarded as having protection derived from the Fourteenth Amendment. The law would say, in effect, to minority candidates: "While you are not protected from competition with other candidates of your own color, you are protected from competition with whites. One of you, by virtue of your color, is entitled to win." Such a candidate-related right would seem to entail a genuine quota system, where a necessary condition for running is that the candidates belong to a particular ethnic group. Of course, they must still get the highest number of votes to win a seat. But they must also belong to a specified ethnic group.

We would respond that while the typical outcome of a single-member-district remedy might give the impression that a quota rule is being applied, this is not in fact the case. The right in question is conferred on an identifiable group of voters, not on candidates. This group of voters has been unable to elect its preferred candidates because of white bloc voting. Section 2 gives the group the right to elect candidates of its choice. Those elected candidates, once a single-member-district remedy has been imposed in a highly race-conscious setting (it is race-conscious because whites will not vote for minority candidates) typically are members of the covered group in question, although not always. So the result may be similar to the result of a quota rule, where rights belong to the candidates. But a different principle is at work, and principle, in matters of fairness, is crucial. This principle says to the voters: "You have previously been prevented by white voters from electing candidates of your choice. We will draw districts so that you, like the white majority, will have that opportunity. *But we do not care what the ethnicity of your preferred candidates is.*"

If critics of this arrangement protest that this is just a subterfuge for requiring minority proportional representation or racial quotas, they are caught in a contradiction.[7] For on that logic, the alternative—an at-large

7. For example, Thernstrom 1987, 237–38, argues that, lacking clear guidelines, the

system in which a white majority bloc usually overrides the minority voters' preferences—can also be described as *requiring* the election of a certain percentage of white candidates (in this case, the overwhelming majority of all winners), and thus is also a subterfuge, but for a white rather than minority quota.[8]

The reader might object that our argument about proportionality so far has been entirely theoretical. But the empirical evidence is consistent with our theoretical assertions. The claim that the Voting Rights Act is tantamount to a general requirement of proportional representation for the protected minority groups falls on its face when confronted with the reality of how few minority officials there actually are, even in states where there has been extensive voting rights litigation and repeated denials of preclearance. It may well be true that in particular challenged jurisdictions a single-member-district remedy will provide something very close to proportional representation, but given the nature of minority residential dispersion, such jurisdictions are the exception. To be sure, the number of black and Hispanic officials has increased sharply since passage of the act. Hispanics in 1990, however, still made up less than 1 percent of all elected officials, although they make up more than 7 percent of the voting-age population. Blacks made up only 1.5 percent, while constituting more than 11 percent of the voting-age population.[9]

Thus we believe the answer to the question of whether section 2 of the act mandates "proportional racial representation" is clear, if by that is meant a racial quota among officeholders. And that answer is no. In a limited number of jurisdictions across the nation, it allows minority voters to elect at least some candidates of their choice, even if white voters seek to prevent it. But requiring fairly drawn single-member-district plans is something very different from a quota system for ethnic groups in America.

---

courts' tendency in adjudicating section 2 claims is to drift toward a standard of proportional representation that "can only lead to a covert system of reserved seats [in legislative bodies] such as those India provides for its 'scheduled castes.'"

8. Of course, as courts have recognized in numerous cases, such as *Citizens for a Better Gretna* v. *City of Gretna*, 834 F.2d 496 (1987) and *City of Lockhart* v. *United States*, 103 S.Ct. 998, U.S. (1983), when other fairer districting alternatives are available, there cannot be an equal opportunity to elect candidates of choice if the election system and the voting patterns are such that minorities are given only the opportunity to elect the *white* candidate of their choice.

9. National Association of Latin Elected Officials 1990, vi; Joint Center for Political Studies 1991, 11. Moreover, the growth rate in the number of black elected officials has decreased in recent years—contrary to what critics of the 1982 section 2 language might have led one to expect.

Has the Voting Rights Act Outlived Its Usefulness?

Some authors have claimed that section 5 of the act—the preclearance requirement—is no longer necessary because the racial climate in covered jurisdictions has radically improved in the past quarter century. It is therefore unfair to require these jurisdictions to show that electoral changes do not have the purpose or effect of harming minority voting rights. Some critics of the act believe that in most situations, even in the South, appreciable numbers of whites are willing to join with the black minority to elect qualified black candidates. Timothy O'Rourke in this volume, for example, emphasizes the number of successful black candidacies in majority-white districts in Virginia. Similarly, Carol Swain emphasizes what she regards as a large number of successful black congressional candidacies in districts that are not majority-black.

We agree that progress is evident, but we are far more skeptical that racially polarized voting is as infrequent as these authors believe, or that southern white resistance to black officeholding has largely vanished.[10] We also do not believe, as other critics maintain, that white Anglo bloc voting against Hispanic candidates is so much less severe than that directed against blacks that Hispanics ought not to be covered by the Voting Rights Act. The empirical evidence showing where minority representation has increased and what the causes of this growth are bear directly on these points of dispute.

10. For example, had Congress done no more than outlaw literacy tests in the South for five years, and had it let section 5 expire in 1970, 1975, or even 1982, it would have encouraged renewed white resistance in the 1970s and 1980s against full and effective black and Hispanic political participation. Arguing for the act's 1982 extension in the hearings before the House Judiciary Committee was the southern historian, C. Vann Woodward, who in the 1960s had given currency to the term *second Reconstruction* as it applied to that era. Woodward is himself a southerner and a close student of American race relations. While not expecting anything so drastic as the disfranchisement that followed the first Reconstruction, he averred in his testimony: "I do think it reasonable to warn that a weakening of this act, especially the preclearance clause, will open the door to a rush of measures to abridge, diminish, dilute, if not emasculate the power of black votes in Southern states" (House of Representatives 1981a, 2001). Woodward was joined in his opinion by many scholars, the voting rights bar, and, perhaps most eloquently and insistently, minority activists themselves, including grass-roots leaders from southern and southwestern communities. If not the pessimists in this national debate, they were at least the skeptics, people whose reading of history or whose personal experience had convinced them that the path of progress in American racial and ethnic relations is often tortuous and sometimes retrograde. They considered the renewal of section 5 and the amendment of section 2 essential for maintaining the tenuous but hopeful position minorities had secured in the less than two decades since the act's passage.

Susan Welch's study of minority representation in 1988 examined all U.S. cities of at least 50,000 people with a population of at least 5 percent but less than 50 percent black or Hispanic. She found it is still true that, in cities electing their councils at large, blacks are underrepresented as compared to blacks in cities with single-member-district systems. Indeed, "all cities with district elections and more than a 10% black population have at least some black representation, while a sizable minority of at-large and mixed cities do not yet have this representation."[11] Even so, the gap in black officeholding between these two types of election plans in the nation as a whole has narrowed appreciably since the 1970s.

In southern cities, too, Welch found that the gap has narrowed. But there was still in 1988 a significant contrast between black representation in at-large and district cities. The mean black "equitability score" (the ratio of blacks on council to blacks in city population) in cities that were at least 5 percent black but less than 50 percent black was 0.71 in at-large cities and 0.95 in district cities—the latter figure indicating almost complete proportional representation. And in those twenty-seven southern at-large cities, 22 percent had no blacks on council, while in the fourteen district ones, none was without black representation.[12] Even so, the equity ratio of 0.71 for at-large southern cities represents a significant increase in black representation since the 1970s.

We suspect, however, that one reason equity may have risen in southern at-large cities is that there are now fewer of these cities than previously as a result of voting rights litigation, and some of the remaining ones are likely to be those where the racial climate was more moderate and black electoral success was sufficient to avoid voting rights litigation. The possibility of such a selection effect must be considered before drawing conclusions about white tolerance from Welch's findings.[13] We also have no way of knowing how many of the blacks elected at large in the South owed their seat to a white-dominated slating group whose interests differed

11. Welch 1990b, 1057. There are many thousands of political entities in the United States today, electing about half a million officeholders: 60.4 percent of the almost 4,000 cities of 2,500 residents or more surveyed in 1986 for the International City Management Association employed at-large elections, as compared to 12.8 percent that used the pure district system (Renner 1988, 15).

12. Welch 1990b, 1059. Welch takes eleven states as her definition of the South.

13. We are coordinating a project funded by the National Science Foundation that uses a longitudinal design to study cities that changed election systems and those that did not in each of eight states. The design permits an evaluation of the magnitude of selection and other effects that may contaminate the usual cross-sectional analyses.

significantly from those of the black community, a phenomenon that is relatively common in at-large systems.[14]

There is a further finding in Welch's study that casts serious doubt on the view that minority candidates running for at-large posts are no longer greatly disadvantaged. In addition to examining at-large and single-member-district cities, Welch examined those employing a mixed plan: some council members elected from districts and some at large. She then compared black success in winning district seats and at-large seats, a comparison, she stressed, that is important for two reasons: first, because mixed systems "have become the modal structure" in the type of cities she examines in her study, and second, because the data from these "self-paired" systems allowed a number of relevant variables to be controlled. Her finding was that although blacks were almost as equitably represented in district seats as their numbers in the city's population would predict, in at-large seats they were dramatically underrepresented. In southern mixed cities, the black equity ratio in district seats was 0.95; in at-large seats, it was 0.20.[15] In other words, blacks in the district seats were very nearly equitably represented; in at-large seats they were underrepresented by a factor of five.

Welch's findings on Hispanics, reported in the same study, provide further grounds for concern about the disadvantaging effects of at-large systems. Hispanics in cities of 50,000 or more with a Hispanic population between 5 and 50 percent were sharply underrepresented in at-large cities—their equity ratio was 0.40. There were no Hispanic council members in 71 percent of such cities.[16] Hispanics were, however, underrepresented in all types of systems. Welch speculated that their low equity ratio in district cities was the result of residential dispersion. This seems logical, because compactness is essential for the creation of majority-minority districts (which is the main reason single-member districts could not be a remedy for the underrepresentation of women); it suggests that section 2 remedies of the sort suggested by Lani Guinier, Edward Still, and others might be more appropriate for Hispanics.[17]

Unfortunately, in Texas, where there has been much voting rights litigation by Hispanic plaintiffs and, in many instances, where Hispanic residential compactness is fairly high, Welch found no district cities that met the demographic criteria for her sample. Thus she could not compare

14. Davidson and Fraga 1988.
15. Welch 1990b, 1059.
16. Welch 1990a, 1066.
17. Guinier 1991b; Still 1984; Still 1992.

representation in the two types of systems in a state where court-ordered district remedies would be most likely to demonstrate a difference between at-large systems and those with fairly drawn districts. What Welch did find in Texas, however, was "negligible" Hispanic representation in at-large cities but "quite high" representation in mixed systems, an equity ratio of 0.83.[18] Moreover, when she compared Hispanic representation in the at-large seats of these mixed cities with their representation in the district seats, the results were equitability ratios of 0.67 in district seats but only 0.07 in the at-large ones, a result that strikingly paralleled her finding for blacks when the same comparison was made.[19] Both blacks and Hispanics in mixed cities are severely handicapped when running at large. Of course, why both groups are less handicapped, relatively speaking, when running in at-large cities than when running for at-large seats in mixed cities remains an important puzzle to be solved.

To summarize, we believe that, generally speaking, both blacks and Hispanics not only have traditionally been more disadvantaged in at-large cities than in district ones but that they continue to be disadvantaged by at-large arrangements.[20] This is particularly so in the South. Districts, while often helpful to Hispanics, particularly in mixed cities, generally help them less than they do blacks because Hispanics are more residentially dispersed.[21]

Bernard Grofman and Lisa Handley approached the question of how minorities fare in predominantly white settings from another perspective, looking at the relationship between voting rights litigation and its concomitant creation of black-majority seats and black electoral success. Their results directly bear on the question of whites' willingness to vote for blacks. Examining southern legislatures, they found that in 1989, only 2 percent of the 1,534 state legislators elected from majority-white districts were black. By contrast, 60 percent of the legislators elected from the 233 majority-black districts were black. In another study, these authors found that among southern members of Congress in 1985, no black was elected from a majority-white Anglo district. Indeed, only 2 southern

---

18. Welch 1990a, 14.

19. In California, where relatively little voting rights litigation under either the Constitution or the Voting Rights Act has been carried out, Welch's data set on large cities shows that Hispanics were *better* represented in at-large cities than district ones, but analysis of a larger sample of cities for which data has been gathered by the Bureau of the Census finds Hispanics considerably better represented in district and mixed systems than in at-large cities, even in California. The authors are currently analyzing this data base.

20. Davidson and Korbel 1981; Engstrom and McDonald 1981.

21. Zax 1990, 353.

blacks were in Congress at that time.[22] This number has since increased to 4 out of 116 southern representatives, or 3.4 percent, in a region whose voting age population is about 17 percent black. The authors concluded that "the congressional data fit the racial polarization model almost perfectly."[23]

Despite these findings, however, we agree fully with Carol Swain's reminder in this volume that, at least at the congressional level and in most state legislatures, blacks are not concentrated enough geographically to create a very large number of new majority-black political units.[24] This is so even in jurisdictions where the other two *Gingles* standards can be met.

Does the Voting Rights Act Harm Minorities?

Questions of law aside, scholars such as Abigail Thernstrom, Katherine Butler, and Timothy O'Rourke have argued that, as it is currently being interpreted by courts, the Voting Rights Act now actually harms minority interests rather than aids them because it helps keep race a divisive political force and "segregates" minorities into preponderantly minority districts.[25] These critics assert that creating majority-minority districts weakens the prospects for coalitions between minorities and whites, making it harder for minorities to achieve major policy goals.

The inability of minorities to elect candidates of their choice because of white bloc voting under certain electoral arrangements (which is what the courts have usually construed minority vote dilution to mean) is one measure of the debasement of a group's voting strength.[26] A rather different measure, as suggested by Gregory Caldeira and also Lani Guinier in this volume, is based on inability to bring about preferred governmental policy.[27] Consider a situation in which blacks or Hispanics are a numeri-

22. Grofman and Handley 1991, 114.
23. Grofman and Handley, forthcoming.
24. Because Hispanics are more residentially dispersed than blacks, increases in the number of Hispanic legislators in the 1990s round of redistricting will also be limited, despite recent dramatic Hispanic population gains.
25. Thernstrom 1987; Butler 1982; O'Rourke 1980.
26. More specifically, minority vote dilution, as the courts have generally understood it, is the degrading of voting strength among a cohesively voting arithmetical minority through a combination of bloc voting by the white majority and the use of certain electoral rules, which together prevent blacks from electing candidates of their choice relative to what would be possible under a fairly drawn single-member-district plan.
27. This is not quite the same as the well-known distinction (see, for example, Caldeira

cal minority in a jurisdiction. Even if the minority's candidates of choice
are elected, the majority on the city council may consistently outvote
those candidates on certain issues and refuse to enact policies that benefit
minority interests. Unlike vote dilution, there is no legal remedy for this
situation.[28]

One can imagine situations in which minority voters' desire to elect
their most preferred candidates to office (candidates who we may suppose
will usually themselves be minority members) conflicts with their desire
to see the enactment of policies beneficial to minorities. Suppose, for
example, that black voters make up only one-fourth of the electorate in
a city employing at-large elections, and they are willing to vote as a bloc
for council candidates who seem genuinely willing to address the particular needs of the black population; the great majority of whites, by
contrast, will not vote for a black candidate. The black voters' candidates
cannot win.

Now imagine two options that blacks might choose between if they
had a decisive voice in the matter. In one, option A, they can choose to
have single-member districts in which black voters constitute a majority
in one-fourth of the districts, with full knowledge that the other three-
fourths of the districts will produce white council members opposed to
the policy aims of the minority bloc of blacks on council. Black voters,
in other words, can elect black candidates of choice, but once elected,
the representatives are unable to bring about the policies favored by their
constituents.

In option B, the same city elects its council at large. Most black voters
forego nominating the black candidates they really prefer, and together
with a minority of whites, are able to elect a liberal majority to the city
council that is sympathetic to black needs, although it is a majority from
which black council members are absent. Thus black voters can constitute

---

in this volume) between policy-based representation and descriptive representation because
we emphasize that what is at issue in voting rights lawsuits is not the opportunity of a
group to elect persons of the same race or ethnicity as themselves, but rather the opportunity
to elect candidates of choice. Admittedly, the results may often be the same; but the processes
are not the same in either law or democratic theory.

Lack of policy responsiveness to minority concerns was once regarded as a supple-
mentary factor that might be used to demonstrate vote dilution, but its importance was
downplayed in the report of the Senate Committee on the Judiciary on the 1982 extension
of the act (Senate 1982b) because proof of this factor was difficult.

28. For a discussion of this problem and an interesting and controversial suggestion
for providing a legal remedy, see Guinier (in this volume and 1991a).

a swing vote without which the white liberal majority on council cannot get elected, and by providing the margin of victory for the white council majority, they can prevent an antiblack coalition from dominating the council and enacting measures that are not responsive to black interests. (Using the same logic, we could construct a similar model, option B_1, in which single-member districts replaced the at-large structure. If district lines are drawn so that blacks are distributed fairly evenly over a number of districts, and black voters, while unable to elect black candidates in such districts, have some degree of influence over the legislators elected from those districts, they can, in this option too, join with sympathetic whites in the city's districts, all of which are majority white, and elect a majority to council whom they can influence by virtue of their swing-vote status.)

Both options B and B_1 might seem preferable, from the standpoint of policy effectiveness, to option A, where black voters are concentrated in a handful of majority-black districts, with little or no influence in the remaining districts. In option A they can elect as their first preference up to one-fourth of the council members, but potential white allies, being walled off from black voters in their own predominantly white districts (each such district composed now of conservative white majorities), will no longer be able to join with the black voters and elect a liberal biracial majority that can control the council. In option A, a political ghettoization has occurred. In options B and B_1, a biracial coalition is possible.

This supposed conflicting set of options, then, is what some critics of the act appear to have in mind when they talk about the trade-off between a minority group's ability to elect candidates of its choice to a legislative body and its ability to get favorable policies enacted by that body. We believe this hypothetical conflict is overblown.

In the at-large setting, the probability seems small that white voters, who according to option B are unwilling to vote for black candidates, would nonetheless sanction policy measures enacted by the coalition's winning slate that would significantly benefit blacks per se. Similarly, in the single-member-district context, the conflict between electing black candidates of choice (option A) and supposed enhanced policy influence if black voters are scattered across districts rather than concentrated (option B_1) rests on the notion that the black minority in those districts will be a swing vote *and* that the representatives who are elected with the aid of that swing vote will be highly responsive to black interests. In the South especially, only sometimes will these two conditions be satisfied.[29]

29. Exactly how often these conditions will be satisfied is an empirical problem to

Nonetheless, critics of the Voting Rights Act have claimed that the creation of black or Hispanic districts as a remedy for vote dilution has led to a deterioration of traditional interracial alliances. In two-party politics, they argue, this has led to a decline in Democratic strength and to Republican gains, thus making it harder for minorities to achieve policy goals, particularly at the state or national level. We believe that the Voting Rights Act gave added impetus to the southern partisan realignment, thus contributing to the new shape of the American political universe, in which "considerations of race are now deeply imbedded in ... strategy and tactics ... in competing concepts of the function and responsibility of government, and in each voter's conceptual structure of moral and partisan identity."[30] But it is one thing to recognize that southern white flight from the Democratic party was initially triggered by the Democratic stance on civil rights in the 1960s and quite another to say that creating more majority-black or majority-Hispanic legislative seats will, on balance, diminish the ability of blacks and Hispanics to enact public policy that would benefit them. This is a very complex question.

As minority officeholders grow in numbers, white flight from the Democratic party may continue, the seeming Republican lock on the

---

which we do not have good answers. It is not sufficient to point to numerous instances where, say, blacks and whites vote together in an at-large minority-black jurisdiction to elect a majority to city council or some other governmental body; such coalitions have existed as long as blacks have been able to vote. It must also be shown that the majority slate has enacted policies of measurable benefit to blacks, including policies that address the special needs of blacks, insofar as these are expressed and known. A systematic study of this issue would require an analysis of winning coalitions in a sample of at-large jurisdictions where blacks (or Hispanics) were a minority, in order to determine if, normally, a) the coalitions succeeded in electing a majority to the governing body; b) they were genuinely biracial, in the sense that minorities played an active and important role in the coalition; and c) the victorious slates were willing and able to enact policies that provided measurable benefits to the minority community. Until evidence for a significant proportion of genuine biracial coalitions is presented, those who emphasize the continued reality of racially polarized voting and racist attitudes, especially in the Deep South, will be unlikely to change their minds. To emphasize a point that is often overlooked in discussing best-case scenarios, racial polarization and hostility may be intense even in many at-large cities where a tradition of black officeholding has been established. The evidence is simply not yet in on whether the typical jurisdiction is one in which there are sufficient white voters willing to form a multiracial coalition capable of winning control of a governmental body for purposes of enacting policies that are clearly beneficial to minorities, even when some minority interests differ significantly from those of whites, as they often do.

30. Edsall and Edsall 1991, 53. See also Grofman, Glazer, and Handley 1992.

White House may strengthen further, and there certainly will be some situations in which the creation of concentrated minority districts will lead to the election of a Republican in a neighboring district.[31] But the other side of the argument needs to be weighed against these possibilities. Quite simply, the presence of minority officeholders makes it harder for racism to persist inside a legislature. In addition, the more natural it becomes to see minorities hold office, the less likely their election will trigger white unhappiness with the Democratic party.

Furthermore, and perhaps most important, the hypothetical conflict between ability to elect candidates of choice and ability to influence policy neglects the role of minority officeholders in vigorously championing minority interests. There simply is no evidence that in the typical case, the addition of minority officeholders to a governmental body, even when they are not a majority on it, *decreases* policy benefits to minority voters.[32] Finally, even if there were some conflict between simple representation and policy influence, it is not clear just what the appropriate trade-off should be. Raymond Wolfinger demonstrated the long-term persistence of white ethnic voting in America.[33] This persistence suggests that the desire to be represented by someone of the same heritage is deeply felt by most ethnic minorities, in part because the simple presence of members of one's own group in government is an important symbol of equality and full citizenship.[34]

31. Thanks to the gerrymandering skills of Democratic cartographers, our preliminary analyses of the opening round of 1990s redistricting suggest that such situations are remarkably fewer than Republicans would like. See also Brace and others 1988.

32. Fraga 1991; Grofman, Glazer, and Handley 1992. One implication of the theory proposed by scholars such as Thernstrom 1987 is that biracial coalitions in jurisdictions with at-large elections would provide more policy benefits to minorities than would be provided in otherwise comparable jurisdictions electing by district where minorities had been "isolated" into majority-minority districts. We know of no evidence to support this view.

33. Wolfinger 1965.

34. Hamilton 1981, 191, has written, "For any number of reasons, voters perceive that one of their own will be more responsive to their needs. They feel a closer tie—call it kinship if you will." In like manner, judging by their tendency to vote as a bloc against minority candidates in many elections, whites may use the ballot box to express feelings of solidarity against minority candidates (Glazer, Grofman, and Owen 1989). In contrast, as Caldeira notes in this volume, "organized labor, for example, has never made a particular point of electing unionists, although some have gone to Congress under the banner of labor. Instead it has cultivated the friendship of politicians from diverse backgrounds and both parties." Caldeira suggests that "perhaps by choice but more probably by lack thereof, blacks and other racial minorities traditionally pursued a legislative strategy along the same

Conclusions

Let us now summarize our stand on the several issues we have raised. First, we reject the claim that the Voting Rights Act is a quota system. Its remedies are contingent on proving case by case that voting is racially polarized and that minority candidates regularly lose, as well as that housing patterns are sufficiently segregated and the minority population is sufficiently large to permit a single-member-district remedy.[35] The process by which a remedy based on creating single-member districts is imposed, in other words, is not proportional representation. Moreover, the percentage of minority officeholders as compared with the percentage of the minority population in the United States today is so small—as is the percentage growth rate of minority officeholders—that accusations that the Voting Rights Act has been subverted into a tool of proportional representation are ludicrous. We would emphasize that the Voting Rights Act operates, in the interest of fairness, within the framework of the fundamentally majoritarian electoral rules of our society. It does not, as a remedy for wrongs, provide entitlements that can be justified only as compensatory redress for previous injustice to members of a given group. Rather, it merely seeks to provide an election system that permits all groups to be fairly represented. Thus it is not surprising to us that voting rights are not as controversial as other areas of affirmative action.[36]

Second, we see minority districts as staging grounds for minority entry into politics. From such districts minorities can build up the visibility and credibility to rise to higher office, sometimes in constituencies that are mostly white. Like Luis Fraga in this volume, we consider the presence of minority officeholders at all levels of government as fostering political accommodation between the minority and nonminority communities rather

---

lines as organized labor and other interest groups. Few members of minorities could, until recently, hope to win a seat in Congress or even a state legislature."

35. As Cain (in this volume) reminds us, Latinos regularly move out of inner-city barrios.

36. We use the phrase *affirmative action* in the voting rights context quite guardedly. Unlike many civil rights activists and many critics of the Voting Rights Act, we do not believe that voting rights fits the usual model of affirmative action case law. See Turner in this volume.

than leading to so-called political ghettoization. We also share Fraga's belief that the incorporation of minorities can lead to a more democratic and inclusive concept of the polity and a shared vision of the public interest that is more than just "fair shares."

Similarly, we are skeptical about the claim made by some conservatives and some liberals that creating majority-minority districts is not in the interest of minorities. Conservatives assert that minority districts harm the prospects for interracial coalitions and lessen the likelihood of a color-blind society. But this argument is naive. It fails to take into account the extent to which patterns of polarized voting are the norm and is based on an unduly optimistic notion of what minority influence would be without the Voting Rights Act. On the other side, some liberals are worried that creating minority districts reduces the net number of liberals— black and white—who will be elected. This is a fundamentally paternalistic argument whose greatest appeal is to white liberal incumbents. Moreover, as Bruce Cain puts it in this volume, whatever may be the extent of this particular problem, it must be "weighed against the losses in system legitimacy and stability when minority voices are not well represented in American government."

Finally, we see the implementation of the Voting Rights Act as what Bernard Grofman in this volume has called the "realistic politics of the second best." We believe that the act has been and continues to be a major force in moving us toward that color-blind society envisioned by Martin Luther King and large numbers of blacks and whites who followed him in his quest. As committed integrationists we consider its recipes for color-conscious remedies necessary as long as there are jurisdictions where race is inextricably bound up in voting decisions and strongly linked to housing patterns.

In a world of race-conscious voting, race-conscious remedies are needed. But that does not mean we have to like the world in which such remedies are necessary or fail to appreciate the limitations of such remedies.[37] We wish to steer a course between a premature optimism, on the one hand, that will lead to the elimination of safeguards vital to the continuing integration of minorities into American electoral politics and, on the other hand, an unrealistic pessimism that insists we will never get beyond

37. See, for example, Bruce Cain's enjoinder in this volume that we need to look to tactics other than voting rights litigation—changes in naturalization policy, easing of registration requirements, campaign finance reform that may benefit minorities—to deal with fundamental issues of minority empowerment.

judging people by the color of their skin and so advocates replacing the quest for a common civic vision with a tribalistic notion of immutable group consciousness and concomitant group rights. We believe that the case-specific and fact-contingent approach embodied in voting rights enforcement steers just such a course.

Appendix

VOTING RIGHTS ACT OF 1965
(as amended through 1982 and as effective on and after August 5, 1984)

AN ACT To enforce the fifteenth amendment to the Constitution of the United States, and for other purposes.

Be it enacted by the Senate and House of Representatives of the United States of America in Congress assembled, That this Act shall be known as the "Voting Rights Act of 1965".

TITLE I—VOTING RIGHTS

SEC. 2. (a) No voting qualification or prerequisite to voting or standard, practice, or procedure shall be imposed or applied by any State or political subdivision in a manner which results in a denial or abridgement of the right of any citizen of the United States to vote on account of race or color, or in contravention of the guarantees set forth in section 4(F)(2), as provided in subsection (b).

(b) A violation of subsection (a) is established if, based on the totality of circumstances, it is shown that the political processes leading to nomination or election in the State or political subdivision are not equally open to participation by members of a class of citizens protected by subsection (a) in that its members have less opportunity than other members of the electorate to participate in the political process and to elect representatives of their choice. The extent to which members of a protected class have been elected to office in the State or political subdivision is one circumstance which may be considered: *Provided*, That nothing in this section establishes a right to have members of a protected class elected in numbers equal to their proportion in the population.

SEC. 3. (a) Whenever the Attorney General or an aggrieved person institutes a proceeding under any statute to enforce the voting guarantees of the fourteenth or fifteenth amendment in any State or political subdivision the court shall authorize the appointment of Federal examiners by the Director of the Office of Personnel Management in accordance with section 6 to serve for such period of time for such political subdivisions as the court shall determine is appropriate to enforce the voting guarantees of the fourteenth or fifteenth amendment (1) as part of any interlocutory order if the court determines that the appointment of such examiners is necessary to enforce such voting guarantees or (2) as part of any final judgment if the court finds that violations of the fourteenth or fifteenth amendment justifying equitable relief have occurred in such State or subdivision: *Provided*, That the court need not authorize the appointment of examiners if any incidents of denial or abridgement of the right to vote on account of race or color, or in contravention of the guarantees set forth in section 4(f)(2)(1) have been few in number and have been promptly and effectively corrected by State or local action, (2) the continuing effect of such incidents has been eliminated, and (3) there is no reasonable probability of their recurrence in the future.

(b) If in a proceeding instituted by the Attorney General or an aggrieved person under any statute to enforce the voting guarantees of the fourteenth or fifteenth amendment in any State or political subdivision the court finds that a test or device has been used for the purpose or with the effect of denying or abridging the right of any citizen of the United States to vote on account of race or color, or in contravention of the guarantees set forth in section 4(f)(2), it shall suspend the use of tests and devices in such State or political subdivisions as the court shall determine is appropriate and for such period as it deems necessary.

(c) If in any proceeding instituted by the Attorney General or an aggrieved person under any statute to enforce the voting guarantees of the fourteenth or fifteenth amendment in any State or political subdivision the court finds that violations of the fourteenth or fifteenth amendment justifying equitable relief have occurred within the territory of such State or political subdivision, the court, in addition to such relief as it may grant, shall retain jurisdiction for such period as it may deem appropriate and during such period no voting qualification or prerequisite to voting, or standard, practice, or procedure with respect to voting different from that in force or effect at the time the proceeding was commenced shall be enforced unless and until the court finds that such qualification, prerequisite, standard, practice, or procedure does not have the purpose and will not have the effect of denying or abridging the right to vote on account of race or color, or in contravention of the guarantees set forth in section 4(f)(2): *Provided*, That such qualification, prerequisite, standard, practice, or procedure may be enforced if the qualification, prerequisite, standard, practice, or procedure has been submitted by the chief legal officer or other appropriate official of such State or subdivision to the Attorney General and the Attorney General has not interposed an objection within sixty days after such submission, except that neither the court's finding nor the Attorney General's failure to object shall bar a subsequent action to enjoin enforcement of such qualification, prerequisite, standard, practice, or procedure.

SEC. 4. (a)(1) To assure that the right of citizens of the United States to vote is not denied or abridged on account of race or color, no citizen shall be denied the right to vote in any Federal, State, or local election because of his failure to comply with any test or device in any State with respect to which the determinations have been made under the first two sentences of subsection (b) or in any political subdivision of such State (as such subdivision existed on the date such determinations were made with respect to such State), though such determinations were not made with respect to such subdivision as a separate unit, or in any political subdivision with respect to which such determinations have been made as a separate unit, unless the United States District Court for the District of Columbia issues a declaratory judgment under this section. No citizen shall be denied the right to vote in any Federal, State, or local election because of his failure to comply with any test or device in any State with respect to which the determinations have been made under the third sentence of subsection (b) of this section or in any political subdivision of such State (as such subdivision existed on the date such determinations were made with respect to such State), though such determinations were not made with respect to such subdivision as a separate unit, or in any political subdivision with respect to which such determinations have been made as a separate unit, unless the United States District Court for the District of Columbia issues a declaratory judgment under this section. A declaratory judgment under this section shall issue only if such court determines that during the ten years preceding the filing of the action, and during the pendency of such action—

(A) no such test or device has been used within such State or political subdivision for the purpose or with the effect of denying or abridging the right to vote on account of race or color or (in the case of a State or subdivision seeking a declaratory judgment under the second sentence of this subsection) in contravention of the guarantees of subsection (f)(2);

(B) no final judgment of any court of the United States, other than the denial of declaratory judgment under this section, has determined that denials or abridgements of the right to vote on account of race or color have occurred anywhere in the territory of such State or political subdivision or (in the case of a State or subdivision seeking a declaratory judgment under the second sentence of this subsection) that denials or abridgements of the right to vote in contravention of the guarantees of subsection (f)(2) have occurred anywhere in the territory of such State or subdivision and no consent decree, settlement, or agreement has been entered into resulting in any abandonment of a voting practice challenged on such grounds; and no declaratory judgment under this section shall be entered during the pendency of an action commenced before the filing of an action under this section and alleging such denials or abridgements of the right to vote;

(C) no Federal examiners under this Act have been assigned to such State or political subdivision;

(D) such State or political subdivision and all governmental units within its territory have complied with section 5 of this Act, including compliance with the requirement that no change covered by section 5 has been enforced without preclearance under section 5, and have repealed all changes covered by section 5 to which the Attorney General has successfully objected or as to which the United States District Court for the District of Columbia has denied a declaratory judgment;

(E) the Attorney General has not interposed any objection (that has not been overturned by a final judgment of a court) and no declaratory judgment has been denied under section 5, with respect to any submission by or on behalf of the plaintiff or any governmental unit within its territory under section 5, and no such submissions or declaratory judgment actions are pending; and

(F) such State or political subdivision and all governmental units within its territory—

(i) have eliminated voting procedures and methods of election which inhibit or dilute equal access to the electoral process;

(ii) have engaged in other constructive efforts to eliminate intimidation and harassment of persons exercising rights protected under this Act; and

(iii) have engaged in other constructive efforts, such as expanded opportunity for convenient registration and voting for every person of voting age and the appointment of minority persons as election officials throughout the jurisdiction and at all stages of the election and registration process.

(2) To assist the court in determining whether to issue a declaratory judgment under this subsection, the plaintiff shall present evidence of minority participation, including evidence of the levels of minority group registration and voting, changes in such levels over time, and disparities between minority-group and non-minority-group participation.

(3) No declaratory judgment shall issue under this subsection with respect to such State or political subdivision if such plaintiff and governmental units within its territory have, during the period beginning ten years before the date the judgment is issued, engaged in violations of any provision of the Constitution or laws of the United States or any State or political subdivision with respect to discrimination in voting on account of race or color or (in the case of a State or subdivision seeking a declaratory judgment under the second sentence of this subsection) in contravention of the guarantees of subsection (f)(2) unless the plaintiff establishes that any such violations were trivial, were promptly corrected, and were not repeated.

(4) The State or political subdivision bringing such action shall publicize the intended commencement and any proposed settlement of such action in the media serving such State or political subdivision and in appropriate United States post offices. Any aggrieved party may as of right intervene at any stage in such action.

(5) An action pursuant to this subsection shall be heard and determined by a court of three judges in accordance with the provisions of section 2284 of title 28 of the United States Code and any appeal shall lie to the Supreme Court. The court shall retain jurisdiction of any action pursuant to this subsection for ten years after judgment and shall reopen the action upon motion of the Attorney General or any aggrieved person alleging that conduct has occurred which, had that conduct occurred during the ten-year periods referred to in this subsection, would have precluded the issuance of a declaratory judgment under this subsection. The court, upon such reopening, shall vacate the declaratory judgment issued under this section if, after the issuance of such declaratory judgment, a final judgment against the State or subdivision with respect to which such declaratory

judgment was issued, or against any governmental unit within that State or subdivision, determines that denials or abridgements of the right to vote on account of race or color have occurred anywhere in the territory of such State or political subdivision or (in the case of a State or subdivision which sought a declaratory judgment under the second sentence of this subsection) that denials or abridgements of the right to vote in contravention of the guarantees of subsection (f)(2) have occurred anywhere in the territory of such State or subdivision, or if, after the issuance of such declaratory judgment, a consent decree, settlement, or agreement has been entered into resulting in any abandonment of a voting practice challenged on such grounds.

(6) If, after two years from the date of the filing of a declaratory judgment under this subsection, no date has been set for a hearing in such action, and that delay has not been the result of an avoidable delay on the part of counsel for any party, the chief judge of the United States District Court for the District of Columbia may request the Judicial Council for the Circuit of the District of Columbia to provide the necessary judicial resources to expedite any action filed under this section. If such resources are unavailable within the circuit, the chief judge shall file a certificate of necessity in accordance with section 292(d) of title 28 of the United States Code.

(7) The Congress shall reconsider the provisions of this section at the end of the fifteen-year period following the effective date of the amendments made by the Voting Rights Act Amendments of 1982.

(8) The provisions of this section shall expire at the end of the twenty-five year period following the effective date of the amendments made by the Voting Rights Act Amendments of 1982.

(9) Nothing in this section shall prohibit the Attorney General from consenting to an entry of judgment if based upon a showing of objective and compelling evidence by the plaintiff, and upon investigation, he is satisfied that the State or political subdivision has complied with the requirements of section 4(a)(1). Any aggrieved party may as of right intervene at any stage in such action.

(b) The provisions of subsection (a) shall apply in any State or in any political subdivision of a State which (1) the Attorney General determines maintained on November 1, 1964, any test or device, and with respect to which (2) the Director of the Census determines that less than 50 per centum of the persons of voting age residing therein were registered on November 1, 1964, or that less than 50 per centum of such persons voted in the presidential election of November 1964. On and after August 6, 1970, in addition to any State or political subdivision of a State determined to be subject to subsection (a) pursuant to the previous sentence, the provisions of subsection (a) shall apply in any State or any political subdivision of a State which (i) the Attorney General determines maintained on November 1, 1968, any test or device, and with respect to which (ii) the Director of the Census determines that less than 50 per centum of the persons of voting age residing therein were registered on November 1, 1968, or that less than 50 per centum of such persons voted in the presidential election of November 1968. On and after August 6, 1975, in addition to any State or political subdivision of a State determined to be subject to subsection (a) pursuant to the previous two sentences, the provisions of subsection (a) shall apply in any State or any political subdivision of a State which (i) the Attorney General determines maintained on November 1, 1972, any test or device, and with respect to which (ii) the Director of the Census determines that less than 50 per centum of the citizens of voting age were registered on November 1, 1972, or that less than 50 per centum of such persons voted in the presidential election of November 1972.

A determination or certification of the Attorney General or of the Director of the Census under this section or under section 6 or section 13 shall not be reviewable in any court and shall be effective upon publication in the Federal Register.

(c) The phrase "test or device" shall mean any requirement that a person as a prerequisite for voting or registration for voting (1) demonstrate the ability to read, write, understand, or interpret any matter, (2) demonstrate any educational achievement or his knowledge of any particular subject, (3) possess good moral character, or (4) prove his qualifications by the voucher of registered voters or members of any other class.

(d) For purposes of this section no State or political subdivision shall be determined to have engaged in the use of tests or devices for the purpose or with the effect of denying or abridging the right to vote on account of race or color, or in contravention of the guarantees set forth in section 4(f)(2) if (1) incidents of such use have been few in number and have been promptly and effectively corrected by State or local action, (2) the continuing effect of such incidents has been eliminated, and (3) there is no reasonable probability of their recurrence in the future.

(e)(1) Congress hereby declares that to secure the rights under the fourteenth amendment of persons educated in American-flag schools in which the predominant classroom language was other than English, it is necessary to prohibit the States from conditioning the right to vote of such persons on ability to read, write, understand, or interpret any matter in the English language.

(2) No person who demonstrates that he has successfully completed the sixth primary grade in a public school in, or a private school accredited by, any State or territory, the District of Columbia, or the Commonwealth of Puerto Rico in which the predominant classroom language was other than English, shall be denied the right to vote in any Federal, State, or local election because of his inability to read, write, understand, or interpret any matter in the English language, except that in States in which State law provides that a different level of education is presumptive of literacy, he shall demonstrate that he has successfully completed an equivalent level of education in a public school in, or a private school accredited by, any State or territory, the District of Columbia, or the Commonwealth of Puerto Rico in which the predominant classroom language was other than English.

(f)(1) The Congress finds that voting discrimination against citizens of language minorities is pervasive and national in scope. Such minority citizens are from environments in which the dominant language is other than English. In addition they have been denied equal educational opportunities by State and local governments, resulting in severe disabilities and continuing illiteracy in the English language. The Congress further finds that, where State and local officials conduct elections only in English, language minority citizens are excluded from participating in the electoral process. In many areas of the country, this exclusion is aggravated by acts of physical, economic, and political intimidation. The Congress declares that, in order to enforce the guarantees of the fourteenth and fifteenth amendments to the United States Constitution, it is necessary to eliminate such discrimination by prohibiting English-only elections, and by prescribing other remedial devices.

(2) No voting qualification or prerequisite to voting, or standard, practice, or procedure shall be imposed or applied by any State or political subdivision to deny or abridge the right of any citizen of the United States to vote because he is a member of a language minority group.

(3) In addition to the meaning given the term under section 4(c), the term "test or device" shall also mean any practice or requirement by which any State or political subdivision provided any registration or voting notices, forms, instructions, assistance, or other materials or information relating to the electoral process, including ballots, only in the English language, where the Director of the Census determines that more than five per centum of the citizens of voting age residing in such State or political subdivision are members of a single language minority. With respect to section 4(b), the term "test or device," as defined in this subsection, shall be employed only in making the determinations under the third sentence of that subsection.

(4) Whenever any State or political subdivision subject to the prohibitions of the second sentence of section 4(a) provides any registration or voting notices, forms, instructions, assistance, or other materials or information relating to the electoral process, including ballots, it shall provide them in the language of the applicable language minority group as well as in the English language: *Provided*, That where the language of the applicable minority group is oral or unwritten or in the case of Alaskan Natives and American Indians, if the predominant language is historically unwritten, the State or political subdivision is only required to furnish oral instructions, assistance, or other information relating to registration and voting.

SEC. 5. Whenever a State or political subdivision with respect to which the prohibitions set forth in section 4(a) based upon determinations made under the first sentence of section 4(b) are in effect shall enact or seek to administer any voting qualification or prerequisite to voting, or standard, practice, or procedure with respect to voting different from that in force or effect on November 1, 1964, or whenever a State or political subdivision with respect to which the prohibitions set forth in section 4(a) based upon determinations made under the second sentence of section 4(b) are in effect shall enact or seek to administer any voting qualification or prerequisite to voting, or standard, practice, or procedure with respect to voting different from that in force or effect on November 1, 1968, or whenever a State or political subdivision with respect to which the prohibitions set forth in section 4(a) based upon determinations made under the third sentence of section

4(b) are in effect shall enact or seek to administer any voting qualification or prerequisite to voting, or standard, practice, or procedure with respect to voting different from that in force or effect on November 1, 1972, such State or subdivision may institute an action in the United States District Court for the District of Columbia for a declaratory judgment that such qualification, prerequisite, standard, practice, or procedure does not have the purpose and will not have the effect of denying or abridging the right to vote on account of race or color, or in contravention of the guarantees set forth in section 4(f)(2), and unless and until the court enters such judgment no person shall be denied the right to vote for failure to comply with such qualification, prerequisite, standard, practice, or procedure: *Provided*, That such qualification, prerequisite, standard, practice, or procedure may be enforced without such proceeding if the qualification, prerequisite, standard, practice, or procedure has been submitted by the chief legal officer or other appropriate official to such State or subdivision to the Attorney General and the Attorney General has not interposed an objection within sixty days after such submission, or upon good cause shown, to facilitate an expedited approval within sixty days after such submission, the Attorney General has affirmatively indicated that such objection will not be made. Neither an affirmative indication by the Attorney General that no objection will be made, nor the Attorney General's failure to object, nor a declaratory judgment entered under this section shall bar a subsequent action to enjoin enforcement of such qualification, prerequisite, standard, or procedure. In the event the Attorney General affirmatively indicates that no objection will be made within the sixty-day period following receipt of a submission, the Attorney General may reserve the right to reexamine the submission if addition information comes to his attention during the remainder of the sixty-day period which would otherwise require objection in accordance with this section. Any action under this section shall be heard and determined by a court of three judges in accordance with the provisions of section 2284 of title 28 of the United States Code and any appeal shall lie to the Supreme Court.

SEC. 6. Whenever (a) a court has authorized the appointment of examiners pursuant to the provisions of section 3(a), or (b) unless a declaratory judgment has been rendered under section 4(a), the Attorney General certifies with respect to any political subdivision named in, or included within the scope of, determinations made under section 4(b) that (1) he has received complaints in writing from twenty or more residents of such political subdivision alleging that they have been denied the right to vote under color of law on account of race or color, or in contravention of the guarantees set forth in section 4(f)(2), and that he believes such complaints to be meritorious, or (2) that in his judgment (considering, among other factors, whether the ratio of nonwhite persons to white persons registered to vote within such subdivision appears to him to be reasonably attributable to violations of the fourteenth or fifteenth amendment or whether substantial evidence exists that bona fide efforts are being made within such subdivision to comply with the fourteenth or fifteenth amendment), the appointment of examiners is otherwise necessary to enforce the guarantees of the fourteenth or fifteenth amendment, the Director of the Office of Personnel Management shall appoint as many examiners for such subdivision as the Director may deem appropriate to prepare and maintain lists of persons eligible to vote in Federal, State, and local elections. Such examiners, hearing officers provided for in section 9(a), and other persons deemed necessary by the Director of the Office of Personnel Management to carry out the provisions and purposes of this Act shall be appointed, compensated, and separated without regard to the provisions of any statute administered by the Director of the Office of Personnel Management, and service under this Act shall not be considered employment for the purposes of any statute administered by the Director of the Office of Personnel Management, except the provisions of section 9 of the Act of August 2, 1939, as amended (5 U.S.C. 7324), prohibiting partisan political activity: *Provided*, That the Director of the Office of Personnel Management is authorized, after consulting the head of the appropriate department or agency, to designate suitable persons in the official service of the United States, with their consent, to serve in these positions. Examiners and hearing officers shall have the power to administer oaths.

SEC. 7. (a) The examiners for each political subdivision shall, at such places as the Director of the Office of Personnel Management shall by regulation designate, examine applicants concerning their qualifications for voting. An application to an examiner shall be in such form as the Director of the Office of Personnel Management may require and shall contain allegations that the applicant is not otherwise registered to vote.

(b) Any person whom the examiner finds, in accordance with instructions received under section 9(b), to have the qualifications prescribed by State law not inconsistent with the Constitution and laws of the United States shall promptly be placed on a list of eligible voters. A challenge to such listing may be made in accordance with section 9(a) and shall not be the basis for a prosecution under section 12 of this Act. The examiner shall certify and transmit such list, and any supplements as appropriate, at least once a month, to the office of the appropriate election officials, with copies to the Attorney General and the attorney general of the State, and any such lists and supplements thereto transmitted during the month shall be available for public inspection on the last business day of the month and in any event not later than the forty-fifth day prior to any election. The appropriate State or local election official shall place such names on the official voting list. Any person whose name appears on the examiner's list shall be entitled and allowed to vote in the election district of his residence unless and until the appropriate election officials shall have been notified that such person has been removed from such list in accordance with subsection (d): *Provided*, That no person shall be entitled to vote in any election by virtue of this Act unless his name shall have been certified and transmitted on such a list to the offices of the appropriate election officials at least forty-five days prior to such election.

(c) The examiner shall issue to each person whose name appears on such a list a certificate evidencing his eligibility to vote.

(d) A person whose name appears on such a list shall be removed therefrom by an examiner if (1) such person has been successfully challenged in accordance with the procedure prescribed in section 9, or (2) he has been determined by an examiner to have lost his eligibility to vote under State law not inconsistent with the Constitution and the laws of the United States.

SEC. 8. Whenever an examiner is serving under this Act in any political subdivision, the Director of the Office of Personnel Management may assign, at the request of the Attorney General, one or more persons, who may be officers of the United States, (1) to enter and attend at any place for holding an election in such subdivision for the purpose of observing whether persons who are entitled to vote are being permitted to vote, and (2) to enter and attend at any place for tabulating the votes cast at any election held in such subdivision for the purpose of observing whether votes cast by persons entitled to vote are being properly tabulated. Such persons so assigned shall report to an examiner appointed for such political subdivision, to the Attorney General, and if the appointment of examiners has been authorized pursuant to section 3(a), to the court.

SEC. 9. (a) Any challenge to a listing on an eligibility list prepared by an examiner shall be heard and determined by a hearing officer appointed by and responsible to the Director of the Office of Personnel Management and under such rules as the Director of the Office of Personnel Management shall by regulation prescribe. Such challenge shall be entertained only if filed at such office within the State as the Director of the Office of Personnel Management shall by regulation designate, and within ten days after the listing of the challenged person is made available for public inspection, and if supported by (1) the affidavits of at least two persons having personal knowledge of the facts constituting grounds for the challenge, and (2) a certification that a copy of the challenge and affidavits have been served by mail or in person upon the person challenged at his place of residence set out in the application. Such challenge shall be determined within fifteen days after it has been filed. A petition for review of the decision of the hearing office may be filed in the United States court of appeals for the circuit in which the person challenged resides within fifteen days after service of such decision by mail on the person petitioning for review but no decision of a hearing officer shall be reversed unless clearly erroneous. Any person listed shall be entitled and allowed to vote pending final determination by the hearing officer and by the court.

(b) The times, places, procedures, and form for application and listing pursuant to this Act and removals from the eligibility lists shall be prescribed by regulations promulgated by the Director of the Office of Personnel Management and the Director of the Office of Personnel Management shall, after consultation with the Attorney General, instruct examiners concerning applicable State law not inconsistent with the Constitution and laws of the United States with respect to (1) the qualifications required for listing, and (2) loss of eligibility to vote.

(c) Upon the request of the applicant or the challenger or on the Director's own motion the Director of the Officer of Personnel Management shall have the power to require by subpoena the attendance and testimony of witnesses and the production of documentary evidence relating to any matter pending before it under the authority of this section. In case of contumacy or refusal to obey a subpoena, any district court of the United States or the United States court of any territory or possession, or the District Court of the United States for the District of Columbia, within the jurisdiction of which said person guilty of contumacy or refusal to obey is found or resides or is domiciled or transacts business, or has appointed an agent for receipt of service or process, upon application by the Attorney General of the United States shall have jurisdiction to issue to such person an order requiring such person to appear before the Director of the Office of Personnel Management or a hearing officer, there to produce pertinent, relevant, and nonpriviledged documentary evidence if so ordered, or there to give testimony touching the matter under investigation; and any failure to obey such order of the court may be punished by said court as a contempt thereof.

SEC. 10. (a) The Congress finds that the requirement of the payment of a poll tax as a precondition to voting (i) precludes persons of limited means from voting or imposes unreasonable financial hardship upon such persons as a precondition to their exercise of the franchise, (ii) does not bear a reasonable relationship to any legitimate State interest in the conduct of elections, and (iii) in some areas has the purpose or effect of denying persons the right to vote because of race or color. Upon the basis of these findings, Congress declares that the constitutional right of citizens to vote is denied or abridged in some areas by the requirement of the payment of a poll tax as a precondition to voting.

(b) In the exercise of the powers of Congress under section 5 of the fourteenth amendment, section 2 of the fifteenth amendment and section 2 of the twenty-fourth amendment, the Attorney General is authorized and directed to institute forthwith in the name of the United States such actions, including actions against States or political subdivisions, for declaratory judgment or injunctive relief against the enforcement of any requirement of the payment of a poll tax as a precondition to voting, or substitute therefor enacted after November 1, 1964, as will be necessary to implement the declaration of subsection (a) and the purpose of this section.

(c) The district courts of the United States shall have jurisdiction of such actions which shall be heard and determined by a court of three judges in accordance with the provisions of section 2284 of title 28 of the United States Code and any appeal shall lie to the Supreme Court. It shall be the duty of the judges designated to hear the case to assign the case for hearing at the earliest practicable date, to participate in the hearing and determination thereof, and to cause the case to be in every way expedited.

SEC. 11. (a) No person acting under color of law shall fail or refuse to permit any person to vote who is entitled to vote under any provision of this Act or is otherwise qualifed to vote, or willfully fail or refuse to tabulate, count, and report such person's vote.

(b) No person, whether acting under color law or otherwise, shall intimidate, threaten, or coerce, or attempt to intimidate, threaten, or coerce any person for voting or attempting to vote, or intimidate, threaten, or coerce, or attempt to intimidate, threaten, or coerce, any person for urging or aiding any person to vote or attempt to vote, or intimidate, threaten, or coerce any person for exercising any powers or duties under section 3(a), 6, 8, 9, 10, or 12(e).

(c) Whoever knowingly or willfully gives false information as to his name, address, or period of residence in the voting district for the purpose of establishing his eligibility to register or vote, or conspires with another individual for the purpose of encouraging his false registration to vote or illegal voting, or pays or offers to pay or accepts payment either for registration to vote or for voting shall be fined not more than $10,000 or imprisoned not more than five years, or both: *Provided, however,* That this provision shall be applicable only to general, special, or primary elections held solely or in part for the purpose of selecting or electing any candidate for the office of President, Vice President, presidental elector, Member of the United States Senate, Member of the United States House of Representatives, Delegate from the District of Columbia, Guam, or the Virgin Islands, or Resident Commissioner of the Commonwealth of Puerto Rico.

(d) Whoever, in any matter within the jurisdiction of an examiner or hearing officer knowingly and willfully falsifies or conceals a material fact, or makes any false, fictitious, or fraudulent statements or representations, or makes or uses any false writing or document knowing the same to contain any false, fictitious, or fraudulent statement or entry, shall be fined not more than $10,000 or imprisoned not more than five years, or both.

(e)(1) Whoever votes more than once in an election referred to in paragraph (2) shall be fined not more than $10,000 or imprisoned not more than five years, or both.

(2) The prohibition of this subsection applies with respect to any general, special, or primary election held solely or in part for the purpose of selecting or electing any candidate for the office of President, Vice President, presidential elector, Member of the United States Senate, Member of the United States House of Representatives, Delegate from the District of Columbia, Guam, or the Virgin Islands, or Resident Commissioner of the Commonwealth of Puerto Rico.

(3) As used in this subsection, the term "votes more than once" does not include the casting of an additional ballot if all prior ballots of that voter were invalidated, nor does it include the voting in two jurisdictions under section 202 of this Act, to the extent two ballots are not cast for an election to the same candidacy or office.

SEC. 12. (a) Whoever shall deprive or attempt to deprive any person of any right secured by section 2, 3, 4, 5, 7, or 10 or shall violate section 11(a), shall be fined not more than $5,000 or imprisoned not more than five years, or both.

(b) Whoever, within a year following an election in a political subdivision in which an examiner has been appointed (1) destroys, defaces, mutilates, or otherwise alters the marking of a paper ballot which has been cast in such election, or (2) alters any official record of voting in such election tabulated from a voting machine or otherwise, shall be fined not more than $5,000, or imprisoned not more than five years, or both.

(c) Whoever conspires to violate the provisions of subsection (a) or (b) of this section, or interferes with any right secured by section 2, 3, 4, 5, 7, 10, or 11(a) shall be fined not more than $5,000, or imprisoned not more than five years, or both.

(d) Whenever any person has engaged or there are reasonable grounds to believe that any person is about to engage in any act or practice prohibited by section 2, 3, 4, 5, 7, 10, 11, or subsection (b) of this section, the Attorney General may institute for the United States, or in the name of the United States, an action for preventive relief, including an application for a temporary or permanent injunction, restraining order, or other order, and including an order directed to the State and State or local election officials to require them (1) to permit persons listed under this Act to vote and (2) to count such votes.

(e) Whenever in any political subdivision in which there are examiners appointed pursuant to this Act any persons allege to such an examiner within forty-eight hours after the closing of the polls and notwithstanding (1) their listing under this Act or registration by an appropriate election official and (2) their eligibility to vote, they have not been permitted to vote in such election, the examiner shall forthwith notify the Attorney General if such allegations in his opinion appear to be well founded. Upon receipt of such notification the Attorney General may forthwith file with the district court an application for an order providing for the marking, casting, and counting of the ballots of such persons and requiring the inclusion of their votes in the total vote before the results of such election shall be deemed final and any force or effect given thereto. The district court shall hear and determine such matters immediately after the filing of such application. The remedy provided in this subsection shall not preclude any remedy available under State or Federal law.

(f) The district courts of the United States shall have jurisdiction of proceedings instituted pursuant to this section and shall exercise the same without regard to whether a person asserting rights under the provisions of this Act shall have exhausted any administrative or other remedies that may be provided by law.

SEC. 13. Listing procedures shall be terminated in any political subdivision of any State (a) with respect to examiners appointed pursuant to clause (b) of section 6 whenever the Attorney General notifies the Director of the Office of Personnel Management, or whenever the District Court for the District of Columbia determines in an action for declaratory judgment brought by any political subdivision with respect to which the Director of the Census has determined that more than 50 per centum of the nonwhite persons of voting age residing therein are registered to vote, (1) that all persons listed by an examiner for such subdivision have been placed on the appropriate voting registration roll, and (2) that there is no longer reasonable cause to believe that persons will be deprived of or denied the right to vote on account of race or color, or in contravention of the guarantees set forth in section 4(f)(2) in such subdivision, and (b), with respect to examiners appointed pursuant to section 3(a), upon order of the authorizing court. A political subdivision may petition the Attorney General for the termination of listing procedures under clause (a) of this section, and may petition for Attorney General to request the Director of the Census to take such survey or census as may be appropriate for the making of the determination provided for in this section. The District Court for the District of Columbia shall have jurisdiction to require such survey or census to be made by the Director of the Census and it shall require him to do so if it deems the Attorney General's refusal to request such survey or census to be arbitrary or unreasonable.

SEC. 14. (a) All cases of criminal contempt arising under the provisions of this Act shall be governed by section 151 of the Civil Rights Act of 1957 (42 U.S.C. 1995).

(b) No court other than the District Court for the District of Columbia or a court of appeals in any proceeding under section 9 shall have jurisdiction to issue any declaratory judgment pursuant to section 4 or section 5 of any restraining order or temporary or permanent injunction against the execution or enforcement of any provision of this Act or any action of any Federal officer or employee pursuant hereto.

(c)(1) The terms "vote" or "voting" shall include all action necessary to make a vote effective in any primary, special, or general election, including, but not limited to, registration, listing pursuant to this Act, or other action required by law prerequisite to voting, casting a ballot, and having such ballot counted properly and included in the appropriate totals of votes cast with respect to candidates for public or party office and propositions for which votes are received in an election.

(2) The term "political subdivision" shall mean any county or parish, except that where registration for voting is not conducted under the supervision of a county or parish, the term shall include any other subdivision of a State which conducts registration for voting.

(3) The term "language minorities" or "language minority group" means persons who are American Indian, Asian American, Alaskan Natives or of Spanish heritage.

(d) In any action for a declaratory judgment brought pursuant to section 4 or section 5 of this Act, subpoenas for witnesses who are required to attend the District Court for the District of Columbia may be served in any judicial district of the United States: *Provided,* That no writ of subpoena shall issue for witnesses without the District of Columbia at a greater distance than one hundred miles from the place of holding court without the permission of the District Court for the District of Columbia being first had upon proper application and cause shown.

(e) In any action or proceeding to enforce the voting guarantees of the fourteenth or fifteenth amendment, the court, in its discretion, may allow the prevailing party, other than the United States, a reasonable attorney's fee a part of the costs.

SEC. 15. Section 2004 of the Revised Status (42 U.S.C. 1971), as amended by section 131 of the Civil Rights Act of 1957 (71 Stat. 637), and amended by section 601 of the Civil Rights Act of 1960 (74 Stat. 90), and as further amended by section 101 of the Civil Rights Act of 1964 (78 Stat. 241), is further amended as follows:

(a) Delete the word "Federal" wherever it appears in subsections (a) and (c);

(b) Repeal subsection (f) and designate the present subsections (g) and (h) as (f) and (g), respectively.

SEC. 16. The Attorney General and the Secretary of Defense, jointly, shall make a full and complete study to determine whether, under the laws or practices of any State or States, there are preconditions to voting, which might tend to result in discrimination against citizens serving in the Armed Forces of the United States seeking to vote. Such officials shall, jointly, make a report to the Congress not later than June 30, 1966, containing the results of such study, together with a list of any States in which such preconditions exist, and shall include in such report such recommendations for legislation as they deem advisable to prevent discrimination in voting against citizens serving in the Armed Forces of the United States.

SEC. 17. Nothing in this Act shall be construed to deny, impair, or otherwise adversely affect the right to vote of any person registered to vote under the law of any State or political subdivision.

SEC. 18. There are hereby authorized to be appropriated such sums as are necessary to carry out the provisions of this Act.

SEC. 19. If any provision of this Act or the application thereof to any person or circumstances is held invalid, the remainder of the Act and the application of the provision to other persons not similarly situated or to other circumstances shall not be affected thereby.

TITLE II—SUPPLEMENTAL PROVISIONS

APPLICATION OF PROHIBITION TO OTHER STATES

SEC. 201. (a) No citizen shall be denied, because of his failure to comply with any test or device, the right to vote in any Federal, State, or local election conducted in any State or political subdivision of a State.

(b) As used in this section, the term "test or device" means any requirement that a person as a prerequisite for voting or registration for voting (1) demonstrate the ability to read, write, understand, or interpret any matter, (2) demonstrate any educational achievement or his knowledge of any particular subject, (3) possess good moral character, or (4) prove his qualifications by the voucher of registered voters or members of any other class.

RESIDENCE REQUIREMENTS FOR VOTING

SEC. 202. (a) The Congress hereby finds that the imposition and application of the durational residency requirement as a precondition to voting for the offices of President and Vice President, and the lack of sufficient opportunities for absentee registration and absentee balloting in presidential elections—

(1) denies or abridges the inherent constitutional right of citizens to vote for their President and Vice President;

(2) denies or abridges the inherent constitutional right of citizens to enjoy their free movement across State lines;

(3) denies or abridges the privileges and immunities guaranteed to the citizens of each State under article IV, section 2, clause 1, of the Constitution;

(4) in some instances has the impermissible purpose or effect of denying citizens the right to vote for such officers because of the way they may vote;

(5) has the effect of denying to citizens the equality of civil rights, and due process and equal protection of the laws that are guaranteed to them under the fourteenth amendment; and

(6) does not bear a reasonable relationship to any compelling State interest in the conduct of presidential elections.

(b) Upon the basis of these findings, Congress declares that in order to secure and protect the above-stated rights of citizens under the Constitution, to enable citizens to better obtain the enjoyment of such rights, and to enforce the guarantees of the fourteenth amendment, it is necessary (1) to completely abolish the durational residency requirement as a precondition to voting for President and Vice President, and (2) to establish nationwide, uniform standards relative to absentee registration and absentee balloting in presidential elections.

(c) No citizens of the United States who is otherwise qualified to vote in any election for President and Vice President shall be denied the right to vote for electors for President and Vice President, or for President and Vice President, in such election because of the failure of such citizen to comply with any durational residency requirement of such State or political subdivision; nor shall any citizen of the United States be denied the right to vote for electors for President and Vice President, or for President and Vice President, in such election because of the failure of such citizen to be physically present in such State or political subdivision at the time of such election, if such citizen shall have complied with the requirements prescribed by the law of such State or political subdivision providing for the casting of absentee ballots in such election.

(d) For the purposes of this section, each State shall provide by law for the registration or other means of qualification of all duly qualified residents of such State who apply, not later than thirty days immediately prior to any presidential election, for registration or qualification to vote for the choice of electors for President and Vice President or for President and Vice President in such election; and each State shall provide by law for the casting of absentee ballots for the choice of electors for President and Vice President, or for President and Vice President, by all duly qualified residents of such State who may be absent from their election district or unit in such State on the day such election is held and who have applied therefor not later than seven days immediately prior to such election and have returned such ballots to the appropriate election official of such State not later than the time of closing of the polls in such State on the day of such election.

(e) If any citizen of the United States who is otherwise qualified to vote in any State or political subdivision in any election for President and Vice President has begun residence in such State or political subdivision after the thirtieth day next preceding such election and, for that reason, does not satisfy the registration requirements of such State or political subdivision he shall be allowed to vote for the choice of electors for President and Vice President, or for President and Vice President, in such election, (1) in person in the State or political subdivision in which he resided immediately prior to his removal if he has satisfied, as of the date of his change of residence, the requirements to vote in that State or political subdivision, or (2) by absentee ballot in the State or political subdivision in which he resided immediately prior to his removal if he satisfies, but for his nonresident status and the reason for his absence, the requirements for absentee voting in that State or political subdivision.

(f) No citizen of the United States who is otherwise qualified to vote by absentee ballot in any State or political subdivision in any election for President and Vice President shall be denied the right to vote for the choice of electors for President and Vice President, or for President and Vice President, in such election because of any requirement of registration that does not include a provision for absentee registration.

(g) Nothing in this section shall prevent any State or political subdivision from adopting less restrictive voting practices than those that are prescribed herein.

(h) The term "State" as used in this section includes each of the several States and the District of Columbia.

(i) The provisions of section 11(c) shall apply to false registration, and other fraudulent acts and conspiracies, committed under this section.

BILINGUAL ELECTION REQUIREMENTS

SEC. 203. (a) The Congress finds that, through the use of various practices and procedures, citizens of language minorities have been effectively excluded from participation in the electoral process. Among other factors, the denial of the right to vote of such minority group citizens is ordinarily directly related to the unequal educational opportunities afforded them, resulting in high illiteracy and low voting participation. The Congress declares that, in order to enforce the guarantees of the fourteenth and fifteenth amendments to the United States Constitution, it is necessary to eliminate such discrimination by prohibiting these practices, and by prescribing other remedial devices.

(b) Prior to August 6, 1992, no State or political subdivision shall provide registration or voting notices, forms, instructions, assistance, or other materials or information relating to the electoral process, including ballots, only in the English language if the Director of the Census determines (i) that more than 5 percent of the citizens of voting age of such State or political subdivision are members of a single language minority and (ii) that the illiteracy rate of such persons as a group is higher than the national illiteracy rate: *Provided,* That the prohibitions of this subsection shall not apply in any political subdivision which has less than five percent voting age citizens of each language minority which comprises over five percent of the statewide population of voting age citizens. For purposes of this subsection, illiteracy means the failure to complete the fifth primary grade. The determinations of the Director of the Census under this subsection shall be effective upon publication in the Federal Register and shall not be subject to review in any court.

[*Note: Section 4 of the Voting Rights Act Amendments of 1982 states: "Section 203(b) of the Voting Rights Act of 1965 is amended by striking out 'August 6, 1985' and inserting in lieu thereof 'August 6, 1992', and the extension made by this section shall apply only to determinations made by the Director of the Census under clause (i) of section 203(b) for members of a single language minority who do not speak or understand English adequately enough to participate in the electoral process when such a determination can be made by the Director of the Census based on the 1980 and subsequent census data."*]

(c) Whenever any State or political subdivision subject to the prohibition of subsection (b) of this section provides any registration or voting notices, forms, instructions, assistance, or other materials or information relating to the electoral process, including ballots, it shall provide them in the language of the applicable minority group as well as in the English language: *Provided,* That where the language of the applicable minority group is oral or unwritten or in the case of Alaskan Natives and American Indians, if the predominant language is historically unwritten, the State or political subdivision is only required to furnish oral instructions, assistance, or other information relating to registration and voting.

(d) Any State or political subdivision subject to the prohibition of subsection (b) of this section, which seeks to provide English-only registration or voting materials or information, including ballots, may file an action against the United States in the United States District Court for a declaratory judgment permitting such provision. The court shall grant the requested relief if it determines that the illiteracy rate of the applicable language minority group within the State or political subdivision is equal to or less than the national illiteracy rate.

(e) For purposes of this section, the term "language minorities" or "language minority group" means persons who are American Indian, Asian American, Alaskan Natives, or of Spanish heritage.

JUDICIAL RELIEF

SEC. 204. Whenever the Attorney General has reason to believe that a State or political subdivision (a) has enacted or is seeking to administer any test or device as a prerequisite to voting in violation of the prohibition contained in section 201, or (b) undertakes to deny the right to vote in any election in violation of section 202, or 203, he may institute for the United States, or in the name of the United States, an action in a district court of the United States, in accordance with sections 1391 through 1393 of title 28, United States Code, for a restraining order, a preliminary or permanent injunction, or such other order as he deems appropriate. An action under this subsection shall be heard and determined by a court of three judges in accordance with the provisions of section 2284 of title 28 of the United States Code and any appeal shall be to the Supreme Court.

PENALTY

Sec. 205. Whoever shall deprive or attempt to deprive any person of any right secured by section 201, 202, or 203 of this title shall be fined not more than $5,000, or imprisoned not more than five years, or both.

SEPARABILITY

Sec. 206. If any provision of this Act or the application of any provision thereof to any person or circumstance is judicially determined to be invalid, the remainder of this Act or the application of such provision to other persons or circumstances shall not be affected by such determination.

Sec. 207. (a) Congress hereby directs the Director of the Census forthwith to conduct a survey to compile registration and voting statistics: (i) in every State or political subdivision with respect to which the prohibitions of section 4(a) of the Voting Rights Act of 1965 are in effect, for every statewide general election for Members of the United States House of Representatives after January 1, 1974; and (ii) in every State or political subdivision for any election designated by the United States Commission on Civil Rights. Such surveys shall only include a count of citizens of voting age, race or color, and national origin, and a determination of the extent to which such persons are registered to vote and have voted in the elections surveyed.

(b) In any survey under subsection (a) of this section no person shall be compelled to disclose his race, color, national origin, political party affiliation, or how he voted (or the reasons therefor), nor shall any penalty be imposed for his failure or refusal to make such disclosures. Every person interrogated orally, by written survey or questionnaire, or by any other means with respect to such information shall be fully advised of his right to fail or refuse to furnish such information.

(c) The Director of the Census shall, at the earliest practicable time, report to the Congress the results of every survey conducted pursuant to the provisions of subsection (a) of this section.

(d) The provisions of section 9 and chapter 7 of title 13 of the United States Code shall apply to any survey, collection, or compilation of registration and voting statistics carried out under subsection (a) of this section.

VOTING ASSISTANCE

Sec. 208. Any voter who requires assistance to vote by reason of blindness, disability, or inability to read or write may be given assistance by a person of the voter's choice, other than the voter's employer or agent of that employer or officer or agent of the voter's union.

TITLE III—EIGHTEEN-YEAR-OLD VOTING AGE

ENFORCEMENT OF TWENTY-SIXTH AMENDMENT

SEC. 301. (a)(1) The Attorney General is directed to institute, in the name of the United States, such actions against States or political subdivisions, including actions for injunctive relief, as he may determine to be necessary to implement the twenty-sixth article of amendment to the Constitution of the United States.

(2) The district courts of the United States shall have jurisdiction of proceedings instituted under this title, which shall be heard and determined by a court of three judges in accordance with section 2284 of title 28 of the United States Code, and any appeal shall lie to the Supreme Court. It shall be the duty of the judges designated to hear the case to assign the case for hearing and determination thereof, and to cause the case to be in every way expedited.

(b) Whoever shall deny or attempt to deny any person of any right secured by the twenty-sixth article of amendment to the Constitution of the United States shall be fined not more than $5,000 or imprisoned not more than five years, or both.

DEFINITION

SEC. 302. As used in this title, the term "State" includes the District of Columbia.

[Note: As enacted, the Voting Rights Act, in Sections 3, 6, 7, 8, 9, and 13, contains references to the United States Civil Service Commission. Because the functions of the Civil Service Commission have been transferred to the Director of the Office of Personnel Management, references in the Act to the Commission have been changed to references to the Director.]

Contributors

Bruce E. Cain
University of California, Berkeley

Gregory A. Caldeira
Ohio State University

Edward G. Carmines
Indiana University

Chandler Davidson
Rice University

Drew S. Days III
Yale Law School

Luis R. Fraga
Stanford University

Hugh Davis Graham
Vanderbilt University

Bernard Grofman
University of California, Irvine

Lani Guinier
University of Pennsylvania Law School

Robert Huckfeldt
Indiana University

J. Morgan Kousser
California Institute of Technology

Thomas E. Mann
Brookings Institution

Laughlin McDonald
American Civil Liberties Union Foundation

Timothy G. O'Rourke
University of Virigina

Carol M. Swain
Princeton University

James P. Turner
U.S. Department of Justice

References

Abraham, Henry J. 1974. *Justices and Presidents: A Political History of Appointments to the Supreme Court.* Oxford University Press.

Abrams, Kathryn. 1988. "'Raising Politics Up': Minority Political Participation and Section 2 of the Voting Rights Act." *New York University Law Review* 63 (June): 449–531.

Abramson, Paul R., John H. Aldrich, and David W. Rohde. 1986. *Change and Continuity in the 1984 Elections.* Washington: Congressional Quarterly.

Acuna, Rodolfo. 1981. *Occupied America: A History of Chicanos,* 2d ed. Harper and Row.

Adler, Selig. 1934. "The Senatorial Career of George Franklin Edmunds, 1866–1891." Ph.D. dissertation, University of Illinois.

Administrative Office of the U. S. Courts. 1979–80. *Annual Report of the Director.* Washington.

Akin, Edward N. 1974. "When a Minority Becomes the Majority: Blacks in Jacksonville Politics, 1887–1907." *Florida Historical Quarterly* 53: 123–45.

Alford, John R., and David W. Brady. 1989. "Personal and Partisan Advantage in U.S. Congressional Elections, 1846–1986." In Lawrence C. Dodd and Bruce I Oppenheimer, eds., *Congress Reconsidered,* 4th ed. Washington: Congressional Quarterly Press.

Alt, James E. Forthcoming. "Race and Voter Registration in the South before and after the Voting Rights Act." In Chandler Davidson and Bernard Grofman, eds., *The Impact of the Voting Rights Act of 1965.*

American Civil Liberties Union. 1988. "Special Report: Congressional Voting Records." *Civil Liberties Alert* (November): 4–17.

Amy, Douglas J. 1991. "Improving Representation for Women and Minorities: Is Proportional Representation the Key?" Paper presented at the annual meeting of the American Political Science Association.

Anders, Evan. 1982. *Boss Rule in South Texas: The Progressive Era.* University of Texas Press.

Andersen, Kristi. 1979. *The Creation of a Democratic Majority, 1928–1936.* University of Chicago Press.

Anderson, Eric. 1981. *Race and Politics in North Carolina, 1872–1901: The Black Second.* Louisiana State University Press.

Applebome, Peter. 1991. "Rights Movement in Struggle for an Image as Well as a Bill." *New York Times* (April 3): A1, A18.

Aptheker, Herbert. 1976 [1935]. "Introduction." In W. E. B. Dubois, *Black Reconstruction*, 2d ed. Millwood, N.Y.: Kraus-Thomson Organization.

Argersinger, Peter H. 1989. "The Value of the Vote: Political Representation in the Gilded Age." *Journal of American History* 76 (June): 59–90.

Asher, Herbert. 1984. *Presidential Elections and American Politics: Voters, Candidates, and Campaigns since 1952*, 3d ed. Homewood, Ill.: Dorsey Press.

Axelrod, Robert. 1984. *The Evolution of Cooperation*. Basic Books.

Bacote, Clarence A. 1955. "The Negro in Georgia, 1880–1908." Ph.D. dissertation, University of Chicago.

Ball, Howard. 1986. "Racial Vote Dilution: Impact of the Reagan DOJ and the Burger Court on the Voting Rights Act." *Publius* 16 (Fall): 29–48.

Ball, Howard, Dale Krane, and Thomas P. Lauth. 1982. *Compromised Compliance: Implementation of the 1965 Voting Rights Act*. Westport, Conn.: Greenwood Press.

Barnes, James A. 1990. "Minority Mapmaking." *National Journal* 22 (April 7): 837–39.

Barr, Alwyn W. 1971. *Reconstruction to Reform: Texas Politics, 1876–1906*. University of Texas Press.

———. 1982. *Black Texans: A History of Negroes in Texas, 1528–1971*. Austin, Texas: Jenkins.

———. 1986. "Black Legislators of Reconstruction Texas." *Civil War History* 32: 340–52.

Bartley, Numan V., and Hugh D. Graham. 1978. *Southern Politics and the Second Reconstruction*. Johns Hopkins University Press.

Bass, Jack. 1981. *Unlikely Heroes: The Dramatic Story of the Southern Judges of the Fifth Circuit Who Translated the Supreme Court's Brown Decision into a Revolution for Equality*. Simon and Schuster.

Bass, Jack, and Walter DeVries. 1976. *The Transformation of Southern Politics: Social Change and Political Consequence since 1945*. Meridian.

Bauer, Raymond A., Ithiel de Sola Pool, and Lewis Anthony Dexter. 1963. *American Business and Public Policy: The Politics of Foreign Trade*. Atherton Press.

Baxter, Tom. 1990. "Primary Wins by Blacks, Liberals May Signal White Flight to GOP." *Atlanta Constitution* (June 7): A1.

Bean, Frank D., and Marta Tienda. 1987. *The Hispanic Population of the United States*. Russell Sage Foundation.

Beitz, Charles R. 1988. "Equal Opportunity in Political Representation." In Norman E. Bowie, ed., *Equal Opportunity*, 155–74. Boulder, Colo.: Westview Press.

Belfrage, Sally. 1965. *Freedom Summer*. Viking Press.

Belknap, Michal R. 1987. *Federal Law and Southern Order: Racial Violence and Constitutional Conflict in the Post-Brown South*. University of Georgia Press.

Bell, Derrick. 1987. *And We Are Not Saved: The Elusive Quest for Racial Justice*. Basic Books.

Belton, Robert. 1990. "Causation and Burden-Shifting Doctrines in Employment Discrimination Law Revisited: Some Thoughts on *Hopkins* and *Wards Cove*." *Tulane Law Review* 54 (June): 1359–1405.

Benedict, Michael Les. 1974. "Preserving the Constitution: The Conservative Basis of Radical Reconstruction." *Journal of American History* 61 (June): 65–90.

———. 1978. "Preserving Federalism: Reconstruction and the Waite Court." In Philip B. Kurland and Gerhard Kaspar, eds., *Supreme Court Review*, 39–79. University of Chicago Press.

Berelson, Bernard R., Paul F. Lazarsfeld, and William N. McPhee. 1954. *Voting: A Study of Opinion Formation in a Presidential Election*. University of Chicago Press.

Berke, Richard L. 1991. "Redistricting Brings about Odd Alliance." *New York Times* (April 8): A1, A11.

———. 1991. "G.O.P. Tries a Gambit with Voting Rights." *New York Times* (April 14): E5.

Berry, Jeffrey M. 1989. *The Interest Group Society*, 2d ed. Glenview, Illinois: Scott, Foresman.

Bickel, Alexander M., and Benno C. Schmidt, Jr. 1984 *History of the Supreme Court of the United States*, vol. 9: *The Judiciary and Responsible Government, 1910–21*. Macmillan.

Binion, Gayle. 1979. "The Implementation of Section 5 of the 1965 Voting Rights Act: A Retrospective on the Role of the Courts." *Western Political Quarterly* 32 (June): 154–73.

Black, Earl, and Merle Black. 1987. *Politics and Society in the South*. Harvard University Press.

Black, Merle. 1978. "Racial Composition of Congressional Districts and Support for Federal Voting Rights in the American South." *Social Science Quarterly* 59 (December): 435–50.

———. 1979. "Regional and Partisan Bases of Congressional Support for the Changing Agenda of Civil Rights Legislation." *Journal of Politics* 41 (May): 665–79.

Blacksher, James, and Lawrence Menefee. 1982. "From *Reynolds* v. *Sims* to *City of Mobile* v. *Bolden*." *Hastings Law Journal* 34.

———. 1984. "At-Large Elections and One Person, One Vote: The Search for the Meaning of Racial Vote Dilution." In Chandler Davidson, ed., *Minority Vote Dilution*, 203–48. Howard University Press.

Blaine, James G. 1886. *Twenty Years of Congress: From Lincoln to Garfield*. Norwich, Conn.: Henry Bill.

Blue, Frederick J. 1987. *Salmon P. Chase: A Life in Politics*. Kent State University Press.

Bobo, Lawrence, and Franklin D. Gilliam, Jr. 1990. "Race, Sociopolitical Participation, and Black Empowerment." *American Political Science Review* 84 (June): 377–93.

Boyd, Thomas M., and Stephen J. Markman. 1983. "The 1982 Amendments to the Voting Rights Act: A Legislative History." *Washington and Lee Law Review* 40 (Fall): 1347–1428.

Brace, Kimball, Bernard Grofman, and Lisa Handley. 1987. "Does Redistricting Aimed to Help Blacks Necessarily Help Republicans?" *Journal of Politics* 49 (February): 169–85.

Brace, Kimball, and others. 1988. "Minority Voting Equality: The 65 Percent Rule in Theory and Practice." *Law and Policy* 10 (January): 43–62.

Braeman, John. 1988. *Before the Civil Rights Revolution: The Old Court and Individual Rights*. Greenwood Press.

Breyer, Stephen. 1982. *Regulation and Its Reform*. Harvard University Press.

Brischetto, Robert, and others. Forthcoming. "Minority Voting Rights in Texas." In Chandler Davidson and Bernard Grofman, eds., *The Impact of the Voting Rights Act of 1965*.

Brown, Peter A. 1991. "Ms. Quota." *New Republic* (April 15): 18–19.

Browning, Rufus P., Dale Rogers Marshall, and David H. Tabb. 1984. *Protest Is Not Enough: The Struggle of Blacks and Hispanics for Equality in Urban Politics*. University of California Press.

———. 1990. "Has Political Incorporation Been Achieved? Is It Enough?" In Rufus P. Browning, Dale Rogers Marshall, and David H. Tabb, eds., *Racial Politics in American Cities*, 212–30. Longman.

Browning, Rufus P., and Dale Rogers Marshall, eds. 1986. "Black and Hispanic Power in City Politics: A Forum." *PS* 19 (Summer): 573–640.

Bullock, Charles S. III. 1981. "Congressional Voting and the Mobilization of the Black Electorate in the South." *Journal of Politics* 43: 662–82.

———. 1982. "The Inexact Science of Congressional Redistricting." *PS* 15 (Summer): 431–38.

———. 1989. "Symbolics or Substance: A Critique of the At-Large Election Controversy." *State and Local Government Review* 21 (Fall): 91–99.

Bunche, Ralph J. 1973 [1940]. *The Political Status of the Negro in the Age of FDR*, ed. Dewey W. Grantham. University of Chicago Press.

Bureau of the Census. 1989a. *Statistical Abstract of the United States 1989*. 109th ed. Department of Commerce.

———. 1989b. "Voting and Registration in the Election of November 1988." *Current Population Reports*, Series P-20, no. 440. Department of Commerce.

Butler, Katharine Inglis. 1984. "Reapportionment, the Courts, and the Voting Rights Act: A Resegregation of the Political Process?" *University of Colorado Law Review* 56: 1–97.

———. 1982. "Challenges to Election Structures: Dilution and the Value of the Right to Vote." *Louisiana Law Review* 42 (January): 851–950.

———. 1985. "Denial or Abridgment of the Right to Vote: What Does It Mean?" In Lorn S. Foster, ed., *The Voting Rights Act: Consequences and Implications*, 44–59. Praeger.

Button, James W. 1989. *Blacks and Social Change: Impact of the Civil Rights Movement in Southern Communities*. Princeton University Press.

Carmichael, Stokely, and Charles V. Hamilton. 1967. *Black Power: The Politics of Liberation in America*. Random House.

Carmines, Edward G., and James A. Stimson. 1989. *Issue Evolution: Race and the Transformation of American Politics*. Princeton University Press.

Carr, Robert K. 1947. *Federal Protection of Civil Rights: Quest for a Sword*. Cornell University Press.

Census Office. 1883. *Compendium of the Tenth Census (June 1, 1880)*, vol. 1: *Characteristics of the Population*. GPO.

Chayes, Abram. 1976. "The Role of the Judge in Public Law Litigation." *Harvard Law Review* 89: 1281–1316.

Chesler, Mark, Joseph Sanders, and Debra Kalmuss. 1988. *Social Science in Court: Mobilizing Experts in the School Desegregation Cases*. University of Wisconsin Press.

Cohen, Richard E., and Carol Matlack. 1989. "All-Purpose Loophole." *National Journal* 49 (December 9): 2980–87.

Cohodas, Nadine. "Strom Thurmond: New Votes, Old Views." 1984. *Congressional Quarterly Weekly Report* 42 (January 14): 70.

Commission on Civil Rights. 1961. *Commission on Civil Rights Report*, Book 1: *Voting*. Washington.

———. 1968. *Political Participation: A study of Participation by Negroes in the Electoral and Political Processes in 10 Southern States since the Passage of the Voting Rights Act of 1965*. Washington.

———. 1975. *The Voting Rights Act: Ten Years After*. Washington.

———. 1976. *Using the Voting Rights Act*. Washington.

———. 1981. *The Voting Rights Act: Unfulfilled Goals*. Washington.

Congressional Quarterly. 1957–88. *Congressional Quarterly Almanac*. Washington.

———. 1975, 1985. *Congressional Quarterly's Guide to U.S. Elections*. Washington.

———. 1981. *Congress and the Nation: A Review of Government and Politics*, vol. 5: *1977–1980*. Washington.

Congressional Quarterly Service. 1968. *Revolution in Civil Rights*, 4th ed. Washington.

———. 1970. *Civil Rights: Progress Report*. Washington.

Congressional Record. 1975. 94 Cong. 1 sess., vol. 121, pt. 13 (June 2), 16284–87; (June 4), 16880–84, 16917.

Conway, Alan. 1966. *The Reconstruction of Georgia*. University of Minnesota Press.

Cotrell, Charles. 1981. "Reflections of a Political Scientist as Expert Witness." Paper prepared for the Conference for Federal Studies, Denver, Colo., September.

Cotrell, Charles L., and Jerry Polinard. 1986. "Effects of the Voting Rights Act in Texas: Perceptions of County Election Administrators." In Charles L. Cotrell, ed., *Assessing the Effects of the U. S. Voting Rights Act. Publius* 16 (Fall, special symposium): 67–80.

Cox, Jane Reed, and Abigail Turner. 1981. *The Voting Rights Act in Alabama: A Current Legal Assessment*. Mobile: Legal Services Corporation of Alabama.

Crofts, Daniel W. 1968. "The Blair Bill and the Elections Bill: The Congressional Aftermath to Reconstruction." Ph.D. dissertation, Yale University.

Curtis, Michael Kent. 1986. *No State Shall Abridge: The Fourteenth Amendment and the Bill of Rights*. Duke University Press.

Dahl, Robert. 1956. *A Preface to Democratic Theory*. University of Chicago Press.

———. 1961. *Who Governs? Democracy and Power in an American City*. Yale University Press.

———. 1971. *Polyarchy: Participation and Opposition*. Yale University Press.

Davidson, Chandler. 1972. *Biracial Politics: Conflict and Coalition in the Metropolitan South*. Louisiana State University Press.

———. 1984. "Minority Vote Dilution: An Overview." In Chandler Davidson, ed., *Minority Vote Dilution*. Howard University Press.

———. 1990. *Race and Class in Texas Politics*. Princeton University Press.

Davidson, Chandler, and Luis R. Fraga. 1988. "Slating Groups as Parties in a 'Non-Partisan' Setting." *Western Political Quarterly*, 41 (June): 373–90.

Davidson, Chandler, and Bernard Grofman, eds. Forthcoming. *The Impact of the Voting Rights Act of 1965*.

Davidson, Chandler, and George Korbel. 1981. "At-large Elections and Minority-Group Representation: A Re-Examination of Historical and Contemporary Evidence." *Journal of Politics* 43 (November): 982–1005.

Days, Drew S. III, and Lani Guinier. 1984. "Enforcement of Section 5 of the Voting Rights Act." In Chandler Davidson, ed., *Minority Vote Dilution*, 167–80. Howard University Press.

Department of Commerce. 1990. *Statistical Abstract of the United States*. Washington.

Department of Justice. 1979. *The Annual Report of the Attorney General of the United States, 1979*. Washington.

———. 1989. *Code of Federal Regulations*, vol. 28: *Judicial Administration*, ch. 1, part 51, "Procedures for the Administration of Section 5 of the Voting Rights Act of 1965, as Amended." Washington: Office of Federal Register, General Services Administration.

———. 1990. *Number of Changes Submitted under Section 5 and Reviewed by the Department of Justice, by State and Year, 1965, April 1, 1991*. Washington.

Department of Justice, Civil Rights Division. 1987. "Voting Rights." In *Enforcing the Law*. Washington.

———. 1990. *Complete Listing of Objections Pursuant to Section 5 of the Voting Rights Act of 1965*. Washington.

Derfner, Armand. 1973. "Racial Discrimination and the Right to Vote." *Vanderbilt Law Review* 26: 523–84.

———. 1984. "Vote Dilution and the Voting Rights Act Amendments of 1982." In Chandler Davidson, ed., *Minority Vote Dilution*, 145–63. Howard University Press.

DeSantis, Vincent P. 1959. *Republicans Face the Southern Question: The New Departure Years, 1877–1897.* Johns Hopkins University Press.

Dinkin, Robert J. 1982. *Voting in Revolutionary America: A Study of Elections in the Original Thirteen States, 1776–1789.* Westport, Conn.: Greenwood Press.

Drago, Edmund L. 1982. *Black Politicians and Reconstruction in Georgia: A Splendid Failure.* Louisiana University Press.

Duverger, Maurice. 1964. *Political Parties: Their Organization and Activity in the Modern State,* trans. Barbara North and Robert North, 3d ed. London: Methuen.

Dworkin, Ronald. 1977. *Taking Rights Seriously.* Harvard University Press.

Edds, Margaret. 1987. *Free At Last: What Really Happened When Civil Rights Came to Southern Politics.* Bethesda, Md.: Adler and Adler.

Edmonds, Helen G. *The Negro and Fusion Politics in North Carolina, 1894–1901.* University of North Carolina Press.

Edsall, Thomas B. 1991. "Rights Drive Said to Lose Underpinnings." *Washington Post* (March 9): A6.

Edsall, Thomas Byrne, and Mary D. Edsall. 1991. *Chain Reaction: The Impact of Race, Rights and Taxes on American Politics.* Norton.

Eisinger, Peter K. 1982. "Black Employment in Municipal Jobs: The Impact of Black Political Power." *American Political Science Review* 76 (June): 380–92.

Elazar, Daniel J., and John Kinkaid. 1986. "From the Editors," preface to Charles L. Cotrell, ed. "Assessing the Effects of the U.S. Voting Rights Act." *Publius* 16 (Fall): 1–4.

Elliott, Ward E. Y. 1974. *The Rise of Guardian Democracy: The Supreme Court's Role in Voting Rights Disputes, 1845–1969.* Harvard University Press.

Engstrom, Richard L., and Charles J. Barrilleaux. 1991. "Native Americans and Cumulative Voting: The Sisseton-Wahpeton Sioux." *Social Science Quarterly* 72 (June): 388–93.

Engstrom, Richard L., and Michael D. McDonald. 1981. "The Election of Blacks to City Councils: Clarifying the Impact of Electoral Arrangements on the Seats/Population Relationship." *American Political Science Review* 75 (June): 344–54.

———. 1985. "Quantitative Evidence in Vote Dilution Litigation: Political Participation and Polarized Voting." *Urban Lawyer* 17 (Summer): 369–77.

———. 1987. "The Election of Blacks to Southern City Councils: The Dominant Impact of Electoral Arrangements." In Laurence W. Moreland, Robert P. Steed, and Tod A. Baker, eds., *Blacks in Southern Politics,* 245–58. Praeger.

Engstrom, Richard, and John K. Wildgen. 1977. "Pruning Thorns from the Thicket: An Empirical Test of the Existence of Racial Gerrymandering." *Legislative Studies Quarterly* 2 (November): 465–79.

Epstein, Lee. 1991. "Courts and Interest Groups." In John B. Gates and Charles A. Johnson, eds., *The American Courts: A Critical Assessment,* 335–71. Washington: Congressional Quarterly Press.

Erie, Steven P. 1988. *Rainbow's End: Irish-Americans and the Dilemma of Urban Machine Politics, 1840–1985.* University of California Press.

Field, Phyllis F. 1982. *The Politics of Race in New York: The Struggle for Black Suffrage in the Civil War Era.* Cornell University Press.

"Flaws in the Solid South." 1882. *New York Times* (July 13): 5.

Foner, Eric. 1988. *Reconstruction: America's Unfinished Revolution, 1863–1877.* Harper and Row.

Foster, Lorn S. 1986. "Section 5 of the Voting Rights Act: Implementation of an Administrative Remedy." In Charles L. Cottrell, *Assessing the Effects of the U.S. Voting Rights Act. Publius* 16 (Fall, special symposium): 17–28.

Foundation for Public Affairs. 1988. *Public Interest Profiles, 1988–1989.* Washington: Congressional Quarterly.

Fraga, Luis Ricardo. 1991. "Policy Consequences and the Change from At-large Elections to Single-Member Districts." Paper presented at the annual meeting of the Western Political Science Association.

Franklin, John Hope. 1961. *Reconstruction: After the Civil War.* University of Chicago Press.

Franklin, John Hope, and Alfred A. Moss, Jr. 1988. *From Slavery to Freedom: A History of Negro Americans,* 6th ed. Knopf.

Freedman, D. A., and others. 1991. "Ecological Regression and Voting Rights." *Evaluation Review.*

Frickey, Philip P. 1988. "Book Review." *Constitutional Commentary* 5 (Summer): 451–56.

Friedman, Leon. 1969. "Salmon P. Chase." In Leon Friedman and Fred I. Israel, eds., *The Justices of the United States Supreme Court, 1789–1969,* vol. 2, 1113–28. Chelsea House.

Fund, John H. 1987. "Voting Law Hurts Blacks, Helps GOP." *Wall Street Journal* (December 21): 18.

Galanter, Marc. 1974. "Why the 'Haves' Come Out Ahead: Speculations on the Limits of Legal Change." *Law & Society Review* 9: 95–160.

———. 1975. "Afterword: Explaining Litigation." *Law & Society Review* 9: 347–68.

Garand, James C., and Donald A. Gross. 1984. "Changes in the Vote Margins for Congressional Candidates: A Specification of Historical Trends." *American Political Science Review* 78: 17–30.

Garcia, F. Christopher, and P. L. Hain, eds. 1981. *New Mexico Government,* rev. ed. University of New Mexico Press.

Garcia, John A. 1986. "The Voting Rights Act and Hispanic Political Representation in the Southwest." In Charles L. Cotrell, ed., *Assessing the Effects of the U. S. Voting Rights Act. Publius* 16 (Fall, special symposium): 49–66.

Garcia, Mario T. 1989. *Mexican Americans: Leadership, Ideology and Identity, 1930–1960.* Yale University Press.

Garrow, David J. 1978. *Protest at Selma: Martin Luther King, Jr., and the Voting Rights Act of 1965.* Yale University Press.

————. 1988. *Bearing the Cross: Martin Luther King, Jr., and the Southern Christian Leadership Conference*, 2d ed. Vintage Books.

Gatewood, Willard B, Jr. 1972. "Negro Legislators in Arkansas, 1891: A Document." *AR Historical Quarterly* 31: 220–23.

General Accounting Office. 1978. *Voting Rights Act: Enforcement Needs Strengthening: Report of the Comptroller General of the United States.* Washington.

————. 1983. *Justice Can Further Improve Its Monitoring of Changes in State/ Local Voting Laws: Report to the Chairman, Subcommittee on Civil and Constitutional Rights, Committee on the Judiciary, House of Representatives.* Washington.

Gillette, William. 1965. *The Right to Vote: Politics and the Passage of the Fifteenth Amendment.* Johns Hopkins University Press.

————. 1979. *Retreat from Reconstruction, 1869–1879.* Louisiana State University Press.

Ginsberg, Benjamin, and Martin Shefter. 1990. *Politics by Other Means: The Declining Importance of Elections in America.* Basic Books.

Glazer, Amihai, Bernard Grofman, and Guillermo Owen. 1989. "A Model of Candidate Convergence under Uncertainty about Voter Preferences." *Mathematical and Computer Modelling* 12: 437–50.

Goldfarb, Joel. 1969. "Henry Billings Brown." In Leon Friedman and Fred I Israel, eds., *The Justices of the United States Supreme Court, 1789–1969*, vol. 2, 1553–63. Chelsea House.

Goldfield, David R. 1990. *Black, White, and Southern: Race Relations and Southern Culture, 1940 to the Present.* Louisiana State University Press.

Graham, Hugh Davis. 1990a. *The Civil Rights Era: Origins and Development of National Policy, 1960–1972.* Oxford University Press.

————. 1990b. "Race, Language, and Social Policy: Comparing the Black and Hispanic Experience in the U.S." *Population and Environment* 12 (Fall): 43–58.

Graves, John W. 1967. "Negro Disfranchisement in Arkansas." *AR Historical Quarterly* 36: 199–225.

Greenhouse, Linda. 1991. "Court, 6–3, Applies Voting Rights Act to Judicial Races." *New York Times* (June 21): A1.

Grofman, Bernard. 1985. "Criteria for Districting: A Social Science Perspective." *UCLA Law Review* 33 (October): 77–184.

————. 1990. "Toward a Coherent Theory of Gerrymandering: *Thornburg* and *Bandemer*." In Bernard Grofman, ed., *Political Gerrymandering and the Courts*, 29–63. Agathon Press.

————. 1991. "Statistics without Substance: A Critique of Freedman et al. and Clark and Morrison." *Evaluation Review*.

Grofman, Bernard, and Lisa Handley. 1989. "Black Representation: Making Sense of Electoral Geography at Different Levels of Government." *Legislative Studies Quarterly* 14 (May): 265–79.

———. 1991. "The Impact of the Voting Rights Act on Black Representation in Southern State Legislatures." *Legislative Studies Quarterly* 16 (February): 111–28.

———. Forthcoming. "Identifying and Remedying Racial Gerrymandering." *Journal of Law and Politics.*

Grofman, Bernard, and Michael Migalski. 1988. "Estimating the Extent of Racially Polarized Voting in Multicandidate Elections." *Sociological Methods and Research* 16: 43–62.

Grofman, Bernard, Amihai Glazer, and Lisa Handley. 1992. "Race and the Defection of Southern Whites from the Democratic National Ticket." Unpublished ms., University of California, Irvine.

Grofman, Bernard, Robert Griffin, and Amihai Glazer. 1991. "The Effect of Black Population on Electing Democrats and Liberals to the House of Representatives." Unpublished paper, University of California, Irvine.

Grofman, Bernard, Michael Migalski, and Nicholas Noviello. 1985. "The 'Totality of Circumstances Test' in Section 2 of the 1982 Extension of the Voting Rights Act: A Social Science Perspective." *Law and Policy* 7 (April): 209–23.

Grossman, Lawrence. 1976. *The Democratic Party and the Negro: Northern and National Politics, 1868–92.* University of Illinois Press.

Grunes, Rodney A. "Book Review." *Tulane Law Review* 62 (March): 849–53.

Guinier, Lani. 1991a. "No Two Seats: The Elusive Quest for Political Equality." *Virginia Law Review* 77 (November): 1413–1514.

———. 1991b. "The Triumph of Tokenism: The Voting Rights Act and the Theory of Black Electoral Success." *Michigan Law Review* 89 (March): 1077–1154.

Haddad, Mark E. 1984. "Getting Results under Section 5 of the Voting Rights Act." *Yale Law Journal* 94 (November): 139–62.

Hamilton, Charles V. 1981. "Response." In *The Right to Vote: A Rockefeller Foundation Conference.* Rockefeller Foundation.

———. 1984. "Political Access, Minority Participation, and the New Normalcy." In Leslie W. Dunbar, ed., *Minority Report: What Has Happened to Blacks, Hispanics, American Indians, and Other Minorities in the Eighties,* 3–25. Pantheon Books.

Hancock, Paul F., and Lora L. Tredway. 1985. "The Bailout Standard of the Voting Rights Act: An Incentive to End Discrimination." *Urban Lawyer* 17 (Summer): 379–425.

Hansen, Jane O. 1984. "More Blacks Win Offices in District Voting." *Atlanta Constitution* (August 26): 1A, 16A.

Harris, William C. 1979. *The Day of the Carpetbagger: Republican Reconstruction in Mississippi.* Louisiana State University Press.

Heard, Alexander. 1952. *A Two-Party South?* University of North Carolina Press.

Heck, Edward V., and Joseph Stewart, Jr. 1982. "Ensuring Access to Justice: The Role of Interest Group Lawyers in the Campaign for Civil Rights." *Judicature* 66: 84–94.

Heinz, John P., and Edward O. Laumann. 1982. *Chicago Lawyers: The Social Structure of the Bar*. Russell Sage Foundation.

Herbert, Hilary A. 1890. *Why the Solid South? Or Reconstruction and Its Results*. Baltimore: R. H. Woodward.

Himelstein, J. 1983. "Rhetorical Continuities in the Politics of Race: The Closed Society Revisited." *Southern Speech Communication Journal* 48 (Winter): 153–66.

Hine, Darlene Clark. 1979. *Black Victory: The Rise and Fall of the White Primary in Texas*. Millwood, N. Y.: KTO Press.

Hirshson, Stanley P. 1962. *Farewell to the Bloody Shirt: Northern Republicans and the Southern Negro, 1877–1893*. Indiana University Press.

Hoar, George F. 1891. "The Fate of the Election Bill." *Forum* 11: 127–28.

Holden, Matthew, Jr. 1990. "The Rewards of Daving and the Ambiguity of Power: Perspectives on the Wilder Election of 1989." In Janet Dewart, ed., *The State of Black America, 1990*, 109–20. National Urban League.

Holt, Thomas C. 1977. *Black over White: Negro Political Leadership in South Carolina during Reconstruction*. University of Illinois Press.

Horowitz, Donald L. 1977. *The Courts and Social Policy*. Brookings.

House of Representatives. 1965a. *Hearings Before Subcommittee No. 5 of the Committee on the Judiciary, House of Representatives, on H.R. 6400*, 89 Cong., 1 sess. Washington: GPO.

———. 1965b. *Voting Rights Act of 1965*. H. Rept. 89-439, 89 Cong., 1 sess. Washington: GPO.

———. 1981a. *Extension of the Voting Rights Act, Hearings before the Subcommittee on Civil and Constitutional Rights of the Committee on the Judiciary*, 97 Cong., 1 sess. Washington: GPO.

———. 1981b. *Voting Rights Act Extension*. H. Rept. 97-227, 97 Cong., 1 sess. GPO.

Huckabee, David C. 1988. *House Apportionment Following the 1990 Census: Preliminary Projections*, CRS report 88-567. Washington: Congressional Research Service.

Huckfeldt, Robert. 1986. *Politics in Context: Assimilation and Conflict in Urban Neighborhoods*. Agathon.

Huckfeldt, Robert, and Carol Weitzel Kohfeld. 1989. *Race and the Decline of Class in American Politics*. University of Illinois Press.

Hume, Richard L. 1982. "Negro Delegates to the State Constitutional Conventions of 1867–69." In Howard N. Rabinowitz, ed., *Southern Black Leaders of the Reconstruction Era*, 129–53. University of Illinois Press.

Hunter, David H. 1976. "The 1975 Voting Rights Act and Language Minorities." *Catholic University Law Review* 25: 250–70.

Hyman, Harold M. 1973. *A More Perfect Union: The Impact of the Civil War and Reconstruction on the Constitution*. Knopf.

Inglehart, Ronald. 1977. *The Silent Revolution: Changing Values and Political Styles among Western Publics*. Princeton University Press.

Institute for Social Research. 1961. *The SRC 1960 American National Election Study*. Ann Arbor, Mich.: Interuniversity Consortium for Political Research.
———. 1965. *The SRC 1964 American National Election Study*. Ann Arbor, Mich.: Interuniversity Consortium for Political Research.
Issacharoff, Samuel. 1989. *The Texas Judiciary and the Voting Rights Act: Background and Options*. Austin: Texas Policy Research Forum.
Jackson, Luther Porter. 1945. *Negro Officeholders in Virginia, 1865–1895*. Norfolk, Va: Guide Quality Press.
Jacobs, Paul W., II, and Timothy G. O'Rourke. 1986. "Racial Polarization in Vote Dilution Cases Under Section 2 of the Voting Rights Act: The Impact of *Thornburg v. Gingles*." *Journal of Law and Politics* 3(Fall): 295–353.
Jacobson, Gary C. 1990. *The Electoral Origins of Divided Government: Competition in U.S. House Elections, 1946–1988*. Boulder, Colo.: Westview Press.
Jaynes, Gerald David, and Robin M. Williams, Jr., eds. 1989. *A Common Destiny: Blacks and American Society*. Washington: National Academy Press.
Joint Center for Political Studies. 1986. *Black Elected Officials: A National Roster, 1986*. Washington.
———. 1990. *Black Elected Officials: A National Roster, 1990*. Washington
Jones, Mack H. 1985. "The Voting Rights Act as an Intervention Strategy for Social Change: Symbolism or Substance?" In Lorn S. Foster, ed., *The Voting Rights Act: Consequences and Implications*, 63–84. Praeger.
Judd, Dennis R. 1984. *The Politics of American Cities: Private Power and Public Policy*, 2d ed. Little, Brown.
Kaczorowski, Robert J. 1972–73. "Searching for the Intent of the Framers of the Fourteenth Amendment." *Connecticut Law Review* 5: 368–98.
———. 1985. *The Politics of Judicial Interpretation: The Federal Courts, The Department of Justice and Civil Rights, 1866–1876*. Oceana Publications.
Karlan, Pamela S. 1989. "Maps and Misreadings: The Role of Geographic Compactness in Racial Vote Dilution Litigation." *Harvard Civil Rights–Civil Liberties Law Review* 24 (Winter): 173–248.
Karlan, Pamela S., and Peyton McCrary. 1988. "Book Review: Without Fear and Without Research: Abigail Thernstrom on the Voting Rights Act." *Journal of Law and Politics* 4 (Spring): 751–77.
Karnig, Albert K., and Susan Welch. 1980. *Black Representation and Urban Policy*. University of Chicago Press.
Katcher, Leo. 1967. *Earl Warren: A Political Biography*. McGraw-Hill.
Keady, William Colbert, and George Colvin Cochran. 1980–81. "Section 5 of the Voting Rights Act: A Time for Revision." *Kentucky Law Journal* 69 (4): 741–97.
Keech, William R. 1968. *The Impact of Negro Voting: The Role of the Vote in the Quest for Equality*. Chicago: Rand McNally.
Keech, William R., and Michael P. Sistrom. Forthcoming. In Chandler Davidson and Bernard Grofman, eds., *The Impact of the Voting Rights Act*.

Kelly, Alfred H. 1956. "The Fourteenth Amendment Reconsidered: The Segregation Question." *Michigan Law Review* 54 (June): 1049–86.

Key, V. O., Jr., with Alexander Heard. 1949. *Southern Politics in State and Nation.* Knopf.

Kibbe, Pauline R. 1946. *Latin Americans in Texas.* University of New Mexico Press.

King, Martin Luther, Jr. 1964. *Why We Can't Wait.* New American Library.

King, Willard L. 1950. *Melville Weston Fuller, Chief Justice of the United States, 1888–1910.* Macmillan.

King, Gary, and Robert X. Browning. 1987. "Democratic Representation and Partisan Bias in Congressional Elections." *American Political Science Review* 81 (December): 1251–73.

Kirschten, Dick. 1991. "Not Black-and-White." *National Journal* 23 (March 2): 496–500.

Kluger, Richard. 1977. *Simple Justice: The History of Brown v. Board of Education and Black America's Struggle for Equality.* Knopf.

Koelble, Thomas A. 1991. *The Left Unraveled: Social Democracy and the New Left Challenge in Britain and West Germany.* Duke University Press.

Kousser, J. Morgan. 1974. *The Shaping of Southern Politics: Suffrage Restriction and the Establishment of the One-Party South, 1880–1910.* Yale University Press.

———. 1984. "The Undermining of the First Reconstruction: Lessons for the Second." In Chandler Davidson, ed., *Minority Vote Dilution.* Howard University Press.

———. 1991. "How to Determine Intent: Lessons from L.A." *Journal of Law and Politics* 7 (Summer): 591–732.

Kutler, Stanley I. 1969. "William Strong." In Leon Friedman and Fred I. Israel, eds., *The Justices of the United States Supreme Court, 1789–1969,* vol. 2, 1153–61. Chelsea House.

Ladd, Everett Carll. 1982. *Where Have All the Voters Gone? The Fracturing of America's Political Parties,* 2d ed. Norton.

Ladd, Everett Carll, Jr., with Charles D. Hadley. 1978. *Transformations of the American Party System: Political Coalitions from the New Deal to the 1970s,* 2d ed. Norton.

Lamar, Cynthia Grace. 1988. "The Resolution of Post-Election Challenges under Section 5 of the Voting Rights Act." *Yale Law Journal* 97: 1765–82.

Lamis, Alexander P. 1984. *The Two-Party South.* Oxford University Press.

Lawson, Steven F. 1976. *Black Ballots: Voting Rights in the South, 1944–1969.* Columbia University Press.

———. 1985. *In Pursuit of Power: Southern Blacks and Electoral Politics, 1965–1982.* Columbia University Press.

Lazarsfeld, Paul F., Bernard Berelson, and Hazel Gaudet. 1968. *The People's Choice,* 3d ed. Columbia University Press.

Levin, Michael. 1990. "Implications of Race and Sex Differences for Compensatory Affirmative Action and the Concept of Discrimination." *Journal of Social, Political and Economic Studies* 15 (Summer): 175–212.

Lewis, David Levering. 1978. *King: A Biography*, 2d ed. University of Illinois Press.

Lewinson, Paul. 1932. *Race, Class and Party: A History of Negro Suffrage and White Politics in the South*. Oxford University Press.

Lichtman, Allan J. 1991. "Passing the Test: Ecological Regression in the Los Angeles Case and Beyond." *Evaluation Review*.

Lichtman, Allan J., and Samuel Issacharoff. 1991. "Black/White Voter Registration Disparities in Mississippi: Legal and Methodological Issues in Challenging Bureau of Census Data." *Journal of Law and Politics* 7 (Spring): 525–57.

Liebling, A. J. 1960. *The Earl of Louisiana*. Louisiana State University Press.

Lijphart, Arend, and Bernard Grofman, eds. 1984. *Choosing an Electoral System: Issues and Alternatives*. Praeger.

Lijphart, Arend, Ronald Rogowski, and R. Kent Weaver. Forthcoming. "Separation of Powers and the Management of Political Cleavages." In R. Kent Weaver and Bert A. Rockman, eds., *Do Institutions Matter? Government Capabilities in the United States and Abroad*. Brookings.

Lipset, Seymour Martin. 1981. *Political Man: The Social Bases of Politics*, expanded ed. Johns Hopkins University Press.

Lipset, Seymour Martin, and Stein Rokkan. 1967. "Cleavage Structures, Party Systems, and Voter Alignments: An Introduction." In Seymour Martin Lipset and Stein Rokkan, eds., *Party Systems and Voter Alignments: Cross National Perspectives*. Free Press.

Loewen, James, and Bernard Grofman. 1989. "Comment: Recent Developments in Methods Used in Voting Rights Litigation." *Urban Lawyer:* 589–604.

Logan, Rayford Whittingham. 1954. *The Negro in American Life and Thought: The Nadir, 1877–1901*. Dial Press.

Lubell, Samuel. 1956. *The Future of American Politics*. Anchor Books.

Luebke, Paul. 1990. *Tar Heel Politics: Myths and Realities*. University of North Carolina Press.

McClain, Paula D., and Albert K. Karnig. 1990. "Black and Hispanic Socioeconomic and Political Competition." *American Political Science Review* 84 (June): 535–45.

McCrary, Peyton. 1978. *Abraham Lincoln and Reconstruction: The Louisiana Experiment*. Princeton University Press.

———. 1984. "History in the Courts: The Significance of *Bolden* v. *City of Mobile*." In Chandler Davidson, ed., *Minority Vote Dilution*, 47–63. Howard University Press.

———. 1990. "Racially Polarized Voting in the South: Quantitative Evidence from the Courtroom." *Social Science History* 14: 507–31.

McCrary, Peyton, and others. 1990. "The Impact of the Voting Rights Act in Alabama." Paper presented at a conference on the Voting Rights Act, Rice University (May).

McDonald, Laughlin. 1983. "The 1982 Extension of Section 5 of the Voting

Rights Act of 1965: The Continued Need for Preclearance." *Tennessee Law Review* 51 (Fall): 1–82.

———. 1988. "Votes of Confidence." *Foundation News*. Washington: Council on Foundations (September–October): 27–31.

———. 1989. "The Quiet Revolution in Minority Voting Rights." *Vanderbilt Law Review* 42 (May): 1249–97.

McDonald, Laughlin, Michael Binford, and Ken Johnson. 1990. "The Impact of the Voting Rights Act on Georgia." Paper presented at a conference on the Voting Rights Act, Rice University (May).

McGuigan, Patrick B., and Dawn M. Weyrich. 1990. *Ninth Justice: The Fight for Bork*. Washington: Free Congress Research and Education Foundation.

McKelway, Bill. 1991. "Live by Politics, Die by Politics." *Richmond Times-Dispatch* (September 22): F1, F3.

McPherson, Edward. 1872. *Handbook of Politics for 1872*. Washington: Phillip and Solomons.

———. 1876. *Hand-Book of Politics for 1876*. Washington: Solomons and Chapman.

———. 1972 [1870]. *The Political History of the United States of America during the Period of Reconstruction (from April 15, 1865 to July 15, 1870)*, reprint ed. Da Capo Press.

———. 1974 [1890]. *Hand-Book of Politics for 1890*, reprint ed. Da Capo Press.

McPherson, James M. 1964. *The Struggle for Equality: Abolitionists and the Negro in the Civil War and Reconstruction*. Princeton University Press.

———. 1990. *Abraham Lincoln and the Second American Revolution*. Oxford University Press.

Maddocks, Lewis I. 1959. "Justice John Marshall Harlan: Defender of Individual Rights." Ph.D. dissertation, Ohio State University.

Magrath, C. Peter. 1963. *Morrison R. Waite: The Triumph of Character*. Macmillan.

Mathews, John Mabry. 1971 [1909]. *Legislative and Judicial History of the Fifteenth Amendment*, reprint ed. Da Capo Press.

Matlack, Carol. 1990. "Questioning Minority-Aid Software." *National Journal* 22 (June 23): 1540.

Matthews, Donald R., and James W. Prothro. 1963. "Social and Economic Factors and Negro Voter Registration in the South." *American Political Science Review* 57 (March): 24–44.

———. 1966. *Negroes and the New Southern Politics*. Harcourt, Brace and World.

May, A. L., and Prentice Palmer. 1988. "Blacks Fighting To Gain Six Seats." *Atlanta Constitution* (July 3): 1B, 4B.

May, Janice C. "The Texas Voter Registration System." *Public Affairs Comment* 16 (July): 2.

Meier, August, and Elliot Rudwick. 1976. "Attorneys Black and White: A Case Study of Race Relations within the NAACP." *Journal of American History* 62 (March): 913–46.

Michelman, Frank I. 1989. "Conceptions of Democracy in American Political Arguments: Voting Rights." *Florida Law Review* 41 (Summer): 443–90.

Mladenka, Kenneth R. 1989. "Blacks and Hispanics in Urban Politics." *American Political Science Review* 83 (March): 165–91.

Montejano, David. 1987. *Anglos and Mexicans in the Making of Texas, 1836–1986*. University of Texas Press.

Morris, Milton D. 1981. "Black Electoral Participation and the Distribution of Public Benefits." In *The Right To Vote: A Rockefeller Foundation Conference*, 164–88. Rockefeller Foundation.

Morris, Thomas R. 1990. "Virginia and the Voting Rights Act." *University of Virginia News Letter* 66 (June): 1–8.

Motomura, Hiroshi. 1983. "Preclearance under Section Five of the Voting Rights Act." *North Carolina Law Review* 61: 189–246.

Moynihan, Daniel P., and Nathan Glazer, eds. 1975. *Ethnicity: Theory and Experience*. Harvard University Press.

Myrdal, Gunnar. 1944. *An American Dilemma: The Negro Problem and Modern Democracy*. Harper.

NALEO Educational Fund. 1988. *National Roster of Hispanic Elected Officials*. Albuquerque.

National Association of Latino Elected and Appointed Officials. 1990. *National Roster of Hispanic Elected Officials*. Washington: NALEO Educational Fund.

National Indian Youth Council. 1986. *National Indian Elected Officials Directory*. Albuquerque.

Niemi, Richard, and others. 1990. "Measuring Compactness and the Role of a Compactness Standard in a Test for Partisan or Racial Gerrymandering." *Journal of Politics*: 1155–81.

1978 Southern Elections: County and Precinct Data, 1950–1972. Louisiana State University Press.

Norrell, Robert J. 1985. *Reaping the Whirlwind: The Civil Rights Movement in Tuskegee*. Knopf.

O'Connor, Karen, and Lee Epstein. 1984. "A Legal Voice for the Chicano Community: The Activities of the Mexican American Legal Defense and Educational Fund, 1968–82." *Social Science Quarterly* 65 (June): 245–56.

———. 1989. *Public Interest Law Groups: Institutional Profiles*. Greenwood Press.

"Official 1990 Count by District." 1991. *Congressional Quarterly Weekly Report* 49 (May 18): 1309–12.

Olson, Susan M. 1990. "Interest-Group Litigation in Federal District Court: Beyond the Political Disadvantage Theory." *Journal of Politics* 52 (August): 854–82.

O'Rourke, Timothy G. 1980. *The Impact of Reapportionment*. New Brunswick, N.J.: Transaction Books.

———. 1982. "Constitutional and Statutory Challenges to Local At-Large Elections." *University of Richmond Law Review* 17 (Fall): 39–97.

————. 1983. "Voting Rights Act Amendments of 1982: The New Bailout Provision and Virginia." *Virginia Law Review* 69 (May): 765–804.

————. 1988. "The Voting Rights Act and the New Theory of Representation." *Benchmark* 4 (Winter): 83–87.

Padgett, James A. 1937. "From Slavery to Prominence in North Carolina." *Journal of Negro History* 22: 433–87.

Parker, Frank R. 1981. "The Impact of *City of Mobile* v. *Bolden* and Strategies and Legal Arguments for Voting Rights Cases in Its Wake." In *The Right To Vote: A Rockefeller Foundation Report*, 98–124. Rockefeller Foundation.

————. 1982. "The Virginia Legislative Reapportionment Case: Reapportionment Issues of the 1980's." *George Mason University Law Review* 5: 1–50.

————. 1987. "Protest, Politics, and Litigation: Political and Social Change in Mississippi." *Mississippi Law Journal* 57: 677–704.

————. 1990. *Black Votes Count: Political Empowerment in Mississippi After 1965*. University of North Carolina Press.

Parker, Frank R., and Barbara Y. Phillips. 1981. *Voting in Mississippi: A Right Still Denied*. Washington: Lawyers' Committee for Civil Rights Under Law.

Parsons, Arch. 1991. "Blacks, Hispanics, Asians Trying to Work Together." *Baltimore Sun* (April 8): 4A.

Parsons, Stanley B., William W. Beech, and Michael J. Dubin. 1986. *United States Congressional Districts and Data, 1843–1883*. Greenwood Press.

Parsons, Stanley B., Michael J. Dubin, and Karen Toombs Parsons. 1990. *United States Congressional Districts, 1883–1913*. Greenwood Press.

Paul, Arnold. 1969. "David J. Brewer." In Leon Friedman and Fred I. Israel, eds., *The Justices of the United States Supreme Court, 1789–1969*, vol. 2, 1515–34. Chelsea House.

Perman, Michael. 1984. *The Road to Redemption: Southern Politics, 1869–1879*. University of North Carolina Press.

Pertschuk, Michael. 1986. *Giant Killers*. Norton.

Pertschuk, Michael, and Wendy Schaetzel. 1989. *The People Rising: The Campaign against the Bork Nomination*. Thunder's Mouth Press.

Petrocik, John R. 1981. *Party Coalitions: Realignments and the Decline of the New Deal Party System*. University of Chicago Press.

————. 1987. "Realignment: New Party Coalitions and the Nationalization of the South." *Journal of Politics* 49 (May): 347–375.

Pettigrew, Thomas F., and Denise A. Alston. 1988. *Tom Bradley's Campaigns for Governor: The Dilemma of Race and Political Strategies*. Washington: Joint Center for Political Studies.

Phillips, Barbara Y. 1983. *How to Use Section 5 of the Voting Rights Ace,* 3d ed. Washington: Joint Center for Political Studies.

Pike, James S. 1874. *The Prostrate State: South Carolina under Negro Government*. D. Appleton.

Pinderhughes, Dianne M. Forthcoming. "How the Lobby Shaped the Law, How the Law Shaped the Lobby." In Wayne Brent and Huey Perry, eds., *Black Politics in the American Political System*.

Piven, Frances Fox, and Richard A. Cloward. 1982. *The New Class War: Reagan's Attack on the Welfare State and Its Consequences.* Pantheon.

Price, Margaret. 1959. *The Negro and the Ballot in the South.* Atlanta: Southern Regional Council.

Rae, Douglas W. 1971. *The Political Consequences of Electoral Laws,* rev. ed. Yale University Press.

Raines, Howell. 1977. *My Soul is Rested: Movement Days in the Deep South Remembered.* Putnam.

Rawls, John. 1971. *A Theory of Justice.* Cambridge, Mass.: Belknap Press.

Reagan, Michael D. 1987. *Regulation: The Politics of Policy.* Little, Brown.

"Redistricting's Harvest." 1991. *Richmond Times-Dispatch* (September 13): A20.

Reed, Adolph L., Jr. 1986. *The Jesse Jackson Phenomenon: The Crisis of Purpose in Afro-American Politics.* Yale University Press.

———. 1988. "The Black Urban Regime: Structural Origins and Constraints." *Comparative Urban and Community Research* 1: 138–89.

Reed, Wornie L., ed. 1990. *Critiques of the NRC Study, A Common Destiny: Blacks and American Society,* vol. 1. Boston: William Monroe Trotter Institutute, University of Massachusetts.

Rendon, Armando B. 1971. *Chicano Manifesto.* Collier Books.

Renner, Tari. 1988. "Municipal Election Processes: The Impact on Minority Representation." In *The Municipal Yearbook 1988.* Washington: International City Management Association.

Rhode, Deborah L. 1982. "Class Conflicts in Class Actions." *Stanford Law Review* 34: 1183–1262.

Rice, Bradley Robert. 1977. *Progressive Cities: The Commission Government Movement in America, 1901–1920.* University of Texas Press.

Rice, Charles E. 1966. "The Voting Rights Act of 1965: Some Dissenting Observations." *University of Kansas Law Review* 15: 159–65.

Rice, Lawrence D. 1971. *The Negro in Texas: 1874–1900.* Louisiana State University Press.

Rich, Spencer. 1988. "1990's Big Winners: California, Texas, Florida." *Washington Post* (January 26): A21.

Richardson, James D. 1900. *A Compilation of the Messages and Papers of the Presidents, 1789–1897.* Washington: GPO.

Richardson, Joe M. 1965. *The Negro in the Reconstruction of Florida, 1865–1877.* Florida State University Press.

Richardson, Leon Burr. 1940. *William E. Chandler, Republican.* Dodd, Mead.

Riker, William H. 1984. *The Theory of Political Coalitions,* 2d ed. Westport, Conn.: Greenwood Press.

Roman, John J. 1972. "Section 5 of the Voting Rights Act: The Formation of an Extraordinary Federal Remedy." *American University Law Review* 22 (Fall): 111–33.

Scammon, Richard M., and Alice V. McGillivray. 1976–88 (biennial). *America Votes: A Handbook of Contemporary American Election Statistics.* Washington: Congressional Quarterly.

Scavo, Carmine. 1990. "Racial Integration of Local Government Leadership in Southern Small Cities: Consequences for Equity Relevance and Political Relevance." *Political Science Quarterly* 71 (June): 362–72.

Schlesinger, Arthur M., Jr. 1991. *The Disuniting of America: Reflections on a Multicultural Society.* Whittle Direct Books.

Schlozman, Kay Lehman, and John T. Tierney. 1986. *Organized Interests and American Democracy.* Harper and Row.

Schuck, Peter H. 1987. "What Went Wrong with the Voting Rights Act." *Washington Monthly* 19 (November): 51–55.

Schuman, Howard, Charlotte Steeh, and Lawrence Bobo. 1985. *Racial Attitudes in America: Trends and Interpretations.* Harvard University Press.

Senate. 1879. *Report on Elections in Louisiana and South Carolina.* No. 855, 45 Cong., 3 sess. GPO.

———. 1982a. *Voting Rights Act,* Hearings before the Subcommittee on the Constitution of the Committee on the Judiciary. No. J-97-92, 97 Cong., 2 sess. GPO.

———. 1982b. *Voting Rights Act Extension,* Report of the Committee on the Judiciary, United States Senate. S. rept. 97-417, 97 Cong., 2 sess. GPO.

———. 1983. *Hearings Before the Subcommittee on the Constitution of the Senate Committee on the Judiciary. United States Senate, Ninety-seventh Congress, Second Session, on S. 53, S. 1761, S. 1975, S. 1992, and H. R. 3112 (Bills to Amend the Voting Rights Act of 1965). January 27, 28, February 1, 2, 4, 11, 12, 25, and March 1, 1982.* Washington: GPO.

Shadgett, Olive Hall. 1964. *The Republican Party in Georgia, From Reconstruction to 1900.* University of Georgia Press.

Shapiro, Walter. 1989. "Breakthrough in Virginia." *Time* (November 20).

Simmons, Ozzie G. 1952. "Anglo Americans and Mexican Americans in South Texas: A Study in Dominant-Subordinate Group Relations." Ph.D. dissertation, Harvard University.

Skerry, Peter. 1989. "Borders and Quotas: Immigration and the Affirmative-Action State." *Public Interest,* no. 96 (Summer): 86–102.

Smallwood, James. 1974. "Black Texans during Reconstruction." Ph.D. dissertation, Texas Tech University.

Smith, Samuel Denny. 1940. *The Negro in Congress, 1870–1901.* University of North Carolina Press.

Smith, Richard A. 1984. "Advocacy, Interpretation, and Influence in the U.S. Congress." *American Political Science Review* 78 (March): 44–63.

Sniderman, Paul M. 1981. *A Question of Loyalty.* University of California Press.

"Some Mississippi Plans." 1882. *New York Times* (July 27): 5.

"Special Report Election '92." 1992. *Congressional Quarterly Weekly Report* 50 (Supplement, February 29).

Stampp, Kenneth M. 1965. *The Era of Reconstruction, 1865–1877.* Vintage.

Stanley, Harold W. 1987. *Voter Mobilization and the Politics of Race: The South and Universal Suffrage, 1952–1984.* Praeger.

Starr, Paul. 1992. "Civil Reconstruction: What to Do without Affirmative Action." *American Prospect* no. 8 (Winter): 14.

Stephenson, Gilbert Thomas. 1969 [1910]. *Race Distinctions in American Law*, reprint ed. AMS Press.

Stern, Mark. 1985. "Legislative Responsiveness and the New Southern Politics." In Lorn S. Foster, ed., *The Voting Rights Act: Consequences and Implications*, 105–20. Praeger.

———. 1992. *Calculating Visions: Kennedy, Johnson, and Civil Rights*. Rutgers University Press.

Stewart, Joseph, Jr., and Edward V. Heck. 1983. "The Day-to-Day Activities of Interest Group Lawyers." *Social Science Quarterly* 64: 173–82.

Stewart, Joseph, Jr., and James F. Sheffield, Jr. 1987. "Does Interest Group Litigation Matter? The Case of Black Political Mobilization in Mississippi." *Journal of Politics* 49 (August): 780–98.

Still, Edward. 1984. "Alternatives to Single-Member Districts." In Chandler Davidson, ed., *Minority Vote Dilution*, 249–67. Howard University Press.

———. 1992. "Modified At-Large Voting as a Remedy for Minority Vote Dilution in Judicial Elections." *Yale Law and Policy Journal*.

Strong, Donald S. 1968. *Negroes, Ballots and Judges: National Voting Rights Legislation in the Federal Courts*. University of Alabama Press.

Sundquist, James L. 1983. *Dynamics of the Party System: Alignment and Realignment of Political Parties in the United States*, rev. ed. Brookings.

Sunstein, Cass R. 1990. *After the Rights Revolution: Conceiving the Regulatory State*. Harvard University Press.

Swain, Carol M. 1992. *Black Faces, Black Interests: The Representation of African Americans in Congress*. Harvard University Press.

Taper, Bernard. 1962. *Gomillion versus Lightfoot: the Tuskegee Gerrymander Case*. McGraw Hill.

Taylor, Joseph H. 1949. "Populism and Disfranchisement in Alabama." *Journal of Negro History* 34: 410–27.

Taylor, Stuart, Jr. 1991. "Electing By Race." *American Lawyer* 13 (June): 50–54.

Thernstrom, Abigail M. 1979. "The Odd Evolution of the Voting Rights Act." *Public Interest* no. 55 (Spring): 49–76.

———. 1987. *Whose Votes Count? Affirmative Action and Minority Voting Rights*. Harvard University Press.

"Threats of Lawsuits Loom." *Atlanta Constitution* (August 26, 1984).

Tindall, George B. 1952. *South Carolina Negroes, 1877–1900*. University of South Carolina Press.

Trelease, Allen W. 1971. *White Terror: The Ku Klux Klan Conspiracy and Southern Reconstruction*. Harper and Row.

Tunnell, Ted. 1984. *Crucible of Reconstruction: War, Radicalism, and Race in Louisiana, 1862–1877*. Louisiana State University Press.

Tushnet, Mark V. 1987. *The NAACP's Legal Strategy against Segregated Education, 1925–1950*. University of North Carolina Press.

"Urban Districts Suffer Big Population Losses." 1981. *Congressional Quarterly Weekly Report* 39 (April 11): 646–49.

"Urban League Takes Neutral Position on Thomas." 1991. *New York Times* (July 22): A8.

U.S. Congress. 1989. *Biographical Directory of the United States Congress, 1774–1989.* Washington: GPO.

Uzee, Philip D. 1950. "Republican Politics in Louisiana, 1877–1900." Ph.D. dissertation, Louisiana State University.

Vincent, Charles. 1976. *Black Legislators in Louisiana during Reconstruction.* Louisiana State University Press.

"Virginia Choices '91." 1991. *Richmond Times-Dispatch* (September 10): A16.

Virginia General Assembly. 1990–91. *Drawing the Line: 1991 Redistricting in Virginia* (newsletter issued approximately bimonthly by the Division of Legislative Services). No. 2 (November 1990); No. 5 (May 1991); No. 6 (July 1991).

Vose, Clement E. 1959. *Caucasians Only.* University of California Press.

———. 1972. *Constitutional Change: Amendment Politics and Supreme Court Litigation since 1900.* Lexington, Mass: D. C. Heath.

Walker, Samuel. 1990. *In Defense of American Liberties: A History of the ACLU.* Oxford University Press.

Walton, Hanes, Jr. 1985. *Invisible Politics: Black Political Behavior.* State University of New York Press.

Warren, Charles. 1922. *The Supreme Court in United States History.* Little, Brown.

Warren, Earl. 1972. "Speech." CBS Library of Contemporary Quotations, May 18, disk 10, side B, cut 10. Copyright CBS News.

Wasby, Stephen L. 1985. "Civil Rights Litigation by Organization: Constraints and Choice." *Judicature* 68: 337–52.

Washington Research Project. 1972. *The Shameful Blight: The Survival of Racial Discrimination in Voting in the South.* Washington.

Watson, Denton L. 1990. *Lion in the Lobby: Clarence Mitchell, Jr.'s Struggle for the Passage of Civil Rights Laws.* William Morrow.

Watters, Pat, and Reese Cleghorn. 1967. *Climbing Jacob's Ladder: The Arrival of Negroes in Southern Politics.* Harcourt, Brace and World.

Weiss, Nancy J. 1983. *Farewell to the Party of Lincoln: Black Politics in the Age of FDR.* Princeton University Press.

Welch, Susan. 1990. "The Impact of At-Large Elections on the Representation of Blacks and Hispanics." *Journal of Politics* 52 (November): 1050–76.

Wharton, Vernon Lane. 1947. *The Negro in Mississippi, 1865–1890.* University of North Carolina Press.

Whiteside, Ruth. 1981. "Justice Joseph Bradley and the Reconstruction Amendments." Ph.D. dissertation, Rice University.

Wiggins, Sarah Woolfolk. 1977. *The Scalawag in Alabama Politics, 1865–1881.* University of Alabama Press.

———. 1980. "Democratic Bulldozing and Republican Folly." In Otto H. Olsen, ed., *Reconstruction and Redemption in the South*, 48–77. Louisiana State University Press.

"Wilder Faces Fight over Redistricting." 1990. *Charlottesville Daily Progress* (February 25): B8.

Williams, Linda F., ed. 1988. *The JCPS Congressional District Fact Book*, 3d ed. Washington: Joint Center for Political Studies.

Wilson, James Q. 1989. *Bureaucracy: What Government Agencies Do and Why They Do It*. Basic Books.

Wilson, James Q., ed. 1980. *The Politics of Regulation*. Basic Books.

Wilson, William Julius. 1978. *The Declining Significance of Race: Blacks and Changing American Institutions*. University of Chicago Press.

———. 1990. "Race-Neutral Programs and the Democratic Coalition." *American Prospect* no. 1 (Spring): 74–81.

Wolfinger, Raymond E. 1965. "The Development and Persistence of Ethnic Voting." *American Poltical Science Review* 59 (December): 896–908.

Wolfley, Jeanette, and Gordon G. Henderson. 1991. "Indian Success in Different Election Systems." Paper presented at the annual meeting of the Western Political Science Association.

Woodward, C. Vann. 1960. *The Burden of Southern History*. Louisiana State University Press.

———. 1966. *The Strange Career of Jim Crow*, 2d rev. ed. Oxford University Press.

———. 1989. *The Future of the Past*. Oxford University Press.

Work, Monroe N. 1920. "Some Negro Members of Reconstruction Conventions and Legislatures and of Congress." *Journal of Negro History* 5: 63–119.

Wright, Gerald C., Jr. 1976. "Community Structure and Voting in the South." *Public Opinion Quarterly* 40 (Summer): 200–215.

Wright, John R. 1989. "PAC Contributions, Lobbying, and Representation. *Journal of Politics* 51 (August): 713–29.

Wynes, Charles E. 1961. *Race Relations in Virginia, 1870–1902*. University Press of Virginia.

Yatrakis, K. 1981. *Electoral Demands and Political Benefits: Minority as Majority, A Case Study of Two Newark Elections 1970, 1974*. Columbia University Press.

Young, Iris Marion. 1990. "Justice, Participation, and Group Difference." Paper prepared for the annual meeting of the American Political Science Association.

Young, Roy E. 1965. *The Place System in Texas Elections*. Austin: Institute of Public Affairs, University of Texas.

Zax, Jeffrey S. 1990. "Election Methods and Black and Hispanic City Council Membership." *Social Science Quarterly* 71 (June): 339–55.

Zuckert, Michael P. 1986. "Congressional Power under the Fourteenth Amendment—The Original Understanding of Section Five." *Constitutional Commentary* 3 (Winter): 123–55.

Index of Legal Cases

General Index

Abrams, Kathy, 288
Affirmative action quotas, 1, 39–40; proportional representation and, 304–05; public opinion on, 194; section 2 and, 77–78; section 5 and, 58; single-member districts and, 304–05; as social regulation, 188–89
Alabama, 11, 13, 19; alternative voting systems, 83–84; at-large elections, 71–72; fraud to disfranchise blacks, 143; minority officeholders impact, 79–80; poll tax, 20; poll watchers in, 20; Selma voter registration drive, 14–16; vote dilution, 25, 30–31
Alaska, 18, 36, 97–98
American Civil Liberties Union, 75, 235, 240, 244n
American Indians. See Native Americans
American Jewish Committee, 235
Annexations, 23n, 94n; section 5 and, 55–56, 58, 61–63
Arizona, 18, 36
Arkansas, 75, 105n
Atlanta, Ga., 76–77, 294n
At-large elections, 24, 25, 26, 27, 71–72, 111; disadvantaging effects, 308–09

Bailout provisions, 18–19, 40, 57, 91–92, 96–98, 111, 193
Ball, Howard, 59–60
Bartley, Numan, 119
Bentham, Jeremy, 239
Birmingham, Ala., 127
Black, Hugo, 54, 86
Black electoral success, theory of, 283n
Blackmun, Harry, 69
Black Power (Carmichael and Hamilton), 296
Blacksher, James, 33, 210, 219, 225, 229n, 297

Black voting rights. *See* Voting rights of blacks
Black Votes Count (Parker), 86, 109n
Blaine, James G., 155
Bond, Julian, 78
Bork, Robert, 230, 256
Boynton, Amelia, 14, 16
Bradley, Joseph P., 164, 170
Bradley, Tom, 133
Brennan, William J., Jr., 69, 100, 106, 166, 200, 212, 213, 219, 221, 225, 297, 302
Brewer, David J., 164
Brooke, Edward, 293n
Brown, David, 81
Brown, Henry B., 164
Brown, Willie, 274
Bullock, Charles, 243n, 294
Bunche, Ralph, 45n
Bunzel, John, 39
Burger, Warren E., 69, 183n
Bush, George, 175
Butler, Katherine, 243n, 310

California: direct democracy, 274–75, 295; minority officeholding, 79, 309n; redistricting, 195–96. *See also* Los Angeles, Calif.
Candidate diminution, 23
Carmichael, Stokely, 296
Carter, Jimmy, 47, 129, 207–08
Carter, Robert, 165
Celler, Emanuel, 17–18
Chase, Salmon P., 163
Child, Lydia Maria, 9n
Civil Aeronautics Board, 180
Civil Rights Act of *1957*, 13, 17, 52, 182
Civil Rights Act of *1960*, 13, 17, 52–53
Civil Rights Act of *1964*, 13, 14n, 17, 126, 182, 184–85

See also Results test; Section 2 of the Voting Rights Act; Section 5 of the Voting Rights Act
Nineteenth Amendment, 31
Nixon, Richard M., 120, 130, 172, 183
Norfolk, Va., 101–03
North Carolina, 18, 19, 26–27, 41, 196
Noviello, Nicholas, 212
Numbered-place laws, 23n, 26
Nunn, Sam, 36

Occupational Safety and Health Administration, 181
O'Connor, Sandra Day, 68–69, 100, 302, 303
Office of Civil Rights, 183
Office of Federal Contract Compliance, 183, 184, 185, 189
Office of Minority Business Enterprise, 183
Oklahoma, 11–12, 232–33
One person, one vote principle, 276
O'Rourke, Timothy, 39, 310

Parker, Frank R., 86, 105–06, 107–08, 109n, 235, 242n
Peckham, Rufus W., 163
Philadelphia plan, 183, 185, 186
Phillips, Wendell, 9n, 136
Plurality electoral systems, 267
Political considerations in enforcement of voting rights, 195–96, 298–99
Political development in South, post–World War II, 119–21
Political equality: color-conscious policies and, 266–69; conditions needed to achieve, 287–89; proportional representation and, 285–87; proportionate interest representation and, 289–92
Political focus on minority power, 275–77
Political incorporation, cultural distinctiveness and, 278–82
Poll taxes, 13, 20, 26, 174
Poll watchers, 19–20
Popular sovereignty, 266, 267
Populism, 11, 133, 134
Powell, Lewis, 54, 92n

Preclearance. *See* Section 5 of the Voting Rights Act
Preface to Democratic Theory (Dahl), 267
Presidential elections, 51; *1880*,141; *1964*, 121–25, 129, 130; of two reconstructions, 156, 159
Proportional representation, 32, 88–89, 109–11, 187–88, 262–63; affirmative action quotas and, 304–05; black political influence and, 295; congressional disclaimer regarding, 106; descriptive representation and, 265–66, 285–86; efficiency and stability, 263–64, 266; fairness, 263; individual and group rights, 264; institutionalization, 107–08; legitimacy, 263, 264; meanings of, 303; narrow and specialized version of, 265; political equality and, 285–87; results test and, 103, 104–06; section 2 "requirement" of, 301–05, 315; semi-proportional systems, 111–12; single-member districts and, 303, 304–05
Proportionate interest representation, 111–12n, 289–92
Proposition *13*, 274, 295
Proposition *98*, 274, 295
Protective League, 233
Public interest law firms, 247–48
Puerto Rican Legal Defense and Education Fund, 235, 240

Quotas. *See* Affirmative action quotas

Racial bloc voting. *See* Racially polarized voting
Racial campaign appeals, 206–08
Racially polarized voting, 75–77, 198–200, 201; absence, 292–93, 296; defining characteristics, 209–13, 221–24; elections relevant to litigation, 213–14; Latinos and, 214, 215–16; legal significance, factors determining, 211–13; minority candidate of choice, 213, 214–15, 224; polarization-cohesiveness relationship, 215–16; validity of polarization data, 216–17
Racial quotas. *See* Affirmative action quotas
Rangel, Charles, 293n
Reagan, Ronald, 38, 40

88; Latinos, coverage for, 35–36; monitoring to determine compliance, 64; negotiated settlements, 60, 61; original intent issue, 171–73; powers of elected officials and, 112–13n; preclearance reaction from states, 86–87; preclearance requirement, 19, 53, 91–92; results test and, 103–05; retrogression test, 56, 93–94, 104; section 2 standards incorporation, 57; states acquiescence to preclearance, 86–87; technical-legal obstacles to compliance, 60–61; unsubmitted election law changes and, 63–64; vote dilution, use against, 27–29

Securities and Exchange Commission, 180

Segregation following black disfranchisement, 11

Selma voter registration drive, 14–16

Single-member districts, 48, 49–50; affirmative action quotas and, 304–05; empowerment objectives of voting reform and, 285; geographic compactness, 218–21; Houston case, 62, 63; minority officeholding and, 73–74, 315–16; proportional representation and, 303, 304–05; Republican support for, 188, 191–92, 195–96; shortcomings, 83, 111, 254, 287–88, 293–95, 311–14, 316

Single-shot voting, 23n, 25n

Slating process for candidates, 204–05; full-slate laws, 23n, 25, 26–27, 30

Smith, Howard W., 18

Smith, Wilford H., 162

Smith, William French, 39

Snyder, Art, 271

Social regulation, 179; affirmative action quotas as, 188–89; civil rights regulation, difference from, 189–91; clientele "capture" of enforcement agencies, 186–88; consumer protection focus, 181; economic regulation as foundation of, 180–81; equal-results standard of enforcement, 183; future risk, focus on, 181–82; legislative style of administration, 181–84; minority preferences, 187–88; public opinion on, 194; quasi-judicial model, 180–81; transition from economic to social regulation, 182–84; Voting Rights Act as, 184–86

Social science testimony. *See* Expert witness testimony

Solicitor General, Office of, 243

South Carolina, 13, 19; at-large elections, 71; disfranchising schemes of late 1880s, 135; gerrymandering, 144, 146, 148, 149; white reaction to black voter mobilization, 81

Southern Christian Leadership Conference, 14–15, 16

Southwest Voter Education Project, 238, 240

Staggered terms, 23n

Stanley, Harold, 243n

Stennis, John C., 36

Stevens, John Paul, 54, 69, 112n

Stevenson, Adlai, 120

Stewart, Potter, 68–69, 93, 95N, 166

Still, Edward, 50

Stone, William J., 150n

Storey, Moorfield, 232–33, 238

Strong, William, 164

Structural discrimination: expansive-constructionist approach to, 48–51; narrow-constructionist approach to, 45–47; stand pat approach to, 47–48

Student Nonviolent Coordinating Committee, 14, 15

Summer, A. F., 29

Supreme Court, U.S.: first Reconstruction and, 160–64; second Reconstruction and, 165–68. *See also specific cases and issues*

Talmadge, Herman E., 18, 36

Taney, Roger B., 163

Texas, 18n; Latinos, section 5 coverage for, 35–36; minority officeholders, 308–09; poll tax, 20; vote dilution, 26, 32–34, 42; white primaries, 12, 233

Theoretical perspective on voting rights. *See* Democratic theory

Thernstrom, Abigail M., 46, 85–86, 107–08, 178, 261, 268, 279, 294–95, 302n, 304n, 310; analysis of her positions, 170–76; criticisms of voting rights legislation and rulings, 39, 58–59, 166–70